COMPUTER HOW-TO
for Normal People

by Miklos Jako

➢ **A quick-reference manual for how to do all the things you don't know how to, or forgot how to.**

➢ **Windows Vista and Windows 7**

➢ **Written by a consumer, for the consumer**

For updates and additions, see *Computerhowtobook.com*

INFINITY
PUBLISHING

ISBN 978-0-7414-7455-1 Monochrome Version
ISBN 978-0-7414-7329-5 Color Version
ISBN 978-0-7414-7330-1 eBook

Printed in the United States of America

Published Fall 2012

INFINITY PUBLISHING
1094 New DeHaven Street, Suite 100
West Conshohocken, PA 19428-2713
Toll-free (877) BUY BOOK
Local Phone (610) 941-9999
Fax (610) 941-9959
Info@buybooksontheweb.com
www.buybooksontheweb.com

IMPORTANT GENERAL INFORMATION

Introduction

Computers are extraordinarily useful... but also extraordinarily frustrating. So often, you cannot logically figure out how to do something; instead, there is some arbitrary piece of information you need to already know. Or there are particular buttons you need to click in a particular order, otherwise, you get nowhere. Or you can't remember how to do something, because it's been a while since you did it last. Or... bad things happen, constantly, out of the blue, and you can't figure out how to fix them!

This manual is an effort to fill in all those gaps.

Topics are arranged alphabetically. Step-by-step procedures are given, with the assumption that the reader is coming to the problem with only minimal computer experience.

THIS MANUAL COVERS MICROSOFT COMPUTERS, NOT MACINTOSH ONES.

This Manual

I am NOT an expert; I am, like yourself, a normal person of reasonable intelligence, but, for that very reason, this manual can be very helpful: It is written from the consumer's perspective, not the computer expert's perspective.

The material reflects the many things that I normally do. If you do other types of operations that I don't cover, I recommend the *Windows Vista for Dummies* or *Windows 7 for Dummies* books by Andy Rathbone.

Note that my grammar and punctuation in these notes are often not strictly correct. Who cares. I just want information to be clear. I'm well aware that commas and periods normally go inside end quotation marks, but I vary it, to make things more clear. I'm well aware that proper grammar requires "his or her" not "their" when the antecedent is singular, that you don't say "is when," etc., etc. But I write colloquially, for clarity.

I cover both Windows Vista and Windows 7; they are essentially the same system, with some improvements in Windows 7.

AR = Andy Rathbone, *Vista for Dummies, Windows 7 for Dummies* author

RS = computer friend of mine

User Friendliness

In my opinion, Microsoft doesn't know the meaning of the words "logical heuristics," "simplify," or "user-friendly." They are too busy trying to dazzle the consumer with more and more. The priority always seems to be on serving the geeks of the world, rather than the average intelligent person who wants to do normal, straightforward, useful tasks.

Also par for the course: Instead of one way to do a function that works consistently, there are usually two, three, or four different ways to perform the same function. The avowed goal is simplicity, but the end result is confusion.

I understand Macintosh is much better in terms of user-friendliness, but, having used Microsoft all these years, I'll stick with what I know, even though it may be a less sensible system. Microsoft's most recent version of Windows – "Windows 7" – has gotten good reviews, compared to the negative ones for "Windows Vista," their previous version. Maybe they're finally wising up and seeing the importance of user-friendliness. (Update: No, they haven't; Microsoft only sees the importance of pretending to be user-friendly.)

Computer Safety

Be aware of your surroundings; a stolen computer can mean not only lost information and money, but also lost time and privacy.

When moving your laptop, be mindful, don't rush. Don't hold it lightly at the edges; you bump your elbow, the computer is on the floor. A dropped computer means serious money to fix it, as well as your being without it for a while. It's also good to get into the habit of never eating or drinking while at the computer. I never do, and I've never had any food spills mess up my laptop.

Though I've never had a problem with this, be careful of static electricity, which can mess up computer components. If you have a deep pile carpet, discharge any build-up by touching a metal doorknob first.

Computer Security

Never open an attachment to any email when you don't know the party sending it (or, if you know the party, but the message seems strange!). Viruses, identity theft, can be a major, major hassle. Have one good virus protection program installed.

Computer Freezing

Because they are complex machines, every so often computers freeze, and nothing works. The way out is simply to reboot: Turn it off; wait 20 seconds; turn it on again. That's the way to unfreeze it. Most often it will retain most of what work you did before it froze, as well as getting a stuck program working again.

You can disregard the warning you get when it starts up again, that you did not close down Windows properly. No kidding, dumb computer, because we couldn't!! And if you can't turn if off in the first place because nothing at all works, then the way to do it is this: press the start button and hold it down for 5-10 seconds; that shuts it off.

Also, when you turn your computer on, always wait until it fully finishes getting turned on, before starting to do anything. For me, it's once my "gadgets" have fully appeared on my screen at the right; then it's ready. Otherwise, if you start doing stuff too soon, it may well freeze on you.

Simultaneous Operations

Usually if some function is being carried out, you can still work on something else in the meantime. For example, if I'm doing my once-a-month virus sweep (which may take an hour or more), I just click on the "minimize" icon at the extreme upper right of the screen (the "–" sign there) to take that function off the screen and put it into the taskbar at the bottom, while I work on something else.

On the other hand, if you are using some software program that is complex (like Windows Movie Maker), or if you are installing a new program, the computer will probably work better if you have nothing else going on at the same time.

Comfort

Don't just accept whatever setup you start with – desk, chair, lighting, wires, etc. Given the huge chunks of time one can spend at a computer, you want everything to be just right. Otherwise, you'll end up with strains and aches.

The two biggest factors in my experience: 1) A laptop stand so I can work lying down instead of hunched over a desk, straining my back. 2) Getting a router, so I can go wireless and use my laptop anywhere in my apartment, without wires always getting in my way.

For any long session, it makes a significant difference if you take a few minutes break every hour.

Help

Sometimes you can figure out stuff from internet sites, but more often than not they just send you around in circles, or try to sell you things, instead of trying to help you.

Sometimes you can figure stuff out by clicking on a question mark icon and typing in the topic, but Microsoft usually presents you with a list of 30 unrelated, utterly useless topics.

Sometimes you can call a phone number and if you can get past a dozen choices, accents you can't understand, and horrible, grating, broken-up music as you wait, sometimes you can actually get a decent answer.

But, basically, you have to resign yourself to the fact that getting help is a long, aggravating process.

HIGHLIGHT KEY

Gray = Basic step-by-step procedure
Green = Key piece of info, without which the procedure will fail
Yellow = Key point
Red = Warning, major screw-up potential
Blue = Windows 7 variation from Windows Vista
Smaller blue font = Secondary material, but may contain useful info

****

0 vs letter "O" – When you have a serial or product number or whatever number, and you don't know whether the circle character is the number zero or the letter O, the difference is that the number is oblong (0), the letter more round (O).

32-BIT vs 64-BIT – I think this has to do with how much information is transferred at a time, in a program or over the internet. The 64-bit rate is the newer, upgraded mode, but many programs do not yet work with it. See "ADOBE FLASH PLAYER" > "32 vs 64-Bit Systems"

ACCENT MARKS – Windows automatically puts in an accent for some words – café, fiancé, sauté – but for others, like "resume," you have to use the Insert tab at top to get the final é: Insert tab at top > Symbol dropdown arrow > More Symbols > select your choice > Insert.

As usual, it's absolute overkill; they have hundreds of weird letters, like ð, or ş or ŭ, but the normal ones you want are hard to find. I finally did find é, and ō, but could not find the n with the squiggle (˜) over it. It's probably there somewhere, but I've wasted enough time. Sorry, Carlos Pena. (Update: Finally found it – 12 rows down, 1st column.)

Keyboard Shortcuts

If you find yourself using a particular accented letter frequently, you can use a keyboard shortcut. Click on the help question mark icon at upper right, type "Keyboard shortcuts for international characters" into the search box at left, click that topic, and it will give you the details.

Aha, now I see how to get the é by keyboard shortcut – CTRL+apostrophe, then "e." And here's the ñ – CTRL+Shift+~ all at once, then "n" – you have to do that exact combination and sequence; pressing the ~ by itself won't do it. (The ~ is on the keyboard at far upper left; first time I ever used it in my life.)

It's hard to remember the above, so your best bet, if you find yourself using the name Peña, for example, a lot, is to make it automatic by using the AutoCorrect function: Type out the name Peña by the above method, block the name, CTRL+C (the name waits, unseen, on the clipboard), Click Review tab at top > Spelling & Grammar at far left > Options > AutoCorrect Options > enter info (Replace: type "Pena," With: CTRL+V "Peña" from the clipboard), Add > OK.

Now, every time you type "Pena" it will automatically give you "Peña." Go Señor Peña.

ACCESS TO PROGRAMS – One way to access programs is through the Start button at lower left (the colored flag icon). But I find it easier to keep icons of my favorite programs on my desktop, so I can just click on them there to open them up. I go through the Start button only for programs I don't use that often.

See also "DESKTOP" topics.

ACCOUNTS – See "ADMINISTRATOR ACCOUNT"

ADD-ONS – Also called Plug-ins. When you're on the internet, they help navigation, and make things smoother with websites. I now keep them all on. I couldn't get videos to play on a "Funny or Die" site. It said I needed "flash" something. Sure enough, one of the add-ons was that one. I had had it disabled. I enabled it; now the videos play.

Tools (upper right) > Manage Add-ons > highlight each, one at a time, and select enable or disable.

Some add-ons can be harmful. Don't download anything if it gets offered completely out of the blue.

ADDING TEXT TO YOUR DOCUMENT – See "EDITING TEXT"

ADDRESS BOX – When you're on the internet, this is the box the sits usually at upper left, and contains the address of the website ("http://www.something.com") you are currently on. This is different than the search box of a website, which sits usually lower down and in the middle.

Windows 7 supposedly has a general topic search feature also built into the address box. When I tried it, it seemed to work sometimes, but other times not. Never could figure out the exact order of things to do to make it work consistently.

Again, the two contemptible features of Windows – 1) even more avenues to do things, ending up confusing, rather than simplifying, and 2) procedures that require arbitrary steps done in an exact order, rather than a few simple and logical steps.

I decided to ignore this new feature; more trouble than it's worth.

ADDRESS – COPY See "COPY – AN ADDRESS"

ADMINISTRATOR ACCOUNT – If you are the owner of a computer, then you automatically have the "administrator account." If other people, like family members, also want to use the computer, you can set up accounts for them, for which they log in with their own password, and the computer opens up to their material only.

I'm the only one using my computer, so I didn't go through this procedure, but the route to setting up such accounts is Start > Control Panel > User Accounts and Family Safety > User Accounts.

See also "GUEST ACCOUNT" for allowing temporary users.

ADOBE FLASH PLAYER – This is a program that enables, or helps, in viewing website videos. I think it comes with your computer or operating system. If not, what happens is that when you try to view a video clip, a window pops up telling you that you need Flash Player. And in that window is a spot to click on for a quick one-minute download of the program.

32 vs 64-Bit Systems

Although it soon will, currently (12/11), Flash Player does not run in most 64-bit browsers. But you can run Flash Player in a 32-bit web browser on 64-bit systems. Go to Start > All Programs > click on "Internet Explorer", instead of "Internet Explorer (64-bit)"; they're listed right after each other. That's it. You should be able to play the clip now.

(I thought at first you have to reset it each time to 32, but no. Once you click on 32, it's set. It kept switching back to 64 for me because I forgot I was still clicking the 64-bit icon shortcut on my desktop. Once I changed the desktop shortcut icon to 32, it opened always to the 32-bit system.)

ADOBE READER – A program which you apparently need to read website stuff. I got a message at one point saying I needed to download it (Adobe 9), to get or read whatever it was. So I did. (It's free.) I assume it replaced an earlier version of Adobe.

RS says yes, you do need Adobe to read PDF files.

Update 2/10

Yes, Adobe PDF Reader is what most websites use more and more, apparently.

Problem: I installed a chess program (from 2003) and next time I tried to check something on a website, it said "Adobe Acrobat/Reader 5" would not open the text. "Adobe Acrobat/Reader 5" is the reader for my old chess program and it was now taking over my reading for other material also, instead of "Adobe PDF."

Solution: Start > Control Panel > Programs and Functions [W7 – Programs and Features] > Uninstall a program > check "Adobe Acrobat/Reader 5" > click Uninstall. THEN, I forget exactly how, I had to select "Abode PDF" to use for reading. Did that, and then things were back to normal.

Copying PDF Text from a Website

Copying text from Adobe Reader into a Word document can be done, but I find it only lets you do it a page at a time. So, your best bet, I think, is to block what you want, or do a CTRL+A, CTRL+C, and then paste it into a Word document. The text is sometimes not editable, or loses formatting, but at least you have it in your computer and can refer to it without going back to the website it came from.

This problem came up several times for me, when I was trying to make a copy of a user manual, so I would have it in my computer for quick reference. Companies these days seldom provide full physical manuals or user guides with their products, but only a quick-start sheet or two. Yet they do maintain full user guides on their websites.

ALPHABETIZING (OR ORDERING BY NUMBER) – Block your desired text > Paragraph box at top > click "A/Z↓" icon > select ascending or descending > OK. It orders that whole segment by number first, then alphabetically. If you have just numbers, it orders them by number. (It used to be that you would have to enter the number 1 as 01, because the ordering was based on proper decimal places for each number, but now, with Windows Vista, you don't have to.)

Note that each word/number must be a different paragraph, that is, you must press the Enter key after each word/number. You can't just type words/numbers along the same line and separate them by commas; they must be in successive lines down the page.

Nifty Organizing Technique for Note-Taking

Put a topic heading word at the start of each note. And no matter how long each note is, keep it to ONE paragraph. After you have tons of notes, alphabetize the whole deal. That puts all of your wide-ranging notes into alphabetical order by topic. And at this point, you can do any other editing you need to.

This technique is much easier than repeatedly blocking sentences and scrolling upward or downward in a long document to find the proper alphabetical spot for those blocks.

Say you're a baseball scout and you have a month's worth of notes on all aspects of the game. You can use this technique to organize the whole deal, much more quickly than laboriously finding, cutting, and pasting each note into its proper category.

Alphabetizing Folders or Documents Inside a Folder

Click the dropdown arrow next to Name at top left (the arrow appears if you put the cursor on "Name"), click "Sort." Click it again to put them in reverse order.

[W7 – Choices are over at the right, next to "Arrange by." Folders, or documents, in alphabetical order is the default setting. (It seems reverse order is no longer available. Good. Why would you want reverse alphabetical order anyway?)]

ALT KEY – At lower left of keyboard. I seldom use this key. Pressing it sometimes brings up a menu for whatever program you're in. Also, pressing it and sliding the right finger up or down on the mouse, changes the size of my chessboard in my chess program. It might do likewise for sizes of other items in other programs.

ANOMALIES – All kinds of weird stuff happens occasionally with computers. Thankfully, a lot of it goes away on its own, after a few days, disappearing as mysteriously as it appeared. For example, I once had a broad, blank white bar frequently show up at the top of my screen. Eventually it just went away on its own.

ANTI-VIRUS SECURITY – See "VIRUS"

APOSTROPHES – STRAIGHT vs CURLY See "QUOTATION

MARKS"

"APPLY" vs "OK" – See "OK vs APPLY"

ARROWS AT UPPER LEFT – INTERNET – When you are on the internet, you can go back to a previous site, or forward to a site you had been on following that one, by clicking on the left or right arrow icons at the upper left. To go all the way back to the first site you called up, just keep pressing the back arrow again and again till you get there.

AUDIOBOOK DOWNLOAD – I like to listen to audiobooks while driving. Now that I have an iPod, I had hoped it would be a simple matter to download audiobooks to it. Yeah, right. God, it's just so deflating; nothing is ever easy.

Figured I would go thru Amazon.com, since I have an account there already. OK, found the book I wanted, found where to click to download an audio version. But then I spent 20 minutes going thru dozens of windows, complications, additional downloads, avoiding some program that costs, re-doing installations, procedures, etc., etc. Finally got it, had trouble finding it, trouble playing it, trouble transferring it to my iPod... but, I eventually got it. Nothing is ever easy; there's always some additional complex procedure to follow.

And every time I try to document exactly the steps I took, it becomes impossible, because there are always so many side avenues, repeated loops, and dead ends.

Also I had to remember to turn "Sleep" to "Never", otherwise the downloading stops when computer goes to sleep.

But, for what it's worth, here is roughly how I downloaded a second book. (This time, I decided to go directly thru iTunes, instead of Amazon.com. That seemed easier when I downloaded an audiobook there a couple of years ago):

To Download an Audiobook

Open iTunes > Click iTunes Store at left > enter author into "Search Store" search box at upper right > a list of names comes up with that author > click on that author's name > icons for his or her books come up > first comes downloadable print books (for reading), then the next section has downloadable audiobooks (for listening); don't get the wrong version > right next to "Audiobooks" is "See all"; click on that > shows all books for that author > click on the book you want > click on "Buy book" > window comes up showing you Apple ID (your email address) and a place to enter your password > enter your password > click "Buy" > had to verify my billing info, because I now have a new computer, not to mention the hassle of retrieving my password. [Principle – you do something all the time, it gets easy; you do it only every so often, it's a pain in the butt. And if some jerk says "It's easy!", say, "No, it's not; it's only easy for you because you do it all the time, you myopic moron."] > I clicked Buy Book again; it showed I've already purchased this item, but haven't downloaded it yet > to download it, it said "Check for available downloads from the store menu"; I checked the OK for that message window, but when I did, it was already downloading (without my checking anywhere yet).

Shows downloading progress at top, but it showed it's downloading 4 items. I hope I'm not downloading the book 4 times! (I did click "Buy Book" several times during this process). Whew, turns out it was only one book, but in 4 parts (*Life*, Keith Richards, $21, 23 hours of material.) Took just over an hour to download.

Now if I click on the left under LIBRARY > Books, it's there. (I accidentally clicked on something and the 4th part disappeared from the list. I went to "Purchased" and all 4 parts were still there.)

When I clicked on the book to play it, it showed that this computer (my new one) is not authorized to play it. (iTunes allows up to 5 computers to play purchased material.) I put in my email and password and clicked "Authorize". Then it showed this computer was already authorized. (?) Anyway, now when I click on the book, it does start to play.

So, finally, what's left is to transfer it to my iPod.

While in the iTunes window, attach the iPod > turn it on > wait 5 seconds for DEVICES to come up at left > click on "Books" under LIBRARY > drag and drop each of 4 book parts into "Books" under DEVICES > took only ten seconds to transfer each part. (The 4th part wouldn't transfer, because, it turns out that that is a separate part, a digital booklet, which I can click on and see pictures. But I don't really want to transfer it to my iPod anyway... oh, I get it: A regular book usually has pictures; so these are the pictures for the audiobook. So I'm guessing this is common – an audiobook will have at least two parts, the text, and then a separate file for the pictures.)

Now the book is on my iPod and it plays in my car as I drive. Hooray. Done.

Final note: It turns out that the booklet section with the pictures is now under Music instead of Books. It may well have zipped over there on its own, not by my mistake. Yet again, Microsoft assuming it's being helpful, but really being confusing.

One Long Track Problem

For a while I thought my iPod-playing car stereo would only play the book in one long track, but I finally figured out that while it doesn't show tracks, if I press the next-track button, it does move it up a full track.

See also "MUSIC / AUDIO TRANSFERS THRU A COMPUTER" > "A. DOWNLOADING MUSIC" > "DOWNLOADING AUDIOBOOKS".

AUDIO RECORDING DIRECTLY TO COMPUTER – See "SOUND RECORDER"

"AUTOCOMPLETE" – This feature guesses what you're about to type into a form and tries to fill it in for you, based on info you had entered in the past, like your email address. Just click on it and it puts it right into the box without your having to finish typing.

If you're not in a secure environment, you might want to keep the categories of this feature unchecked, so that this information is not available to other people's eyes. If you're in a situation like mine and rarely have people nosing around your computer, you might as well keep most of the categories checked. It's a choice of security vs convenience.

To change settings here: Internet Explorer > Tools > Internet Options > Content tab > AutoComplete section, Settings > check or uncheck selections > OK.

AUTOCORRECT – AUTOMATICALLY CORRECTED WORDS

MS Word automatically corrects many misspellings automatically. If you type in "recieve," it will immediately correct it to "receive" as soon as you press the space bar.

If you tend to misspell certain words constantly, you can add those particular words yourself to their big list of automatically corrected words.

You can also use this function to have Windows automatically change an abbreviation to a full word. Speeds up your typing considerably.

For example, I don't like spelling out "Christianity" all the time. So I put "Xity" onto the list: Click Review tab at top > Spelling & Grammar at far left > Options > AutoCorrect Options > AutoCorrect tab > enter info (Replace: "Xity" With: "Christianity") > Add (or Delete if you want to drop one) > OK.

Very useful function.

Keeping the Original Word (or Abbreviation or Misspelling)

Sometimes I want to keep the abbreviation instead of the full word. After it puts in the full word, just CTRL+Z it back one step to the abbreviation. CTRL+Z doesn't erase the word, but puts it back to the original form you typed it in (a second CTRL+Z erases it). Convenient. Otherwise, you have to fiddle with it, going backwards letter by letter, to produce the original abbreviation or word.

AutoCorrect Options Button

A little icon (blue and yellow) often shows up right on top of your text when some autocorrect or auto-formatting action took place (like automatic numbering). If you click on it, it gives you correction options. If you just keep typing, it disappears on its own.

But I find it very annoying, popping up so much and hiding part of my text. To get rid of this function: Review tab at top > Spelling & Grammar at left > Options at lower left > AutoCorrect Options at upper right > uncheck "Show AutoCorrect Options buttons" > OK > OK > x out the window.

And, as usual, redundancy leads to confusion: That little icon and its choices seem to override the very same choices I made under AutoCorrect. Even though at one point I had automatic numbering unchecked, it kept doing automatic numbering, because I left the same feature still checked under the small icon dropdown arrow options. So I had to order up those small icons to appear again, so I could get my option choices in both places matched (to unchecked). I'm sorry I ever clicked on that small icon. But OK, I'm back to no automatic numbering now.

It's unbelievable how often MS tries to make things easier by offering different routes to the same function, and ends up just causing more problems and aggravation.

AUTOCORRECT – SYMBOLS – If you want to get a symbol into your text more easily than by inserting it from the Symbol selection, you can use the exact same procedure as above for automatic word replacement:

Use Insert, Symbol, to get it into your text for the first time, so you can do a copy (CTRL+C) of it, which puts it onto your clipboard. Then click Review tab at top > Spelling & Grammar at far left > Options > AutoCorrect Options > when you get to "Replace:", type in the letters you want to represent the symbol. Then for "With:", you do a CTRL+V, pasting the symbol you have on the clipboard into the "With:" box > Add > OK.

That way, next time, when you type your chosen letters, you get the symbol up in its place automatically.

Useful ones for me:
"= =" to get ≠
"dg" to get °
"cents" to get ¢
"(c)" to get © [W7 – does this one automatically]

Besides this automatic replacement feature, you can also get symbols up quickly by making CTRL key shortcuts. See "SHORTCUTS – CUSTOM SHORTCUTS FOR SYMBOLS"

AUTO-SAVE – See "SAVING – AUTOMATIC"

BACK / FORWARD NAVIGATING – When you've visited multiple websites, you can use the large arrows at upper left to navigate back to a previous website (or forward to the next one you had visited). You can do likewise for document folders.

BACKING UP YOUR MATERIAL – It's a good idea to do so, in case your laptop is lost or damaged. And, because your computer's hard drive will eventually die (4-6 years life?) and you'll lose all your material!! There are many ways to accomplish this. I've settled on the following as my preference:

1. My Documents – Frequently to a Flash Drive

I back up "My Documents" (normal "ongoing" documents or folders), every month or so on a flash drive. And, if I'm working hard on a particular document, I may even do a daily backup for that one document.

I had preferred backing up material to re-writable DVD disks rather than flash drives, because they are easier to store, label, and not lose, and they are cheaper. And there's plenty of room. My "My Documents" folder is less than 1 GB, and the disk is 4 GB.

However, I now prefer flash drives to DVD disks. I've had some problems with disks. (Once it wouldn't let me delete a document until I erased the whole disk and re-formatted it. Also, it wouldn't let me erase and re-format some old disks, though I had no problem when using new disks. This weird stuff could be the virus I had in my old computer still lingering; I don't know.)

At any rate, I'm switching to flash drives rather than disks. They're faster, less fragile, more stable, more reliable than disks, in my experience.

2. Major Folders – Twice a Year to External Hard Drive

I back up my four major folders ("Libraries" in Windows 7) – Documents, Pictures, Music, Videos – two or three times a year to an external hard drive. See "EXTERNAL HARD DRIVE"

Set Material

I keep a separate big folder called "Set Material" of stuff I know I'm not going to change; that way I don't have to pointlessly re-copy that material every time I do a backup. I keep a copy of that folder on both my laptop and my external hard drive, so that is IS backed up, but, I don't need to keep re-backing it up.

Say you have a ton of pictures. Keep two folders – Old Pictures and New Pictures. That way you can avoid constantly re-backing up the old ones, which constitute "Set Material."

Backing Up vs Moving

Note this key distinction: When backing up material onto a disk, or flash drive, or external hard drive, by DRAGGING AND DROPPING, you are making a copy. But when dragging and dropping material from one location to another on your computer, you are NOT copying the material but are moving it, so that it no longer remains in the original location.

For example, if you drag and drop a document from a folder onto the desktop, you get the actual document on the desktop, not a copy; it is now gone from the folder you moved it from.

Backing Up a Shortcut Icon

Along with the above caution, note that if you have shortcut icons on your desktop, and drag and drop one of those to an external device, you are only copying that shortcut, not the actual file it represents! So that file is NOT backed up! Be sure you are dragging and dropping actual files, not their shortcuts.

Now, if you have that external device plugged into your computer, and click on the shortcut on it, it will bring up the actual file; but, that's only because the file is still in your computer, and the device can access it when it is plugged in. But if you had deleted the file from your computer, it would be gone, and the shortcut would not work, because the actual file is NOT on your device, only the shortcut is.

Confusing Dates

Also note this wrinkle, which I think applies to transfers to either disk or flash drive: If you drag and drop material and you already have a document or folder there with the same name, a window pops up asking you if you want to copy and replace that older version. If you click on that option, it does copy and replace, BUT, it retains its old date when you hover the pointer over its icon, even though it is NOW in fact the newer version. Can be confusing! And alarming, to look at your list of backup items weeks later and think you didn't save your latest version of a big document, when in fact you did; it's just that the date label stayed the same.

I usually delete the old version from the backup device first, and then import that new version from my computer, so that it gets labeled with the correct current date.

But, even then, some big folders may keep their old date, because you may not have changed them, only the stuff inside them.

To check if a backup is current, instead of looking at the date of the My Documents folder or a big folder, look inside it at another folder or document you recently worked on, and those will show you the actual date they were last edited. In other words, a folder may show an old date, but the files inside it will show you the latest version.

How to Back Up Material to a Flash Drive

1. Insert the flash drive into a USB port
2. Window for it comes up (may take more than 5 seconds)
3. Click on "Open folder to view files" at bottom
4. Make the resulting window (showing the contents of the flash drive) smaller, and move it to the right. [W7 – just drag the window by its top, deep into the side and it pops into a half-screen size]
5. Open whatever folder the desired folder is in. (For example, the "Documents" folder, so you can back up the "My Documents" folder inside it.)
6. Make its window smaller and move it to the left
7. Now you have the two windows up side-by-side
8. Drag and drop the file from the left to the right
9. That's it. You now have a copy of the file on the flash drive
10. Unplug the flash drive

I definitely think this method is the easiest. But if you're not familiar with dragging and dropping or setting windows side-by-side on the desktop, you could also right-click the file > CTRL+C > CTRL+V it into the flash drive.

Note that to back up a My Documents folder, you click on the bigger "Documents" folder, so that the "My Documents" folder is listed. If you click on the My Documents folder itself and open it, you'd have to drag and drop all the numerous items inside it individually.

How To Back Up Material to a DVD–RW

For a Blank DVD–RW Disk

1. Insert blank DVD-RW
2. Dialogue box automatically comes up
3. Click "Burn files to disc" (not "Burn a DVD video disc")
4. Type in Disc Title (the default title is the current date)

[If you click the down arrow for "Show formatting options," it shows the default "Live File System" checked. That's the one you want, a computer data disk. The other choice, the "Mastered" format, is for making a video disk to play on a DVD player.) [W7 – has now labeled these two options more clearly: "Like a USB flash drive" and "With a CD/DVD player."]

5. Next, Yes. Wait [W7 – takes less than one minute] as it formats the disk
6. "AutoPlay" window comes up, click "Open folder to view files"
7. That opens the disk window
8. Make the window smaller
9. Drag it to the right (by dragging the top part of the window)
10. Open whatever folder holds the desired folder
11. Make that window smaller and drag it to the left
12. Now you have the two windows side by side (computer at left, disk at right)
13. Drag and drop items from left to right. (For me, on my new computer with Windows 7, it transferred material at the rate of approximately 100 MB per minute.)
14. That's it. It makes copies, not cuts. The material is on the DVD disk now.
15. With a Sharpie marker, write the current date on the disk

Once you've formatted and used a disk, DON'T erase the disk (Computer > right-click Drive E > "Erase this disc"); rather, just delete the files on it. That way it stays formatted and you don't have to re-format it.

For a DVD–RW Already Being Used

1. Insert DVD-RW
2. AutoPlay window comes up
3. Click "Open folder to view files," delete the old files you had on the disk
4. Make the window smaller
5. Drag it to the right (by dragging the top part of the window)
6. Open whatever folder holds the folder you want to back up
7. Make that window smaller and drag it to the left
8. Now you have the two windows side by side (computer at left, disk at right)
9. Drag and drop items from left to right
10. That's it. It makes copies, not cuts. The material is on the DVD disk now.
11. With a Sharpie marker, write the current date on the disk, having crossed out the previous date.

Cautions

You CAN edit the material on the disk (add, delete, move, etc.), just like you do on the computer hard drive. BUT, I would NOT do so, because then the info on the disk will no longer be the same as the info on your hard drive, and hopeless confusion looms on the horizon. Computer hell is not knowing which of several versions contains which of numerous updates.

Trust me; it can get very complicated very quickly. Use that disk ONLY for backup or transfer, not for working on or editing.

Deleting a document from the disk, deletes it completely. It does NOT go to the Recycle Bin. (Though you still have the original document on your hard drive.)

Windows Automatic Backup – Ugh

There is a way of having your computer do an automatic backup. BUT, I think my current method is FINE. Otherwise, things get obsessive. My accidentally deleting stuff is very rare anyway.

Besides, when I tried it out, I couldn't get it to work anyway. Windows Vista Backup Program: Start > All Programs > Maintenance > Backup and Restore Center > Files > options... Supposed to only change the stuff you've changed; non-changed stuff simply stays as is... I think. But when I tried it, it kept stalling. Wouldn't work. So, forget it. I'll stick with my normal manual backup to flash drives and external hard drive.

I don't see the point anyway. It's like a complex program that requires your ongoing attention to keep gas in our car. Leave me alone! I know when I need gas – when the tank is low – and I don't want to be constantly nagged when my gas level is fine.

Update for Windows 7 automatic backup: Start > Control Panel > System and Security > Backup and Restore > attach external hard drive > "Set up backup" at right > in the backup destination box, click on the external hard drive > Next > Let Windows Choose (saves documents, music, pictures, videos) > click "Change Schedule", set it to what you want > Save Settings and Run Backup. So it does a backup right away and will do regular backups according to your schedule.

But again, what's the point? You have to have your destination device attached each time, on a set schedule Seems easier to simply do it on my own, manually, when I want to. Not only that, but it doesn't let you choose selected material from what it landed in your external hard drive; you have only overall "Restore" options to click.

Bottom line, for me, it just makes everything MORE complicated, not less complicated. I'm sticking to simple manual backing up!

Hard Drive Life

Though they last many years, your hard drive will eventually die, losing all your info, so I've read. So you DO need to do backup, especially if your laptop is getting very old.

BACKUP – MUSIC – See "MUSIC"

BACKUP OF PRINTED PAGES – See "SECOND SIDE PAGES"

BANKING ONLINE – I have no experience here. I'm sure that, once you learn how to do it, it's easier than regular banking. BUT, I am very uneasy about security. I mean, if I were a cyber thief, I would focus on online banking, in hopes of scoring big hits. Online banking – not for me.

Also, from Jean Chatzky, Newsweek 10/30/11 – *"Unfortunately, switching banks is an administrative nightmare, particularly for people who bank and pay bills online. This is by design."*

BATTERY FOR LAPTOP – The battery for a laptop gets charged automatically when you have the computer plugged in. Once it's charged, you can use the laptop unplugged. It does all the same operations.

How much battery time is left shows on the battery icon at lower right. Put the cursor on it, and it shows percent left. If your battery is about to run out, the computer automatically warns you. And if it runs out as you're working, it automatically saves what you did right up to just before it ran out.

Well, I experimented with letting the battery run out, and here is what happened: If I had opened a document, worked on it, saved it, and then did some more work on it without saving it, then when the battery ran out, it DID automatically save the new unsaved stuff, in a Document Recovery panel on the left (choose the latest one). But, if I opened a document, worked on it but did not do an initial Save yet, it did NOT save it.

Then I tried it again, and this time it did not save it, despite an initial Save. Conclusion: sometimes it saves it, other times not. Best to remember to always click Save whenever your computer is not plugged in and may run out of battery power.

The battery in my new computer shows percent left, and, usually also gives me an approximate estimate of time left in hours and minutes. Also, the green light of the ON/OFF button starts blinking, as a warning, when the battery is down to about 10%.

Battery Life

Battery life has improved over the years. Depends a lot on the type of operation you're doing. For example, printing uses it up quickly, whereas simple typing uses it up slowly. Watching a DVD would be somewhere in the middle. For simple typing, for me, on my old computer I get maybe an hour's time; on my new computer, several hours' time, maybe up to 4 hours.

The battery lasts longer if you let it run out, or close to it, maybe once a week. So I consciously, but not religiously, use my laptop fairly often unplugged to let it run low.

Note that as a battery gets older, it lasts less and less time. My old computer battery, after only 2½ years was down to about 10-15 minutes per full charge.

Also, batteries do run down in an unplugged laptop, even if you're not using it.

Battery – Replacement

Removing it from the bottom front should be fairly easy; for mine, I just move the two locking clips over.

Needed a new battery. Comp USA is out of business, as is Circuit City. Went to Best Buy. They said they don't stock computer batteries for the most part, since they are too many types. Went to a store down the road called Batteries Plus. They had it. Otherwise, I would have had to get it online from SONY.

Cost – $106, $96 with $10 mail-in rebate. (Used to cost $250!)

Guy said I should charge it for 4 hours, let it run out, then repeat that 3 more times, so that it gets well adjusted to the laptop (or something to that effect). Then, every week, once a week, let the battery run out. You get better mileage out of it that way. Yeah, OK, but no thank you. The battery runs out every so often in my normal course of using it anyway; it works fine. I don't want my epitaph to say "He dedicated his life to good battery maintenance."

Battery Installing

Note that some computers, like my new Sony Vaio, have the left and right battery release switches on the battery itself, not the computer.

One time, when I got a new battery, it seemed to run out right away. I detached the battery and put it in again. Then it was OK. Might not have been clicked in all the way.

BAY – CD / DVD DRIVE BAY – I use this bay a lot. It is a mechanical mechanism, so I'm not surprised that after 4 years it started acting up and not playing some CDs or DVDs that it used to play fine. Got it replaced at a computer place (about $125). New one works fine.

See also "CD DISK REMOVAL" or "DVD – PLAY".

BLACKBERRY – I don't have one, and have no experience with them. It's a hand-held device with many capabilities – it's a phone, it does email, functions as a planner and address book, has some picture and video capabilities, etc., etc.

I don't know if it has internet capabilities. I'm pretty sure the iPhone (a similar device) does; you can access the internet just like a computer, except it's a hand-held device, with no wires! It's pretty popular and cutting edge... but I resist it, for now. Don't want my life revolving around a hand-held device. Will wait till I feel a definite and practical need for one.

BLANK PAGE – SUDDEN APPEARANCE OF – This is spooky. You're typing along and all of a sudden a blank page appears. Oh no! Did I just lose three hours of work!! No, what happened is you accidentally pressed CTRL+N, instead of CTRL+something else. CTRL+N orders up a new, blank document. But, the document you were working on is still there. Just "x" out the new document and the document you were working on is back, just as you left it, ready to continue work on. Whew!

BLOCKING – Means selecting a text, or some chunk of material, so that you can make an adjustment to it, like changing its font, or typestyle, or size, etc. Or, moving it, copying it, deleting it, etc.

For example, if you want to change a paragraph of text from regular typestyle to italics, you would block it first, then press CTRL+I.

Blocking a Section of Text – Three Methods

1) F8 KEY – Position the cursor > press F8 key > use arrow key, to scroll down > order the change you want. (Sometimes the block does not hold beyond the bottom of the page.)

2) SHIFT KEY – Position the cursor > Shift key > use arrow key, to scroll down > order the change. (I like this method; it holds the block thru the end of the page to the next page.)

3) MANUAL DRAG – Position the pointer > press left of mouse > drag the pointer thru the text. (This is the method to use for blocking text off the internet, since the other two methods do not work there.)

Note that, for MANUAL DRAG, the lower you hold the pointer below the text, the faster it will block. It goes even faster if you hold it below the bottom edge of the page and wiggle it back and forth.

Note also that blocking internet text can be tricky. You often have to try it several times to get just the section you want, since internet texts are often made up of imbedded chunks or sections already.

More Consistent INTERNET Blocking – Caret Browsing

Hey, guess what, there IS a way to make the SHIFT method work for internet blocking. You CAN get a cursor in there and move it with the arrow keys, to get more accurate, consistent blocking of internet text:

While on the internet, press F7 key > a window comes up asking if you want "Caret Browsing" on > Click Yes > Then you can click on a spot and that puts a movable cursor into the internet page, so you can use Shift and arrow keys to block more accurately. (Doesn't always work well; gets hinky sometimes. If the down arrow sticks as you're scrolling, use the right arrow, and then the down arrow again, to continue.)

Note that this feature will stay on as you browse other sites in the same session, but when you open up a new browsing session, you have to re-order it, to get the movable cursor up into the webpage.

Blocking the Entire Text

To block the entire text of a document, press CTRL+A.

For websites, unless you really want everything on that page, it's usually not a good idea to use CTRL+A, because it will include all kinds of extra embedded junk. Better to block just the desired area or text.

If you made a mistake in blocking, just undo it by CTRL+Z and do it again. Or, if you're on a website, move the pointer outside the text area and left-click it to get rid of the mistaken highlighting.

See also "HIGHLIGHTING (BLOCKING)"

BLOG – A blog (a blend of *web log*) is a website where people share ideas and opinions. It is usually hosted by a single person, who makes regular entries. Blogs are usually subject-specific – politics, sports, whatever. You can google "free blog" to find free blog sites, and then sign up with one to create your own blog.

A blog might be visited by only a handful of friends, or, have millions of visitors. The most popular blog is The Huffington Post (politics, news), which has an estimated unique monthly visitors of 54 million!

BLU-RAY DISKS – These are disks that hold hi-definition (very clear) video. Regular DVD players will not play Blu-ray disks (they use different types of lasers to read the info); you need a Blu-ray player (which are not that expensive – can get one for under $100 at Walmart).

On the other hand, Blu-ray players WILL play regular DVDs as well as Blu-ray disks.

The disks hold 5 times as much info as regular DVDs. You can burn hi-def video (that you imported from a hi-def camcorder to your computer) to a Blu-ray disk, but, few computers have a Blu-ray burner. You can buy a separate Blu-ray burner (about $200) to attach to a computer and burn the disk. (At least, I think so. This is part of my future plans; after all, what's the point of having a hi-def camcorder if you can't burn hi-def (Blu-ray) disks?)

BLUETOOTH – This is short-range radio technology that enables you to use devices wirelessly. Wireless communication between mouse, keyboard, and printer is a common application.

BOOKS – AUDIO – See "AUDIOBOOK DOWNLOAD" and also "MUSIC / AUDIO TRANSFERS THRU A COMPUTER" > "A. DOWNLOADING MUSIC" > "DOWNLOADING AUDIOBOOKS"

BORDERS – To get a border around a word or section of text: Block it > Paragraph box at top > Borders and Shading icon at lower right of the box > dropdown arrow > select option (usually "Outside Borders"). It will put a rectangular border around your blocked material, all the way to the edge if you blocked a whole line or paragraph, just around the word if you blocked just the word.

Block the material again, click that dropdown arrow again, and click "Borders and Shading" at the bottom, and it gives you options to change the border width, color, shading, etc. Note how I have some procedures here in this manual bordered in black or red.

I also find that putting a border around an individual word is sometimes a good way to emphasize that word.

Often, borders will do odd things, and you have to spend time fiddling with them to get exactly what you want.

BRACKETS – Much easier to use the keyboard keys to get brackets (directly above Enter and quotes keys) than to use Insert and Symbols.

BREAKS – See "SECTION BREAKS"

BRIGHTEN OR DIM – SCREEN – Fn key+F6 to brighten screen; Fn key+F5 to dim. Goes up or down one level per press. If nothing happens, that means it's already at maximum or minimum. I always keep it at max. See also "OUTDOORS – SCREEN BRIGHTNESS"

BROWSER – A browser is a program that one uses to search for websites on the internet. The Windows' browser program is "Internet Explorer", the icon with the large blue "e" in it.

Other browsers are Firefox, Google Chrome, Safari.

BROWSING HISTORY – WEBSITES – Computers keep a history of the websites you visit. Click the white star at upper right ("View Favorites, Feeds, and History"). [I used to have these options under a yellow star "Favorites" icon on the left; I don't know where that went. It may simply be the new setup under Internet Explorer 9.]

Under the History tab, Windows shows you the websites you've visited, for the past 20 days. I don't find this feature useful at all. I suppose it's for getting back to a site you liked, but if I like a site, I already know it, or I make a note of it, rather than search thru a huge list of them under this History feature.

Deleting Browsing History

1. You can delete a single site from this history: right-click it, and click Delete.

2. You can delete the entire history list: Tools at upper right > Internet Options > General tab > Browsing History > Delete > Delete > OK. But, of course, the feature itself is still on and it starts a new history next time you browse the net.

3. You can turn off this feature, so it won't keep a history: Tools at upper right > Internet Options > General tab > Browsing History > Settings > "Days to keep pages in history" at bottom > set at "0". (What's the difference between doing that and checking the "Delete browsing history on exit" option in that same window? I don't know.)

Keeping Password Info

Now, the problem is, if you do set the number of days to keep history to "0," you no longer have website info saved, and you therefore have to enter your user name and password EVERY TIME you want to access a website account you have (for me, my Yahoo email, my Netflix account, my Match.com account, and a few others.)

So, what kind of setup should I have, to maintain privacy in websites visited, yet have quick access to my accounts?

Read some internet stuff, that people have had the same trouble I had, in setting this balance. And also in trying to clear browsing history; often it doesn't seem to work; stuff keeps coming back like unwanted dinner guests. Part of the problem may be that settings takes affect only after you restart your computer. That seemed to be the case sometimes; other times not! I tried all kinds of things and combinations, unsuccessfully:

– Tools, Manage Add Ons, disabled most of them – no go.
– Tools, Internet Options, Advanced tab, reset, restart computer – no go.
– Tools, Internet Options, Settings, Advanced tab, reset, check Delete Personal Settings, restart computer. No go.

– Tools, Internet Options, General tab, browsing history Settings, set days to "0" from "20", OK – No go. Also checked "Delete Browsing History on Exit" – no go! [Actually, here I must have done something in the wrong order or combination, because this one IS the key. See below.]
– Safety, Delete Browsing History, uncheck top box (Preserve Favorite Website Data). Note that top box is SEPARATE from the delete button below; the bottom six get deleted if checked, but the top one is simply checked or unchecked to stay as such... I think. Very confusing. Nothing seems to work, but other times, it does.
– In theory, under the Google search box, you can click on the red "X" at the right of each (it says "Delete"!) but after it deletes, they are all still there next time!

One "workaround" solution I came up with:

1. Clear your history, up to this point, so that all old info is gone.
2. UNCHECK your "Delete Browsing History on Exit," so that it will gather new info.
3. Open up your email and the other few sites for which you need a password, so that it gathers this new specific browsing history.
4. Close each of those sites.
5. Then, open up the browsing settings window again, and now CHECK your "Delete Browsing History on Exit" so that it now deletes any further new history from this point on, but keeps your password-required sites info that you just accumulated. That should do it.

Of course, if you "Delete Browsing History" in the future (step one), you'd lose that password-required sites info. And if you uncheck "Delete Browsing History on Exit" in the future (step two), it would be back to gathering ALL new history info.

Another possible solution:

Put sensitive sites under your Favorites list and name the folder something different (like "Recipes," instead of "Bank Account" or "Laundry.com" instead of "Howtokillyourmotherinlaw.com"). Then only access those sites through your Favorites (star icon), so that you never have to type them in again, bypassing the History gathering feature.

Best Solution:
Keep the browsing history feature fully on, but use "InPrivate Browsing".

InPrivate Browsing

Internet Explorer > Safety > InPrivate Browsing. This keeps your history private, and also any further tabs or links or new sites you type in and visit during that session. For any new session, you need to re-select InPrivate Browsing. As long as you see the "InPrivate" word in blue at upper left, and then go to Google or whatever, this function is in effect.

See also "PASSWORDS FOR WEBSITES – SAVE"

BULLETS – Block the text > Paragraph box at top > "Bullets" icon upper left of box > dropdown arrow for choices. It puts bullets in front of each new paragraph, and moves the text a bit to the right.

Note that you can delete those bullets by backspacing, but it's usually easier to re-block the text, click the dropdown arrow of the Bullets icon, and select "None."

Also, as with automatic numbering, press Enter key twice to end that automatic action at the end of your text list.

BURN vs RIP – BURN means copying something from the computer to a disk. RIP means copying something from a disk to the computer (hard drive).

BUSINESS CARDS – You can make your own business cards.

The Avery.com website (labels) has a template for business cards for free downloading. I recommend their site; I use their templates for address labels also. You type material into already correctly positioned spots. Avery.com > Find Templates > Cards (at left) > business cards > download. Their templates fit whatever product number is on their label packages, which you can buy at Staples, or even CVS.

Here's the exact procedure: Google "Avery. Com" > "Office Supplies – Office Products & Labels / Avery" shows up; right there click on "Find a Template" > Template for Business Cards > scroll selection (about 5 pages in, is "Business Card – Wide, 10 per sheet") > click "Download at right (or click on the title if that doesn't work) > type in name and email > check "No, not at this time" for no ads > Submit > "click here" if doesn't download automatically > Save > select destination folder > type in the name you want for it ("Business Card") > Save. That lands it (a template for business cards, with business card rectangles already correctly positioned) into your destination folder. Open up that file and you can type in whatever you want, in whatever fonts, sizes, format you want.

Types of Avery Templates

Last time I checked they seem to have moved their blank card templates to the top of their list. I like the ten per page one.

I kinda prefer their blank business card templates, otherwise you have to work within their specific designs.

On the other hand, you can adjust the several boxes of info within each card design, like dragging the box corners to different sizes, changing fonts or colors, etc. Then, having adjusted the boxes in the first one at top left, block and copy each box to the next card, which means a bit of work, replacing three or four boxes for each card. But, it's not too bad. Once you get your ten cards done, then you're all set.

Pre-Scored Sheets

Staples carries (not in their labels section, but in their paper section) nice pre-scored sheets for business cards. They separate remarkably cleanly, with smooth edges. (I got these because if I do my own cutting with a hand cutter, the cards never come out exactly rectangular.)

My Old Method

Card size is 2 by 3½ inches. I designed one card (Arial Black font, different sizes, embossed font, background color, border, etc.), then made 5 copies of that down the left side of the page. You have to do considerable fiddling with sizes to get the five evenly spaced down the page. I used these margins: top .5, bot .5, left .4, right 5.3, and these font sizes for successive lines: 9,14,13,13,12,12,6 9, 9 9,14,13,13,12,12,6 9, 9 etc.

Used Photo matte paper (much crisper than regular card stock.) Made a copy, at "best quality" printing. After printing those five cards on a page, I ran same side page thru again, this time upside-down, to end up with a sheet of 10 cards. Then I cut them to size.

BUTTONS – Usually refers to physical buttons to push on your computer, other than the keyboard keys. Computers vary for what they have for buttons. They may have buttons for sound volume or screen brightness, etc. At the very least they'll have an ON/OFF button.

If you can't figure out why you have no sound, sometimes it's because you accidentally pressed a "Mute" button.

Buttons can also refer to labeled rectangular icons to click on, in a dialogue window, like [Delete] or [Next].

CABLE TV – Quick note on Comcast service: If your remote is working very sluggishly despite good batteries, or, if you lose your picture suddenly without having changed anything and your DVR shows "EAS," call them. They can fix both quickly by rebooting your DVR. Before you talk to a person, they offer to "refresh" your program by your just pushing the #1 key on your phone; that didn't work for me, but once I talked to a person, their "rebooting" did the trick almost immediately.

Recent Discovery

When timer-recording a sports game, the DVR gives you the option of a half hour of extended recording, in case the game goes long. Myself, to play it extra safe, I always used to record the next three half-hour programs after Celtic games. But, I now realize that that half-hour extended time option can be clicked on and adjusted to an extra TWO hours. Much easier to do this than to record the following programs.

Sports Tip

If I'm watching a repeat of a game already played, and the program has news text crawling across the bottom, to avoid accidentally looking at the text and finding out who won, I fold a sheet of paper lengthwise, 4 times, and scotch tape it to the bottom of the screen to hide that crawling text.

CABLE WIRE – At the end of the wire (called the "ethernet" cable) that connects your computer to the modem, there's a plastic "boot" or piece that clicks or locks your wire into your computer port so it won't fall out. Mine was partly broken and often failed to lock, coming loose and causing me to lose my internet connection intermittently. You can get a replacement at Radio Shack for $14.

Or, do what I did: reverse ends, plugging the loose connection into the modem and the stable end into your computer (both ends are identical). The end that plugs into your computer is the end that gets the most jiggling, whereas the modem end doesn't get much jiggling and should be fine with a less than perfect locking mechanism.

CALCULATOR – Start > Programs > Accessories > Calculator. Neat feature, if you don't have a regular calculator handy. I often like to know percentages of things. Calculator shows on screen and you click on the numbers, the operation, and then the equal sign. [W7 – has more extended features here than Vista.]

CALENDAR – You would think you could get a calendar from Windows easily, to insert into a Word document, but I find they just keep trying to sell you stuff. Leave me alone! All I want is a calendar for the month!!

I like this site: "Timeanddate.com" > copy selected material to a Word document. That's it; no BS, no signing up for anything. You can adjust the format after you land it into your document.

CAMCORDER – I keep separate extensive notes for my camcorder instructions. Like everything else in electronics, it takes a while to learn all the stuff, and if you don't use it often, you forget how to do things.

I just note a few key concepts here:

I'm pretty sure that tapes and disks are on the way out. It's now hard drives or memory cards. It's great not to have to worry about tapes or disks.

I have a Sony hi-def camcorder now. Camcorders are much smaller than they used to be. They usually come with a USB cord that connects from the camcorder to your computer, so you can import material to your computer hard drive. They have all kinds of features, a lot of which are kind of pointless, since using the default settings is usually just fine.

Biggest tip: When you know you're going to be using it, especially for something important, practice with it for several days beforehand, so that doing the operations is automatic and you can concentrate instead on the shooting and subject matter, and not fumble, be confused, or forget something. I keep a list of things to check on before going out to shoot. Fully charged battery is a key one. Also, a tripod is important for steady shooting.

Built-in Camcorder in Computer

See "VIDEO RECORDING WITH THE COMPUTER ITSELF"

"Flip" Pocket Camcorder

I bought one, and it's pretty neat. It takes decent HD video, it's very portable (it's a little bit bigger than a deck of cards), and the operating instructions are refreshingly simple and straightforward. So far the one big drawback is that when you move the camcorder at all, the picture gets wobbly. It doesn't have image stabilizing, like regular camcorders do.

Update: Yeah, it's really a bad, wobbly picture if you hold it by hand, or move around with it; MUST use a tripod!!

Update: Recent Consumer Reports article says the video quality of these pocket camcorders is definitely inferior to even the lowest end regular camcorders. I believe it. So, as convenient as it is, I think I'm better off with a second regular camcorder, even a cheap one.

CAMERA (See also "PHOTOS / PICTURES") – Like camcorders, modern digital cameras come with a CD that you put into your computer and it automatically gives you directions for installing the program. From that point on, you just connect the camera to the computer with the USB cable that came with the camera (small end to camera, large end to computer USB port), turn on the camera ("display" mode, not picture-taking mode), and it automatically imports the pictures you've taken, usually to Owner, Pictures folder. They usually land as a folder automatically named the current date. Before importing, It gives you an option to "tag" or name the pictures, so you can find them more easily (otherwise, they get automatically labeled by numbers like 093, 094, 095, etc.)

If it doesn't automatically import the picture, unplug the USB end of your cable > wait a few seconds > plug it back in > AutoPlay should come up > check "Always do this for pictures" > click Import Pictures and Videos. Now it should automatically import pictures from your camera.

Another method: Windows Photo Gallery > click File at upper left > Import from Camera > select your camera from the list of devices > click Import.

Afterwards, don't forget to erase those pictures from your camera. I think Windows automatically detects and does not import pictures you've already imported, even though those old ones are still in your camera. I know for iPod pictures, it does that.

Pictures automatically land in BOTH "Pictures" folder (under Owner [W7 – under Libraries]) and Windows Photo Gallery. I think they are actually stored in the Picture folder, but Windows Photo Gallery accesses them and displays them also. **However,** if you delete a picture under either place, it automatically deletes it from the other place also!

Most cameras today are digital. They take excellent pictures. They also shoot video, though not for any extensive length, or in as good quality as a camcorder. (Conversely, most camcorders also take still pictures, though not in as good quality as a camera.)

Note that if you delete pictures from your camera, THEY ARE GONE. However, if your camera simply runs out of battery life, the pictures still stay in there, and are available again when you put fresh batteries in.

Windows 7

For Windows 7, you don't even need the camera CD program that came with it. You just attach the camera, using the cable that comes with it, and Windows recognizes it and imports pictures automatically.

If not, type "Scanners and cameras" into the Start search box > "View scanners and cameras" should come up; click on it > click Add Device > (Yes), Next > choose manufacturer and model > Next > type in a name for the device > Next > Finish.

This feature is for installing drivers for older cameras. So, use it if simply attaching the camera, or using the CD program, doesn't work.

Memory Cards

You can also transfer photos to your computer using a memory card. You need to buy a memory card reader ($20) that matches your camera's memory card. You plug it into your computer and then plug the card into it. See "MEMORY CARDS"

Batteries

Cameras drain batteries very quickly. I don't take that many pictures, but I find it best to use long-lasting lithium batteries. I've read they last 8 times longer than regular ones.

They're expensive, but well worth it, I think, for your peace of mind, knowing you're not likely to run out of power at the wrong time. I remember how I used to use regular batteries and was surprised how quickly they ran out, and how that constantly put me into an anxious frame of mind.

In fact, a regular battery has to be pretty new to work; a half-empty regular battery will run many things, but not a camera, I find.

A geek guy once told me rechargeable batteries actually work better than regular ones also.

I've read that trying to take pictures when the battery is low, is not good for memory cards.

CANCEL PRINTING – Most printers have a "Cancel" or "Waste Basket" button to push, if you suddenly realize you don't want to print the material after all, or don't want to print it just yet. On my Epson 810, there's no separate physical "Cancel" button, but once you order a print job, then a "Cancel" choice shows up on the printer display screen, which you can then press.

If your printer doesn't have a cancel button, you can cancel the job thru your computer: Start > "Devices and Printers" at the right > right-click your printer > "See what's printing" > right-click the job > Cancel.

See also "PRINTING" > "Cancelling a Print Job"

CAPACITY – Refers to the amount of digital information a computer, or storage device, can hold. A "byte" is a small bit of digital info, maybe one letter's worth. A kilobyte (KB) is roughly a thousand of those. A megabyte (MB) is a thousand of those. And a gigabyte (GB) is a thousand of those.

My old laptop (1999) had 6 GB capacity. My next one (2007) had 160 GB capacity. My current one (2011) has 585 GB capacity.

The Vista or Windows 7 operating systems take up about 30 GB of space just by themselves, I believe. Regular "Word" documents take up very little space. Pictures and music take up much more space. Video takes up the most.

To see how big any file is: Right-click, Properties.

Typical Capacities

Numbers vary hugely: it depends on the program being used, on the amount of formatting, etc., etc. If you want to get an estimate, check how much you have so far, and then extend that figure mathematically. For example, if you estimate you are ¼ of the way thru your project, get that amount by right-clicking and checking under Properties; then multiply by 4. Much safer doing an estimate this way than using other people's estimates. Your project has its own unique amount of capacity being used.

Here's some rough, sample numbers I got for my own files:

– One page Word doc: 50 KB; 250 pages: 2 MB
– One color picture: 1 MB
– One song: 4 MB; 500 songs: 2 GB
– 2-minute video clip: 21 MB; 4-minute video clip: 67 MB; 5-minute video clip: 317 MB. All over the place; don't really know why the big differences. I find a one-hour movie I've made is usually 2-4 GB.

Making Space

"Clean Disk" and defragging operations clear up some computer space. See "MAINTENANCE"

CAPITALIZATION

Block > Font box at top > click on "Aa" icon > pick choice.

Note that "Capitalize Each Word" also capitalizes "a" and "the." So if you are making a title out of a bunch of words, you need to manually change those little words back to non-caps.

Also, to get sentence case, out of an all-caps line, you may have to change all the words to lowercase letters first, THEN order up "Sentence case." Otherwise, it sometimes doesn't work.

A good technique for making many capitalization (or bolding or color) changes: Do one, then put the cursor into the next word, and press the F4 repeat key, and continue that way.

CASE – See "LETTER CASE"

CDS AND DVDS FOR SAVING FILES – You can save regular files, documents, texts on either CD or DVD, just like you used to save stuff on a floppy disk. You can then transfer this material to another computer if you want to.

I usually don't use CDs for data (files, documents), but only for music.

See also "BACKING UP YOUR MATERIAL"

CD / AUDIO EDITING – See "MUSIC / AUDIO TRANSFERS THRU A COMPUTER" > "B. EDITING"

CD DISK REMOVAL – Press the disk bay button on the side of your computer, wait a couple seconds, and it ejects the disk. See also "EJECT"

Computer must be on for it to work. Some computers have a small hole near the bay, into which you can press the end of a paper-clip, and that ejects it when the computer is off. My old one did that, but my new one (Sony Vaio) doesn't.

CD – PLAYING A MUSIC CD – Insert CD into disk bay, a music program automatically comes up – like iTunes, or Windows Media Player – and starts playing the first song. If you want to play a different song, maximize that window, right-click on an empty spot, click on whatever option you think will bring up your track list (I find options constantly vary), double-click on the track to play it.

If a program did not come up to play the disk you inserted, double-click Computer, double-click Drive E, and that will bring up a program.

You can set or change which program plays your music: Start > All Programs > Default Programs > Change AutoPlay Settings > CD dropdown arrow > make selection > Save.

Note that most computer speakers are not that great; if you want good sound, use earphones, or buy separate speakers for your computer.

CD PROGRAMS – INSTALLING "SOFTWARE" – Most programs ("software") come on CDs that you put into your computer. The CD starts automatically and tells you how to proceed to install the program to your computer. For example, if you buy a printer, it comes with a CD. You put the CD in, follow instructions to install the program; and then you can take the CD out and put it away.

Usually you need to restart the computer to finish the installation; it will tell you.

If the CD does not start automatically, click Start > Control Panel > Programs > Programs and Features > How to install a program, and Windows Help gives you further info.

See also "PROGRAMS" > "Programs – Installing and Removing"

CD – THOMPSON'S BIBLE CD – This is a good example of a CD program which condenses tons of material onto your computer. I used to have 15 different versions of the Bible in my bookcase. Now I just keep a few actual Bibles, but have 22 different full versions in my computer. Takes up much less space.

Once you learn the program and how to use it, you have access to all kinds of info quickly. For example, if I want to check the Sermon on the Mount, and can't remember just where to find it, I do a word search for a phrase I remember like "Blessed are the poor," and it will show me chapter and verse.

CELL PHONE – Several years ago I switched to using only a cell phone, no landline. Cheaper. Works out well; quite satisfied. They let me have my old landline number. I am not a big phone user at all. So, for me, charging it for two hours, every 4th or 5th day, does the trick. Sound quality is not quite as good as a landline, but of course the portability is a major advantage. And, it has its own answering machine, photo-taking capability, texting, etc., etc. The newer, more expensive ones, like the "iPhone", even have internet capability.

Consumer Reports, Jan, 2011, says 25% of people now keep only a cell phone, and *"we think that dropping your home landline and making all calls – including 911 calls – on a cell phone is generally a safe bet..."*

It's good to know how to set your phone to "vibrate: for occasions when ringing is a disruption (movie, restaurant, etc.).

Note that having a cell phone number in the phone book costs money; it's not free like landline phone listings are. And, as yet, there is no national cell phone directory, or the equivalent of traditional phone books. It's still a matter of debate; people don't want telemarketers bothering them.

Tip

Using the phone as a recorder – If I remember something in the middle of the night, instead of turning on the light and writing down a note for myself, I just grab my cell phone, which is right by my bed, and in the dark turn on the camcorder function and say, "Remember xyz at 4 o'clock tomorrow." (Don't forget to press Save.) And then I put the phone back on the night stand in a different spot to remind myself I have a note on the phone.

CELL PHONE – PICTURES AND VIDEO – I'm not up on all the latest gadgets, but I know that things are much easier with the more recent hand-held devices – sending pictures, importing them to your computer, printing them. These days, importing pictures and video is just a matter of attaching the device to the computer with a USB cord that comes with the phone, and the material automatically imports itself to your "Pictures" or "Videos" folder. Very easy.

If you like taking pictures and video with your cell phone, get yourself a cell phone that transfers material easily. Mine, a primitive basic one, 5 years old, is a nightmare to use for getting material into my computer and then onto a disk (for video). Twenty or more steps, memory cards, adapter, etc., etc. Forget it.

A few tips I found to be key: Know exactly which way your lens is pointing. Keep your finger away from the lens. Keep the lens clean.

CENTERING – You can center text horizontally, and also vertically.

Centering – Horizontal

Block a text, or position the cursor inside a paragraph of text, CTRL+E (or, Paragraph box at top, click centering icon 2nd from left). That arranges the text to the center of the page, horizontally.

Centering – Vertical

Page Layout tab at top > Page Setup box, dropdown arrow at lower right > Layout tab > Vertical alignment dropdown arrow > pick "Center." That arranges your text to the center of the page, vertically.

This is actually a killer annoyance if you happen to accidentally set it at "Center" instead of "Top," and didn't realize it. You can't figure out what's going on as you type the first word of a page and it keeps popping down to the center of the page!! Happened to me once.

[Odd note here: No longer in Windows 7, but in Vista, shaded text on screen would often show clear space between lines, but when you actually print the text out, there is no space; the shading is solid, the way it should be.]

Centering – Spread-Out Words Problem

If you suddenly get words spread out over a full line, like above, see "JUSTIFYING TEXT" > "Words Suddenly Spread Out on a Line"

CENTS SYMBOL (¢) – Insert tab > Symbol dropdown arrow > More Symbols > select ¢ under Font (normal text), (7 down, 2 across) > Insert. Or, you can set it up so that every time you type the word "cents," it automatically changes it to ¢. See "AUTOCORRECT – SYMBOLS"

CHARTS – See "TABLES"

CHECKS (✓) – Insert tab > Symbol dropdown arrow > More Symbols > Font at left > dropdown arrow > Wingdings 2 > select ✓ (4 down, 1 across).

My shortcut command for a ✓ is: "CTRL+/"

Problem

Some years ago, when I had my old computer and was using, I think, "Windows 98," I suddenly lost my check marks. They all disappeared from my documents, replaced by odd marks! And my Wingding symbol selection box (from which I got the ✓) had disappeared! And bullets under "Numbering and Bullets" turned into odd symbols. Called MS. Tech guy suggested reinstalling MS Word 2000. Did that, and it worked! Hooray! Everything corrected itself. Got Wingdings back, etc. See procedure below:

Word 2000 CD > Start > (Settings) > Control Panel > Add/Remove Programs > Install > Next > Finish > Repair Word.

[W7 – There is a "Repair" option under Start > Control Panel > Programs > Programs and Features > click on the program > click Repair at top. I think if "Repair" does not show up as an option, the program is supposed to be OK.]

CHECKBOXES – Are usually situated to the left of a word in a windows list. Self-explanatory; you click in the box to select, or un-select, the item. But, note two things: 1) Sometimes there is no checkbox UNTIL you hold the cursor over the word, THEN it appears. Actually, this is the default setup for folders and documents! 2) For some situations, like items you've downloaded, there is a checkbox at the upper left with the word "Name." If you check this one box at the top, it checks ALL the boxes of the items below. A nice shortcut.

Be careful. You may want to delete an item, but forgot that you still have other items also checked. It will delete ALL those checked items. So, when it asks you "Are you sure?" look carefully at the items that are checked. If it says items, plural, and you thought you were in the process of deleting only one item, start over. Usually it names an item if there is only one, but with more than one, it uses the phrase "these 2 items" or "these 6 items."

Checkboxes Disappear

One day the checkboxes next to folders and documents on my screen, simply disappeared. I used the Help icon, and typed in "Checkboxes" to learn how to get them back: Start > Control Panel > Appearance and Personalization > Folder Options > View tab > scroll down to near the bottom, check "Use check boxes to select items" > OK.

CHESS CD – I bought a chess program called "Chessmaster 9000." Here's what I wrote after I first got it: *"Don't like it. As usual, it does all kinds of things, but simply playing... geez – physically awkward to use laptop, strain on the eyes, pieces are not that distinct (hard to recognize), the captured piece box is not convenient (too small – those pieces are actually bigger than the board pieces, so you have to expand the box to see all the pieces), often hard to figure out what piece was just taken. Much prefer a stand-alone physical chess computer, with real pieces."*

I have since completely changed my mind!! I now have a "laptop lounger," which is like a supported bed tray and makes watching stuff on a laptop very comfortable. I made adjustments on the chess program so that pieces are more clear and at a better angle, and various parts of the screen resized for greater convenience, etc., etc. I learned how to use it better. Now I love it. No pieces to fall off or lose. No having to laboriously reset pieces for each new game. Everything is quick and automatic. Plus it keeps track of your results. It gives you an accurate actual chess rating based on your games, etc.

And, it's a great program (Josh Waitzkin, the little kid chess wiz of the "Searching for Bobby Fisher" movie, designed it.) You can play against players based on real people, their level of play, their style. Even provides bios and pictures of these people.

I'm proud to say I can occasionally beat Josh... well, at age six. At age seven... that's a lot tougher.

Note that if you do a "system restore" – see "RESTORE SETTINGS" – then your Chessmaster stats revert to the date you restored your computer settings to. I had done a "restore" to a point one week earlier and the games I played during the last week disappeared from my stats.

Windows Chess Program

I didn't realize this till years later, but Windows comes with a chess program already installed, called "Chess Titans." It's much more pared down than "Chessmaster 9000," but it's good. Straightforward, five different levels of play. I prefer "Chessmaster 9000" because of the ratings feature (a more accurate sense of where I am ability-wise), plus I like feeling like I'm playing against actual people instead of a machine.

Update 8/11

I successfully installed the program on my new computer. It was working. But then, after I starting using a router, it no longer worked. It wouldn't open; it wouldn't allow re-installation. Don't really know why. Maybe their software allows only one computer per CD, if there is a router involved.

I wanted to download a newer version of the program anyway, so I searched the internet for an hour, going in circles, seeing a wide variety of prices for the same product ($5 to $80).

Finally found one (Direct2Drive.com) that seemed to have clear downloading instructions, for $10. Attempted that. It stalled, with a complex message, with the heading "Runtime Error." Checking the progress bar, I figured that maybe it stalled because my computer went to "Sleep" mode automatically after 10 minutes the way I normally have it set. I set it to sleep "Never" (under the Power Options, "Change when the computer sleeps"), so it would stay on, and hooray, that did it! Still had to press the right buttons, wait, register, put in an activation code number, etc. But I got it; it's working.

Took a good hour to download, if I remember right. And it turned out not to be a new version, but the same one – 2003, but, I'm OK with it. This downloaded version doesn't require putting in the disk to renew it every two weeks or 15 sessions. So, that's an improvement.

Fascinating to read online reviews of Chessmaster vs Fritz programs, especially by elite players. And all the technical problems people encountered. Same old story: not enough emphasis on user-friendliness by these damn companies.

CLEANING COMPUTER – Just vacuum keyboard, delicately, with brush attachment of vacuum cleaner every so often. Have never done this myself; have had no problem.

CLEANING PRINTER – Used to have to clean my first printer (I'm on my third one now) by using diluted rubbing alcohol on the rubber rollers every so often. Over time, the rollers would pick up bits of paper (like lint) and subsequently feed sheets less consistently. But, with my current printer, I don't need to do any cleaning. Never did with my previous Epson, and it fed beautifully throughout its life. (Maybe there's no more rubber rollers involved?)

CLEARING WEBSITE HISTORY – See "MAINTENANCE"

CLICKING – A double click opens a document, folder, or icon; a single click will open a website. You can also open items by right-clicking and selecting "Open." Also, right-clicking shows you a bunch of other options to select to perform on that file – cut, copy, delete, etc.

If you prefer to have a single click open items instead of a double-click, you can change the setting: My Documents folder > Organize tab dropdown arrow at upper left > Folder and Search Options > General tab > select "Single click" > OK.

CLIPBOARD – When you cut or copy a text, it puts the text onto a "clipboard" which is out of sight; then you go to where you want to land the text, do CTRL+V, and that copies it from the clipboard and puts it into your target.

After you've pasted the material, it still stays on the clipboard, so you can paste the same material repeatedly into additional places. Then, once you put something new in there, it pastes the newest material.

To actually see what you have on the clipboard: Home tab at top, Clipboard down arrow, and a window opens on the left showing what you have. I think it holds up to 24 items. Click on any of them and it inserts it into your current text where your cursor is. Can be very useful if you have, say, 50 letters to write with three different texts; as you go to each letter, click the appropriate clipboard text of the three. It very quickly inserts it. You have the Clipboard window at the left, the text window at the right.

CLOCK – At right on the taskbar at bottom, the time of the day is shown. Hold your cursor over it and it shows day of the week and date also. Click the time on the taskbar and it shows a handy calendar for the month. And it gives you a spot there to click for changing the date and time settings. To get rid of that window, just click once elsewhere on the screen.

See also "Gadgets." I keep a time and date one up on my desktop.

"CLOUD" – This computing term refers to a concept that may take stronger hold in the near future – instead of keeping all your data on the hard drive of your computer, you let companies keep it on their servers and you access the info via the internet. Just like you do currently for your email info, except now they keep... everything. And you can access your info thru handheld devices also.

But I don't know. I have a visceral reaction against this trend. I don't like trusting others to keep my stuff; I like to keep my own stuff. We'll see what the future holds here. To me, the idea of cyber thieves jumping into a whole new field for theft opportunities creeps me out.

"CTRL" KEY – See "SHORTCUTS"

COLOR MANAGEMENT – Sometimes devices need different settings to get the correct color. You may need to go to Start > Control Panel > Classic View on left > Color Management. But, usually the default settings are fine.

COLORS – Highlight what you want colored, then from the Font box at top, click the dropdown arrow to get your choice of colors, either from the Text Highlight Color icon (crayon icon, second from the right) or the Font color icon (farthest right in the box). The text one shades the area of your highlighted text. The Font one put the font into the selected color.

"Text Highlight Color" vs "Shading"

"Shading" (paint can icon in the Paragraph box) gives you more color choices than "Text Highlight Color" (crayon icon). And it can shade both words and whole paragraphs.

Note that Text Highlight Color (crayon icon) takes precedence over Shading (paint can icon). Say you have a yellow text highlight color and you want a lighter shading of yellow, and you order it thru the Shading icon. Nothing will change, because you have the stronger text highlight color still on. You need to change the highlight color to "No Color" first to get rid of it; then the shading will apply.

Seemingly Inconsistent Shading

Sometimes it seems as though shades you thought you knew are changing (3rd one down now looks more like 4th one down, for example), but I find that that is not the case. It's the angle of your screen that makes shades appear darker or lighter. Sometimes you can't even see a very light shade, but then when you adjust the screen angle, you can see it clearly.

COLUMNS – To put a text into columns, highlight the text, (or don't highlight anything if you want to put the whole document into columns) > Page Setup box at top > click Columns > select number of columns you want. You can click "More Columns" at bottom for more options, like having a line between columns, getting more than 3 columns, etc.

I find this feature very useful, because columns are easier to read than text that goes all the way across a page (note how newspapers and magazines use columns), and, you don't waste paper. I most often put text into two columns, with a line in between.

Double Columns Are Short

If both your columns end evenly across the page, partway down, instead of the left column reaching the bottom of the page and the right one starting at top and going partway down, click ¶ in the Paragraph box at top (this shows your section breaks) > delete the section or page break at the end of column two > Click ¶ again, to again hide the command symbols.

Conversely, if you do want your columns to end up evenly on the page, position your cursor > Page Layout tab > Page Setup box > Breaks > Section Break > Continuous.

Mixed Columns

If you have cobbled together several documents into one, and then try to put the whole thing into a double column, you may get a computer message that your columns are not sized right or something like that, and it won't do the operation for you. To fix that:

Under Paragraph at top, click the paragraph symbol "¶" > that makes "page breaks" and "section breaks" show up. Delete all of them one by one (usually at spots where you followed a single column with a double one); re-adjust, putting line spaces back in. THEN it allows you to double-column the whole deal.

In other words, I think it won't allow you to do columns for the whole document unless the document is without page/section breaks between sections having different numbers of columns.

Conversely, if you want, say both 2 columns AND 3 columns on one page, you need to put in section breaks: Position your cursor > Page Layout tab at top > Breaks > Section Break > Continuous. Each time you click Continuous, from that point on from where your cursor is, you can order up a different number of columns. "Continuous" here means that the text continues right from this point, but under your newly ordered different number of columns.

Column Changing Problems

Computer wouldn't let me change from double column, 8½x11, to single column, 5½x8½ (i.e. the final format for a book.) I put the whole thing to single column first, THEN made the margins consistent, THEN changed the page size. That worked.

5/05 Update: Tried to change an 8X11 double column text portrait to an 5X8 triple column text landscape. What I needed to do was block the 8X11 material, put the text into a single column, then open a new document and move the text there. THEN change it to 5X8, and then triple-column it. If I remember right, that's what allowed it to work, though you never know for sure what factor messes things up. My sense is that the more you cobble together stuff, the more likely the computer will refuse to follow orders.

When you try to make any column change, and the preview image at lower left of the Page Setup window is blank, then you know it won't work. That preview image at lower left must show text lines. If it's just blank, something is not right. Usually, change the text to a single column first, then it works.

COMPUTER FREEZES – Sometimes, due to whatever odd combination of operations you did, the computer just freezes and won't respond to anything you do. (Maybe because you started doing things before it finished booting up fully. Maybe because you did some complex operations too fast. Who knows.) In that case, you need to reboot the computer:

Start > click right arrow to right of lock icon > Restart > wait a few minutes for it to boot up again. That invariably unfreezes the computer.

If the computer completely freezes and nothing at all responds and you can't shut it down, you CAN, and should, shut it down by this last option: Press and hold down the On/Off button for 5-10 seconds [W7 – 4 seconds]. That will shut your computer down.

Wait a minute or so before turning it back on. When it opens, a message will scold you for not shutting off the computer properly. Ignore that message and just press the Enter key to get the computer going again.

Also, note that when your pointer/arrow is offscreen, the computer does not respond; it seems frozen. Just click the pointer/arrow back onto the screen. (Move it with your right finger across the pad, and then left-click.)

If the computer suddenly acts erratically after you have installed a new program, uninstall that program and install it again, or, do not install it. See also "RESTORE SETTINGS"

****

COMPUTER – GETTING A NEW COMPUTER

[This is a major section]

OVERVIEW

I compare getting a new computer – or upgrading your operating system from older versions of Windows to Windows 7 – to getting your taxes done by H&R Block. Instead of going thru the uneasiness of doing it yourself, you go to an expert. You pay, but you get peace of mind, and less aggravation. So my recommendation is to put as much as you can into the hands of those who do this for a living. I've had good experiences with Best Buy. Staples strikes me as another good choice. Unless you know them well, I would avoid smaller places; I think they are less likely to be reliable and trustworthy.

That being said, here's what I went thru in getting a new computer and setting it up. I tried to do as much as I could myself. A little more involved than one would hope. I'm reasonably sure most of the steps and information below correlate pretty well to what the average person experiences when buying a new computer.

From Best Buy, I bought a new Samsung laptop. $1,200, plus about $300 of other stuff including Geek support from the store, plus an anti-virus security program. Note that once you buy the computer, they have to prepare it (unless they have one already prepared) – installing Windows, security, and getting rid of "Bloat-ads" (I think he called it) and any extra junk that came with it. So I had to come back the next day to pick it up.

Like getting a new car; you have to adjust to a lot of little different things – where things are on the dashboard, how to open the trunk, the windows, etc. After a week, I decided to exchange it for a Sony (Best Buy is very good about exchanges, within a two week period).

The Samsung is a nice machine, but 1) I didn't like its large keyboard with the extra key bank on the right for numbers, etc. Several keys I use a lot, like Home and End, are scattered in amongst those keys and are hard to locate quickly, the way I'm used to. I note that there seem to be two standard keyboards – regular, and wide with the extra keys at the right. I do not like the extra bank of keys on the right. Overkill, for me.

And 2) Sony is one of the few companies that includes their own DVD-playing program in their computers ("InterVideo WinDVD") and I like its controls better than Windows Media Player.

So, I got a Sony Vaio, 14", with Windows 7 ("Home Premium"), 585 GB Hard Drive, white, $800, SKU: 1892044, Model: VPCEA46FM/W.

My operating system is Windows 7; my web browser Internet Explorer. I think the other two major operating systems are Mackintosh and Linux. Other browsers: Firefox, Google Chrome.

(FYI, I heard that computer hard drives last maybe 6 years, at which point you should think about buying a new computer or a new hard drive.)

INITIAL SETUP

1. Unpacking – Unpacked the box, being careful not to damage the box in case I needed it to return the computer. Taped to the outside of the box is my security program CD (Norton). Inside are the computer, the battery, a power cord, instructions, and 3 Best Buy Geek Squad recovery disks (in case I ever need to re-install Windows 7).

2. Model Number – On the first page of the "Safety Information" booklet it tells you that the model number and serial number are on the bottom of the computer, and to make a record of those numbers. My model number is PCG–61317L. (What? A second model number? Why is everything always so complicated in the computer world?) There are half a dozen other numbers there, any of which might be the serial number. So the heck with that; they're there on the bottom; I'll ask a rep which one it is, if I ever need it.

3. Recovery Disks – Looked thru the "Recovery, Backup and Troubleshooting Guide," and decided to bring the computer to Best Buy if I ever have a problem with my computer not operating properly or being infected with a virus.

4. Quick Start Guide – Read thru the "Quick Start Guide" and followed the steps, basically installing the battery and connecting the power cord. (The battery lock and unlock switch is on the battery itself, not the computer.) Once connected, for future reference, you can access their on-screen Vaio manual: Start > Help and Support > Use my Vaio > select the appropriate user guide. The Vaio also has a green dropdown arrow right at the center top when on the desktop, if you hover the pointer over that spot; clicking on that gives you a bunch of Vaio info. Annoying. I hate multiple avenues to the same info.

I put all the above paperwork (which is not that much, hooray) away in the cellophane bag it came in.

5. Quick Start Guide Steps – Pressed the "On" button at upper right. Takes a few minutes for first startup.

Window came up saying "Battery health status is excellent." Clicked OK. Screen showed 7 icons on desktop: Libraries, Computer, Recycle Bin, Microsoft Office 2010, Norton AntiVirus, Sony Pictures BD Live, and Best Buy.

Note that the "Libraries" icon – a "superfolder" containing the 4 major categories – Documents, Music, Pictures, Videos – is roughly equivalent to Vista's old "Owner" icon.

The taskbar at bottom showed 7 icons: Start button, Internet Explorer, Windows Explorer, Windows Media Player, 4G Wimax tutorial (not for me), Windows Live Messenger (not for me), and Intel Wireless Display (not for me).

Normally, Windows wants all users to log on, but since I'm the only one using my computer, I got rid of the "Welcome" screen that pops up, which shows an "Administrator" icon for me (the owner) and a "Guest" icon, by right-clicking desktop empty spot > Personalize > Screen Saver at lower right > unchecking "On resume display logon screen" > OK.

6. DVD Player Bay – I inserted a DVD, to make sure that feature worked. It played fine. The window gave me choice of Windows Media Player or WinDVD. I picked WinDVD and checked "Always do this for DVD movies." Aha, that's what the "BD Live" icon represents – Sony Vaio's DVD player. And it's pretty much the same as the "WinDVD" on my old computer.

There's no eject button to press; must press DVD bay manually; but, it's quite responsive. So, no problem.

Update: I notice when I clicked on the "BD Live" icon, it plays a damn ad! Oh, I hate that! I deleted that icon, and then went to Start > All Programs > Corel > right-clicked "Corel WinDVD" > Send to > Desktop (create shortcut). Now I have the actual program shortcut up on my desktop, instead of a damn ad first.

7. Desktop Icons – I set up icons on the desktop for the folders, programs, and websites I use the most. I used a screenshot of my normal desktop, that I had stored in a document, to set it up exactly the way I had it on my old computer. I will still need to send the rest of my program icons to the desktop, once I install all my programs.

I also made a new folder called "Misc Desktop" under My Documents, sent it to the desktop, and dragged into it icons on the desktop that I normally do not need (like Best Buy icon, extra Epson printer icons, etc.) Just to clear up space on the desktop and yet to have that stuff in case I need it.

Note: Use right-click and "Send To" for putting program, folder, and document icons onto desktop. If you just drag and drop, you're putting the program/folder/document itself up there instead of just a shortcut. I noticed this after I dragged a document to the desktop and saw I no longer had it back in its normal folder. I dragged it back and used "Send To" instead.

The icon on the desktop should have the blue arrow at lower left designating "shortcut"; if not, it's the actual file.

One of my document icons would keep migrating on its own to the Left. Geek guy couldn't figure out why; just an anomaly. Computers are constantly doing weird things. See "MIGRATING ICONS"

MAJOR TASKS / ISSUES

1. Transferring Data – OK, now a big step – transferring all my data. First, all my documents and folders, and then pictures, music, and video. (Best Buy will do this for you, if you don't have an external hard drive, or flash drive, to use as a transfer device.)

Went back to my old computer and transferred My Documents to an external hard drive.

I decided to enter no new information of any sort to my old computer, and to enter all new info of any sort ONLY to my new computer from this point on. A crisp decision like this, is very important; otherwise, you end up never knowing just what you have where. Believe me, this kind of ambiguity can be a nightmare; it gets exponentially more complex and confusing at every step, if you don't make this clear decision: no new stuff on the old one; new stuff on the new one.

I plan to keep my old computer simply as a back-up in case my new one is "in the shop" for a few days, or if I'm traveling. I'll put new material on a flash drive, transfer it to the old computer desktop, work on it from there, then transfer it back to the flash drive and then to the new computer later. But, I will avoid allowing any new material to stay on the old computer on any regular basis.

I kept all my programs, as is, on the old computer. Will also, of course, have to also install them all on my new computer. See "INSTALLATION OF PROGRAMS" below.

I transferred my "My Documents" folder from my old computer to an external hard drive. I plugged in my new computer and attached the external hard drive to it. It automatically installed a device driver for the external hard drive, in a few seconds. I clicked "Open folders to view files" of the external hard drive.

On the new computer, I clicked Libraries > Documents > My Documents, and dragged and dropped My Documents into there. It was 450 MB and it only took 2 minutes to transfer.

Then when I clicked on "My Documents" to make sure I had it, a Microsoft Office window opened for "Office 2010". I clicked "Use Office Starter 2010".

Windows 7 is an Operating System; "MS Office" is a major program in it. And "Office" includes features for most of what I do, and, I think most normal people do – typing, pictures, music, video). Other major programs in "Office" are PowerPoint (for presentations), Excel (for business), Outlook (managing email), OneNote (managing notes), etc. It's mind-boggling overkill. I mostly just use Word. You can do all that other stuff on your own anyway; you don't need their intrusive, complex "help" to organize things for you. That's my feeling.

Now... the "MS Office Starter 2010" version is a free, reduced functionality version. (See below for the full story – "Getting Rid of Ad Panel at Right".) I've read that Microsoft Word used to come pre-installed for free, but now they do this "starter" version thing; you get basic functions for free but have to pay for the regular full version.

After clicking "Use Office Starter 2010", I clicked Use > Open > Yes (takes about 2 minutes) > Puts its icon on the desktop > I put in my name and initial for their "User Name" window that came up > OK > Accept > checked the "Use Recommended Settings" small circle > OK > Yes. I x'd out the window, and it's ready to go. Click on a folder or document and it opens up for you, like I'm used to.

I already had all my pictures, music, and video, on my external hard drive. So I transferred that material also into the appropriate big folders – Pictures, Music, Videos, under Libraries. The music took only ten minutes. I was surprised it let me transfer all 10.3 GB of material in one operation. I guess the RAM capacity of 4 GB does not apply to transferring material in, but only material out, I guess. Transferred my pictures (1.4 GB) in one minute.

Ultimately decided not to transfer my videos; I have hard copies of that material anyway.

That completes the "data transfer" operation. Again, Best Buy can do that for you, if you don't want to do it yourself. I recommend doing it yourself, but, if you're going to have them do the installing of your programs anyway (a more difficult task) you might as well have them do both data transfer and program installing.

2. Internet – Tried the internet. Clicked Internet Explorer icon on taskbar. No go. Showed the typical "Internet Explorer cannot display the webpage" when your computer is not connected to the internet. Clicked "Diagnose Connection Problems." Clicked "Skip this step" (modem issue), and "Continue trying to fix this problem." Came up with "Problem found – 'Local Area Connection doesn't have a valid IP configuration.' " Whatever that means. Clicked explore additional options, got nowhere. Tried earlier suggestion of turning off power to modem for 10 seconds, then turning it back on. A window came up. Clicked "Home Network." Waited for "Set Network Location" window to do its thing. Showed "Connecting to your network and applying settings..." That kept going for more than 10 minutes.

I minimized that window, came back 20 minutes later, and, hooray, now the net comes up when I click on the Internet Explorer icon. Although it is quite possible, if not probable, that it didn't work at first simply because my internet wire was loose.

Update: After I tried getting the net and my email on my old computer (see "Email below), then when I re-attached my new one, I couldn't get internet. That same window came up showing "Diagnose Connection Problem." It suggested shutting off the modem for ten seconds and then putting it back on, clicked "Click here" (either before or after that, don't remember), and it came up with "Problem found – Local Area Connection doesn't have a valid IP configuration." I clicked "Close" and then when I clicked on Internet Explorer, it was back! I guess attaching a different computer to a particular modem will mess up the configuration.

Update: Yep, it seems any time I try to switch computers, it won't allow internet, until I click on "Diagnose Connection Problem"> a window opens ("Windows Network Diagnostics"); wait while it goes thru "Resolving problems" > turn off the power to the modem for ten seconds > turn it back on > click "Check here to see if the problem is solved" > shows "Problems fixed", "Local Area Connection doesn't have a valid IP configuration", "Fixed" > close. Now it works. Apparently I have to do this every time I switch computers and want to use the internet, with this modem.

Update: Lately both my laptops work fine now without any adjustments. Why? I don't know. I guess all the stuff I did above fixed the problem for good.

3. Security – Norton security window came up saying I need to activate it. Need to be connected to the internet for this. Clicked a button there. When I connected to the internet, that activation window had disappeared, and the program was already working! Clicked for a

quick scan, and it worked fine. Very clear. Best Buy guy says he has Norton himself and thinks it's the best; they used to be so-so, but are now tops, in his opinion.

I didn't have to do anything; I just left everything at default settings, which includes a weekly full scan. It's working. I don't think I need to check it from this point on, unless I get a message from it.

4. Email – Don't remember how I got my personal email function. I think I googled Yahoo.com and then clicked My Yahoo, and signed in with my User Name (email address) and password, and there it was, just like with my old computer.

But, for my website email (my second email account), to get it accessible again, I had to call the company that hosts my website. What a hassle! Who could know that differently labeled lines one and two – Email address and User Name – want the same exact info for both lines – your email address in both places?! Did they want my home email address or my site email address? Why did none of the website control panel icons on the desktop work, but the small one down on the taskbar did? Why did I first get a completely different format for my site email, with no Trash bin, and then later, going thru a different avenue, I got back the format I'm used to? Who knows?! As usual, if you stick with it long enough, and make phone calls at the right time, you end up finally, suddenly, getting it.

Later on, checking to see if I still had my email on my old computer when I attached it to the internet cable, I had to struggle for 20 minutes to get it back. Somewhere along the line I clicked "Home" under Set Network Locator. Didn't work at first (I think sometimes things take a minute to get operational); then suddenly I had internet... but not email. Put "Yahoo Mail" into the Google search box and I got a window to sign in. I did that (email address, and password) and hooray, I got my email back, for my old computer.

5. Printer – Installed my printer (Epson 810) so I can print. See "INSTALLATION OF PROGRAMS" below.

6. Home Page and Search Engine – I wanted to have Yahoo as my home page, so I can open up right to my email; and I wanted Google (which I prefer to Yahoo) as my default search engine. Forget where, but I clicked to have Google as my default search engine, but, Yahoo stayed there and there was no search box at upper right like I always had. Then, suddenly I got my old setup back with the search box at upper right, except it had Bing instead of Google.

"Bing" is Microsoft's search engine. I entered Yahoo.com there, clicked on Yahoo mail, my mail came up. In the middle at top it has a button for making Yahoo your home page. Clicked that and now when I click on Internet Explorer, my Yahoo mail comes up. Excellent.

At the Bing search box at upper right, I clicked the dropdown arrow, clicked "Find more providers", and selected Google as my default search engine. Now I have the Google search box at upper right, the way I like it.

(I don't know how good Bing is, but, out of sheer resentment, I will not give it a chance, because Microsoft has fixed that big damned intrusive advertisement panel on the right side of the screen.)

Note that "Google Chrome" is an actual browser (like Internet Explorer), not a search engine for a browser.

Update: Once I downloaded the latest version of Internet Explorer (9), I lost that setup – Yahoo as home page, with Google search box at upper right. Tried all kinds of things. Was not able to get it back to what I had. Settled for this: I typed Google.com into my Yahoo search box, and when the site list came up, I clicked on "Google" which showed a nice big, plain search box. I added that site address to my Favorites. So now the tab for this Google search box page is always right there at top left on my Favorites bar. It's just one click away from my Yahoo home page. I can live with that.

7. Mouse Tapping Function

The mouse tapping functions on the Sony seem better than on the Samsung (maybe because the mouse size is one I am used to and I don't accidentally rest my left finger on the left edge, triggering unwanted results); nevertheless, I hate this feature. I think one time I spread two fingers accidentally and it changed the size of my desktop icons AND their arrangement, and I had to laboriously put them back!

So, I disabled the tapping functions: Start > Control Panel > Hardware & Sound > Devices & Printers > Mouse > Device Settings tab > Settings > uncheck Pinch Zoom, Rotate, and Tapping > Apply, then OK each.

DO NOT DISABLE EITHER "Synaptics TouchPad" or the "Buttons" under Device Settings, or you will simply disable the mouse and have to struggle to get it back!! See "MOUSE – TAPPING FUNCTION"

8. Getting Rid of Ad Panel at Right

How to get rid of that annoying, intrusive, space-wasting "Getting Started" panel at right!? After two hours of trying, I found out – you can't, unless you buy "Microsoft Office 2010." That panel is part of "Microsoft Office Starter 2010," which is a simplified, ad-funded version of "Microsoft Office 2010" that comes pre-loaded and ready to use on your computer, once you click on it.

To get rid of that panel, you have to buy the regular "MS Office 2010," for $140. And even that was a hassle (trying to enter a new password made up of their encrypted squiggly letters I couldn't read). I said the heck with it, but then later realized I DO need the full version, because that has many functions I'm used to, which the Starter version does not have.

The "Starter" version has overall reduced functionality – less tabs at top, less picture formatting, does not support "programmable content" or "running macros," whatever that means, etc. I suspected my picture-formatting, and setting CTRL shortcut commands for inserting symbols, would be fully available with the full version. ["Macros" = *"a set of instructions that is represented in an abbreviated format."*]

I clicked on stuff in that "Getting Started" panel, to get the full service free trial (2 months), and yes, I now have those functions, plus all the tab options at top that I was used to.

AND, that damned ad-supported panel at the right is now finally gone!

See also "10. Buying 'MS Office' Full Version" below.

9. "OneNote" Issue

Geez! I go to print and it won't! A message says you have to have the "OneNote" program start at least one time first. I typed "Microsoft OneNote" into the Start search box, to find that program. Don't remember what happened next, but it ends up, when you go to print, you have to send your material to "OneNote" first, which I did, at which point the printing window shows a spot where you can uncheck

"OneNote". Did that, but, the "OneNote" window still came up when I did a Ctrl+P.

Then, once I got the printing window up at the left, under Printer dropdown arrow, I selected my printer, instead of "OneNote" and that did the trick. OK, but, it's infuriating!

I am incensed!!! I hate Microsoft! I hate Bill Gates! I hate the army of geeks who come up with these ideas! Here they try to force you into doing THEIR idea of organizing notes and material. And, so typical, they tout – oh, you can do this, you can do that, you can keep track of this and that, and dates and times, etc., etc., etc., you know, stupid far-out stuff for anal-retentive types. But simply how to turn the damn thing off, that they won't tell you!

It's so intrusive; you can't go about your work, but have to use their complex system or try to figure out how to get rid of it, which of course they don't want you to do. And it's not just one extra step, it's a whole layer of different steps.

They want you to get enmeshed in their world, so you feel you need it... resulting in more money for them, and further "validation" for their jobs. George Bernard Shaw once said, "Every profession is a conspiracy against the layman."

If I weren't at least reasonably computer-literate, I never would have been able to figure out how to turn the damn thing off. As it was, I spent more than an hour figuring it out.

Update: And it's STILL doing it (inserting and giving priority to "OneNote" program options by default) when I try to print something from the internet. Researched the issue some more. Did this: Start > Control Panel > Hardware & Sound > Devices & Printers > right-clicked my Epson printer > Set as default printer > right-clicked "Send To OneNote 2010" > Remove device, yes.

OK. Finally, I'm back to normal. If I ever meet Bill Gates in person, I'm going to give him a piece of my mind, unvarnished. It never ends. IT NEVER ENDS! There's always some new frustrating thing suddenly popping up to gum up the works. Because of the computer world's focus on "more, more, more, more bells and whistles" instead of "simplicity, consistency, and user-friendliness."

10. Buying "Microsoft Office 2010" Full Version

After a couple of weeks, I decided to go ahead and buy the full version. Called them and ordered the CD. (I prefer a physical CD for a program, rather than downloading it.) Came within a week. I didn't have to install it, since the free trial full version was already installed. But I had to "activate" it with the 25-character product key code:

Start > type "Office" into search box > click on Microsoft Office 2010 > shows "I already purchased Office 2010, click "Activate" [the other choice is "Go online to purchase Office 2010," "Purchase] > message: need valid product key > OK > Yes > enter 25-character product key (on CD package, inside cover) > Continue > Accept, Continue > (uncheck "Include free MS Office Professional 2010" trial), click "Install Now" [I don't know if this means install "Office" itself or install the activation of it. At any rate, I did not have to use the CD at all. I just have it for back up], wait 5 minutes > Close > shows "Completing Office setup (one minute). That's it.

You get free tech support for 90 days. Their Quick Start guide says online support is at "support.microsoft.com/office2010" or "answers.microsoft.com". And, *"For a complete list of support telephone numbers – "support.microsoft.com/officephonesupport"*

11. Getting Rid of Old Computer

I'm keeping mine. But if you want to get rid of your old one, I suggest bringing it to Best Buy to recycle it. It costs $10 but they give you a $10 gift certificate; so it's basically free. And, key thing, they take out the hard drive and give it to you, so you don't have to worry about a thief accessing sensitive info.

INSTALLATION OF PROGRAMS

Installing programs is sometimes easy, sometimes a nightmare. On the more complex ones, it seems there are three phases to the process: 1) Downloading – getting a program into your computer from the CD or from the internet. 2) Installing – getting the program operational from your download. 3) Activating – registering it with the company so that they know who's using it and maybe so that other people can't use it without your ID and password.

Note that if you buy software along with a new computer, there's a good chance the store will install it for you for free.

If you originally downloaded the program from a company rather than downloaded it using a disk, you need to go the company's website to download it again, which they should allow for free, since you already bought the program. They should have a record of your purchase. This is the way I was told to do it, and the one time I did, that's the way it worked. See "11. Bibles Program" below.

I installed all my programs and put shortcut icons for each one on the desktop.

1. Windows 7

Put in by Best Buy upon purchase. This is not a program as such, but an overall "operating system." Windows 7 is Microsoft's latest generation of operating systems, supplanting Windows Vista.

2. Norton Anti-virus Security Program

Put in by Best Buy upon purchase. Webroot security program has always been fine for me, but the store already had my computer set up with Norton. Update: I like Norton even better. Can just leave it alone with its default settings and it works with no further attention from you, unless it warns you of something trying to get on your computer. At which point you just click a button in the window that popped up, to do a scan and get rid of it.

3. Printer – Epson 810

Approximate time – 10-15 minutes.

With printer connected and on, I put Epson 810 CD in (window came up about installing a device driver; can ignore it because the drivers get installed as you go thru the upcoming process) > click Run SETUP.exe > Yes > Install, at bottom > Accept > Install driver for direct USB connection > Next > "Installing..." (several minutes) > it put "Epson Scan" icon on desktop and I got the message "Your device is ready to use."

However, there was another "Next," which led to installing the CD printing feature of my particular printer: Next > Next > Installing Epson Print CD > it put an icon on my desktop for that feature. [I need the CD printing feature because I produce CD's and DVD's, and sell them.]

Somewhere along the line I exited or canceled choices for Network and for Fax, since I use neither.

Another "Next" led to product registration. I filled all that info out, declining any email offers, etc. and clicked "Submit."

Ready to go; printer works now.

4. Chess – ChessMaster 9000

Approximate time: 5-10 minutes.

I put my first "ChessMaster 9000" CD in > Run autoplay.exe > Install > Yes > Next > Yes > Next > "Typical", Next > wait > Picked "Never Register" Yes > Yes > Next > Next > Finish > OK > removed disk and inserted the second ChessMaster disk > OK > Run autoplay.exe > Next > Finish > Play. Hooray, it works! This, despite, the usual weird dead ends, pointless windows, contradictory indications, etc. You just forge ahead as logically as you can, and it usually works.

5. Encyclopedia – MS Encarta

Approximate time: 15 minutes.

Put CD in > Run, Autorun.exe > Next > check "I accept" > Install, OK > Yes, wait > Next > Copy to Hard Drive, Next > uncheck "Encarta for Kids, Next > Next > Install, wait a good ten minutes > Exit Setup. Done, except it did not, like most programs, automatically put its icon on the desktop. Needed to type "Student Encarta" into Start search box to see the program, right-click it, and send a shortcut icon to the desktop.

6. Dictionary – Merriam-Webster

Approximate time: 5 minutes including restart.

Put CD in > Run, Autorun.exe > Install > Yes > Yes > showed "error extracting files"; I x'd out the window to start over, but underneath was another window offering "Next", so I clicked that > Yes > Next > Next > Next > No (to read) > Finish > Save > Restart. Got it; icon is on desktop; program ready to use.

7. External Hard Drive – Seagate

I have their CD, but when I simply attached the drive, it worked fine. Not sure if it needs a driver, but if it does, it quickly put it in by itself. I think it's the same deal with flash drives; they just work; you don't need to do a program installation.

8. Camcorder Sony Handycam

Approximate time: 10-15 minutes.

Put "Handycam" disk in > Run Install.exe > Yes > Install > Next > Next > Next > I accept, Next > Standard, Next > Install, wait, shows progress in green > Yes, wait about one minute > "PMB was successfully installed" > Next > "Connect your device, such as a Sony camcorder, to this computer. You will be able to install features related to the specific device" > Finish > Restart now.

On my desktop now appear these icons – "PMB", "PMB Help", "PMB Launcher". ("PMB" stands for Picture Motion Browser.) It's for importing video and pictures and managing them. I don't know if I will use it. I'm not sure, but from my limited experience with it so far, my sense is that it interferes with my normal importing of video and just makes things more complex and confusing. It's one of those extensive programs that tries to take over everything and organize it for you, resulting instead in total confusion. Like having two head coaches for the same team; not a good idea.

Not sure, but I think I don't even need this program. Windows Media Player imports video automatically to your Videos folder anyway.

9. Camera – Canon

Approximate time: 5-10 minutes

Put "Canon" disk in > Run Install.exe > Yes > USA > United States > English > Easy Installation > OK > Install > Yes, wait, 2 minutes > Next > No, to register, Next > Restart. It put 4 icons on my desktop, which I dragged into my Misc Desktop folder, since usually you don't need to click on those icons; pictures get imported automatically by Windows Media Player anyway, just like for video material, as mentioned above.

I think that your material (pictures, video) is stored somewhere on your hard drive, and many of these device programs, like the camera one here, do not literally make a copy of all that stuff to keep inside their programs, but merely enable themselves to have access to these materials, from the hard drive, as they organize the names of these files on their own programs, and display the info to you.

10. OCR Program – Nuance Communications (OmniPage 15)

Time: lengthy, an hour?

Put CD in > Open folder to view files > double-clicked the one file there > this will extract OmniPage 15 installation file, OK > Unzip > "unzipped successfully", OK > Yes > English > Start installation > Next > I accept, Next > entered my name and the serial #, which I had noted on package > Next > Next > Next > Install, wait about a minute > Finish > skipped registration by x'ing out window. Says you need to activate it: "Activate Now" > OK > said it was retrieving data from server and said to enter new serial number. Waited. Nothing. That's as far as I could go.

OK, I typed OmniPage 15 into the Start search box, and I see that I do have the program in (I right-clicked it and sent a shortcut icon to the desktop), but I still need to activate it. Called them (407 241-1827) and it turns out when it says to put a new serial number in, it means for you to re-enter your old one. Geez!

I'm all set; it's activated and works now. Normally they charge for technical support, but since this was simple (just identifying my serial number), no charge. Future assistance will cost.

Up-to-date version is OmniPage 17 (Legacy is the company now, I think) and I can order it in the future by calling 1 800 654-1187.

11. Bibles Program – Bible Apologetics Library (Geisler)

Approximate time: one hour.

Got nowhere on my own. Called. Number not working. Checked website; got a new number (1 800 875-6467). Called, and got good help. Told me my disk is old. Best to download newest version (no charge). He led me thru it. If I had tried to do it using my old disk, I NEVER would have succeeded. Lesson: Never be determined to do it yourself no matter what; know when to cut your (time) losses and seek help. Once it was downloading, it was the usual Run, Run, Yes, Next, I accept, etc.

They've changed the plethora of account info you needed formerly (ID, user name, account number, password, etc., etc.) to just two items: your email and your password. Good move.

Download time: 10 minutes. Phone time: 20 minutes. Total time, including before phone call: one hour. The program is now set up somewhat differently, but retains all the books and functions of the original program.

12. Pinnacle/Studio (movie making program)

Approximate time: 2½ hours trying to figure it out along with phone call; 5 hours downloading time (it's a big program); 30 minutes installation procedure.

I don't have a CD for this program; I had purchased and downloaded it over the internet.

Tried to call them for advice (650 267-5196, tech support). What a hassle. So typical. Needed to purchase a "Service Code" to talk to anybody. Tried to get free online chat help; needed a new password; they send you one by email; except that's a temporary one; from there you need to enter yet another new one. Didn't work because the one I choose matched one of my old ones; finally entered a new one successfully. Went thru the process of signing up for chat help; it finally showed "action not available." So typical: phone help sends you in circles, getting you nowhere, finally advising you to check their website; website help sends you in circles, getting you nowhere, finally advising you to call them!

Called again; got info on how to apply for (purchase) a "Service Code" so I could talk to a human. (www.pcle.com/ studio/asc) No luck. Of course, their site shows five (5!) different ways to get help. Did any of them work? No! It's SO stupid. Just like Microsoft; they work hard at selling the IDEA that they are helpful instead of following thru and actually being helpful! And it's not the fault of the individual tech people you finally talk to; they do their best; it's the higher ups, the bosses, who are oblivious to the aggravation customers go thru.

I'll never forget a piece "60 Minutes" did on Netflix. They were interviewing the CEO, and told him how some customers in Maine had some problem but could find no number to call. He laughed at the absurdity of that claim. The interviewer challenged him to find the number. He couldn't! He couldn't! I loved it. (Actually I am a fan of Netflix; they are in fact very good at help, and maybe, I'm speculating, as the result of that embarrassing moment on national TV.)

Anyway, I finally found a place to click on to get a "Service Code" number ($10). And finally reached a human being who guided me thru doing a download. The download itself took about 5 hours (the program is 2.8 GB big). Now I need to install it. (Remember, download and install, are often two different things.)

Unbelievable the plethora of things you have to go thru, requiring your user name, or password, or new password, or serial number, or order number, or service code, or product number, or customer care number... geez! I think I ended up purchasing a service code number a second time ($10); at one point I eventually saw I had one already. But, I don't care, I'm not going to try to get reimbursed, because I'll probably have to go thru more numbers and multi-step processes. I can't take any more!

OK, I've got it downloaded, but I still have to install it. I got an email from the tech guy explaining how to install the program:

Studio 14 icon > Pinnacle Studio > Welcome > Extract All > Extract (2 min) > Pinnacle Studio > Welcome > Yes > Install Studio 14 > English > entered old serial number (guy emailed me both old and new 25-digit serial number, actually letters) > OK > no go, timed out, tried again > (worked this time) entered name, address info > entered new serial number > OK > OK, preparing to install... > Next > I accept > four more Nexts (kept all default choices) > Install (7 min) > Finish > OK (for plug-ins) (5 min) > English> Next > I accept > Next > Next > Install (1 min). Done. Familiar multi-colored Studio pinwheel icon is now on desktop, and the program is working. Hooray.

Lesson learned: Whenever possible, buy the software CD rather than buy and download over the internet. It's easier to install, easier to get it onto a new computer. (Plus, you don't have to be concerned with viruses.)

13. Gadgets

Approximate time: 30 minutes.

I put my gadgets up at the right.

Typed "Gadgets" into Start search box > Desktop Gadgets > Right-click, Add > Don't like their selection, clicked "Get more gadgets online" at lower right > Windows Live Gallery > Added "Weatherbug" (the one I like) > Download > Install > Save > Desktop > Save > right-click icon > Install > clicked on popup wrench icon to adjust > put in zip code > Search > OK. Now I have the weather gadget I'm used to. Had to put in my zip code again elsewhere. You often have to fiddle around quite a bit to get what you want.

Worked my way thru putting a couple others up also. The weather one, and a good date/time one. But I couldn't find the same stock market one I had before, a straightforward simple one I liked. Ain't that typical? I could find the Turkish (!) stock market one, but a simple American Dow Jones Average one, no. Finally found an acceptable one.

14. iTunes

Approximate time: 20 minutes.

Googled "iTunes" and clicked on the "iTunes Official Store." But that led me to downloads that cost money! Checked Wikipedia to see if iTunes program is still supposed to be free. Yes. Latest version is 10.2.2.

So I googled "iTunes version 10.2.2 free download" > clicked 4th selection down "iTunes 10.2.2 – Apple – Support" > clicked "Download button at upper right > clicked "Download Now" at left > Run, wait 7 minutes or so > Next > I accept, Next > Install > Yes, wait a minute > Yes, wait a minute or so again > Finish > a video tutorial page comes up ("Watch the video"), which is pretty good, 9 different topics (iPod, importing CD's, etc.). Set to go.

The iTunes icon is automatically put up on the desktop. First time I bought a song, I had to confirm my billing info, but that was quick, no problem.

MINOR TASKS / ISSUES

32 vs 64 Bit – Somewhere along the line I was given a choice between 32-bit or 64-bit web browser (bigger chunks of info at a time, making your browser – Internet Explorer, in my case – a bit faster). Since I have a 64-bit computer, I was told that's what I should select. You can find whether your computer is 32- or 64-bit by right-clicking Computer and then clicking Properties.

However, I picked 32-bit, because many programs do not yet run on 64-bit; see "ADOBE FLASH PLAYER"

Adobe Flash Player – Got automatic notification that an update is available. Clicked on "Install", etc., and it was done in less than a minute. Supposed to help in viewing videos. See "ADOBE FLASH PLAYER" for more info.

AutoCorrect Shortcuts – I put in a few autocorrect shortcuts I find useful, like "esp" for especially, "Xity" for Christianity, etc. See "AUTOCORRECT – AUTOMATIC REPLACEMENT OF WORDS"

AutoCorrect Symbols – Entered a few AutoCorrect symbols (Cents for ¢, = = for ≠, etc.) See "AUTOCORRECT – SYMBOLS"

Automatic Formatting – Review tab > Spelling & Grammar > Options, at lower left > AutoCorrect Options > there are 5 tabs, choose your option preferences under each.

Myself, I left Math and Action tabs alone > AutoCorrect tab > unchecked all 4 items, including "Automatic bulleted lists" > unchecked Straight quotes with smart quotes > OK > under AutoFormat As You Type tab > unchecked "Automatic bulleted lists" and "Automatic numbered lists" > OK > OK > OK.

I don't like too many things done automatically, because often it's not what I want.

Automatic Numbering and Bulleting – DISABLE – See "NUMBERING WITHIN THE TEXT – AUTOMATIC" > "Getting Rid of Automatic Numbering"

(Note that the "MS Starter 2010" program has items reached thru different routes. Regular version, for instance, has this function under Review tab, Spelling & Grammar; "Starter" version has it under File > Options > Proofing.

Camera – Wasn't importing my camera pictures automatically. Did this: Attach camera > turn it on > Canon icon shows in taskbar; click on it > double-click Change general settings > "When this device connects to this computer" dropdown arrow > Import pictures and videos > OK > click "Import" (not sure if it's completely automatic now; seems I still need to actually click on "Import" button after connecting, but that's fine) > sends the picture to Pictures folder under Libraries, in a folder with the current date.

CD Printing – My CD label files would not open up. Long story short, with help from Epson tech guy on the phone: I typed "Print CD" into the Start search box (that was the name of the Epson program for CD printing); otherwise I was not able to locate it. ("Epson" was not enough; "Epson Print CD" was too much. That's the odd way the Start search box often works: You have to put just the right number of words. Say a program is entitled "Smith Graphics Tools." You put in "Smith", no go. You put in "Smith Graphics", you get it. You put in "Smith Graphics Tools", no go again.

Opened it up > File > Open > browsed to my CD label files > Open > that put the list under the Folder heading > clicked on the desired file > OK. That brings up that file, to edit or print.

I right-clicked the program under Start and sent a shortcut for it onto my desktop, so I don't have to search for it each time.

Update: Aha. Once up, for each label file, I clicked Save at top, and it sent it to my labels folder as a file I could now just click on to open up. I deleted the corresponding old files that would not open up.

"CTRL" Shortcuts for Symbols – Entered two CTRL orders for symbols: 1) Ctrl+/ for ✓ and 2) Ctrl+> for → . Initially this would not work, even though it does on my old computer. I know now it's because "MS Office Starter" has reduced functionality. Once I bought the full "MS Office 2010" program, it worked. See "SHORTCUTS – CUSTOM SHORTCUTS FOR SYMBOLS"

Desktop Background – Changed my desktop background to a plain color.

Desktop Icons – Align – Right-click desktop > View > check "Align icons to grid" > uncheck "Auto arrange icons" (which stacks them all on the left). Arranged them the way I like instead.

Double Hyphens – Windows 7 puts double hyphens automatically into dashes, but only after you type in the next word. And, if double dashes are at the beginning of a paragraph, it automatically puts in a square bullet. I do not like either of these two automatic operations. I like to be able to see the change to a dash right away, and, to use dashes sometimes at the beginning of a paragraph and have them stay dashes.

Did this: Review tab > Spelling & Grammar > Options, at lower left > AutoCorrect Options > left Math and Action tabs alone > AutoCorrect tab > Replace: -- With: pasted in a dash – > Add > OK > OK. Now my double hyphens change to a dash, even at the beginning of a paragraph, not a bullet, and they always change to a dash right away.

Font – Loss Of – After I transferred My Documents from my old computer to my new one, I noticed that all my text in Arial Narrow, which I use a lot, now shows as script! Even though the font box at top indicates that it's in Arial Narrow. And, there is no Arial Narrow in the font list!

I restarted the computer; the font suddenly came back – Arial Narrow text in the document, and also in the font list. I guess if a font is not on the font list, after restarting, it puts any new font from an imported document, automatically into the list and makes it functional... I think.

However, if that is not the case, and you're missing a font from your old computer that you want in your new computer, you can transfer it. See "FONT – INSTALLING A NEW FONT" > "Transferring Font from Old Computer to New Computer"

Grammar Checking – Got rid of default green grammar-error underlining. Home tab > Proofing box at right > Spelling & Grammar > unchecked "Check Grammar" > Options at lower left > unchecked "Mark grammar errors as you type" > OK > closed window. I like to keep the red underlining for spelling, but not the green underlining for grammar.

Update: Now I keep the grammar on also. Helps catch miscellaneous errors, and spacing errors.

Lid Closing Setup – Put it to my preferences. See "COMPUTER ON / OFF BUTTON – SIMPLIFY" > "Laptop Lid Closing – Setting"

Number Keys at Right – Disable – See "NUMBER LOCK"

Pointer Style – Made pointer larger and dark, so I can see it better than the default style it comes in. Typed "Pointer" into Start search box > "Change how the mouse pointer looks" > chose "Windows Black (extra large)."

Print Quality Setting – I used to use "Draft" as my default setting, but at the moment I'm going with their default "Regular" setting. So, I didn't change anything here. See "PRINTING" > "To Set 'Draft' Quality as Your Default Print Quality"

Quote Marks and Commas – Curly vs Straight – Got rid of default curly ("smart") quote marks. Home tab at top > Proofing box at right > Spelling & Grammar > Options at lower left > AutoCorrect Options > AutoFormat As You Type tab > uncheck Replace As You Type "Straight quotes with smart quotes," OK.

Screen Dim Out Times – I changed the default settings to my preferences. See "COMPUTER ON / OFF BUTTON – SIMPLIFY" > "Windows 7 Update"

Sony Vaio Controls at Top – My new Sony Vaio has a toolbar ribbon that pops up at the very top; or if you put the pointer at the very center top spot, this Vaio toolbar shows up. Very annoying. Most of the stuff is redundant. Seems every company tries to take over, from the other companies, what you do on your computer. I already have picture features, etc., etc. The only two functions here I might use are 1) the User Guide, 2) the webcam. And those items, and the rest, are listed anyway under Start, All programs (webcam is under "ArcSoft Webcam Companion 3" > "Launch"). I don't need that toolbar popping up all the time.

It would even pop up with one-line current news flashes. How wonderful!! No, you bastards, leave me the hell alone!! If I want to get news, I'll go get news. Stop distracting me!! Research shows multitasking makes you dumber, not smarter!

At one point I saw an X option at upper right, clicked on that, and, hooray, that toolbar finally stopped popping up. But then later, it started popping up again!

Solution: Just to the left of that X, is a "Close Settings" icon > click on that > click No for "Load at startup". That finally did it.

Spelling Addition – Added my first and last name to the dictionary, so they won't get underlined in red all the time as misspellings. Right-click on the name, Add to Dictionary.

Tab Size Preference – Put in .2 tabs as my preferred default size. See "TABS"

Taskbar – Disappearing – At one point my taskbar disappeared. To get it back: Press Start key on the keyboard (since the Start icon has disappeared along with the taskbar!) > type "Taskbar" into the Start search box > Taskbar and Start Menu > uncheck Auto hide. See also "TASKBAR"

Taskbar Cleanout – Cleaned out taskbar of programs I don't use, by right-clicking each icon and clicking "Unpin this program from taskbar." Some of the odd ones that hang out at the right, I just left there because they did not seem to have that unpin option. Note that among these odd ones are also several key ones to keep, namely battery, volume, time, and date.

Website Favorites – Entered a few websites I use often under "Favorites." See "FAVORITES – WEBSITES"

DIFFERENCES – VISTA vs WINDOWS 7

Calculator – Instead of just basic functions, Windows 7 calculator has expanded ones (scientific calculator, conversion feature, etc., under the View tab).

Document Creating – Instead of Windows Office button at upper left > New > Create at lower right under Blank Document, you go to File tab at upper left > New > Create at lower right under Blank Document.

Problem: Until you have a document open already, there is no "File" tab to check! And doing a Ctrl+N under My Documents does nothing. So how do you get your first document of your new computer created (if you didn't transfer one from your old computer)? Solution: Start > All Programs > MS Office Home and Student > click "MS Word 2010" > that opens up a new document.

Update: Hah, another, easier, way. I sort of knew this but it didn't occur to me till now: Press the ALT key and that brings up a menu with File at upper left. See also "FILE" TAB DISAPPEARED

DVD Disk Preparing – Instead of the two unclear choices – "Live File System" or "Mastered" – Windows 7 has now labeled these choices: "Like a USB flash drive" or "With a CD/DVD player". More understandable, namely, a choice between using the disk as a computer data disk (to hold information on), or as a video disk (to be watched).

Also, it took less than a minute to prepare; and, no problems. With my old computer with Vista it would sometimes take a long time, or freeze, especially after I had that virus. Things seem more stable with Windows 7.

Also erasing a disk only took a few seconds.

Eject Disk – Seems there is often no eject button to click (I don't know if this is Windows 7 or just my new computer.) However, the physical eject button at the disk bay is very responsive: push it once, wait a few seconds, and it ejects. My old one I sometimes had to push it half a dozen times to get it to work.

File Icons – Instead of clicking View at the top of a folder, to change how your documents are listed (large, medium, small icons, or list), you click the "Change your view" icon (six little squares) at the top right.

File Listings – Folder and document lists show in one column, instead of two. I prefer two columns; can see more. Solution: Click on "Change your view" icon at upper right (6 little squares) and check "List" instead of "Details."

Files Selecting – As a default setting, a window of files may not have "☐ Name" at upper left. To get it back, click the "Change your view" button at upper right, several times thru the variations, till you get it (namely "Details" instead of "List"). This ☐ Name is a good feature, because clicking the box before "Name" will check ALL the files in that window at once. Lot easier than checking each one individually.

Folder – Creating New Folder – When you are in a folder, there is a "New Folder" button at top, whereas under Vista you right-click an empty spot > New > Folder.

Fonts – May not have all the same ones as Vista, though I think it is largely the same list.

A Humanist font text I had, turned into a script font when I transferred it from my old computer. And occasionally, a font changes into the default Calibri font when I copy a text to another document. In both cases I had to block the text and select the original font to change it back. (Actually, you can fix this second case by: Home tab > Font box dropdown arrow > select a font, upper left > "Set as default" lower left > "This document only." Then, next time you import text to this document, it will land in the font you set as default... maybe; or, more likely, having gotten rid of Calibri as the default font, text will land in the document in the same font as it was when you copied it from the other document.)

Gadgets – Instead of being restricted to the "Sidebar" panel at the right side of the screen, gadgets can be positioned anywhere on the desktop. But I still keep them at the right; that's a good spot for them.

Lost Documents or Folders

Instead of only two steps from accidentally losing a document or folder forever – Deleted, and then Emptied from Recycle Bin – Windows 7 provides an extra safety feature; it retains 20 days of previous versions of a document or folder, even if they have been deleted from your Recycle Bin. See "DOCUMENTS – RETRIEVING OLDER VERSION"

ON / OFF – Instead of 3 or more minutes, Windows 7 boots up faster, closer to 2 minutes. (I assume it's Windows 7 rather than the newer computer that makes the difference, but I don't know for sure.

Picture Editing – Instead of being able to only rotate a picture, as is, with Windows 7 under Windows Live Photo Gallery, you can actually straighten subject matter, with automatically adjusted new borders: Windows Live Photo Gallery > Edit > "Straighten" at top.

See also "PHOTOS / PICTURES – BASIC OPERATIONS" > "EDITING THE PICTURES" > "Windows 7 Straightening Feature"

Also, a nice improvement: Instead of having to put in numbers to crop a picture, you can now crop by dragging edges. See "PHOTOS / PICTURES – BASIC OPERATIONS" > "EDITING THE PICTURES" > "Size and Cropping"

Printing – Selecting Odd or Even Only Sides

Instead of ordering range of pages first, then odd only/even only option (say, pages 1-7, odd only), Windows 7 requires that you set the odd/even command first, THEN set the page range, otherwise the page range command doesn't stay in effect; it just disappears. You must set the odd/even command first, THEN the page range command.

Program Names – Windows Movie Maker is now called Windows Live Movie Maker; Windows Photo Gallery is now Windows Live Photo Gallery.

Quote marks – Instead of "straight" quote marks as the default format, Windows 7 has "curly" quote marks as the default.

Restart

A black screen comes up and tells you to click "Cancel", and close any remaining open file. Then you can click "Restart" again. Wait a few second and it proceeds.

Sony – New vs Old Sony

Speaker sound is poor, worse than old one, which was so-so. (I think that's one of the differences between an $800 computer and a $1,200 one.) But, sound is good when using earphones, and quality sound directly from the computer speakers is not that important to me.

Has 3 USB ports on right, another one on left. Old one had just 3 at right.

Is already set up to go into Sleep mode upon closing lid.

Has 585 GB capacity vs 160 for the old Sony. (Compare that to my first Sony in 1999 – only 6 GB.)

Shut Down – Instead of "Shut Down" being one of the options after you click the arrow at the lower right of the Start window, Windows 7 has "Shut Down" as an immediate option before you click the arrow.

And a dark window comes up showing the computer shutting down items you currently had in the taskbar. (If there is something you need to close down on your own, it gives you an option of canceling, shutting that item down yourself, and then starting the shut-down procedure again. As always, MS makes things more annoying, complex, and confusing than necessary.) Basically, you can just ignore all the stuff it says there, and just wait for it to close down on its own.

Taskbar – Hidden Icons – Instead of to the left, the Hidden icons arrow points upwards.

Taskbar at Bottom – Default taskbar is a little bigger. I like the taskbar smaller: Right-click it > Properties > select Small Icons.

And, when you place the pointer on an icon there, instead of just a name popping up, a thumbnail picture pops up; a bit more informative, I guess. Each item that pops up can be closed by clicking the red "x" that appears at its top right if you put the pointer there.

At one point, for whatever reason, those thumbnail pictures wouldn't pop up anymore; I just get the name of the item, which is fine by me; that's all I need. [Update: now suddenly the thumbnails are back. They're actually pretty good, like little preview windows, making it easier to recognize and click on the one you want.]

Another difference: If your Internet Explorer icon is on the taskbar, you can right-click it to bring up a list of recent sites visited, to click on.

Toolbar – When in a Word document, you can quickly minimize the toolbar "ribbon" at top, to get more screen space, by clicking a caret arrow at upper right, right next to the question mark icon. Click the same caret arrow (now pointing down) to get it back. In both Vista and Windows 7, you can also hide the ribbon by double-clicking the name of the active tab, then again to get it back.

Video – Windows Media Player has a different look. I thought it was QuickTime at first. Looks like it, but it's Windows Media Player. Shows up at upper left when you click on a video file.

Window Resizing – Besides dragging an edge or corner of a window to change its size, you can make a small window pop into full-screen size by dragging it and bumping it into the top of the screen.

Windows Side-by-Side – You can get two windows side-by-side by dragging one deeply into the right edge and the other deeply into the left edge. Probably my favorite improvement over Vista. In fact now that getting windows up side-by-side is less of a hassle, I find I use this feature more often. See "VIEW DOCUMENTS SIDE BY SIDE"

Word Search – When you do a Ctrl+F, instead of a window right on top of your text, you get a bigger more complex one at the left, called "Navigation." See "FINDING – A WORD (WORD SEARCH)"

****

COMPUTER – FREEZES – See "FREEZING"

COMPUTER – LAPTOP vs DESKTOP – They both can do all the same functions. The desktop is bigger, with mouse and keyboard attached to the monitor by wires. The laptop is smaller, portable, with mouse, keyboard, and monitor all in one unit.

COMPUTER – ON... WAIT – When turning on the computer, don't start doing anything until it FULLY boots up (i.e. the desktop is fully settled, the gadgets on the right fully up); otherwise things tend to stall or go very slowly, or, also very likely, the computer will freeze and you have to reboot, if you try to start a function before the computer is fully on. At least, that's been my experience.

COMPUTER ON / OFF – SIMPLIFY – Instead of clicking Start > arrow > Shut down, and waiting for it to shut down – as I had been doing for years – you can shut down the computer, or turn it on, by pressing just the ONE keyboard Power button (upper right, for me), if you set it up like this: Start > Control Panel > Hardware & Sound > click Power Options > "Choose what the power button does" > select "Shut Down" from pull down menu > click "Save changes". Now, just pressing the On/Off button turns computer on or off.

But!!! I don't recommend this. See next paragraph:

When you normally close a text document, it will automatically remind you to save it, but if you use this one-button method, it is very easy to miss that reminder, as you instinctively press that button and close the lid very quickly... and lose your latest typing!!!

A much safer technique: Set your laptop to go to "Sleep" mode when you close the lid, so that even if you shut the lid and forget to save something, the material will still be there, as it was, next time you open it. This "Sleep" setting is much safer, and much more convenient. See "Laptop Lid Closing – Setting" below.

You just put the lid down, and it goes to sleep. You lift the lid, press the On button, and it opens the computer, in just 5-10 seconds. No more need to wait 2-3 minutes for it to power up, or power off. It keeps up whatever you had (files, programs, etc.) and resumes within seconds. Very convenient.

Nowadays I rarely close my computer down. Usually only if it freezes, to unfreeze it.

I note that I'm the only one using my computer. If you are sharing one, you may prefer not to have your material up front and center like this, and may prefer traditional "Shut down" for your lid and button settings.

Laptop Lid Closing – Setting

Start > Control Panel > Hardware & Sound > Power Options > "Choose what closing the lid does" at left, select Sleep > Save Changes. Now, closing the lid puts it to sleep.

I recommend: For both "On battery" and "Plugged in," for both power button and lid – select "Sleep". ("Choose what the power button does" is on the same list on the left as the "Choose what closing the lid does" option.)

[W7 – The default mode when closing the lid is Sleep (the On button slowly blinks orange, as opposed to a steady green when it's fully on). Open the lid, press any key, and you're back in business in seconds. Computers vary. If pressing a key doesn't work, pressing the On button will wake it up again.]

Sleep vs Hibernation

There is another setting option – Hibernation (at least in Windows 7; I don't see "Hibernation" in Vista). Start > Control Panel > Hardware & Sound > Power Options > "Choose what closing the lid/button does" at left, select Hibernate > Save changes.

[To change the hibernation after x minutes time: Power Options > "Change when the computer sleeps" at left > "Change advanced power settings" at lower left > "Advanced settings" tab > scroll down to "Sleep", click on the + button > "Hibernate after", click on the + button > change the minutes > OK.]

Hibernation is a deeper sleep; it uses a bit less power and takes a bit longer to wake up than Sleep. Pointless overkill, in my opinion. Sleep uses very little power anyway. If the computer is not plugged in, when a battery charge gets critically low, Windows automatically switches from Sleep to Hibernation.

I've read that if you forget to Save material, and your battery runs out, Windows automatically saves data for you at that point, before shutting off. (And that has been my experience.) YET, I also read in the Sony User Guide – "If the battery pack runs out of power while the computer is in sleep mode, you will lose all unsaved data" [!!??]. I click on Save a lot anyway, just to play it safe. When you shut the computer fully off without saving... that's when you definitely lose data for sure.

Wakes on its Own Problem

Recently, several times, after some hours of having closed the lid, I noticed the computer was back on, on its own; the orange light was now green, and my computer screen was on, despite the lid being closed. Thought at first it was Windows waking it up to add an update, but no; checking my update history, I saw that the times didn't match.

Sent an email thru "esupport.sony.com" site and got a two-page answer, suggesting either a "system restore" or an advanced power options adjustment. Did the advanced power options suggestion; and it worked. Hooray:

Start > Control Panel > Systems and Security > Power Options > "Change plan settings", at right next to "Balanced (recommended)" > "Change advanced power settings" at lower left > click the + sign next to "Sleep" > click the + sign next to "Allow wake timers" > on both "On battery" and "Plugged in", click on "enable" to change it to "disable" >

OK That did it. Now the computer stays asleep till I physically wake it by lifting the lid and pressing the ON button.

Of course, now the orange light keeps disappearing after some time. But that's fine; it still takes only 30 seconds or less to wake up the computer in the morning. I'm pretty sure what it is, is the "Hibernation" setting under "Sleep" has a default time of 4 hours, after which the computer automatically goes into Hibernation mode (a deeper sleep mode) instead of Sleep mode. Hence the disappearing orange light.

Automatic Sleep mode after 10 minutes, and automatic Hibernation mode after 240 minutes (4 hours), are default settings that are fine with me. I like my computer to turn off after 10 minutes of non-use during the day. And I like my computer to go to Hibernation deep sleep overnight.

I suspect this whole problem came about because the Sony computer power options were competing with the Windows operating system power options. All behind my back, the little bastards. Of course, I can't really tell if these are competing programs, integrated programs, or what.

Green light = ON. Blinking orange = Sleep. No light = Hibernation, or computer off. (Blinking green = battery low.)

Wake Up Times

Wake up time from Sleep = 5-10 seconds; Wake up time from Hibernation = 25-30 seconds. Wake up time from Off = 2-3 minutes (my old Vista – 3 minutes; my new Windows 7 – 2 minutes). Screen wakeup from blackout is instantaneous upon pressing any key.

Update: I got tired of waiting 30 seconds for the computer to wake up from hibernation, so I changed the default setting so that it never goes into Hibernation, but only into Sleep: Start > Control Panel > Hardware and Sound > Power Options > "Change plan settings" at right > "Change advanced power settings" at lower left > scroll down to Sleep, click on the + sign > "Hibernate after", click on the + sign > "On battery, click on "60 Minutes" > scroll down to "Never" > "Plugged in", click on "240 Minutes" > scroll down to "Never" > OK. Now my computer consistently wakes up in about 5 seconds after I push the ON button. Or, if the computer is still on (steady green light), pressing any key puts the screen back on.

From Baycongroup.Com Vista Tutorial

What do you mean when you say my computer is in sleep mode?

In sleep mode, your computer consumes very little electricity. When you need to use your computer again, you can press your computer's power-on switch to resume work quickly. Instead of shutting your computer down when you are not using your computer, you should put your computer in sleep mode.

I am using a laptop. Won't putting my computer in sleep mode drain my computer's battery?

A sleeping computer uses very little energy. Microsoft, the maker of Windows Vista, recommends that you put your computer, whether a desktop or a laptop, in sleep mode when you are not using it. A sleeping computer should not drain your computer's battery. However, if your power becomes dangerously low, Vista saves your work to your hard drive and then shuts your computer down.

COMPUTER REPAIR – Once, my laptop slid off a low table onto a soft carpet, but landed on its corner, messing it up; would no longer work. I had gotten careless when moving it! Place I used to get it fixed: Rapid Response, 1 Wall St. Hudson, NH, off Rte 111, 603 898-4357; $125/hr 5-7 days, $250/hr for 2-day service. They were good, though expensive.

Now I use Best Buy for repair service. Staples also has computer repair. And I just saw a TV ad for Infinity (Comcast); they also offer home networking, PC tune ups, and virus removal.

My advice is to stick to these major companies. See "VIRUS" > "MY VIRUS SAGA"

COMPUTER – SPEED – Can presumably speed things up a bit by lowering the quality of the graphics. Tried it. Didn't notice much difference in speed, but I noticed I don't like the stripped down graphics, so I put it back to where it was.

Start > Control Panel > System and Maintenance > Performance Info and Tools > Advanced Tools at left > Adjust Appearance and Performance of Windows > Adjust for Best Performance (fastest), or Adjust for Best Appearance (best graphics), OK. Or, what I went back to: select "What's Best for my Computer."

COMPUTER – TECHNICAL INFO – Can find technical info about your computer – which version of Windows you have, computer model number, 32- or 64-bit system, RAM, etc. – from Start > Right-click Computer > Properties.

"COMPUTER" WINDOW – You can open your "Computer" window by clicking Start, then Computer (at right). The window shows you all the major stuff you have on your computer. On the right: Local Disk (your basic hard drive where most material is kept), and Drive E (any disks you put in). If you attach a camera or camcorder, or a flash drive, to a USB port, an icon for it shows up in this window.

On the left: the "Computer" window shows your major folders (Pictures, Music, etc.) and all the folders under them. You can successively click on items and their sub-categories, to reach what you want.

I like the "Computer" window icon on the Desktop, for quicker access. To get the "Computer" icon up on your Desktop, if it isn't already there: Start > right-click Computer > Show on Desktop.

CONTROL PANEL – Click on Start and listed at the right of the Start window is "Control Panel," which allows you to change computer settings, uninstall programs, etc. (Sometimes you need to wait till all your programs show up in your control panel.) Clicking on Control Panel opens a window listing a number of categories, like System and Security, Programs, User Accounts, Appearance, etc. Note that each of these categories (in green font) have subcategories beneath them (in blue font). Clicking on the green heading will open up more subcategories than just the blue ones initially shown. The blue ones are just the most commonly used ones.

"Setting" windows arrived at thru the Control Panel, can also usually be arrived at by: right-clicking an item, then clicking Properties.

CONVERSION WEBSITE – "OnlineConversion.com" is a good website to use to convert measurements – lengths, weights, temperature, etc. [If you're offline, Windows 7 calculator has a conversion feature; see "CALCULATOR"]

COOKIES – DEFINITION – Small files stored on your computer by websites to save info, such as log-in information. They help speed things up. I don't like them; I don't like information gathered on me; don't know where it will end up. But, I understand no website can view another website's cookies, and, I don't really want to have to sign in every time I check my email, or Netflix account, etc. So, under the "Safety" tab at upper right and under the "Delete Browsing History" window, I keep every item on that list checked (for "on"), for the sake of convenience.

You can delete the information accumulated by checking the categories there and clicking the Delete button at bottom. Or, you can uncheck the ones you don't want accumulating, and close the window. (That retains those settings; there's no OK button to click.)

See also "BROWSING HISTORY – WEBSITES"

COPIES USING YOUR PRINTER ONLY – Usually you print out stuff from your computer, with the computer controlling the printer. But if you want to just make a copy of a document you already have – like a standard "copy machine" – most printers these days can do that. On my Epson 810, I put the original face down to the left of the glass > select Copy > OK > Start. It makes a copy.

COPY – AN ADDRESS – When you enter a search term into a website search engine, like Google, you don't have to be exact. It can guess what you meant. BUT, for an email address, or for a website address entered into the website address box, you need to be exact. Most often it's best to block an address, copy it, and paste it into the address box, so that it is exact. Note also that if you accidentally included a space at the end of the address, then that is not exact, and it won't work. When some program or website requires you enter an ID number, the same concept applies: if you include an extra space, it may not work.

COPY – FILE – To make a copy of a file (document, picture, audio, or video): Right-click its icon when it is closed > Copy > find where you want to land it > then CTRL+V to paste it there.

Note that if you make a copy of a document into another folder, so that you have it in both places, and if you add something to one of those copies, it does NOT make the same change in the other copy! So now you have two documents that do NOT have the identical data in them. Keeping a document, that you often add to, in two different folders, is NOT a good idea. You'll end up with two significantly different documents with the same name. Better to simply decide which folder is the most logical one to keep that one document in... unless you know you're never going to add info to it, then it's OK to put it into two different folders.

Accidental Multiple Copies

When you paste with CTRL+V, just press the keys ONCE, don't hold them down, or you'll get several copies!

COPY – TEXT – Block the text > CTRL+C > find the new spot > CTRL+V (paste) it there.

I don't like to use the Copy and Paste icons at upper left under the Home tab; I much prefer using CTRL+C and CTRL+V.

COPY PROTECTION – ON COMMERCIAL CDS – Some CDs have copy protection on them, so you can't rip them to your computer.

COPY PROTECTION – WINDOWS MEDIA PLAYER – I think this setting is usually turned off anyway by default, but if it isn't, you probably should want it off, so you don't get problems not being allowed to use your own material, or songs you've already purchased from iTunes. Windows Media Player > ALT key to bring up menu > Tools > Options > Rip Music tab > uncheck Copy Protect Music.

CORD – POWER CORD – It's an excellent idea to always keep a spare power cord in your laptop case for use when you are away from home, in case you forget to disconnect and pack the one you normally use at home, or simply because you can't stand constantly disconnecting and re-connecting that cord.

Note that a spare cord may not be that easy to get, since it might be "proprietary," i.e. you need to get that particular cord from that particular company; a generic one may not work. (That used to be the case with Sony; you couldn't just go to a Radio Shack and buy a generic cord. But, I think that's changed now.)

Watch out that you don't step on the end of the power cord when you're carrying it around. You might squish the end of it where it attaches to the computer, ruining the cord.

CPU – HIGH USAGE ALERT – CPU = Central Processing Unit. It carries out the instructions of a computer program. Kind of like the inner brain of the computer.

At one point I kept getting a popup message warning of high CPU usage. I don't think it's any big deal; I just x'd it out; had no problems. But, it's annoying to get the message. Had Best Buy guy check it out. He said it was my "network sharing" feature using a lot of whatever. He turned it off and the message stopped popping up.

Start > Control Panel > Network and Internet > Network and Sharing Center > "Change advanced sharing settings" at left > turned off Network Discovery and Public Folder Sharing > Save Changes.

Update: Turning off Network Discovery, turned off connection to my printer. Had to put that back on.

Update: It's still popping up! Long story short, here's how to get rid of it: Open Norton > click "Settings" on window that comes up > then, not on the scroll list, but at bottom is a category "Miscellaneous Settings" with a picture of a wrench > click on that > then scroll down to "Norton Task Notification" > "High Usage Alert for" > click all 4 under that OFF (CPU, Memory, Disk, and Handles) > Apply > OK. Now it logs that stuff but doesn't alert you.

Note that you do have to click both Apply and OK (in other programs you often just need to click either one).

Norton phone help: 1 800 441-7234; or 1 800 745-6061 x4.

CRASH – A condition where a computer or program stops working. See also "FREEZING" for some solutions. Usually re-starting the computer solves the problem.

CREDIT CARD THEFT – This isn't strictly a computer issue, but I include it because it happened to me once when I bought something over the internet.

Last year I got a call from, allegedly, VISA, about recent suspicious activity on my card. The caller sounded legit, but I eventually decided he might not be. He told me of several suspicious charges in the past few days, which I knew were definitely not mine. He also told me of one legit automatic charge, the amount for which he got slightly wrong. So I said good-bye to him, and called the number on the back of my card instead, and talked to another guy.

Turns out the first guy WAS legit; it was not a scam. When we tried verifying me, my mother's maiden name was listed as "Cox" instead of what it really was. So he figured, yes, somebody has compromised my card. Someone in the Mid-West was charging stuff I never buy, on my card.

We went through a quick process to get me a new card, new number, new password. I should be getting it in the mail in a few days. Can't use current card now.

Final thing was he said I should call the Credit Bureau companies to inform them of this activity. Called Equifax (1 866 640-2273); they gave me this number to call – 1 800 525-6285 – to get "Fraud Alert" put on for free for 90 days. She said it lapses after 90 days. When I voiced concern that they might start charging me for it after 90 days if I forget about it, she said no, it automatically stops; I need to actually call to renew it, if I want to.

Also, they automatically inform the other two major companies (Experian 1 888 397-3742, TransUnion 1 800 680-7289). Don't need to call them. So, I think I'm all set now. But it was certainly a hassle, and I am without a card for a few days. Also, I'll need to fill out some form they'll send me, to verify which charges weren't mine.

Man, do I hate thieves! They are so unconcerned with the pain they cause their victims. If I were Jesus up on the cross, I would have said, "Sorry, pal, too late!"

Credit Score Report

To get a free credit report, you can go to annualcreditreport.com, the Internet site maintained by the three companies – Equifax, Experian and TransUnion. But watch out; you have to sign up for a free trial. And then you have to cancel your account before the free trial expires, or else you'll be paying $15 or so each month for pointless (to me) ongoing monthly information.

When I tried this a few years ago, I ended up paying $15 for my "free" info. Just did it again recently: Equifax website > filled out the info > and they immediately give you your credit score number from all three companies. I had 30 days to cancel, which I did, by calling the next day (between 8 and 3 EST, 7 days a week) 1-866-547-2622 (found number under "Contact Us" at upper left). Had to go thru the usual garbage to reach a person, and then listen to them trying to get you to buy the product. Had to give them all my info, though not my password, oddly enough.

Overall, it went reasonably well and I got my scores for free with not too much trouble.

"CTRL" KEY– This key is located at the far lower left of your keyboard. It is a function ordering (or "command") key, which, when pressed in conjunction with another key, will perform a particular function. For example, to make a text bold, you press CTRL+B.

(The + sign here simply means "and"; it does not mean you press the "+" key. You press two keys – CTRL and B, not three keys – CTRL, the + sign key, and B.)

Many computer functions can be performed by either of two basic methods: clicking an icon, or using the CTRL key. So for bolding a text, you click the "B" icon in the Font box at top, or, press CTRL+B. The CTRL key can be referred to as the "keyboard shortcut" key.

Go with what you find most convenient. I like to use the CTRL key for maybe a dozen of my most often used functions. Like CTRL+V instead of the Paste icon in the clipboard box at top. Some functions, like Undo (CTRL+Z) and Redo (CTRL+Y), don't have icons.

CURSOR / ARROW / POINTER – The thing that moves on the screen when you move your mouse. It's an arrow when it's outside a page, and turns into an I-beam-looking thing when you are inside a page's text.

And when you left-click it in a spot in a text, the cursor – a vertical straight line – appears right where you were holding the I-beam-looking thing. The cursor sits and blinks at that spot, and that's where typing gets entered when you start pressing the letter keys.

Identifying the Function of an Icon

If you hover your arrow/pointer over any icon, usually a few words identifying what that icon is for, pops up.

Arrow Visibility – Changing Arrow Style

Often it's hard to find and see the cursor or arrow against particular backgrounds. To get a heavier version of the pointer: Start > Control Panel > Hardware and Sound > Mouse > Pointers tab > Scheme dropdown list (it's a long list, I picked "Windows Black extra large") > Save As > OK. Then, under "Customize" selection, I picked "Text Select" (heavier I-beam) > OK. Might have to screw around for a while to get exactly what you want, but I now have a heavier, more visible arrow and I-beam.

Arrow Sticks, Moves Erratically

Sometimes the arrow moves very slowly or erratically as you use the touch pad. May be due to static electricity; I don't know. If you slide your finger across the pad very softly, sometimes that helps. Usually it clears up on its own after 5-10 seconds.

Hey, lately I find that blowing some warm breath on my finger makes it work!

And, the other big thing is that unknowingly resting your left finger on the pad, even a tiny bit, keeps the pointer from moving properly!! Get that left finger off the pad!! (Try it. Move the pointer with your right finger, then touch the pad – not the clicker, the pad – with your left finger; it stops the pointer dead in its tracks.)

DATA TRANSFER – To transfer material, you basically set up two windows – one for the computer, the other for the transfer device – and then drag and drop items from one window to the other.

Using floppy disks to transfer material is outdated; floppy disk capacity was pretty small, about 1.44 MB. CDs hold about 700 MBs; DVDs hold 4.7 GBs (about 6 or 7 times more than a CD).

Current devices for transferring material to another computer by making a copy of the material are:

A) Disk (CD or DVD)
B) Flash drive (a small device that plugs into your USB port)
C) External hard drive

(There are also memory cards, but I have little experience with them.)

The procedure for transferring material is pretty much the same for all three, except that the disk must be formatted first:

A. Disk

1. Insert a blank RW (re-writable) disk, either CD or DVD (you can use a regular non-rewritable "R" disk but then you can't erase and use it again)
2. AutoPlay window comes up
3. Click on "Burn files to disc"
4. Title the disk (or keep the default title of today's date)
5. "Like a USB flash drive", Next, to format the disk
6. Wait (should take only a minute or two, though I've had it take longer)
7. AutoPlay window comes up
8. Click "Open folder to view files"
9. Click on "Restore Down" icon at far upper right (next to the red x) so that the window becomes less than full-screen
10. Drag that window to the right (by dragging the top part of the window)
11. Open My Documents, or desired folders, on your computer
12. Make or keep that window small and drag it to the left
13. Now you have the two windows side by side (computer at left, disk at right)
14. Drag and drop items from left to right
15. That's it. It makes copies, not cuts. (You still have the original in your computer.)
16. To make a copy to another computer, insert the disk into the other computer and just do the same procedure in reverse, opening two windows side by side, dragging and dropping items from right to left, disk drive window to computer window
17. Usually, don't erase the disk ("Erase Disc" at top), because then next time you'll need to format the disk again. Better to just delete the files on the disk, leaving the formatting intact and the disk ready to use next time.

Remember that when you delete material from a disk, it's gone for good; it does not go into a recycle bin where you can retrieve it. Of course you'd still have the original material on your computer. (The disk is just a transfer device.)

You can also do a transfer by right-clicking files > CTRL+C and CTRL+V. Just avoid using CTRL+X, because then you wouldn't be making copies, but cuts, and you would no longer have the item on your computer.

B. Flash drive

1. Insert flash drive into USB port (correct side up; they only go in one way*)
2. AutoPlay comes up
3. Click "Open folder to view files"
4. Click on "Restore Down" icon at far upper right (next to the red X) so that the window becomes less than full-screen
5. Drag that window to the right (by dragging the top part of the window)
6. Open My Documents, or desired folders, on your computer
7. Make or keep that window small and drag it to the left
8. Now you have the two windows side by side (computer at left, flash drive at right)
9. Drag and drop items from left to right
10. That's it. It makes copies, not cuts.
11. To make a copy to another computer, insert the flash drive into the other computer and just do the same procedure in reverse, opening two windows side by side, dragging and dropping items from right to left, flash drive window to computer window.

* The white plastic slider should be up; or, if there is no slider, look inside the tip, half is black, half is open, the open side goes up.

The third category, an external hard drive, is good for big capacity stuff – music, video, etc. Good for transfer as well as storage (to free up space on your laptop).

C. External Hard Drive

1. Plug external hard drive into to USB port(s)
2. AutoPlay comes up
3. "Open folder to view files"
4. Click on "Restore Down" icon at far upper right (next to the red X) so that the window becomes less than full-screen
5. Drag that window to the right (by dragging the top part of the window)
6. Open My Documents, or desired folders, on your computer
7. Make or keep that window small and drag it to the left
8. Now you have the two windows side by side (computer at left, external hard drive at right)
9. Drag and drop items from left to right
10. That's it. It makes copies, not cuts.
11. To make a copy to another computer, just do the same procedure in reverse, opening two windows side by side, dragging and dropping items from right to left, external hard drive window to computer window.

See also "EXTERNAL HARD DRIVE"

DATE AND TIME SETTINGS – Just place the cursor right on the time at the lower right corner of the screen, and it shows you the date also. Left-click the time and it shows you the month's calendar and gives you option of changing date and time settings. To get rid of that calendar box, click the time again.

Computers continue to keep the time correctly even when the computer is turned off.

DATING – INTERNET DATING – People put a profile of themselves on a dating website – interests, history, what they are looking for, pictures of themselves, etc. Others view the profiles, then click somewhere to show interest, or start emailing. They email back and forth, or call, and then meet, and from that point on, it's a normal date.

I've been doing it for years, and it works reasonably well.

Some thoughts:

– "Match.com" is the biggest and therefore the best bet, I think. Several dates per year for me. I found eHarmony disappointing; huge hype on proper matching on their part, but I got a constant stream of people who live 5 states away, despite my repeated indications that I was looking for people within 50 miles. Had only ONE date for the entire year I was on it.
– Short coffee meetings are best for a first meeting. For both parties, who wants to spend a whole evening with someone you knew in three seconds you weren't going to be interested in?
– Always meet in public place for a first meeting.
– Predominant outcome for me is "no match" but a good conversation. I

suspect it's similar for most people.
– People are nuts if they spend huge amounts of time emailing and thinking they've found their soul mate before even meeting the person.
– I guess many people misrepresent themselves to make themselves appear more attractive (like posting non-current photos), which seems kinda pointless to me. Do guys really think that once they get a date, their personality will outweigh their dishonesty? I have to say, I have not experienced any significant misrepresentations by women.
– I think women who do not include a photo of themselves get far fewer responses from men. Match.com openly says so.
– One thing I keep in mind for profile photos that are borderline attractive to me: A woman is not likely to look better than her photos. What women will look at 100 photos of herself, and decide to pick the 54th best one? The ones I see are probably the best.
– I think until you meet, you can only get a ballpark estimate of what the person is like. Once you meet the person in person, then you can tell if there is chemistry.

In terms of computer how-to, navigating a dating website is usually reasonably straightforward. Though, of course, if you're new to the computer world, you'll need to spend time at it to learn it.

DEFAULT PROGRAMS – Most of the time Windows knows which program to use to open a file. Just double-click on any file and it opens up the file with a "default" program (the one set as the usual program to open this type of file).

Most files (documents, pictures, music, video) can be opened by more than one program. For example, a video clip can be opened by Windows Media Player, by Windows Media Center, by QuickTime Player, etc. I recommend just leaving default settings for programs as is, unless you have a specific reason for changing.

Rathbone says if you have Windows Media Player AND QuickTime, they tend to compete for being the default player. Try to stick to ONE program, if you can.

For documents, I use Microsoft Word 2010. For pictures, I use "Windows Photo Gallery," usually editing a picture there, then copying it to a Word document. ("Paint" is another option a lot of people like for editing pictures.) For music, iTunes automatically uses QuickTime, since that is Apple's (iTunes) program. For video, Windows Media Player is good, but I prefer my built-in Sony video-playing program (WinDVD) as my default player.

To set a default opening program: Start > Control Panel > Programs > Default Programs > Set Your Default Programs; pick one, OK. I leave most of these overall settings alone (the default programs listed on the left); I don't want things all over the place suddenly being different.

Instead, I occasionally do an opening program change for single instances: Right-click the file > "Open with" > select preference. You can also set your default program in this same dialogue box ("for this kind of file"): Right-click the file > Open with > "Choose default program," at bottom > pick, OK. There's a dropdown caret arrow to click for "Other Programs" if you want to look for other programs not initially listed. This window includes an option to check or uncheck, at lower left – "Always use the selected program to open this kind of file."

Note that you may have a video that may not open in one program but only in another. If you get a window saying "Windows can't open this file," use the options in the lower half of that window to find a suitable program to open the file.

(Note that to get the "Open with" option, you need to click on a file, not a folder.)

DEFAULT "WORD DOCUMENT" FORMAT – When you create a new Word document, Vista (and Windows 7) opens it in this set default format: 11-point Calibri font, one-inch margins, and an automatic line space at the end of each paragraph.

I do NOT like this! I like 10-point Times New Roman (or 11-point Arial Narrow), narrow margins, with no embedded line spaces. It's a major pain to adjust the format each time I create a new document!

To Change the Default Font

Home tab at top > font box dropdown arrow; that opens a dialogue box > select a font in the list, style, and size > click "Set As Default" at lower left > "All documents based on the Normal template" > OK.

To Change the Default Margins

Page Layout tab at top > Margins dropdown arrow > Custom Margins (at bottom) > Margins tab; change margins to your preference > "Apply to:" dropdown arrow, "Whole document" > click "Set As Default" at lower left > "Do you want to change the default settings for page setup?" > Yes.

To Change the Default Line Spacing

Home tab at top > Paragraph box > "Line and Paragraph Spacing" icon (middle, lower row) dropdown arrow > Line Spacing Options (third from bottom) > Indents and Spacing tab > Spacing, both "Before:" and "After:" at "0" points > Line Spacing at "Single" > "Set As Default" at lower left > "All documents based on the Normal template" > OK.

Now, when you create a new Word document, whether by pressing CTRL+N while already in a document, or by clicking File > New > Microsoft Word Document, while in a folder window, those new settings should now be your default formats for any new document.

I'll spare you the details, but originally I had all kinds of difficulty trying to supplant the damned Microsoft default settings for settings I prefer for new documents. I did eventually figure out a couple of ways to do so, but the above is, I think, the proper way to do it.

This is why I hate Microsoft; they make the most common operations difficult. You really should be able to set a default format of your preference much more easily.

Before figuring out the above procedures, I had settled into the following method. I find it works pretty well, so I still use it:

Getting the Page Format You Want

1. Create a folder called "Current – Blank"
2. Create a new Word document in that folder
3. Put that document into the format I like (font, size, margins, line spacing)
4. Save it as empty page, as a document called "Current"
5. Make 10 copies of that document by right-clicking > Copy > and CTRL+V 10 times

6. When I want a new document, I open "Current - Copy 10," work on it, save it, name it, move it to a desired folder
7. Then, next time, I open "Current – Copy 9" and so on till I get down to last copy, whereupon I make 10 more copies.

I keep a shortcut icon for that "Current – Blank" folder on my desktop, and double-click on it whenever I want to create a new document. Works well. It's actually easier than you might think.

DELETING – DOCUMENTS, FOLDERS – Right click the document or folder icon > select Delete.

Note that every so often, when you right-click a file, the option list that comes up does not have "Delete." Haven't figured this one out yet, but usually just do it again and on your second try, "Delete" is included. Might have something to do with just where on the icon you click. I don't know.

Deleting Several Documents

Single click to the left of each document name, which checks and highlights them. Then, with the pointer on one of these highlighted documents, right-click to delete the whole bunch. Or, if you have a bunch right in a row, you can "lasso" them by dragging the cursor straight down through them while holding down the left of the mouse, then right-click, and Delete. Deletes the whole bunch.

Sometimes the lassoing doesn't work. In fact, you could unintentionally move your documents by dragging the pointer down thru the documents. Instead, I find that if I start at the lower right and drag the cursor UP to the left thru the documents, that is a much more consistent "lassoing" technique.

Recovering a Document from the Recycle Bin

Recycle Bin, check the item to the left of it, click "Restore this item" at top. That sends it back to where it was deleted from.

Remember, once you've deleted an item from the Recycle Bin, or emptied the whole Bin, those items are GONE. I think it's not a good idea to obsessively clean out your Bin. Let it fill up a bit for a week or two, then empty it. Every so often you realize a day or two after deleting an item, that you still need it.

Also remember that deleting an item from a disk, or from a flash drive, does NOT send it to the Recycle Bin; that item is GONE. (External hard drives, on the other hand, DO send deleted items to the computer Recycle Bin.)

Also, if you restore an item from the Bin, watch out you don't happen to have all the other items in your Bin also checked, or you'll get them ALL put back where you deleted them from!

Trouble Deleting a Document

Usually a document has to be closed to be deleted. If the document is closed yet it still won't let you delete it (by right-clicking and deleting), try 1) dragging it to the Recycle Bin ("Restore Down" the My Documents window so that it's smaller, drag and drop the document onto the Recycle Bin icon), or, 2) If you restart the computer, then it usually lets you delete a document it wouldn't let you delete before.

DELETING – PROGRAMS – (See also "PROGRAMS – INSTALLING AND REMOVING")

Best to think of "deleting" programs as "uninstalling" them, rather than "deleting" because you can't delete them by just clicking on a "Delete" button. Must go to Start > Control Panel > Programs > Programs and Features > Uninstall a Program > find and click on the program to check it > click Uninstall (at top) > Yes. That's it.

DELETING – VIDEO CLIPS – Right-click and Delete. If you still have Windows Media Player on, you need to close it in order to delete a video clip you've just been watching on Windows Media Player. In fact, any file will refuse to delete if it is still open.

DESKTOP – Refers to the screen in front of you when you first turn on your computer, showing "what you have" in your computer. The screen has icons spread across it, representing your programs and folders. You double-click on those icons to open a program or folder.

Adding and Deleting Desktop Icons

You want your desktop to have the programs and folders that you use most often, so you can access them quickly. And you want to remove icons of programs you seldom use, so that they don't clutter up your screen.

To add a program to the desktop: Start > All Programs > scroll down to find the program > right-click on it > Send to > "Desktop (create shortcut)". That puts its icon on the desktop, as a shortcut, i.e., an opening "button." You just need to find it and drag it to the spot on the screen where you want to keep it. You can put folders or documents on the desktop in exactly the same way – very useful. If I'm currently working on a document over a week or two, I put a shortcut for it on the desktop, for quick access.

To delete a program (or program shortcut) from the desktop: Right-click it > Delete. Note that almost all the icons on the desktop are "shortcuts." They have a blue arrow at the lower left. And when you delete them, you are not deleting or uninstalling the program, but only deleting the shortcut!

I notice on my desktop that the only icons that are NOT shortcuts are the very basic ones: Owner, Computer, Internet Explorer, and Recycle Bin.

Adding a WEBSITE Icon onto Desktop

To save a WEBSITE icon onto the desktop: Open the website > click Page at upper right > Save As, select Desktop > Save. That puts it up on the desktop. (Find it there and drag it to the position you want.) If there is a website you visit all the time, it's a good idea to put its icon on your desktop, for quick access. Or, put it into your "Favorites" section – see "FAVORITES")

Another way to get a website icon onto the Desktop: While on a website, make the window smaller ("restore down") > click on the site icon at upper left (very left of website address bar, to the left of "http"), and drag it to the desktop. Now you have a shortcut icon on the desktop that you can click to get to that site quickly.

For a website, like a newspaper, that is updated daily, sometimes you get stuck with a constant repeat of the same OLD-date material. I'm not sure, because there seems to be no clear, consistent pattern, but I think the first method above (Page, Save As) tends to give you a static page, but the second method (dragging and dropping) tends to give you the daily current material.

Navigation Method – Getting to What You Are Looking For

A basic way to access your programs is through the Start icon at lower left. Scroll thru your programs and then click your desired program, or click on one of the basic programs at the right of that box. BUT, I much prefer having all my key programs with a shortcut icon on the desktop! Particularly useful for me is to set up four major icons, in descending order of size, at the far upper left of the desktop: 1) Owner [W7 – File], 2) Computer, 3) Documents, 4) My Documents. With these four I can quickly access most everything I normally need to access.

Arranging Icons on Desktop

Can drag and place them wherever you want on the screen. A good idea is to right-click on an empty spot on the desktop, View, and "Align to Grid." That way the icons line up nicely. Best to arrange them by some sort of logic, like putting similar categories in a bunched group, so you can find them more easily. [W7 – For some reason, a single document icon on the edge of a group often migrates on its own over to another group on the left. See "MIGRATING ICONS"]

Don't click "Auto arrange icons" by accident; it'll put all your icons over on the left, and then you'll have to put them all back laboriously.

Icons Suddenly Re-Arranged

Sometimes when you're trying to do something complex and the computer freezes, after you re-start it, you find many of your desktop icons have suddenly moved to new positions! Don't know how to prevent that, but what I do is keep a screen shot of my preferred desktop arrangement in a document, so I can refer to it, to put the icons back where I like them.

In fact, any time you make adjustments to the desktop, it may re-arrange your icons. For example, making changes to the desktop background; I don't experiment with that anymore, because I'm sick of re-arranging my icons back to where I like them.

Changing Icon Size – DON'T!

Once you have your icons arranged the way you like them and in the size you like (I like medium), don't go experimenting with size changes, because that will completely re-arrange them! And clicking back to the previous size will NOT put them back into order; you have to laboriously do it yourself, dragging icons to preferred spots.

Icons Disappear

If all your icons, have suddenly disappeared from your desktop, right-click the empty desktop, and under View, check "Show Desktop Icons."

Changing an Icon's Name

Can do so by right-clicking, Rename. And I found this to be a good idea, since some of my desktop icons are not that readily recognizable to me. For example, I have a Bibles program with a long odd name; I replaced it with simply "Bibles."

Getting Back to Desktop Easily

When you close all the files you've been working with, the Desktop shows. But, you can also get back to the Desktop by right-clicking the taskbar at bottom on an empty spot, and clicking on "Show the Desktop."

Or, press the Windows icon (flag) key (between Fn and Alt at lower left of keyboard) and D. Goes right to Desktop.

DESKTOP FORMAT OR BACKGROUND – CHANGES

Right-click an empty spot on the desktop. That brings up a window where you can make changes, under View for icons (size, arrangement, etc.) or under Personalize for your preferred background. I like medium size icons, aligned to grid, with a solid-color background.

Picture as Desktop Background

I prefer a solid color as my background, given that I have at least 50 icons on my desktop and I don't want any more visual clutter. But, if you want a picture as a background: Right-click an empty spot on the desktop > Personalize > Desktop Background at bottom left > at upper left, click on the "Picture location" dropdown arrow, for choices of colors or pictures > click on one of the pictures they offer, (or, if you want one of your own pictures as a background, click the Browse button; find your Pictures library or folder); click on the picture you want > Saves Changes at bottom right; that's it; now the picture is your desktop background.

I had some trouble locating some of my pictures; found them under the "Picture location" dropdown arrow > "Pictures Library", rather than under "Browse."

You can also use an internet picture as your desktop background: Right-click on the picture > "Set as background" > Yes.

DESKTOP – GADGETS – See "GADGETS"

DESKTOP vs LAPTOP COMPUTER – They both do the same functions, but the laptop is portable. Recently learned from knowledgeable Best Buy guy that laptops are taking over; less and less desktops are being sold.

DIALOG BOX – Refers to all the boxes or "windows" that pop up showing you your options to choose from.

DICTIONARY – You can get synonyms by right-clicking a word, and then clicking "Synonym."

If you are online, you can get a dictionary definition by clicking the Review tab at top > Proofing box > Research icon > type in the word at top right > click the green arrow.

But if you're not online, the synonyms are all you can get. I bought a Merriam-Webster Dictionary CD ($10) from Staples years ago. Installed it, keep a desktop icon for it, and use it when I'm not online.

(Geek guy suggested to me not to download any dictionary off the internet, since you can't verify the source. Update: Saw some good reviews for a free dictionary program called WordWeb. But, guess what, it's only free for 30 days, then you have to buy it.)

Best bet: When you are online, use "Dictionary.com" – excellent for everything. Includes thesaurus tab, and encyclopedia tab.

DIGITAL VOICE RECORDERS – See "1. Digital Voice Recorders" under "MUSIC".

DIRECTORY – Double-click Computer, and the window that opens shows your directory of folders in a panel at the left. You can click on any of those to see what is inside. And then double-click items from there, to open them.

Note this normal progression: The "Documents" folder contains the "My Documents" folder which contains folders, which contain Word documents.

"DISK CLEANUP" – This function clears up space on your hard drive, deleting unnecessary files. Double-click Computer > right-click Local Disk C > Properties > General tab > Disk Cleanup at lower right; lists bunch of no-longer-necessary files, including temporary files (only a couple are checked by default; I leave the default settings there as is; I'm not struggling to save space; I'm more worried about something screwing up if I check other selections) > OK > "Are you sure..." ; Delete Files. Usually doesn't save that much space, unless you haven't done this for a long time. ("Disk" here refers to your computer hard drive, not to a CD or DVD.)

DISK CLEANING – To clean CD or DVD disks, use a smooth cleaning cloth. Wipe from center to edge, not around in circles, which may cause scratches along the grooves. Rub gently; disks break easily (DVDs more so than CDs). Can use rubbing alcohol according to internet, though Best Buy guy was against it. I think a 20% alcohol, 80% bottled water (not tap water) is best.

DISK CAPACITIES – CD / DVD – Rathbone: A DVD stores 5 times as much info as a CD. Let's see, does that make sense? The disks I buy from Best Buy are standard ones: CD – 700 MB, and DVD – 4.3 GB. About 1,000 MB = one GB. 5X700= 3,500. Uh, close enough. Internet says DVD has 7 times as much capacity as a CD. But it's good to use the conservative figure so you don't get into trouble trying to get too much material on.

A blu-ray DVD (abbreviation – BD), incidentally, can hold 5 times as much info than a regular DVD. They are more expensive. (At Best Buy summer 2010 – $59 for five – more than $10 each, compared to maybe $1 or less each for regular DVDs. But, I think lately the price has come down significantly.)

Note that Blu-ray players can play either type of disk, but regular DVD players cannot play blu-ray disks; you need a Blu-ray player!

DISK COPYING – You can copy both audio and video disks by ripping material onto the computer, then burning it back to a blank disk. See "Music" for details. Of course, commercial, copyrighted material from a store, usually will not copy. You can download and burn iTunes songs to a disk.

DISK ERASING – This of course would be for RW disks (re-writable), not regular R disks, which cannot be erased.

Insert disk > double-click on Computer > click on Drive E, "Erase this disc" at top > Next > Finish.

Note that if you erase a DVD on your computer, that's not good enough to make it ready to record on, in a DVD recorder. You have to erase it also on the DVD recorder. At least that has been my experience.

DISK INSERTED – HOW HANDLED BY COMPUTER – For audio CDs or DVD movies, to change the way the computer treats the disk: Start> Control Panel > Hardware and Sound > "Autoplay" > check "Use AutoPlay for all media and devices" to have disks start automatically > then select from the dropdown arrow choices, for "Audio CD" and "DVD Movie", for default choices, so that when you put a disk in, it automatically uses that choice > Save.

For blank CDs, Autoplay window comes up and you have a choice between making a data disk ("Burn files to disc") or a music disk ("Burn an audio CD", or "Create a CD"). There is also a checkbox for "Always do this for blank CDs."

DISK PLAYING – Usually when you put a CD or DVD into your computer, it starts playing automatically. If it doesn't, you can set it to normally do so automatically: See "DISK INSERTED – HOW HANDLED BY COMPUTER" above.

Or, for a single instance, you can double-click on Computer and then double-click on Drive E, to start it.

I like Windows Media Player for playing CDs, and my Sony WinDVD for DVDs. Though Windows Media Player for both, is a decent default setting.

Note if your Drive E indicates "DVD/CD–RW," then your computer plays and burns CDs, but only plays DVDs, not burns them. If it says "DVD–RW," then it plays, and writes, both. Most modern computers do both.

DISKS (CD OR DVD) – SAVING MATERIAL ON – See "BACKING UP YOUR MATERIAL"

DIVISION SIGN (÷) – See "MULTIPLICATION SIGN / DIVISION SIGN"

DIVX PLAYER – Some kind of program that plays video. According to Geek Brian, you may need it, in order to play some things. I've never needed it as far as I know.

Update: I uninstalled it. It was starting to make folders of itself all over the place. Very annoying. (But then it came back on its own. At least it stopped being so intrusive. Maybe I'll need it someday.)

DOCUMENT FORMATTING – You normally want to open any new document, with your preferences already set – margins, font, line spacing, etc. – rather than ordering up all those specifications each time you create a new document. See "DEFAULT 'WORD DOCUMENT' FORMAT" > "Getting the Page Format You Want"

DOCUMENTS – "MY DOCUMENTS" FOLDER – This is the main folder in which you should keep all the normal Word Documents you type.

DOCUMENT CREATING – Here's 4 ways; take your pick:

1. When inside a document, press CTRL+N

2. When inside a document, click colored "Office Button" [W7 – "File"] at far upper left > New > Create, at lower right under Blank Document

3. When inside a folder, right-click an empty spot > New > Microsoft Office Word Document

4. When inside a folder, click File at upper left, New, Microsoft Word Document.

Note this key concept: Normal procedure for creating a document is to create it first, then send it to a desired folder. BUT, you can also go to a desired folder location first, create the document there, and Save it right there. I used to do it that way for years, until I settled on a kind of a hybrid procedure as my preference (see "DEFAULT 'WORD DOCUMENT' FORMAT" > "Getting the Page Format You Want").

See also "SAVING" > "Save vs Save As"

Missing "FILE" Tab in Windows 7

W7 – Typical computer problem – a detail they tell you nothing about, but which can stop you from getting anywhere: Under Windows 7 default settings, there is no "File" tab at top of folders anymore! That toolbar is gone. There's a File tab when you're in a document, but, not when you're in a folder! And, if you are creating your first document, under My Documents, there is no File tab, and CTRL+N does nothing!

It's insane; all of a sudden now with Windows 7, you can't even create a document!!

Solution: Start > All Programs > MS Office Home and Student > MS Word 2010 > that opens up a new document.]

Update: To get that toolbar back (the "Folder Menu" or "Menu Bar" as it's called) with the FILE tab in it, just press the ALT key.

But to KEEP that toolbar up, you need to do this: While in a folder, click Organize dropdown arrow at upper left > Folder and Search Options > View tab > "Always show menus" > OK.

A lot of former Vista people, including me, are used to having that "File" tab up there! AR notes its absence in Windows 7 and refers to that toolbar as *"... menus that users have come to depend on for the last decade."*

And, of course, to typically make things even more unnecessarily complex, Microsoft actually has TWO places for that same option, and if you have either one unchecked, you won't get that menu bar. The other place is the "Layout" option just above the "Folder and Search Options": Click Organize dropdown arrow > Layout > check the Menu Bar, to keep the FILE tab up.

Default Format

Default format of a new document is: 11-point Calibri font, one-inch margins, automatic skipped line after a paragraph. If you prefer a different automatic format, as I do, see "DEFAULT 'WORD DOCUMENT' FORMAT"

DOCUMENT CLOSING – Click the "x" at far upper right. Or, press CTRL+W.

DOCUMENT COPYING – Right-click the document icon > Copy > navigate to your desired new location > CTRL+V.

Note that usually you need to left-click inside the window first, before it allows you to paste a document in that window. Otherwise, when you press CTRL+V, nothing happens.

Be aware that making copies of documents can have serious negative effects: You now have a copy in two places; if you add to the document, you have to remember to add to it in BOTH places. Making changes in one copy does NOT automatically make the changes in the other copy! Strong suggestion: Do not, as a rule, make copies unless you know you will not be adding anything to the document in the future.

DOCUMENT DELETING – Right-click the document icon > Delete. That sends it to the Recycle Bin, where it stays till you either delete it from there, for good, or decide to restore it to the original location. You delete folders the same way as documents.

If you are deleting multiple documents, always check that you have the right number. It asks if you want to move these x number of items. If you want to delete 3, make sure it says 3, not 4, because it is VERY easy to forget you also had another one checked, and you may end up unknowingly deleting that one also!

Note that clicking on the "x" at the far upper right, closes the document, not deletes it.

DOCUMENT FINDING – First of all, try to store your documents and folders in a logical way, by rough categories. For example: Letters folder, Work folder, Finances folder, Health folder, etc. Good organization makes things easier in the long run.

Then, if you can't find a document or folder you are looking for, use the Start search box, at the lower left. Type in what you think the name of the file is, or even just a key word or phrase inside the text of that file (like "Grandma's visit"), and the computer will list for you all the files containing the word or phase.

Works pretty well, usually. For example, if I type in the word "giraffe," it brings up a half dozen files of mine with the word "giraffe" in it.

If your desired file is in the list, double-click on it to open it. Or, to find out just where it is located, for future reference, right-click it, Open File Location, and it opens the file and shows you at top the progression of files that led to that location. For example: "Owner ▸ Documents ▸ My Documents ▸ "Cars" folder ▸ "Ford" document.

Note that the Vista index of files slows down eventually, and you need to rebuild (update) it. See "Index – Updating."

To make my most used documents easier to find in a folder, I CAPITALIZE the names of the ones I use a lot. Very helpful. Instead of your eye going down the full alphabetical list, it tends to focus first on the few that are capitalized.

See also "LOCATION OF FILE – DETERMINING"

Tip – If you want to have a document appear in a list of documents at the top, or at the bottom, so it's easier to find, and you don't have to scroll thru a long list every time, type in an "A" or a "Z" as part of the first letter of its name. Instead of "Latest Stats", have "ALatest Stats" or "ZLatest Stats".

DOCUMENT MOVING – Right-click the document icon > Cut > navigate to your desired new location > CTRL+V. (Don't get confused by the word "Cut" and the use of the letter "C": CTRL+X = Cut; CTRL+C = Copy, not Cut.)

To move multiple documents, click just to the left of each one to put a check into the box that pops up there > put the pointer on one of these document icons > right-click > Cut > find location > CTRL+V. (You can also "lasso" them by dragging the pointer up thru them to highlight them.)

If you have a document you are constantly adding to yet want to retain the original, a good technique is to make a copy, and name it the same but with the current date. For example: "Poem 8-12-10," "Poem 8-15-10," "Poem 8-16-10," etc. Note that if you forget when you created or altered a document, you can always right-click it > Properties > General tab will tell you when you created it, modified it, accessed it.

DOCUMENT NAMING – If you've created a document while under a folder (from "File" at upper left > New), type in the name where "New Microsoft Word Document" is highlighted in blue > press Enter key.

If you've created a new document while already in a document (by pressing CTRL+N) after you click Save, you type in the name and click Save again.

Document Renaming

Right-click the document's icon under My Documents > click Rename > type in the new name > press Enter key. Note that a document must be closed to rename it.

DOCUMENT ICON STYLE – To change the style of icons listing your files, click View (at top of any folder) > select your preference. [W7 – can also use the 6-squares icon ("Change your view") at upper right for preferences.] I usually like the "List" style, rather than small, medium, or large icons; that way I see more information in a smaller area.

The same options apply to lists of other types of files in a folder (music, video, etc.).

DOCUMENTS – RETRIEVING OLDER VERSIONS – If you accidentally delete a document or folder or other kind of file, you can retrieve it from the Recycle Bin (check it > Restore this item). But once it has been deleted from the Recycle Bin, it's gone forever.

HOWEVER, Windows 7 has a new feature, not for an item already completely gone, but for an item with several versions: In other words, it's not for restoring deleted items, but for restoring items you've already edited, saved, and moved on from. Windows 7 automatically retains previous versions of a file.

Right-click your current version > Restore Previous Versions > select the one you want from the chronological list it shows > open it > copy it.

(If you click "Restore" for that file, that deletes your current file! So that's why I say open it and make a copy, rather than click "Restore," in case you change your mind again. Windows Help icon: *"The file or folder will replace the current version on your computer, and the replacement cannot be undone."*)

SO DO NOT CLICK "RESTORE"!!! Theoretically, you could lose years of work!

This is a nice feature for when you decide you liked a previous, or original, version better. Or, if you like your current version, but prefer a section of a previous version, you can copy just that section and paste it into your current version.

Note "Limitations" below though.

I've always had an aversion to cluttering up my computer, but this feature is actually pretty good. It doesn't get in the way of anything; it stays out of sight until you need it.

Limitations

It's confusing trying to figure out how long this feature keeps previous versions. It shows previous versions of folders dated only for the past 20 days or so, updated for every three days during those 20 days, i.e., 7 versions. BUT, if you open any of those folders, it contains documents that may be many years old.

So, best I can figure, it keeps previous versions of files for the past 20 days (whether you changed them or not), updated every three days during those past 20 days. (If you haven't touched a document for years, it makes 7 versions of the same untouched document, giving each a recent date though, indicating when the version was updated/copied, not when it was created.)

I'm pretty sure it does not keep multiple previous versions you did long ago; it just keeps the one latest version you did long ago. And it keeps recent (last 20 days) previous versions of any document you currently have.

And, it does not keep a copy of any file you deleted to the Bin and then deleted from there.

Note that having changed the name or location of a document or folder may frustrate your "previous version" search.

DOUBLE-CLICK OR SINGLE-CLICK – Sometimes programs open with a single left click, sometimes with a double-left click. A right click brings up choices, including an "Open" option.

You can change your settings to get single clicks to open items instead of double-clicks (I prefer to stick to the default double clicks, but if you want single clicks): Start > Documents (at upper right of Start window) > "Organize" tab dropdown arrow > Folder and Search Options > select single click > OK.

DOUBLE COLUMN FORMAT – Page Layout tab at top > Page Setup box > Columns > select Two. That puts your whole current document into double columns. If you click on "More Columns" lower down, you get more options, like putting a line between the columns, selecting 4 or more columns, space between columns, etc.

Block a section if you want to double-column only a section.

To navigate the cursor through the columns use the mouse pointer (much easier than using arrow keys to navigate laboriously from column to column.). Clicking the mouse pointer puts the cursor at the spot in the text where the pointer is.

I use the double column format quite a bit, because it fills the page fully, yet is easy to read because the columns are narrow, rather than all the way across the page. Narrow columns are easier to read, newspapers and magazines being good examples of that.

See also "SECTION BREAKS" > "Importance of Deleting Section Breaks"

<u>**"DOWNLOADS" FOLDER**</u> – Can always reach this folder by typing "downloads" into the Start search box. [In Windows 7, if you click on Libraries, the window that opens up has "Downloads" at the left.]

<u>**DOWNLOADING AUDIO**</u> – Usually audio downloads land automatically in your "Music" folder, but if they don't, and you don't know where it landed, download the item again and at the point where it shows you a window for saving it, check what location it shows at top, then change that location to "Music" folder, or whatever other location you want, by clicking amongst the folders at the left.

See also "MUSIC"

<u>**DOWNLOADING vs "INSTALLING"**</u> – I bought and downloaded a video editing program called "Studio 14." Couldn't get it to work. Solution: I had downloaded it, but had not yet "<u>Installed</u>" it. Gotta do that. "Downloading" does not necessarily equal "installing" (although with some programs it <u>does</u>). Studio tech guy helped me thru the process. Then it worked fine.

Also, I note that every time I install something, there always seems to be some step or two that I'm quite unsure of, whether I chose the right selection; but, most often, it works anyway.

<u>**DOWNLOADING A PROGRAM – "RUN" OR "SAVE"**</u> – At some point when you're downloading a program from a disk or from a company over the internet, a window shows the option of either "Run" or "Save." I spent hours on the internet trying to get a clear answer as to which one you should chose.

My conclusion: **Click "Save" and that gets the program on your computer, to stay, for use any time in the future. <u>Then</u> click "run" and that installs or activates the program, usually opening it up for immediate use.** So, I would say, click Save first to get it; then click Run to see it in operation. (Though, most often, no matter which you click, the other option gets presented also to you somewhere during the process.)

If you click "Run" only, then you only get temporary use; the program will not be there for you to use next time. When I open an attachment to my email, it offers "Open" or "Save." That might be the best way to think of it: "Run" means "Open" the program.

Clearest internet quote:

<u>"Run</u>
- *The file is downloaded to the temp folder.*
- *It will automatically be played/run/executed when the download is complete.*
- *It will automatically be deleted after a set time period.*

<u>Save</u>
- *Lets you download the file to the location of your choice.*
- *Preferable if you want to keep the file or installer for future use.*
- *You have the choice of when to play/execute it."*

Technicalities aside, I think it comes down to this: "Save" saves it; "Run" installs it temporarily and opens it up.

<u>**DOWNLOADING A PROGRAM – SAMPLE**</u>

[See also "PROGRAMS" > "Programs – Installing and Removing" and "COMPUTER – GETTING A NEW COMPUTER" > "Installation of Programs"]

I already have a "Chessmaster 9000" program, but they also offer a free sample game. So this is how I downloaded that, to practice downloading:

1. Googled "Chess program downloads"
2. "Download Chess – Free" over on the right
3. Download Free Game
4. Type in email address, AND check "no ads" box at bottom
5. Start Download
6. Gives "Run" or "Save" option, clicked "Save"
7. It downloaded in about two minutes
8. Clicked "Run" and immediately "Run" again. NOW (!) it installs.
9. Next, Agree, Finish
10. Chess board comes up and you have 49 minutes to play a free game.

I ran thru the procedure a second time, and at step 6 picked "Run" instead of "Save." It <u>downloaded</u> the program in two minutes. "Run" came up again. I clicked on "Run" and it <u>installed</u> the program.

I guess it works with either choice; I try to click on both at one point or another.

<u>Trying to Download a "Free" Chess Program, Unsuccessfully, Demonstrating Why We Hate Computers:</u>

1. Googled "Free chess program download" > 2. Picked the one at the top > ... ... > 6. Brought up, instead of "Run" or "Save" window, a "Find" or "Save" window > ... ... 12. Clicked "Use the Web service to find the correct program" (to open it), OK > ... ... 14. Checked the top "Open this file" **(This is why I hate the computer world – now I'm downloading a program, to enable me to download a program!!)** > ... ... 25. Browse, and looked for that second "opening" program – "ParetoLogic" > 26. Couldn't find it listed > ... ... Now the window shows "FileCure" checked as an opening program, clicked OK > ... ... 37. Typed in name and email, Submit > 38. Well, guess what!? It costs $30! So much for my "free"' download > 39. I uninstalled both the programs.

Ain't that just so typical of computer stuff? You spend an hour (39 steps!) going around in circles getting nowhere.

I went thru a similar unsuccessful process for a free Scrabble game download. Got to a point where I had to give my email address and select a password. Whenever I'm required to create a password, I say, that's it, I'm not interested. Also I read a review of this program, which said that after a few games, you need to pay.

During this attempt I got the impression that "Run" installs a program, more likely than "Save." I guess my conclusion is: if one doesn't work, try the other. They seem to lead to each other at different times, with different programs.

Tried another free download. Got a screen full of hieroglyphics! Have I mentioned how much I hate the computer world?

DOWNLOADING – SAFETY – Never download something from the internet if it's offered to you out of the blue. Only download if you ordered it yourself and from a trustworthy company. Also, be wary of free stuff. It may sound good, but may come bundled with stuff that costs. Also you may end up getting constant email ads from them!

DOWNLOADING – VIDEO – Right-click image, Save Target As, then Save As. Usually it gets sent to Owner, Downloads, but if you have been sending stuff elsewhere the last time you used your computer, it may send it there instead. Before you click "Save As", check that you have the location you want. Select your desired location from the choices on the left.

Wrong Location

At one point it suddenly put downloaded video to my desktop. In the "Save As" window, at top, you need to select where you want to land it. For me: Owner, Downloads. It usually stays there for the next time, but occasionally it sticks it some other random place, or in some competing program. So, check that the window does say "Downloads" as your destination. If you don't know where the heck it sent the previous one, download it again and look at the destination the window shows, and change it to Downloads, from the selection on the left.

Won't Play Video

Some internet clips only play through some other program besides Windows Media Player, like QuickTime. You may have to install the other program. But, basically, for me, just stick with WMP. It plays most everything, and competing programs are just a source of frustration.

YouTube

Videos from YouTube are not downloadable. I'm sure there's some way around it, but YouTube's intent is for their video material to be seen rather than downloaded and saved. (If I see something I really like – like video on Wilt Chamberlain – I resort to the lowest form of video quality: I play it on my computer and record it with my camcorder aimed at the laptop screen. Pretty primitive, hah. Actually, if it's spoken word material, and the video quality is not that important, this is a good way to save something from YouTube.)

"DOWNLOADING" vs "UPLOADING" – Usually, downloading means moving material from the internet to your computer, i.e., getting stuff. Uploading means moving material from your computer to the internet, i.e., sending out stuff.

"DRAGGING AND DROPPING" – This is a basic technique for moving a file. With your right finger on the mouse touchpad, move the pointer to the icon of the file (document, folder, program) that you want to move, hold down the left of the mouse, slide your right finger to move the icon to the new location, then release the left finger, to drop it there. Have the point of your pointer positioned right on the middle of the folder you're dropping the item into, otherwise it may land outside the folder.

If you do this for a document icon and drop it onto a folder icon, it puts that document into that folder. You can also put folders into other folders this way.

If you do this for a document, folder, or program icon, and drop it onto the desktop, it puts that actual material onto the desktop, and the material no longer exists in its original location. Note this critical difference: Dragging and dropping to and from an external storage device (disk, flash drive, external hard drive) makes a COPY, whereas dragging and dropping within your computer moves the material from one location to another, and it no longer exists in its original location!

Note that when you get a message that "The source and the destination file names are the same," that is MS's muddled attempt to say, "This file is already in this folder."

Now, the other basic technique for moving a file is to right-click it and select Cut, find the new location, and then CTRL+V it there. Your choice. I find the drag and drop method easier.

DRIVERS – A driver is a program that lets the operating system communicate with the hardware gadgets you plug into your computer. In most cases Windows automatically applies the necessary driver. Or, it will inform you that you need to download an appropriate driver and it usually gives you a button to click on for that.

I had bought a thing for $40 to identify all drivers I use and indicate which ones I should update. Geek Brian says, no, not worth it. Drivers are fine as they are, already in your computer, unless you have a problem. Installing new ones often can bring major problems! So I got rid of that driver ID program.

DRAWING – The drawing feature of Vista is pretty neat, although I usually only use the "Shapes" category.

Insert tab at top > Illustrations box > Shapes.

Click on a shape, it changes your pointer into a "+" sign, position the + at the target spot in your document, and left click. That places an average-sized image of that shape right there.

Then, you can adjust that shape any way you want: move it, change its size, its outline color, fill it in with a color, pull an edge with a handle to elongate a square into a rectangle, etc., etc.

For an arrow shape, you left-click to start it, slide your right finger to elongate it, and left-click again to set its length there. Then if you left-click on it again, it produces "handles" which you can drag to make the arrow point in whatever direction you want, or further elongate or shorten it, etc. You move the arrow itself from the middle; you move the direction of the arrow by its ends.

Takes some playing around with, to see all the options and get proficient. But it's fun. Kids will love it. I used to use it a lot for SAT tutoring in geometry problems. You can even get text inside a shape, using the Layout options: Right-click the shape you landed into your text > Format AutoShape > Layout tab > Behind text > OK.)

To delete the shape, left-click it to bring up the handles, press Delete key.

WordArt – (Titles)

You can get some excellent fancy big titles, preset with shading, etc. Insert tab at top > Text box > WordArt > click on your choice > OK. That drops it onto your text. Then you can right-click it and make any adjustments you want in size, color, etc.

Sample:

Your Text Here

Problem

Lately, when I click on WordArt, the selection doesn't appear, but instead just a series of A's (which you work with for a heading, but it's a whole different thing). Then other times, the selections do appear. Damn computer world. I found if I fiddled with it, or did a restart, or just tried the next day, the selections came back. (Of course, now the A's are gone, if you liked that feature.)

DROPDOWN ARROW OR MENU – When there is a heading with an arrow to the right of it, you can click on that arrow and it opens up a list showing your choices under that category. Sometimes that arrow does not appear there until you place the pointer over the word.

Neat Tip

If it's a long list of words, instead of scrolling down, press a letter key, to immediately arrive at that letter. For example, if I want to select "Impact" font under the very long font list, I just press the "I" key and that puts me to the beginning of the I's, highlighted in yellow. If you go ahead and press a second or third letter ("Imp"), then it will immediately take you to the first word that starts with those letters.

DUPLEX PRINTING – Simply means printing on both sides of a sheet, as opposed to "simplex" printing (printing on only one side of the sheet at a time). Some printers can print on both sides, though the way they actually do it, is not print on both sides at the same time, but, with a "duplexing unit", they send the same sheet back to go thru again, without your having to feed it back in manually.

My printer has this feature. It's very convenient. You order up two-sided printing, press Print, go to the bathroom, come back, and the job is done. The process of the machine sending each sheet back in for the second side is actually a bit slow. So if you really want the job done quickly, I would go with the old-fashioned way: do one-sided printing (selecting Odd pages), put the stack back in, then do the second side (selecting Even pages). Though less convenient, it's actually quicker.

Note that depending on how your printer feeds, you may have to reverse-collate all the individual first side odd-numbered sheets, before backing them up. For example, my Epson prints on the bottom of blank sheets, and they come out print side up, page one ending up obviously on the bottom of that stack. I need to reverse collate each page so that for the run-thru for the even-numbered second sides, page 1 is back on top, print side up, page 3 next, print side up, etc.

DVD – BURNING DOWNLOADS ONTO DVD – Use Windows DVD Maker program > click "Add items" at upper left; that sends you to your Download folder > select the items you want to add [If you have many items, check the top left box of that whole window, which checks all the items at once, with the "View" option on "Details"; much easier than checking each one individually] > "Add" at lower right > Next (transfers stuff from Downloads folder to Windows DVD Maker) > insert blank DVD > Burn [After you press Burn, a window may come up saying "Existing data on disk. The disk in the DVD burner already has content on it. Do you want to override the content?" Click "Yes."] > Next (encodes and burns) > progress shows at lower right > automatically ejects when done. (1 min took 5 minutes for me; 20 minutes took 20 or more minutes; takes a long time. Windows 7 seems faster that Vista.)

Works OK in my DVD players. Chapter layout is a bit different from my DVD recorder – need to press Play or Titles.

Best to erase a DVD–RW disk first (either on your computer or in your DVD recorder), otherwise it might stop in the middle of burning and say "error." In fact, it's probably a good idea to erase the disk in both your computer and in your DVD recorder. I've noticed that if I erase a disk in the computer, it will not record in my DVD recorder until I erase it there also.

DVD – COMPATIBILITY – Most current DVD players play all the various kinds of DVD disks. (Though you do need a Blu-Ray player to play Blu-Ray disks.)

I like DVD+RW disks. I use them all the time, like the old traditional blank videotape cassettes: I record TV programs on them, erase them, use them again. You don't even need to "finalize" them. They can simply be added to at any time if you have space left. For example, you record two programs, watch one, put the disk back in, delete that program, record another two programs, and you have the other old one and the two new ones ready to watch.

Every so often a disk goes bad – glitches or stalling. I clean it; that often fixes it. If not, I toss it. Saving 50¢ Is not worth the aggravation of having a disk constantly stall on you! Sometimes, usually with disks I've used for a while, the disk suddenly won't play, or plays in a player but not in my computer, or vice versa (showing "Disc Error" message); I toss it and use a new one; not worth the aggravation of having it work sometimes, but other times not.

Note that for recording DVD disks on a DVD recorder, which recording format you use to record is key! When you first put a blank disk in, to initialize it, you are offered the option of VR Format, or Video Format. VR allows more editing flexibility, but does not play on most DVD players, including TVs with a DVD player in them.

You must, therefore, record in Video Format, which is what commercial DVDs are in, and which allows play in most DVD players including TV/DVD players. (I checked this out in a Toshiba player, and an RCA player).

[One of my early religion DVDs wouldn't play on some DVD players. What I did to make it compatible, is simply transfer my original master (recorded in VR format, since I didn't know yet that I should record in Video format) to another disk, recorded in Video format, which plays on almost all DVD players.

Actually, for regular R disks (as opposed to RW ones) there is no VR option, since you can't erase and edit; Video format is the default and only format.

To retain my separate chapters, I copied the master in 6 chapter sections, otherwise, I'd get one long chapter. Note that the DVD recorder must be stopped to define each segment as a chapter. As opposed to my "Microboard" copier (see below), which does not need to be stopped (nor can it be); it transfers chapter titles just as in the original, each separate.

Update: Now I use a movie-editing program in my computer (Studio 14), rather than dealing with primitive manual editing on a DVD player and a DVD recorder.]

DVD – DEFECTIVE – I've find that recordable DVD disks occasionally become defective, over time and use. I've had one or two regular DVDs become unplayable for no particular reason. And for DVD–RW disks, which I use all the time for recording TV programs, I've had several go bad, for no reason. Sometimes they are still playable in my DVD player but not in my computer, sometimes vice versa. I write a question mark on that disk, and if it falters again, I toss it.

For any critically important material, start with a brand new disk, and make a backup copy.

DVD – COPY FROM MICROBOARD COPIER – I have a disk copier, a "microboard" disk copier, from Long's Electronics. It makes DVD and CD copies in about 5 minutes.

Once in a great while a copy "fails." I also get, every so often, a copy that works, but "hangs" (stalls) at a spot or two. Happens so rarely I don't bother to check any more, but if I have a very important copy to send someone, I can check if it came out OK by running (playing) it through the laptop, at 60X speed. If it has any hanging spot, it will hang at 60X speed as well as 1X speed. So I can check the whole disk in a matter of less than 20 seconds.

See also "Long's Duplicator", under "Music" > "Backing Up Material"

DVD–MAKING FROM CAMERA/CAMCORDER VIDEO

1. Record video on the camera.
2. Attach camera to computer with Camera-USB cord.
3. Turn Camera on. (May need to be in playback mode.)
4. It automatically imports your pix and flix. Wait; it gives progress at lower right.
5. It might bring up Windows Photo Gallery, which has access to both pictures and videos. I like to keep pictures separate from video. So I close out Windows Photo Gallery, and open "Windows DVD Maker."
6. Click "Add items" at upper left
7. Browse your Video folder and check the items you want.
8. Click "Add" at lower right
9. Next at lower right (transfers material to Windows DVD Maker)
10. Burn at lower right
11. Insert blank DVD

(If another disk playing program pops up trying to play that blank disk, X out that program.)

("Yes" to overwriting existing data on disk if it asks.)

12. Starts burning the disk at that point. Progress shows at lower right; takes a while.
13. Automatically ejects when done, ready to play in any player.
15. Click "Close" to another copy? Click "Yes" or "No" to save the project.

DVD – MAKING A DVD OF CELL PHONE VIDEO – Essentially it's the procedure above. If you have a fairly new cell phone, where importing material is automatic by simply attaching the connecting wire to the USB port, it should be fairly easy.

On the other hand, if you have an old cell phone, it can be a nightmare. See "CELL PHONE – PICTURES AND VIDEO"

DVD – MAKING A DVD FROM CAMCORDER VIDEO – As usual, you would think it's easy, but all kinds of complications come up. Sometimes stuff works, next time it doesn't, etc., etc. Part of the problem, I think, is competing programs. I uninstalled "Divx" because it kept showing up doing nothing. Then, I think "PMB" – the program that came with my camcorder – was "stealing" clips from my Pictures folder so that I couldn't access them. At least I think that was what was happening.

If you have a stand-alone DVD recorder, that may be the simplest way to get camcorder material on a DVD disk. Just attach the camcorder to the recorder with the three-color wire, select the correct "source" input, play the camcorder and record with the DVD recorder.

But, here are various ways to make a DVD disk thru the computer:

Note that your source material devices are key. Regular camera video, and regular camcorder video work fine. But, iPod-recorded video and hi-def camcorder video do not, unless you use third party software. Update: I found I CAN make a DVD from iPod video thru Windows 7; see "iPOD" > "iPod Video to DVD Disk".

First – Get the Material Into Your Computer

1. Record video on camcorder.
2. Attach camcorder to computer with Camera-USB cord.
3. Turn camcorder on.
4. Camcorder should be in Playback mode. Press "USB Connect" on the camcorder (left one for video, right one for pictures), or press "DVD Burn", or whatever your particular camcorder instructions are. (I have a Sony.)
5. Click "Import" at lower right of window that comes up on your computer screen, if it doesn't import material automatically. It imports to Owner [W7 – Libraries], "Videos" folder.

Initially, it shows a window with the landed material. I close that out and go to my Videos folder to access the material.

Then, here are various methods to produce a DVD of the material:

A. – Using "Windows DVD Maker"

This is my recommendation for your go-to program for making DVDs. It's the same technique/steps as for camera video. See "DVD – MAKING A DVD FROM CAMERA VIDEO" above.

B. – Using "Windows Media Player"

Ha ha. Good luck. I couldn't do it. Don't know if it's my fault or what, but after hours of experimenting, over various sessions, I found, that with either Vista or Windows 7, I could only get the material playing on the computer. I could not get it to play on my DVD player.

Tried all kinds of things. No Go. You can burn a CD thru Windows Media Player, but for a DVD I think you have to use Windows DVD Maker.

C. – Using "Windows Movie Maker"

After making your movie, you click on the icon at far upper left ("Movie Maker" dropdown arrow) > Save Movie > Burn a DVD > Save > that opens up "Windows DVD Maker" program > Next > Burn > insert a blank disk > overwrite content, yes, if necessary > lower right shows progress as computer burns the disk > it ejects when done.

When you want to get just one clip on a disk, you should use "Windows DVD Maker" right off the bat; when you want to put several clips together to make an actual movie, use "Windows Movie Maker." Then note how "Windows Movie Maker" eventually sends you to the very same "Windows DVD Maker" program for the actual burning of the disk.

D. – Using "PMB" Program

This is the program that came with my camcorder; I assume most camcorders have a similar program that gets installed onto your computer when you first attach it. (PMB = Picture Motion Browser") This worked consistently for me.

1. Start, All Programs, PMB
2. PMB window opens
3. Click on the desired folder on the left, to bring it to the window
4. Click on the desired clip, to highlight it
5. "Create Discs" dropdown arrow at top
6. "Create DVD-Video Format Discs (STD)"
7. Clip should be checked. Next.
8. Insert a blank disk
9. Start
10. For RW (re-writeable) disks, Erase existing data – Yes
11. Wait while it erases the disk
12. Starts to burn disk, showing progress in green. Wait.
13. Finish
14. Disk ejects, ready to play

However, because I can't stand redundancy, even though this program worked nicely, I ignore it.

E. Windows Media Center

Windows Media Center > press down arrow key till you reach "Tasks" (well below the initial screen) > use arrow key to move over to "Burn CD/DVD" > click on that > insert a disk > click on Retry once window comes up > Yes > Video DVD > Next > erase disk (if your disk was not blank to begin with) > type in a name for the disk > Next > Video Library > Next (that takes you to your Videos folder > browse that to get what you want > click on the clip > click again on its icon when it comes up > look at lower left to see that you've got the item there > if you want more clips, click Next, Add More, gets you back to your Video Library to select another one > when ready, at lower right, click "Burn DVD" > shows progress at lower right > remember that an hour's worth of material will take more than an hour to burn > ejects itself when done.

It's now ready to play in DVD players.

I had never used Windows Media Center to make a DVD, but a Geek guy told me he likes it for burning DVDs. Works pretty well; fairly straightforward, once you learn the sequence of steps.

What I liked about it was that when I tried to burn iPod video, or hi-def video, it had the courtesy to say "Unsupported file type", instead of saying and doing nothing.

F. "Studio" Movie-Editing Program

This is a purchased program I have. If I did not have this, I would be using A. "Windows DVD Maker" as my go-to program. But, I do have it, so I use it as my go-to program for DVD-making. It's set up along the lines of C. "Windows Movie Maker" for editing many clips before burning to a disk.

See "STUDIO"

Hi-Definition Material

Note that if you try to use hi-def material under "Windows DVD Maker," as you go to add items from your Videos folder and click to open your folder with the hi-def clip in it, it shows nothing! Even though it IS there when you go to your Videos folder directly. That's because the computer cannot burn hi-def material.

You can import hi-def video from a hi-def camcorder into your computer, and at least with Windows 7, you can play it in hi-def with Windows Media Player on the computer. However, you cannot burn hi-def material onto a regular DVD disk. I believe hi-def material needs a different kind of laser burner, as well as a blu-ray disk. (Hi-def and blu-ray are roughly synonymous.)

Few computers have hi-def burning capability yet, though you can buy a separate hi-def burner, use blu-ray disks, and a blu-ray player, to get hi-def material on your TV screen, to watch... I believe. I think you need all five elements – hi-def camcorder/material, hi-def burner, hi-def disk, hi-def player, and hi-def TV.

Now, you can watch hi-def material from a hi-def camcorder attached to your hi-def TV directly. But, come on, you want to watch from a disk, and not have to keep the material permanently inside your camcorder in order watch it when you want to!

So, that, at least for me, is the future – getting everything hi-def. I mean, really, what's the point of a hi-def camcorder if you can't keep hi-def material on disks?

DVD – PLAY – Just put the disk into the bay and close it. If doesn't start automatically, open Windows Media Player and click on the Play icon at bottom center. The controls are fairly straightforward. Use the "Maximize" icon at upper right for full-screen size. See "WINDOWS MEDIA PLAYER."

I find watching DVDs on a laptop, using it as a portable DVD player, works very well. I lie in bed, have a laptop stand so that that computer is right in front of me, and use earphones. A very comfortable way to watch a DVD, either commercial DVDs (Netflix) or programs I've recorded from TV with my DVD recorder. I use RW DVDs, just like I used to use videotape cassettes: I record TV programs, erase them after I've watched them, and then record new ones.

Note that Windows Media Center duplicates most the functions of Windows Media Player, but, most people don't use it. I usually don't, though I do like the way it fills the entire screen. See "WINDOWS MEDIA CENTER."

How to use the controls for Sony WinDVD

I have a Sony laptop, which has its own DVD-playing program – "InterVideo WinDVD." I prefer it to Windows Media Player; I'm used to the controls.

When WinDVD is opened, it shows thumbnail pictures of the programs you've recorded. Click on the one you want and it starts playing. The control icons are on the bottom; they're fairly self-explanatory. Clicking on the screen shows or hides the control bar [W7 – resting pointer at top or bottom shows control bar; resting it in between, hides the control bar.]

Once a program is running, if you want to stop it and select another one, you can bring up titles and chapters on the right by right-clicking the screen. "Titles" are your programs ("01", "02", "03", etc.); "Chapters" are segments of the programs. Click on your desired title to play it.

I've found the easiest way to fast forward or rewind is to click repeatedly on the left, or right, double arrows, to get 2X, 4X, 8X, 20X, or 60X speed. Past 60X speed, it reverts back to normal speed. (On DVD–RW disks you can click on or drag the timeline marker/slider for even quicker movement; but, DVD+RW disks don't show any marker on the timeline.)

Stalling

If you hit a sticking point (very aggravating) and can't get past it, you can right-click the screen and then select the chapter just AFTER the problem spot, to continue from there; or, you can try rewinding from that chapter start, back to the sticky spot. At any rate, if I clean the disk and find it still sticks in the same spot, I toss it. Not worth the aggravation; much easier to just use a new disk (only 50¢).

DVD – RECORDING MOVIES ON A DVD RECORDER

A DVD recorder of course is a separate item from a computer. But, it's good to know some of this stuff.

When I bought a new LG brand DVD recorder in July 08, it turned out that they are getting more stringent on recording movies. Now, on this new recorder, it only allows some movies (20% I find) to be recorded on DVD one time only (no further copies), and the rest (80%!) not to be recorded at all! Shows "Copyright Protected" or something like that. Only allows free recording of regular TV programs.

Bummer. A third of the stuff I record is movies. So with this new recorder I can no longer record movies on disks and watch them on my laptop when I am away from home.

Therefore, I returned the recorder and had my old one – which does allow free recording of movies – serviced (it had started to get a bit hinky, stalling occasionally).

Guy at electronics shop said that he's surprised my old one allowed movie recording. He said some did. And he said, they do sell some device you can get fairly easily that unscrambles the movie signal so that you can record movies.

Update 2009: Bought a new Magnavox DVD recorder from Radio Shack. It allows recording any movie that's broadcast. Hooray.

DVD STAND-ALONE RECORDER – TWO TYPES – Solution to question as to why some DVD recorders are much cheaper than others ($150 vs $250): the cheaper ones do not have a tuner, and require a cable box to record TV stations. That's why I was not able to get stations with the cheaper one I bought at first. The more expensive ones – like the Panasonic one I have – have a tuner, and I can record TV stations without a second cable box in a second room!

DVD – STILL CAPTURE – If you want to get a snapshot of a specific frame of a video, you can do so. A neat feature, I think, especially with hi-def video; you can get decent quality still shots from video material. You can get a shot of the exact moment Bob fell into the wedding cake, or Jane scored the winning goal.

My Sony video playing program – WinDVD – does not allow image capture with the Print Screen key. Windows Media Center does, but only at small-screen size, not full-screen size. But, hooray, Windows Media Player does allow full screen image capture with the Print Screen key:

1. Open Windows Media Player
2. Insert DVD disk
3. Get the disk up, usually by double-clicking on "DVD (E)" at left of your Windows Media Player window
4. Click on the clip (title) you want to play
5. Get full-screen size by clicking on Maximize icon at upper right
6. Pause it at the still capture spot
7. Put pointer at middle edge of screen so that controls disappear from screen after 5 seconds (otherwise the controls get included in your image)
8. Press "Prt Sc" key at upper right (sends image to your clipboard, unseen)
9. Minimize or x out Windows Media Player
10. Open a Word document
11. CTRL+V the image there
12. Trim edges and adjust size to your desire
13. You now have a still capture, of pretty decent quality
14. Print it out

Notes:

a. If it doesn't work with a DVD–RW, use a DVD–R. For me, it used to not work with RWs, but lately it has been working – ?
b. Whether the DVD is recorded in SP speed or XP speed, I was not able to discern any difference in still-capture image quality.
c. You can actually press Prt Sc key while the video is moving. Don't have to pause it, but if you pause it, you can see exactly what you're going to get.
d. You can similarly capture a still from a commercial video disk as well as material from TV that you've recorded on disk with a DVD recorder.
e. You can similarly capture a still not from a disk but from video material on your hard drive in your Videos folder.
f. For me, using my Studio program is actually a better way; it has a nice still capture function.
g. Can also use Windows Movie Maker to get a still shot: Get the video material on your hard drive first, in your Videos folder > Windows Movie Maker > Import Media [W7 – "Click here to browse for videos"] > check the file you want > Import [W7 – Open] > play clip and stop it at desired spot (can use the left and right frame buttons to move to the exact frame) > Tools [W7 – "Add" box, "Create a snapshot of the preview" icon at center of box] > Take Picture from Preview [W7 – Save] > that automatically sends it to your Pictures folder > from there you can make a copy to a Word document and edit and print it.

Note that, generally, pressing Prt Sc captures the entire screen, whereas pressing Alt+Prt Sc captures only the active window.

EASE OF ACCESS – Start > Control Panel > Ease of Access. Provides various options for the physically challenged.

The one item I found might be useful for me, is the magnifying glass feature. You can always increase the size of the entire screen, to see better, but if you want to operate the pointer like a magnifying glass, over a specific area, instead of increasing the size of the entire screen: For Windows 7 – Start > Control Panel > Ease of Access > Ease of Access Center (must click on green heading) > Start Magnifier, at upper left > small control window comes up (at upper left of your screen, not your "Ease of Access Center" window) > Click + to increase size > Views > Lens > then when you go to a Word document or internet site, a rectangle follows wherever you move your pointer, and the area inside the rectangle is magnified. Pretty neat.

A magnifying glass icon stays on screen (usually upper left), and you can click on that to bring that small control window back up (or click on it on your taskbar at bottom), in order to make adjustments. You can change the size of the rectangle magnifier by clicking Options (gear icon).

To get rid of this function, click on the "x" of the small control window. (And if the control window has disappeared, as well as the magnifying glass icon, you can click on this feature's icon now on your taskbar below, to bring it up again, to x it out. Geez, I hate Microsoft! I was stuck for 15 minutes not being able to get rid of the magnifying function, till I found the icon for it on the taskbar.)

You would have to practice some with this feature to see if it's really useful for your situation.

This feature on Windows Vista is simpler, without options: You click on Start Magnifier and it simply shows a wide magnified window at the top (depicting the area that your pointer is in down below).

See also "NARRATOR – COMPUTER TALKS TO YOU"

eBAY – This is an online auction and shopping website, for all kinds of goods and services. It's shopping online, but you buy from other people instead of a store, and people bid on items over a set period of time. I have limited experience here. I tend to avoid it; don't want to bother learning all the rules and procedures. But I'm sure some people love it and get great deals.

EDITING TEXT – Find your document, open it up, move the cursor to the desired spot, do your adding, deleting, revising, etc., then CTRL+S when done. Note that you should keep all your text documents under the "My Documents" folder. You don't have to, but it makes finding material much easier.

Changing Text Format

To change text appearance, "block" the segment (hold the left of the mouse down while dragging the pointer from the beginning of the segment to the end), then click the desired icon, or use the keyboard shortcut.

For example, after blocking, you can click (in the Paragraph box at top) icons there for aligning text left, center, or right, or justifying it. Or you can produce the same results by using the keyboard shortcuts: CTRL+L, +E, +R, or +J to align left, center, right, or to justify.

Same deal for changing the font or font size. Block the segment, go to the Font box at top, click the dropdown arrows for options.

Note that if you continue typing from any spot within a text, the text will continue automatically in the same font and size.

That whole comprehensive "Styles" box at top I never liked. I prefer to manually set the text format according to my own tastes.

EJECT – Most often the screen has an Eject tab at top to eject a disk, or just open the disk bay. Sometimes not, in which case you need to physically push in the disk bay button. I notice my new computer reacts much better than my old one. I press it once, wait two seconds, and the bay pops out; sometimes with my old one I had to press the button half a dozen times to get it to work. Note that if you double-click on Computer, then click Drive E, there's almost always an Eject tab at the top there.

E-MAIL – OVERVIEW AND BASIC OPERATIONS – E-mail is a great way to send mail, instantly and at no cost. E-mail programs are set up a little differently under different companies (the big three are Microsoft, Google, and Yahoo), but they essentially have the same features, and buttons, and tabs, and options, somewhere. But you have to look for them; not only do different companies have items in different places, but the same companies constantly change their own setups. So that the procedures I provide ahead, are just general signposts. You have to slog thru your own setup and learn by practice. Sorry.

I think most people have web-based email programs – your email is stored on the web and you need to be connected to the internet to access your email. But, there are also PC-based email programs, like Outlook Express or Windows Mail, but they are more difficult to set up and may not work with all email addresses, according to AR.

I use Yahoo.com. I'm not a big emailer, but here's some basic information:

To Sign Up for E-Mail

I forget how I signed up. If you google one of the providers – Hotmail, Yahoo, Gmail, AOL Mail – their website will guide thru the process. It involves selecting an email address and a password.

Email addresses are in the form of a name of your choice, the "at" symbol – @ – and the company. For example: john-smith@yahoo.com The part before the @ symbol is called the "user name"; the part after the @ symbol is called the "domain name."

Most addresses end in ".com." Government organizations end in ".gov." Schools in ".edu."

I have a personal email address, and also one for my website: mjako@confrontingbelievers.com

To Send E-Mail

Internet Explorer (if that does not automatically open up your email window, then click Start, type in your email company name, like "Yahoo," and then click on that to open up the window) > Mail > New > insert receiver's email address > type in a subject title if you want to > type your letter > Send. That's it. They receive it within seconds.

Whenever possible, copy and paste someone's email address into the address box, rather than typing it in. Less chance for error. Email addresses must be exact, or they won't work.

You CAN send email between a Microsoft computer and a Mac. They have compatible software for regular emails.

Formatting Texts

You can type in bold, underlined, or italic. I think, if you want to retain more complex formatting than that, you'd have to do it in a

Word Document and then send that document as an attachment. That's one way to keep formatting, if you want to send something with lots of color or whatever.

My current email setup has a toolbar, which includes formatting options like bold, underline, italics, etc. In the same toolbar is a spell-check icon, which you click after you've typed your message, and it then underlines misspellings in red.

Often, formatting changes once an email arrives. For example, tab indents for new paragraphs tend to change; it's best not to use them, but skip lines between paragraphs instead. To check to see exactly what arrives (at least if the recipient is using the same company as you are), you can send email to yourself. Or, you can check your "Sent" folder.

To Receive E-Mail

Internet Explorer, Mail, Inbox, place the pointer on the text below "Subject," click, and there's the letter to read.

Note that your email company holds your mail until you turn your computer on to see it. (But you don't have to keep your computer on all the time, in order not to miss mail.) And, you can access your email from any computer anywhere that is online, as long as you have your user name (email address) and password.

To Print E-Mail

Block the text you want printed and press CTRL+P. You can also click on a Print button at top if you want to print the entire page instead of just the text.

To Delete E-Mail

Internet Explorer, Mail, Inbox, check the box to the left of the selected letter, Delete. That sends it to your Trash folder (which is just like your computer's Recycle Bin).

You can restore a letter from the Trash folder, by checking it, Move, Inbox. I find that my email in the trash folder gets deleted at no particular time limit, or amount limit. It varies! This is what it says there: *"Deleted messages are moved to the Trash folder temporarily, where they are subject to deletion at anytime."* Yet, my other email address for my website seems to save everything!

To Save E-Mail

Given that companies vary in their policies on automatic permanent deletion from the Trash folder, if you really want to save an email, highlight the page and save it to a Word document.

To Send an Attachment

To send material that's fairly large, or say a document that you already have fully typed out, you can send it as an "attachment."

Click "Attach Files" (usually has a paper clip icon by it) > Browse, keep double-clicking folders till you get to the desired document > check that document > click Open (which does not open it but attaches it) > click Browse to do more if you want more than one file attached > click Attach Files, wait > click Send when you're all ready with your email. 25 MB size limit.

To Send a Picture

There may be other ways to do so, but the way I know is to simply send it as an attachment. You can also send sound files, or video files this way, as long as they are below 25 MB size.

To Open an Attachment Received

Click on the file icon near the paper clip, Download File, Open (to see or play it) or Save (to save it to desired location). Note that if it doesn't open, that usually means it was sent under a program you do not have. Says Stokes, *"Think of it this way: Computer software programs are a language. Your computer needs to speak the same language as the attachment in order to read the attachment."*

WARNING: NEVER open an attachment sent by someone you don't know! I understand that that is the primary way by which computers get infected with a virus!

My new computer with Windows 7 automatically scans any attachment I open and tells me if it detects any virus.

To Send an Email with a Link to a Website

So that the recipient can just click on an underlined address to open that website, instead of having to type it into the search box his or herself: Minimize ("–" icon at upper right) the email you're writing, so that it goes to the taskbar at bottom > click on Internet Explorer > bring up the desired website > highlight its URL (website address) in the box at upper left > CTRL+C it to put it on your clipboard (unseen) > click on your email icon on the taskbar to bring your letter up again > find the spot in your text you want > CTRL+V the link into that spot. That address, now in your text, will appear as an active, clickable link for the recipient to click on.

To Use a Contact List

To send email to a person on your contact list: Click "Contacts," check his or her box at the left, double-click on the person's address (in blue) at the right, type your letter, Send.

To add to your contact list: Click "Add Contact" at top, fill in the info, Save. It puts the new address into your list at the left, alphabetically.

Sports Alert!

If you taped a big sports event that you are going to sit down and watch later, if your email program displays the latest news, close your eyes! The result may be already be splashed on the opening page, ruining your watching pleasure! One year I found out by accident who won Wimbledon just before I was going to sit down and enjoy the match.

E-MAIL – MULTIPLE E-MAILS

To send copies of an email to more than one person – CC (old abbreviation for carbon copy) – I think you need to have already put all those addresses into your contact list first, INDIVIDUALLY. Then when you do a multiple email, click "CC:", the contact list opens up, check the desired addresses, and click "Insert Checked Contacts." That puts all those addresses into the "CC" line. Then when you send that email, all those addresses get it.

If you don't want people to know that you sent the email to the others, click "Show BCC" to bring up a BCC line, which means Blind Carbon Copy. Put the contact addresses into that line.

I haven't done much with multiple emails, but I resorted to the following technique of keeping groups of people separate: I put a key letter or letters in front of each address of a person in a particular group. For example: For tennis contacts, I use TNbillsmith@... , TNjohnbrown@... etc. For religion contacts, I use RRevJohnson@... RPastorChip@... etc. That way my contacts are grouped and I don't have to search everywhere on my list to pick them out.

Making Separate Category Lists

You can make a separate contact list by clicking the Contacts tab, Add a Category, name, Save. I suggest doing this if you send out a lot of multiple emails.

To add an address from the "All Contacts" main list to a separate category list: Contacts, check the desired address, click "Categories: Unfiled • Add," check the category, DONE.

To access these lists: Mail, New, Insert addresses, Categories, click the category, check the ones (usually all) you want, "Insert Checked Contacts."

When I tried doing multiple emails, I had mixed results. It wouldn't do 20 at a time, but it did do bunches of 5...? Also, note that if you delete an address from your main list, it will ALSO automatically be deleted from the separate category list! So, I'm sticking to my grouping by key first letter technique, instead of grouping by making separate categories.

E-MAIL PROBLEMS

Sign-in

For me, my Yahoo email program, as a safety measure, requires me to sign in with my username and password every two weeks. In that window it has a spot to check for how long you want to be kept signed in (so you don't have to sign in each time) UP to two weeks. I keep it at two weeks.

You can set that two-week period to a shorter time by changing your choice under My Account, even though there is no "My Account" to click on where it claims that there is. (What else is new?) I got there by clicking Help > Edit Account Information > Sign-In and Security > Sign me out every – they give you only two selections, every 2 weeks or every day > Save.

Sign-In Problem

If you do not like your computer keeping track of websites and passwords, and have that feature shut off, then you'll have to sign every time you want to open your email account!

For options and solutions to this problem, see "BROWSING HISTORY – WEBSITES"

SPAM

Spam, as you probably know, is the email equivalent of junk mail. My email has automatic filtering that filters out most of it. I quickly check the Spam folder to see if there are any legit emails there. Then I click "Empty" next to the Spam folder, to delete all the stuff in it. If I see spam in my regular inbox, I check it, click "Spam" at top, and that sends it to the Spam folder and, additionally, sends any future mail from that sender automatically to the Spam folder.

Similarly, if a legit one arrives in your spam – like a receipt for an order did for me recently – you can check the Move box at top and move it to the regular Inbox. And, I assume, from that point on, email from that source will now get into your regular box.

Unfortunately you can't do much else to get rid of spam coming in. It's the nature of the beast. I'll keep quickly checking my spam box, simply because occasionally I do get some legit mail there.

(I recently thought maybe I got some legit mail in my spam box, because it indicated one person I knew saying something about another person I knew. But the contents made no sense, and I was pretty sure these two people did not know each other, even though both are on my email contact list. So that is yet another scamming technique: They try to get you to click on something by using two names on your address list they somehow got, trying to get you to think the sender is someone you know. But, the contents of several of these were either nonsensical regarding the two people, or vile garbage. I did NOT click on anything inside those emails. Do not let your curiosity get the better of your common sense.)

So you can't prevent spam. But, most email programs do a decent job of flagging uncertain content or questionable email addresses. I think clicking on Spam and using the options there to order certain filtering words, will help filter them to the Spam folder.

Just read an interesting quote in *Time* magazine by Bill Gates: "Two years from now, spam will be solved." That sounded encouraging, but then I read the small print and the date of that quote... 2004!

Tips from Yahoo

Never respond to unsolicited email.

Never respond to the spam email's instructions to "remove me from this list". This is a ploy to get you to react to the email and will alert the sender that your email address is open and available to receive mail. If you reply, your address may be placed on more lists, resulting in more spam.

Never click on a link or web site address listed within a spam email.

Never sign up with sites that promise to remove your name from spam lists.

Spam and Virus Recognition

I've found that spam, and phony "fishing" emails, invariably have grammatical, spelling, or idiom errors. So, for me, a former SAT tutor, I spot them right off the bat. Email from legit companies use proper English. They don't spell "your" – "yuor." Or write "...in respect of your inheritance fund" instead of the proper idiom – "with respect to your inheritance fund."

I recently got one pretending to be Yahoo.com and asking for people to "verify" their accounts. Here's "flags" I quickly spotted:

1. It was not sent to my specific email address, but "undisclosed recipients," always a giveaway.
2. "Due to the congestion in all Yahoo! users accounts, Yahoo! would be shutting down all unused..." [Should be WILL be shutting down.]
3. "Please **LEAVE** all information requested." [The word "leave" is in caps and bolded for no good reason.]
4. "Date Of Birth.................." ["Of" capitalized; should not be]
5. "Country Of Residence..........." [The 5 dotted lines of the 5 categories end ragged, not justified.]
6. "inconvinience" [Should be spelled "inconvenience."]

Thieves – people who want to get ahead the easy way – invariably, with that mentality, have never learned proper grammar, spelling, or idiom. When you get legitimate stuff from a bank for instance, they always use solid English and grammar. And solid idiom – the accepted, proper, way to express ideas in the English language. For example, we say "We need your account information," not "We are needing the account information of yours."

Server Popup Problem

Suddenly, whenever I was offline, I started to get a message "The e-mail server is currently unavailable. Please try again later." Kept popping up EVERY FEW MINUTES! Tried a bunch of things. No go. Still kept popping up. Major pain, trying to watch movies.

Figured out a temporary solution: Right-click at top (blue part) of that message. Gives option to close or to move. Closing does no good; it pops up again minutes later. But, click Move and drag it down to the lower left of my screen; that way it stays there, which is not bad. You still see 99% of the screen.

Emailed SONY for help.

Did their email suggestion: Did a "system restore." Not a complete one, which would mean re-installing Vista, but a "restore to an earlier time":

Start > All Programs > Accessories > System Tools > System Restore > (Turn on System Protection) > Choose a Different Restore Point > Next > Create a "restore point" (The one they gave me was for last fall, but my problem has only been here for a week or two; I clicked "Show restore points older than 5 days"; I picked Aug 2 (two weeks ago) > Next > Finish > Computer restarts.

Result? Good! Popups are gone. Basically I think it was one of Windows' automatic updates that messed it up for me.

If you had installed any program AFTER that restore date, you have to re-install it.

Picture Blocked with Red "X"

Luckily this is rarely a problem, but sometimes you get email from a company with images not showing, but marked by a little red "x." To show the picture, I was advised: Internet Explorer > Tools > Internet Options > Security tab > uncheck Block Images.... Yeah, right; it doesn't even have such a category to uncheck. Ain't that typical. I guess things are constantly changing. I'll have to experiment next time I get such a picture.

Maybe this will work, which I read on "Windows Help": *"Double-click a message that contains blocked images to open it. Click the Information bar at the top of the message to download and display the pictures in the current message."*

I remember once something at the bottom (of such a page with hidden images) referring to "Showing full information" or something. If you click on that – if that is there – it should show the pictures then.

Good luck.

Server Type Request (POP or IMAP)

Every so often I try to send an email to some company thru their website and they require I tell them what my email incoming server and outgoing server are (POP3 – Post Office Protocol, or IMAP – Internet Message Access Protocol) and I never know what that is. Went around and around for two hours. Got nowhere. Bottom line – forget it. I only get this server request rarely anyway.

Getting help from Yahoo, either online or by phone, is ridiculous. As is the norm, they ask you all sorts of questions, then you ask them the question, and they send you elsewhere, several times, until the final person sends you to their worthless online help site, from which you started, two hours ago. And, as usual they finish off their utter unhelpfulness by giving you a long worthless incident ID number, and cheerily asking if there is anything else they can help you with. The more appropriate question is "Is there anything we can help you with?" And the answer is, no, apparently not.

I always get the impression the help sites are not there to help you, but to sell you more stuff!

Solution

Well, still got nowhere trying to go through the email function at a website, BUT, then I simply took their email address and sent it though MY regular email, and it worked fine. I guess that server info requirement only applies to when you are sending email through THEIR website directly. I don't know. I think maybe POP is website email service and IMAP is your personal email service.

I read that IMAP is more versatile, and is a more recent protocol. Also read that Yahoo does not support IMAP, so I assume I have POP...? Another annoyance of the computer world – often the more research you do on the internet on a technical issue like this, the more confused you get, admittedly, because it's not that simple. Various programs have various features that work or don't work in various environments.

EMOTICONS – These are punctuation marks or letters used to represent a facial expression, to express a writer's mood. I think the most common ones are :) for a smile and :(for a frown. In fact when you type :) in, Windows automatically changes it to ☺. And :(to ☹. Note that if you want to get from the face back to the punctuation, do a CTRL+Z. Same for any automatic replacement word – CTRL+Z gets it back to the original thing you typed, and then a second CTRL+Z deletes it.

ENCYCLOPEDIA – If you are online, the entire internet is an enormous encyclopedia. Type the topic into your search box at upper right and it will bring up tons of info.

If you're looking for just basic knowledge on a topic, go to the "Wikipedia" website and type the topic into their search box. I highly recommend it. It's one of my favorite and most useful sites. See "WIKIPEDIA"

You can also use Dictionary.com, clicking on their Encyclopedia tab.

Offline

I like to have an encyclopedia program installed on my laptop so that I have an encyclopedia available when I am offline. Bought one ("Student with Encarta Premium 2008" encyclopedia, $30). Installed it. But, I don't really like it. It's more collections of articles on topics rather than one comprehensive yet succinct article on each topic, like Wikipedia is. I much prefer Wikipedia, but you have to be online to get it.

"ENTER" KEY – For typing text, the Enter key moves the cursor to the next paragraph. For windows offering options, the Enter key makes the computer take action on the option you chose. Pressing the Enter key = execute my choice. Occasionally a program window gives no "OK" or arrow button to click on anywhere; press the Enter key, and the computer should take action on your choice.

If you check a document under a folder, and then press the Enter key, it will open the document. Some people like to use the Enter key rather than double left-clicking, for opening files.

ENVELOPES – You can print envelopes. Most printers have adjustments you can make to run them thru. On your computer, you can use Mailings tab at top > Create box > Envelopes, where there is a template into which you can type and choose options. Then, of course, you have to make physical size adjustments to your printer tray, to run those envelopes thru.

I don't bother with printing envelopes any more. Don't want to deal with printer adjustments. Instead, I print labels on 8½ by 11 multiple-label sheets and then stick them on the envelopes. See "LABELS"

EQUAL SIGN FOR MATH – The "equal" key is at the upper right of the keyboard.

If you want to use the equal sign in typing out math problems dealing with fractions, it's a bit tricky. You could type: 4/5 = 8/10, but if you want to make them look better, here's what I used to do (admittedly a bit labor intensive):

Use three lines, in order to get the equal sign positioned properly as the middle of the three lines. For the middle line, make the divisor line 4 hyphens (which turn into 2 dashes in a row, i.e., the divisor line), then 2 spaces, then equal sign, then 2 spaces, then 4 hyphens again. Then fill in your numbers or letters in the first line and third line, spaced appropriately. Digits and letters are necessarily spread far apart.

$$\frac{X}{20} = \frac{5}{10}$$

"Greater than" (>) or "less than" (<) signs, are right on the keyboard – Shift comma and Shift period. Don't need to use Insert and Symbol.

ESCAPE - "ESC" KEY – Top left key. A quick way to get out of some windows, like a full-screen video to a partial screen one.

ETHERNET CABLE – This is the cable that runs from your wall to your computer, and carries internet signals. A modem is connected to a router also by an ethernet cable.

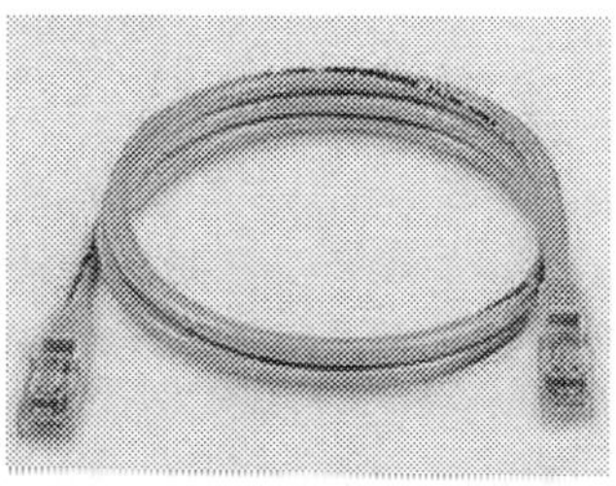

EXPONENTS – To type a letter or number in superscript (smaller and slightly high) or subscript (smaller and slightly low), use the X^2 or X_2 icons in the Font box under Home tab at top.

Exponents in math are probably the most common superscripts – x^2. Footnotes in a scholarly text are normally flagged by superscripted numbers also, like this.[8]

EXTERNAL HARD DRIVE – Your computer has a "hard drive" on which it stores all your info. An "external hard drive" is one that you can use to store stuff in a similar way but outside your computer. They're usually just a little bigger than a card deck. Cost maybe $150.

Disks or flash drives can store several GBs of material. External hard drives can store much more – hundreds of GBs.

I bought one called Seagate (indicated as "Sea_Disc" under Computer). This one you don't have to plug into an outlet; just plug the two USB cables (it has two) into your laptop and it gets powered on, and automatically puts a window for itself up on your screen.

Click the bottom choice ("Open Folder to View Files"), or click "Computer" on desktop and click "Sea Disc."Restore Down" the window, and move it to the right. Click My Computer, to get the desired source folders or documents, "Restore Down" that window, and move it to the left. Then just drag and drop items, left to right. That's it.

Transfer rate (Vista) is about 100 MB/min. [Windows 7 – Most recent transfer I did was much faster – 524 MB in less than one minute!]

When you drag and drop, it makes copies, not cuts. I could do cuts by the old method of right-click, cut, move, but I should not do so, since I always want to play it safe and keep my original on my laptop.

Sometimes, in order to save space on my laptop, I do store some of my big stuff (video) on my external hard drive device only. But I always make sure I have several hard copies of that video material on DVDs first. Never want to spend months on a video project and have something go wrong and lose it!

Recycle Bin

If you delete material from Seagate (I assume other hard drive devices are similar) it sends the material to your COMPUTER Recycle Bin. Note this important difference: When you delete material from a disk or flash drive, it's gone, but, from an external hard drive, it goes to the computer Recycle Bin.

Transfer Size Limits

Transferring material that is over 2 GB approximately doesn't work. My computer's transfer capacity ("memory," "RAM") is only about 2 GB. So I don't transfer full, finished video disks. Don't really need to, once I have a bunch of hard disk copies.

Be careful when you are transferring material close to 2GB size. It might look like it's going thru the process yet end up, in fact, not transferring. Always make sure it did work, before you delete the original from your computer (if ever)!

Not sure why yet, but sometimes the amount of material I think I have on the external hard drive doesn't quite match what it shows I have. I have 74 GB used on the sea disk, but it shows 93...?

Best External Hard Drive Transfer Procedure

Best procedure, I've found, is to delete the outdated material on the external hard drive FIRST (the outdated material goes to the Recycle Bin of computer) and THEN move new ongoing material to the external hard drive. Otherwise, it keeps stopping and asking you each time if you want to replace each smaller same-named old folders that are still there. So instead of doing other things, you have to stay there at the computer, while it transfers EACH folder and asks you EACH time. Though, I suppose you could select the "Do this for the next 8 conflicts" option, to speed things up. But I worry about weird things happening, like folders getting put inside other folders, something getting messed up partway thru, clicking the wrong spot, the computer freezing, etc. I prefer simplicity: Delete old stuff, transfer new stuff; then, if there's a problem, I can start over clean; I've got the new stuff still on my computer, and the old stuff freshly landed in my Recycle Bin. I'll know where I am, and I won't be hopelessly confused about where what material is and in what stage.

I assume most people are like me; under My Documents, they have scores of folders and hundreds of documents.

"F4" KEY – The F4 key is the repeat key. Press it and it repeats the last function you did. For example, if you just bolded a word, put the cursor into another word, press F4, and that word will also be bolded. Or if you want to put a certain word into caps, do it for one instance, put the cursor into the other instances of that word and press F4. A good time saver.

Works for larger functions also. If you want certain paragraphs indented (into a narrower column), indent one paragraph, put the cursor inside any other paragraph, press F4 and those paragraphs will be equally indented.

Very helpful whenever you have to repeat a function that takes several little steps; F4 key reduces the operation to one step.

I find the Repeat key very useful for deleting columns or rows in tables; delete one, put the cursor into any other one, press F4.

Another good trick using the repeat key: To get a lined sheet of paper, put in say 5 lines by pressing Shift key and holding down the underline key, block those 5 lines, CTRL+V them at that point, then keep pressing F4 to get the whole page lined quickly.

FACEBOOK – This is a social networking website. It's kind of like public email, for people you have designated as "friends." It's extremely popular, and as a way of communicating with like-minded people it can be quite a force (regime change in Egypt, for example). But, I have an aversion to it. I signed up for it, but for me it's like suddenly having dozens of people I'm supposed to keep up a correspondence with. I don't want that. I'm a busy man; I have to watch the Celtics and other things.

I don't even know how to use it. But I'll stay on it; I may find it useful someday.

FAVORITES – WEBSITES – To put an icon of a favorite website onto a Favorites list: While on that website, click the "Favorites" icon (white star at upper right) > click "Add to Favorites" (not the dropdown arrow), window opens showing that site's name > click Add. Now it's listed under that white star icon and you can click on it there to open it up. You can also put that site's icon into a folder there on your list (Add to favorites dropdown arrow > Organize favorites > New Folder), or use the normal right-click functions, to move, rename it, etc. Shortening the names so you can see them on your list more easily, is a good idea

For Windows 7, it's a bit easier. While on the site, just click the "Add to favorites" yellow star icon at left, that's it, the site gets immediately added to the quick-access Favorites bar right there by the yellow star. Note that the yellow star at left doesn't actually put that site into your Favorites list under the white star at right. You have to go to the white star at right to literally add it to your actual list, or to make any adjustments to it, like renaming it, etc. But, just having a site on the "yellow star" bar is all you need really; the icon stays there; just click on it, and up comes the site.

I use this Favorites bar a lot, keeping my top 4 or 5 websites there. I used to use site icons on my desktop more, but now I find using the Favorites bar is easier; it's right there to click on; I don't have to take the extra step of going back to my desktop.

Microsoft puts in several of their sites into your Favorites section automatically, trying to sell you stuff. Damn them! Mercenary bastards. I deleted those site folders.

FAX – A fax (short for "facsimile") is a document sent over a telephone line. A fax machine looks like a printer of sorts. You feed a document thru it and it reads it and transposes the visual info into something it can send over the phone lines. With a fax machine at the other end, the info gets re-transposed into the visual info again and gets printed out.

Businesses use it a lot, for quickly sending copies of needed documents. It's more secure than sending info over the internet. I have little experience here, but I did recently send a fax. A company needed a signed document from me. Went to Staples, where they have self-service fax. Loaded sheet face down > pressed Start > put in fax number of company (or maybe I put in the number first and then pressed Start; don't remember) > the sheet gets fed thru and read > maybe 15 seconds later the machine prints out a sheet of what you just sent > you go to the cashier to pay (costs about $1.50, for one sheet).

One wrinkle: the printed sheet had the bottom info cut off – my signature – which was the point of sending it. Guy at the store assured me the signature was in fact included on the copy that was sent. I guess the extra info at the top of this copy/receipt sheet pushes text lower, cutting off the bottom; but the actual full page does get sent.

Many printers have fax capability. Mine does, but I don't use it. I may send a fax only once every few years.

FILE – A "File" is a block of arbitrary information, which is available to a computer program. Files can be text document files, audio files, video files, picture files, whatever.

I'm not clear on when a computer shows a file's extension after its name, but every file has an extension indicating what kind of file it is, or what software program it needs in order to be read. ".doc" is a Word document; ".wav" is a sound file; ".jpg" is a picture file, etc.

You can see a file's extension or type, by right-clicking it > Properties > General tab > "Type of file:" near the top.

FILE ICONS – A file type can usually be identified by their appearance: A Word document file has a blue "w"; an audio file has a blue musical note; a picture file is orange or shows a square picture; a video file shows a filmstrip; etc. If you click on Start, All Programs, you can see all the different icons of the programs at the left of the program names.

"FILE" TAB DISAPPEARED – Windows 7 doesn't have the traditional "File" tab at upper left of a folder window as a default setting. To get the "File" tab back at the top of a folder window, just press the ALT key. To keep that toolbar up (the so-called "Folder Menu" or "Menu Bar") with "File" in it – "Organize" at upper left of any folder >

Folder and Search Options > View tab > Always show menus (2nd one down) > OK. Or, click Organize > Layout > "Menu bar".

FILE TRANSMISSION ERROR – When I work with tables, every so often, especially when I make quick additions or changes, it refuses to Save, indicating a "File transmission error." Very annoying. The best way around this, I found, is to make a copy of what you just added, close the document without saving it, re-open it, then paste in what you just copied into the appropriate spot. Now it should allow saving.

Of course, if you did a lot of work on it and can't really sort out all the material you added, then you have to make a copy of the whole document (CTRL+A, CTRL+C), open a new document, and paste the entire thing there, and Save it. That usually works. Delete the old document, then rename the new one to the name of the old one.

FILE – "WINDOWS CAN'T OPEN THIS FILE" MESSAGE – Pops up when Windows does not recognize the exact kind of file it is. Click "Select a Program from a List of Installed Programs" > OK > select one to open the file > then check the box "Always Use the Selected Program to Open This Kind of File.

If that doesn't help, click the lower option – "Use the Web Service to Find the Correct Program." Windows searches the web and suggests links for downloading the correct program to use.

FILTERING – See "SORTING – FOLDERS OR DOCUMENTS"

FINDING ANYTHING – See "SEARCH BOX – 'START' ICON"

FINDING – A WORD (WORD SEARCH) – You can find a particular word or phrase by pressing CTRL+F > then type in what you are looking for > click Find Next. (Or you can click "Find" at the far upper right of the Home tab. That brings up the very same window.)

Remember that to get any search box functional, you need to first click inside it to get your cursor in there to start typing.

Windows 7

[W7 – (I've found the Windows 7 word search function to be a nice improvement over the Vista one, once you get used to it.)

When you do a CTRL+F, a panel called "Navigation" opens, now on the left. It lists the instances of the word, with a chunk of the text it is in, making it easier to identify which one you want, as you scroll down the panel. When you click on the chosen instance, it shows that instance in your text at the right, with the word highlighted in yellow. You can then x out the panel and do your editing in your text at the right.

The subtle but definite improvement over the Vista search function, I think, is that you can scroll down the panel at left, seeing each instance of the word in context, without having to scroll thru large chunks of your actual text without that word. And rather than seeing only one instance of the word at a time as you click "Next," you can see half a dozen or more instances at a time. Overall effect is to make it easier to find which instance you're looking for.

Plus, it solves the problem of the dialogue window sitting right on top of your text, hiding portions of it. (See "Tips" below.)

To match letter case, or other options: Click on the dropdown arrow next to the blue "x" > Options > check your choice.]

The navigation pane at left actually has three tabs – browse the headings, browse the pages, and browse the results from your current search. The third one is the one you usually want. Sometimes the tabs seem to switch on their own.

Note 1) If you don't click on either the panel at left, or your text at right, when you x out the panel, the text at right reverts to the top instead of staying at that spot. 2) After doing some editing, the list in the panel on the left disappears! To get it back, click the down arrow just above the panel's scroll bar, to continue looking for further instances of your word, from the very point it left off from.

The "Replace" (CTRL+H) function remains the same as for Vista; a window opens at the right. And, actually, if you don't like the Windows panel on the left for a word search, you can press CTRL+H, instead of CTRL+F, and the familiar Vista dialogue box opens, which includes the familiar Vista "Find" tab. So you can still do it the old way if you want to. I find the new way significantly better though; it didn't take too long to get used to it.

Tips

For Vista, if you're searching thru a long document for instances of a word, it will go faster if you drag the dialogue window to the far right (even partially off screen, as long as you can access the "Find Next" box). That way you can just keep on clicking for the next one without the window box covering parts of the text.

If you're searching thru a long double-column text, it's probably easier if you temporarily re-format it to a single column. (CTRL+A > Page Layout tab at top > Columns > One.) Searching up and down double columns is a pain.

Find and Replace

Under the same CTRL+H window, you can click the Replace tab and then type in a word to be replaced with another word. Usually click "Replace All." Very useful function, especially for a word you've misspelled consistently or a word you now realize should be capitalized.

For capitalization (say you want to replace every "east" with "East"), you need to click the "More" box at lower left and select "Match Case." (Don't forget to uncheck "Match Case" afterwards.)

A neat trick to find out how many times a particular word appears in your document, is to order the word to be replaced by itself, the very same word. The window tells you how many instances there were. Now you know how many times it appeared, without actually having changed anything. And, to play it safe, do a CTRL+Z back to what you had, just in case you did something wrong, like replaced not only his with His, but 30 instances of this with tHis without realizing it!

Won't Work

A couple times the word search function simply did not work at all for me. I closed the document, opened it again, and then it worked.

Finding Last Stopping Point Trick

If you're working on a long document over several days, a quick way to find your last stopping point, is, each time you finish working on your text, at that point, enter "xxx" and then Save. Then next time, simply do a word search for "xxx" to get to that point quickly, rather than scrolling laboriously trying to remember where you stopped.

I use the same technique for marking things I need to check on (a spelling, a fact, whatever): I leave a "kkk" at the spot. Then when I'm done, I do a word search for "kkk" to find those issues I still need to address. Very useful! Scrolling a long document trying to find something is an annoying time waster.

Finding a Word in an Internet Article

Use CTRL+F just like finding a word in a Word document. But, instead of a dialogue window, you get a search box at upper left, where you type in the word. It immediately shows, and highlights, the first instance. Then you click on "Next" slightly to the right of the search box, to find further instances. (You could also use the Edit tab at upper left, and click on "Find on this page". Brings up same search box at upper left as CTRL+F does.)

FINDING – A DOCUMENT – If you can't remember where you have a document or folder, click the Start icon at lower left, and type into its search box your best guess of the document name (or even some text inside it). It searches and puts up a list, hopefully including the one you're looking for. Then, right-click on it, Open file location.

You can also go under Documents or My Documents and type in the name (or, just a piece of text) in the search box at upper right.

If you have no idea what the name of the document is, but remember you mentioned poodle in it, type in poodle and it should list all documents with the word poodle in it. Also, if you put the word or phrase in QUOTES, then it will narrow its search to just that exact word or phrase. For example, if I put in darken the sea, it might find a dozen documents containing the word darken. But if I put in "darken the sea" it will find the ONE document I have that contains that exact phrase.

Or, at least, that's what I've read. Sometimes it works for me, sometimes it doesn't.

Finding By Date (While in a Folder)

In "My Documents" or any other folder, you normally have folders and documents listed alphabetically. But if you're looking for a file you've recently worked on, click the Date Modified tab at top and then items are listed according to the date last modified, and you can check near the top of the list for your item. (You may have to have the "Details" option checked under "View.")

[W7 – Has this feature (at upper right "Arrange by" > "Date modified") and it arranges all your documents by Yesterday, Last Week, Earlier This Month, Earlier This Year, A Long Time Ago. Can be quite useful, when you can't find a document by name but you remember clearly WHEN you worked on it.]

FINDING A FILE – FROM CATEGORIES ON THE LEFT – If you are in a window – browsing for a file to attach to an email would be one example – and your various categories and folders are shown on the left, you click on the category you want, working your way down to smaller and smaller categories or folders within those folders, until you find the specific one you want.

If you want to start all the way up at your desktop, you may have to click on the up arrow (it's more like a caret than an arrow) to get there. In other words, if the category you want is not shown, click on the up, or down, arrow to navigate to it.

FINDING A PROGRAM – Click Start > All Programs > scroll down to find it.

Note these complications: The program may not be under the exact name you are looking for, but a different name. It may be in the lower part of the list (you have a bunch of programs listed alphabetically, but then another big bunch of programs in folders in a second alphabetical list below that top list). The program may be listed as a subcategory under another folder (for example, "Calculator" is under "Accessories.")

Lastly, it may not be on that list, even though it's in your computer somewhere. To find it: Start > type in the name of the program in the Start search box and it should show at the top of the resulting list. Click on it, to open it. Note that, often the program will pop up after the first word, but then disappear if you type in the second word!! For example, the "Sticky Notes" program shows once you've typed in "Sticky," but disappears once you type in "Notes." Crazy.

Note that deleting a program icon from your desktop does not delete the actual program, but just the icon (the shortcut button). Also, "deleting" a program from the names on that list under "All Programs" does not delete it either; you have to "UNINSTALL" it to actually remove it from your computer. The names in that "All Programs" list are shortcuts to the programs, not the actual programs.

Adding a Program to the Start List

Find the program by typing its name into the Start search box > it should show at top > right-click it > Send To > "Desktop (create shortcut)", so that you now have a shortcut icon for it on the desktop > return to Start and click Start > right-click All Programs > Open > double-click Programs > right-click on an empty part of the "Programs" window > New > select "Folder" > name it > press Enter key > then open that folder > make the window small so you can go directly to the desktop > drag and drop the shortcut icon on the desktop into the new folder > close the window. That should put that program onto your Start program list.

(Thanks to the eHow website; they're very helpful; I never could have figured that out on my own.)

FIREWALL – A security program that helps prevent programs from connecting to your computer when you did not request their company. It should be on by default. You can check its status under Start > Control Panel > System and Security > Windows Firewall.

If it is blocking a program, but you want it allowed thru: Start > Control Panel > System and Security > Windows Firewall > "Allow a program..." at left > click the "Change Settings" button > "Allow another program..." > highlight the program > Add > OK.

The firewall on a router keeps people and software from accessing your router network.

FIREWALL – DESKTOP "WEBROOT" FIREWALL EPISODE

At one point a "Webroot" security window kept popping up every time I opened my laptop. Needed to click it out every time. VERY annoying. I don't need the desktop "Webroot" firewall. Geek guy says one is all you need (the Microsoft one already in the computer); more than one just causes trouble.

I went to Start, Programs, deleted it. (Though remnants of it still show up. I opened it; it's still there, though no longer on my Program list. I set it on Allow, so that stupid block/allow box doesn't show up at the lower right every time. The one that used to show up in the middle of the screen at least no longer does.)

6/15/08 Update – Still can't get rid of it completely.

6/16/08 Update – Finally got rid of it by going through Uninstall procedure. See "Uninstall a Software Program." (I think what I didn't realize at the time was that deleting a program on the Start list, is not deleting the program but only deleting its shortcut there in the Start list.)

FITTING MATERIAL ONTO A PAGE – MANY OPTIONS – If you have text that is a little too big to fit onto ONE page, or a little too big to fit onto 8 pages instead of 9, or whatever variation, there are a number of different options to accomplish this:

– Edit your text so that it is succinct. Get rid of unnecessary paragraphs or words. (He is taller ~~by comparison~~.)

– You could decrease the margins. See "MARGINS"

– You could change the font to a narrower font. See "FONT – SELECTING FONT TO USE" (Arial Narrow is a good choice here.)

– You could decrease the size of the font, including half sizes. See "FONT – SIZE" > "Half Sizes"

– You could squeeze the text. See "SPACING BETWEEN LETTERS". You could also squeeze the line spacing (Paragraph box > Indents and Spacing tab > Single > At: .8 or .9 > OK.)

– You could put the text into two, or three, columns. That saves significant space. And, make the space between columns narrower.

FLASH DRIVES – Flash drives are small storage devices that plug into your computer's USB ports. You can transfer material to and from them.

1. Insert flash drive into USB port (look inside the tip, half is black, half is open, the open side goes up, or, if it has a white slider thing, like the picture above, that's the side that goes up)
2. AutoPlay comes up
3. Click "Open folder to view files"
4. Keep or make that window small ("Restore Down" icon at far upper right)
5. Drag that window to the right (by dragging the top part of the window)
6. Open My Documents, or desired folder, on your computer
7. Keep or make that window small and drag it to the left
8. Now you have the two windows side by side (computer at left, flash drive at right)
9. Drag and drop items from left to right
10. That's it. It makes copies, not cuts.
11. To make a copy to another computer, insert the flash drive into the other computer and just do the same procedure in reverse, dragging and dropping items from right to left, flash drive window to computer window.

Note that if you delete material from the flash drive, IT IS GONE; it doesn't go to your computer Recycle Bin. Even if you drag and drop a file from the flash drive window to the computer Recycle Bin window, the file does NOT go there; it is permanently deleted!! If you want to play it safe, right-click and copy the file to your Desktop for retrieval if something goes wrong. (I tried making a copy directly into my Bin, but it would not go! But, you can make a copy to your Desktop, and then delete it to your Bin.)

Procedure Variations

If you are using the flash drive (sometimes referred to as a "thumb drive" also) for the first time, it may prompt you to install the driver for it first. Just follow the instructions that pop up, click on a couple of things, and it's ready for use, in less than a minute.

Also, if no window for the device shows onscreen automatically when you insert it, you can bring it up by: Double-click Computer > double-click "Removable Disk (F)", that brings up a window for the files on the device.

"LaunchU3" File

My flash drives have a file embedded on them called "LaunchU3." I think this file has to do with using applications or programs, rather than just Word documents or pictures. I've experimented, and found, on both my old (Vista) computer and new (Windows 7) computer, that not clicking on this file to prepare the flash drive pull-out, or, simply totally ignoring this "LauchU3" file, made no difference. I still could transfer Word documents and pictures. I find I don't have to do anything other than just plug the thing in, transfer material, and pull it out. Any "Unsafe Eject" message refers to, I think, parts of applications or programs rather than the literal files.

Sometimes if you drag and drop a document to the flash drive, it doesn't go the first time (something to do with its trying to involve your disk bay). Just do it a second time and it works.

"FLIP" POCKET CAMCORDER – See "CAMCORDER" > "Flip" Pocket Camcorder

FLOPPY DISKS – These are the square-encased disks that used to be used for making copies of files. They're outdated, because they have such little capacity – 1.44 MB, maybe 300 pages of text only.

A higher capacity disk called a Zip disk (238 MB), is, I think, also outdated. The storage devices currently used are: Flash drives, CDs or DVDs, or external hard drives, or memory cards. The smallest flash drive holds 1 GB. External hard drives can hold up to (I've seen advertised) a TB (a thousand GBs)! See "DATA TRANSFER"

Fn KEY – This is a "function" or modifier key at lower left, right next to the Ctrl key. It's like the Ctrl key – when you press it in conjunction with another key, it performs a function. I rarely use it, except for lowering (Fn+F3 key) or raising (Fn+F4 key) sound volume. Wikipedia says, *"It is mainly for the purpose of changing display or audio settings quickly, such as brightness, contrast, or volume, and is held down in conjunction with the appropriate key to change the settings."*

FOLDERS – Computer "folders" work just like real folders. You put stuff into them, usually documents on the same topic – financial documents under a folder you name "Financial", job documents under a folder you name "Job" etc. Besides documents into folders, you can put folders into folders. For example, a "Pets" folder might have a subcategory "Dogs" folder under it, and then a "German Shepherd" folder under that, etc.

Navigating a Folder Window

Any folder window has back and forward arrows (at top left) for moving to other folders you've opened. It has an address box, which shows the progression of locations that took you to your current location (for example, "Libraries ▶ Documents ▶ My Documents ▶ Maps ▶ Maine"). It has a search box at upper right. And it has a list of major locations in a panel at the left for navigating to those places.

Creating a New Folder

Creating a folder is just like creating a document: Right-click on any empty spot in a folder (usually the "My Documents" folder) > New > click on "Folder" (instead of "Microsoft Word Document") > type in a name > press Enter key.

Note that you can also create a folder by right-clicking on an empty spot on the desktop, but then your new folder sits on the desktop, as the actual folder, not just a shortcut icon. (I like to be consistent and just keep folder shortcuts on the desktop, otherwise, at some point, I might accidentally delete an actual folder instead of its shortcut.)

Moving and Storing Folders

If you open a chosen folder (by double-clicking on it), you can create a document right there inside that folder. Or, you can create a document inside any folder, and then decide to move it into a chosen folder, by "dragging and dropping" that document into that folder. Likewise, you can drag and drop folders into folders.

Another way to move documents, or folders, into folders, is to right-click it, cut (CTRL+X), find the target folder, and then paste (CTRL+V) it there.

Try to store all your text documents under the "My Documents" folder, all your pictures under "Pictures" folder, all your music under "Music" folder, etc. Vista tends to send those types of files into those folders automatically anyway.

My own "My Documents" has mostly folders in it under broad categories like "Health" or "Finances," but I also keep some isolated documents under "My Documents" that don't particularly fit into any broad category.

Note that "My Documents" is under the broader category folder of "Documents." I keep a shortcut icon for "My Documents" on my Desktop, for quick access. See also "DESKTOP" > "Arranging Icons on Desktop"

To Delete a Folder

Right-click it > Delete > it goes to the Recycle Bin. Note that deleting a folder deletes all the folders and documents inside that folder.

Also note that any file that ends in .exe, .config, .sys, .bak, and .dll ... do not tamper with. Leave it alone. These are integral programs for running your computer. Although, I have to say that all kinds of programs automatically stick their folders onto your computer, which, when I click on them, I find empty. And I do delete those; I hate clutter. I hate the way all these factions in the computer world try to take over your computer.

To Rename a Folder

Right-click it, click Rename, type in the new name. Don't rename a folder the same name as another folder, especially a major one like Documents, Pictures, or Music. That confuses Windows.

To find a folder

If you can't find a folder, use the same technique I describe under "DOCUMENT FINDING"

FONT – AUTOMATIC RED CORRECTIONS – Some people like to see corrections made to a text in red. I don't really like this feature, and I don't recommend it, unless you're an editor, and are willing to get familiar with all the options here, and can figure out how to keep all kinds of editing marks from repeatedly popping up suddenly when you thought you already got rid of them!

Review tab at top > Tracking box > Track Changes > Track Changes > that puts all the new changes into red underlined font. Click "Track Changes" again, to stop this red tracking, from that point on.

Now, if you want (as one normally would want) that text to remain as part of your revised text, in normal black color now, not red, underlined, you cannot change it into black by blocking it and ordering black font! Instead, to get rid of the red/under-lined format, you must go to the top right of that box and click Final Showing Markup and click "Final." [DON'T click on "Original", because that doesn't get rid of just the redness of the changes but the actual changes themselves that you've just made!] That gets rid of the tracking red and puts those changes into black font... it does? Hah, only for the time being!

Actually, all the red stuff keeps on showing up, again and again, every time you open up the document! You need to click "Show Markup" and uncheck each box!!

Guess what? The red corrections are STILL showing up every time I open up the document! Hiding the changes does NOT delete them! To really get rid of the red, you need to "accept" or "reject" the changes, like this:

Getting Rid of the Red for Good

1. Under the Review tab, go to the Changes box, NOT the Tracking box.
2. Click "Accept" dropdown arrow
3. Click "Accept All Changes in Document"

That should do it. You have your changes, but the redness and underlining of those changes are gone for good and won't keep reappearing.

(If you had entered any editing comments yourself, go to the Comments box (to the left of the Tracking box) and click Delete, to get rid of those.)

Unbelievable! Typical Microsoft! A normal person wants to get rid of the red once he or she is finished editing a text. That's the normal thing one would want to do. Instead of making that function clearly and logically available, Microsoft makes it a struggle to figure out. Who would think you have to move over to the next box, instead of staying in the Tracking box!?

Microsoft always gives you all kinds of needless options, but the main thing one normally needs to do – getting rid of the red in this case – that, that is hidden somewhere like the Holy Grail!

I think, for the normal person, this red editing feature is way too much trouble to bother dealing with. Though, in fairness to Microsoft, if you're an editor or teacher, and once you get familiar with it, the program can be quite useful.

FONTS – BIG FANCY TITLE FONTS – See under "DRAWING"

FONTS – CHANGING DESKTOP / DISPLAY FONTS – You can change the fonts of the Desktop, Menus, Taskbar, etc.: Start > Control Panel > Appearance and Personalization > Change the Theme > select choice (I picked "Windows Vista" – a simple Arial type font I think) > Apply, wait > OK.

I would advise against experimenting here, if you're satisfied with what you have. It is typically the type of thing that you would think is a matter of only one minute, yet, because Windows is so terminally afflicted with overkill, you'll find yourself confused as to procedures, stuck in things you can't get out of, having to redo your whole desktop, and spending a huge chunk of time at it instead of only one minute!

I've had an episode or two where adding or dropping a font automatically changed my display fonts! It put my icon fonts and window fonts into italics, etc. Very annoying. I had to use the above procedure to get fonts back to what I had.

FONT – INSTALLING A NEW FONT – Haven't installed a font for quite a while. The numerous ones already there are fine for me. But, if you want to install a font (you can buy a CD with fonts on it, or download a font online), here are the BayconGroup Instructions:

[I had mixed success with these steps. See "Downloading a Font", further below for what finally worked for me.]

How do I install a new font?

You must purchase or otherwise obtain the font you want to install. Then:

1. *Click the Start button.*
2. *Click Control Panel.*
3. *Click Appearance and Personalization.*
4. *Click Install or Remove a Font, which is located under Fonts. The Fonts window appears.*
5. *Click File, which is located on the menu bar of the Fonts window. Press the ALT key if you do not see the menu bar.*
6. *Click Install New Font.*
7. *Specify the drive and folder where the font you want to install is currently located. The fonts appear in the List of Fonts box.*
8. *Highlight the font you want to install.*
9. *Select Copy Fonts to Fonts Folder (this puts a copy of the font you are installing into the Fonts folder).*
10. *Click Install. If you are prompted for permission to continue, click Continue. Vista installs the font.*
11. *Click Close. The Add Fonts dialog box closes.*

Mixed Success at Downloading Fonts

I tried to download a font for free and just got into a big mess. I ended up with an image of the font letters, rather than the usable font itself. It seems if you really want a font, it costs money. Plus whatever site you go to, all the presumed "free" stuff seems to be bundled in with other stuff they are trying to sell you. I suppose there is a way to get "Abadi MT Condensed Light" font for free, but after an hour of trying, it wasn't worth my time to continue.

Then I downloaded a different free font from "1001free-fonts.com" and it downloaded but I could NOT get it installed. I followed the above directions carefully, but step 7 never worked. No matter where I put the font – regular folders, temporary folders – it never showed up in the "List of Fonts" box. The only thing that ever showed up in that box was the list of fonts I already have, when I clicked on the Fonts folder.

I even tried putting the font on a CD and then dragged it to the Font folder, and it said it's not a valid font style and cannot be installed!

I made a copy of the font to My Documents, brought up My Documents, brought up my font list from the Control Panel, set up one window on the left, the other on the right, and tried dragging and dropping the font to my Font folder. No go. Again it gave me a message that this is not a valid font style and cannot be installed.

I tried another font from the same freefonts.com site. This time it worked! Tried it again with another font and again it worked. The icon for these looked different, a blue "T." I don't know if that means a "true" font compared to other types. Anyway, those worked. They didn't show up right away in my font list, but when I opened a document and clicked the font dropdown arrow at top, they were there, and I could use them.

Unfortunately, that 1001 freefonts site does not have "Abadi MT Condensed Light." Will try another site. That's the only font I'm interested in now. It's condensed yet very readable.

If I copy a chunk of Abadi from an old document, I can actually continue typing from a point within that text and it will continue in Abadi font. But, I cannot change a block of text already typed in another font, to Abadi. Nor is the Abadi font in my font folder.

Other sites, again, 1) "free" fonts are attached to some promotion you have to sign up for, 2) can't find Abadi, they don't have it in their list, even though the site specifically says you can download that font for free! Kept going. Another site, gives you a free font, but the Abadi one costs $20. Another site specifically said there are "no free Abadi fonts."

Decided to go back to the fonts I already have and look for one similar to Abadi (by blocking a text, then scrolling down thru the list, which changes the blocked text into each choice as I scroll, so I can get a good idea of what it looks like.) Also, I went back to the 1001 site to check there again.

Final Update on Abadi Font

Guess what, after more exploring, I find that Humanist 521 Cn BT (which I have in my Font folder) matches Abadi almost exactly – if not exactly – in looks and space. A condensed yet readable text.

However, I think I'll stick to Arial narrow as my go-to font for condensed text. Humanist 521 is a bit too small (and if I increase the size, it starts to no longer save space).

Downloading / Installing a Font

1. 1001 Free Fonts site
2. Pick a font
3. Click "Windows Download"
4. Save As, to the Desktop
5. Get Fonts folder up (Start > Control Panel > Appearance and Personalization > Fonts)

6. Make the Fonts folder small and move it to the right
7. Drag and drop the new font from the desktop into the Font folder (takes only two seconds to copy) The dragging and dropping does the installing.
8. That, hopefully, should do it. Your new font should be in your Font folder now, ready to be used.

However, sometimes it won't do it. It's crazy. One font I tried wouldn't go. The next one I tried, no go again; ended up with a message that this "might not be a true font."

Windows says that besides installing a font by dragging and dropping, you can also do it by right-clicking and clicking "Install." So I tried that; I went back to the first one that wouldn't go. I had to click "Extract" first before an "Install" option came up. [Note that after you download some of these fonts, you can see that their file type includes the extension ".zip", meaning, I figure, that you have to unzip them first (i.e., click the "Extract" option.]

I then right-clicked and clicked "Install." Hah! It worked this time! I now have a nice calligraphy font called *Baroque Antique Script*.

But, then I tried the same thing with the other font, and got nowhere.

Tried another one [Download > Save As, to the Desktop > Save > right-click folder > "Extract All" > "Extract" > right-click folder > click "Install > window comes up showing that it's installing. Got it. A font called "AlphRev".]

So, I think some fonts you just can't get, but most you can, if not by the drag and drop method, then by the right-click > extract > right-click > Install method.

Good luck.

Last wrinkle: On fonts that open up to half a dozen files, right-click each one to see if it gives you an "Install" option. If it does, it may well give you at least some variation of that font. I tried that with a chess font, and I got chess icons installed. I press K, I get ♔ ; I press Q, I get ♕ , I press B, I get ♗ , etc.

Ha ha, I like this one: "Carbon Type". **You can type a letter making it look like you typed it on an old typewriter.**

Transferring Font from Old Computer to New Computer

Tried a bunch of things but the only thing that seems to work is, hooray, the simple drag and drop method:

Attach transfer device (flash drive, disk, or external hard drive) to old computer > Open folder to view files > then, on the computer, Start > Control Panel > Appearance and Personalization > Fonts > make windows small so that you now have the Font window and the transfer device window side by side > drag and drop font onto transfer device > remove transfer device > attach to new computer > do the same drag-and-drop procedure, this time from device to Font folder of new computer. That's it. Font should be fully functional.

Software Fonts Automatically Added

When you install some programs, their fonts are sometimes automatically put into your font folder. From my chess CD I had gotten a "ChessMaster" font, and from my Bibles program I got several Hebrew and Greek fonts. (Actually, now I can't find any of them. I think they got left in my old computer.)

Deleting Fonts

Follow the above procedure for adding a font, but when you get to your list of fonts, check the font, right-click it, and Delete.

FONTS – MOST USEFUL FOR ME

Times New Roman

Great basic font, looks just like text you see in magazines or books.

Arial Narrow

My go-to font for saving space and ink. This manual is in Arial narrow. Note that Arial regular, though very popular, wastes both space and ink.

Humanist 521 Cn BT

Great for condensed yet readable text.

Courier New

A non-proportional font (the "i" and "m" take up the same amount of space). Good for aligning stuff.

Freestyle Script

Good for hand-writing-looking text. (Just need to increase its size 3 or 4 points.)

"Freehand 521" is pretty good also.

TITLE FONTS

ARIAL BLACK – GOOD FOR TITLES.

IMPACT – FOR MORE CONDENSED TITLE LOOK.

FONT – REVERSE LETTERS (WHITE ON BLACK) – Block the text > Home tab at top > Paragraph box > shading (paint can) icon dropdown arrow > click the black square.

Also works with the dark red square.

Of course, you can order up any combination of shading colors and font colors (shading from the Paragraph box, font color from the Font box).

Note, however, that printers do not have white ink. White font text is literally no ink for the letters, surrounded by a shade. In other words, you need white paper to get white text. If you order up white text with no shading, and use, say, yellow paper, you get only... yellow paper. If you surround the text with a shade, the text letters will show as yellow (the paper itself).

FONT – SELECTING FONT TO USE – Home tab at top > Font box > click the dropdown arrow by the current font name at the upper left of that box > click on your selection. Text you type from that point on will be in that font. To change a section of text to a different font, highlight the section and follow the same procedure, clicking on your selection.

Note that all these fonts can be italicized (CTRL+I), bolded (CTRL+B), or underlined (CTRL+U), by using those three keyboard commands, or, you can use the three icons in the Font box at top – B, *I*, U.

FONT – SIZE – The most common sizes for normal reading, I would say, are 10, 11, or 12 point size. This font is 11 point. 72 point font = one inch high.

To get font sizes: Home tab at top > Font box > dropdown arrow next to the number in the top middle > select size of your choice. From that point on your text with be in that size. You can also block a text and then order a size to change the whole block to that size.

The other method of ordering font size is by pressing CTRL+[, to decrease size, CTRL+] to increase size, by one size each time you press the bracket key. If you want to go smaller than 8 point, you have to use CTRL+[since, at least on my computer, the numbers in the dropdown list only show down to 8.

Or, you can just type in the size number you want and press Enter.

See also "SPACING BETWEEN LETTERS" for how to condense or expand fonts.

Half Sizes

You can actually get half sizes by clicking inside the Font Size box and just adding .5 to whatever number you type in there and then pressing Enter.

Desktop Font Size

You can adjust your font size on the Desktop by Start > Control Panel > Appearance and Personalization > Fonts > "Change font size" at left > Apply. I just leave it at default size, which is fine. Changing the Desktop font size often messes up the arrangement of icons you have there, and then you have to laboriously put them back into the positions you like.

FONT – SPACING – See "SPACING BETWEEN LETTERS"

FONT – STYLE OPTIONS – Besides selecting a font, its size, its color, etc. there are a number of other nifty options under the Font box dropdown arrow (lower right of box) window > Effects: ~~Strikethrough~~, Outline, **Shadow**, etc.

The "Shadow" style, FYI, only works effectively with large letters. In fact, you're probably better off using "WordArt" titles instead, for shadow-like effects. See "DRAWING > WordArt – (Titles)"

FONT – TRANSFERRING A FONT TO A DISK – Start > Control Panel > Appearance and Personalization > Fonts > Install or remove a font > check the desired font > Edit at upper left > Copy > insert a disk (CD or any external transfer device) > paste.

With the font now on a disk, you can transfer it to another computer (by dragging and dropping it into the Font folder).

Sending a Font by Email

You can even send a font by email to another person who wants the font but doesn't have it: Send the font as an attachment to your email. The recipient receives the email, downloads the attachment, saves it, goes to the Downloads folder, right-clicks the font file, and installs it. Pretty sure that works.

(I had gotten a religious-looking font from a CD, for my book, and sent it to the publishing company this way, so they could use it for my book.)

FOOTNOTES – To get a superscripted number in your text to indicate a footnote[13], click the Superscript icon ("x^2") in the Font box under the Home tab at top, then type the number.

[13] See also "EXPONENTS"

FOOTERS – Refers to footnotes, or page numbers, at bottom of the page. See "HEADERS & FOOTERS"

FORMATTING – INFORMATION – If you are not sure what font or formatting a text is in, block it and press Shift+F1 key. That brings up the full formatting information of that text in a window at the right. X out the window when you're done.

FORMATTING A DOCUMENT – You normally want to open any new document with your set preferences – margins, font, line spacing, etc. – rather than ordering up all those specifications each time you create a new document.

See "DEFAULT 'WORD DOCUMENT' FORMAT" > "Getting the Page Format You Want"

FORMATTING CHANGES – Block the section of text you want to change, click on the desired icon (bold, italicize, size, line-spacing, whatever) at the top tabs.

Won't Allow Margin Change

Sometimes I've tried to make a change – usually in margins – and the computer would not let me. Under Page Layout tab > Page Setup > Margins > Custom margins, it shows "Margins, columns, etc. too wide for page" or something like that. And the "Preview" image of the page (lower left) under the Margins tab, does not show the lines as usual but just has a blank page.

Once you can get that "Preview" page to show the lines, then it will let you make the change. The way to do that – at least this worked for me – is to make sure the text is under ONE column first, not two or more. I think this was usually my problem, given the fact that I change column formats quite often and I probably didn't clear it back to a single column format first.

Formatting Stuck

When you scan something in, or you pasted it in from a website, re-formatting is always tougher. Lots of stuff comes, it seems, with embedded formats, so it often takes a lot of work to fix it the way you want it.

See also "INTERNET – COPYING MATERIAL FROM THE INTERNET"

Mixed Formatting to Consistent Formatting – Tip

If you have text with mixed formatting (bolds, italics, underlining) and you want to change it to just regular text, you don't have to re-block each section several times for each style change. Just block the section once, order one style choice once, then the other style choices twice. That gets rid of those styles.

For example: To change "**these** *few* words" to "these few words" – Block them, do a CTRL+B once, CTRL+I twice, and CTRL+U twice. That's it; you don't have to re-block for each order.

Very convenient if you have, for example, a huge text with many italicized and bolded words, and you decide you prefer just normal-style text.

See "TEXT FORMATTING – REMOVING ALL" for the best way to remove all formatting.

Using the F4 repeat function key is another option (do the first one, put the cursor into the next one, press F4); but, that does only one word at a time and one style change at a time. This may be your only option if you want to make many specific changes (like less bolded words, more italicized ones, a few all-caps words, etc.) rather than put everything into the same style. In other words, you can quickly reduce a variety to one style, but changing a variety to another variety will be more labor-intensive.

FORMATTING – EMPTY SPACE AT BOTTOM OF PAGES

If your text doesn't reach all the way to the bottom of some pages, it's probably because you have "Widow/Orphan Control" checked. "Widows" and "orphans" refer to single isolated lines of a paragraph at the bottom or top of a page. "Widow and Orphan Control" keeps those lines attached to the rest of a paragraph so that you don't get those isolated lines. Instead, you get empty space. A matter of opinion which looks worse – empty space or single lines.

For normal typing, if you just want that space used so that the page is filled up: Home tab > Paragraph box dropdown arrow > Line & Page Breaks tab > uncheck Widows/Orphans Control.

If you still have some spaces at bottoms of pages, and the above doesn't work and using the deleting keys (either the Backspace key or Delete key) also doesn't work, you can manually cut and paste lines from the top of the next page into that empty space at the bottom of the previous page.

FRACTIONS – Some common fractions, like ½ and ¾, automatically get reduced in size as soon as you type them. Others, you can express with a number, slash, and a number – 5/6, 7/8, etc.

Wanting Your Fractions to be a Consistent Size

If you type 1 slash 2, it automatically puts it into the small-sized form – ½; but if you want to keep that fraction in normal-size font, one way to do that is to type it backwards, the 2 first, press left arrow key, slash, left arrow key, 1.

But, easier is this: Type it, then just "CTRL+Z" it out once. One CTRL+Z puts it back to regular-size font – 1/2 instead of ½. A second CTRL+Z would take it all out. Try it.

You can use the AutoCorrect function, to get other frequently-used normal sized fractions to automatically switch to smaller-sized ones: Type a normal sized one, superscript (x^2) the numerator, slash, subscript (x_2) the denominator, then copy and paste the result into the AutoCorrect "Replace with:" box. That way, you can get 7/8 to come out as $^7/_8$ every time.

You can also use Insert, Symbols options. They have ⅛, ⅜, ⅝, ⅞ selections there.

FRAMING – See "BORDERS"

FREE OFFERS ON INTERNET – If something is offered free, usually, don't get it. Most often, I find, it's more trouble than it's worth. They're trying to sell you something. It's an ongoing battle: The consumer wants something for free; the seller wants to lure you, one way or the other, honestly or deceptively, into buying something.

FREEZING – If your computer freezes completely and won't do ANYTHING, you can unfreeze it by holding down the "On/Off" button for 5-10 seconds; the computer shuts down. Then restart it and the freeze is gone, though you may have lost unsaved material. (You can ignore the computer's warning that you did not shut it down properly... because, you couldn't! Then when it starts up again, press the Enter key to get it going faster.)

Another option is holding down CTRL+ALT+Delete key all at same time; that brings up a green page. Click Start Task Manager > Application tab > End Task. That might unfreeze things.

Otherwise, do the first option – shut off the computer by holding down the On/Off button for 5-10 seconds, wait 30 seconds, then restart it. (I don't think it causes any damage if you don't wait, but I've read several places that it's good to wait 30 seconds before turning the computer back on, so that it has time to complete tasks.)

RS refers to shutting down computer as "powering-down" and turning on computer as "powering-up." Same as "rebooting."

AR suggests this order of efforts to unfreeze a computer: 1) Press Esc key twice. 2) The above CTRL+ALT+Delete procedure. 3) Reset button, if you have one. 4) Hold down the On/Off button till computer turns off (5-10 seconds) and then turn it back on.

Number 4 is my preference. I end up having to do it maybe once every two months.

One Item Frozen

Once I clicked a category under the Control Panel and it would do nothing, yet all the other categories were responding. Restarted the computer; that fixed it.

Text Page Frozen

If a text page seems frozen, usually it's not. You just need to put the pointer on the page and click once, to get things active. This usually happens when you are away from the document working on something else and then come back to the document. You need to click inside it, once, to get it going again.

If an internet page freezes on you, pushing the "Refresh" button might restart that page for you. "Refresh" button is located at the end of the URL address box – it's the double blue arrows (or the blue semi-circle arrow) to the left of the X. Or, you can press the F5 key, which is the Refresh key.

(Note that the F5 key is the Find and Replace key when you are in a document, as opposed to the Refresh key when you are on the internet.)

Re-Installing Vista

I think one can uninstall Vista and then re-install it (a "reformat") and that may well help a computer work more smoothly. A fresh computer tends to work more efficiently, with less glitches, freezes, etc. BUT, I'm pretty sure you have to save everything first (all your big stuff onto an external hard drive), and then re-install ALL your programs. I fear untold extra tasks and complications may result! So I am not going to do a full "reformat" unless I find I really need to. As it is, my laptop works pretty well, and only freezes occasionally.

If I ever need to re-install my operating system, I'll probably have Best Buy do it.

RS says you can get software to help clean up your computer, but he does not recommend it. Doesn't work that well, I presume. Or, it may not make much difference.

If your computer is becoming very slow, I recommend taking it to Best Buy.

GADGETS – Are single-purpose application icons that sit on your desktop, usually at the right side. For example: date and time, a clock, the current weather, the current stock market. (Those are the four that I keep up.) Very convenient.

They are connected to the internet and are updated continuously. They come with Vista/Windows 7.

They show up on your desktop automatically when you turn the computer on. If they are not up there, you can get them up by: Right-click any empty portion of the desktop > click Gadgets (near bottom) > right-click the gadget of your choice > Add. That puts it up on your screen ready for use.

[W7 – Gadgets can now be positioned anywhere on the desktop; they are no longer restricted to a panel at the right of the screen.]

You can get all kinds of additional gadgets online.

At the lower right of the Gadgets selection window, click on "Get more gadgets online" > Windows window opens up > click Gadgets at upper right > explore and click on "Get it now" or "Download" under your selection > Install > Save As > Save, to the Desktop (Windows automatically runs a security scan) > icon for the gadget appears on Desktop; drag it to where you want > double-click to open it; may have to click on Install again > that, or some variation of the above steps (things change...) should do it.

Deleting Gadgets

Put the pointer on the gadget icon on your desktop. A small "x" and "wrench" icon appear just to the right of the gadget icon. Click on the "x".

Gadget Adjustments / Details

Click on either the icon itself, or the "wrench" icon that comes up at the upper right of the icon when you hover your pointer over it. You can see more details, or make adjustments like changing the size of the info, or changing the home location for your weather gadget.

To drag the icon to a different place on your desktop, you need to drag it with the "drag gadgets" icon spot just below the wrench icon. Otherwise, you can't move it.

For the weather one (I have the "Weatherbug" one rather than the "Weather" one), you can get a daily forecast for the week, or an hourly forecast for the next 24 hours. For the stock market one, you can get neat graphs of the Dow Jones Average for 1 day, 1 month, 3 months, 5 years, 10 years, or the entire history of the stock market.

Gadgets – Suddenly Missing

Sometimes the gadgets you had on your desktop simply disappear on their own, for no known reason. Right-click an empty spot on the desktop, then click on "Gadgets" (near the bottom of the list). That should bring them up again. Or, type "Gadgets" into the Start search box, and Gadgets should appear at the top of the resulting list. Click on that.

If that doesn't work, you'll simply have to put them up again, by right-clicking selections and clicking "Add."

If individual gadgets have disappeared, usually the problem is that they have drifted on top on one another, and the solution is to drag one down or up to reveal the other one beneath it.

Restoring Original Vista Gadgets

At one point, for whatever reason, my gadgets disappeared. I brought up the Gadgets window, but I couldn't find the same ones I used to have, and liked. Tried the "Get More Gadgets Online" (lower right), but 1) I was afraid of a virus, and 2) they didn't have the same good ones I had originally selected. Plus I didn't want to scroll thru 5,000 gadgets.

For Windows 7, I didn't see some of the older options, or selections. I just had to go ahead and pick new ones from the online selection.

For Vista, I did this: Right-click the Windows Sidebar icon on the taskbar at bottom (may have to use the little left-pointing arrow to un-hide it) > Properties > Restore Gadgets Installed with Windows. This doesn't send the gadgets to your sidebar, but sends them to the choices window you get when you click on the "+" at the top. From there, you can add them to your sidebar.

If the "Restore Gadgets Installed with Windows" option is grayed out, I think that means you already have all the original gadgets in there.

Weather Gadget – Stuck on Same Day

Often my weather gadget shows the same day for several days, instead of staying current. On Thursday it's still showing Monday's weather. I find if I just click on it, it usually updates to the current day. If clicking on it doesn't do it, then clicking on "Extended Forecast" does it.

Other Glitches

One time I accidentally moved a shortcut icon for some other program inside the sidebar area and I couldn't get it out (or do anything with it). Had to right-click a spot in the Sidebar and click "Close Sidebar", leaving that lone shortcut icon there. Then I was able to move it. Then I clicked the Sidebar icon on the taskbar at bottom, and that brought the Gadgets Sidebar up again, without that shortcut icon inside it.

Another time my stock gadget kept showing up on top of Word document windows. I hovered my pointer over it, to bring up the tools to the right, and x'd it out, and then went to Gadgets and added it again.

Another time, my stock gadget said it needed an update, so I downloaded the update, but it wouldn't work. So I downloaded it again, ran it, opened it, saved it, installed it, gave it a kiss upon the forehead, and it finally worked. In other words, just keeping trying different stuff and it usually works. I think the key here for me was that I had not actually installed it, despite doing all the other stuff several times. The "install" button didn't show up for a long time.

GAMES – Vista comes with several games, including chess and solitaire. To get to them: Start > Games (at right of window) > double-click on your selection to open it. If you buy and then install a game, Vista automatically puts that game in this same Games folder.

You can right-click a game and click "Add to Quick Launch," so that you get an icon for it on your taskbar at bottom. Makes for quicker access. You can also right-click that icon and click "Send to Desktop," to get that icon on your desktop.

The Vista chess program is a nice, simple, straightforward, user-friendly program. It's not as elaborate as my "Chessmaster 9000" that I bought, but it plays at five levels, including a very high level, and keeps track of how you've done.

I'm always amused – I swear this has happened half-a-dozen times to me – when I see someone locked on a computer, consumed in gravitas, obviously seeking to save the world, or solve the mysteries of existence. I am so impressed by their deep sense of purpose. Then, as I walk to a different angle, I can see that all they're doing is playing Solitaire.

GO TO PAGE – If you want to get to a particular page of your document quickly: CTRL+G > enter the page number > click Go To.

GOOGLE – Google is a major search engine for the internet. Type in a word or phrase in its search box, and it will come up with numerous websites related to that word or phrase. It's quite an amazing and comprehensive information retrieval system!

GOOGLE EARTH – Another amazing program. It's a maps system of the whole planet. It uses actual satellite photographs. You enter an address, press a button, and "fly" to the spot; you choose how close. You can actually see streets and houses.

I can make out the bulkhead of the house I used to live in!

And it's free. Comes with Vista. If you don't have it, you can google "Google Earth" and download it.

GRAMMAR – If you have the Spelling feature on (at the left, under the Review tab), it underlines misspellings in red. If you have the Grammar feature on, it underlines grammar concerns with a wavy green line. Since the grammar "corrections" are complex and are often just suggestions rather than errors, I keep the grammar function off.

To keep the spelling on, the grammar off: Review tab > Proofing box at left > Spelling and Grammar > click Options > knock out all checks except Spelling as You Type and Use Contextual Spelling > OK.

Update: Lately I've been keeping the grammar function on. It picks up punctuation errors I might have missed. As well as, accidental double spaces between words, a frequent error of mine.

GRAPHS – See "TABLES – GRAPHS"

GRAYED OUT – If an option in any window is grayed out or faded, that means it is not active, or not applicable. Very often you have to click some other main option to get the grayed out one active.

For example: When working with pictures, you need to click one of the "Wrap Text" options first, to activate the "Rotation" option, which is initially grayed out. Another example: In my printer options window, the "Selection" option is grayed out UNTIL I do in fact block a selection of text first; then the "Selection" option is activated.

GRAYSCALE – If you want to save color ink and print a colorful text or a color picture in just black and white, you can print in "grayscale." CTRL+P > Properties > Advanced tab > Print Options > check "Black/Grayscale > OK. Your printer may have a different setup, but the grayscale option will probably be somewhere under "Properties."

GRIDS – See "TABLES"

GROUP SELECT – DOCUMENTS OR FOLDERS – To select multiple adjacent files, hold left of mouse, then drag pointer to include the group you want, just like using the pointer to select text. Like lassoing them. (I find dragging from lower right, up thru the group, to upper left works best.) You can see it putting in the check to the left of each document. Then you can right-click and cut (move) or delete the whole group at once.

Note that if these documents or folders are not grouped together, then you need to check each one individually, then right-click while on one of them, to move or delete all of them.

Checkboxes Disappear

Well, guess what? After years of having checkboxes next to my list of documents, suddenly they disappeared! So far I haven't figured out how to get them back. BUT, here is a "workaround" method for selecting multiple NON-adjacent files: Hold down the CTRL key, as you click on each desired document.

Update: OK, figured out how to get the checkboxes back: See "CHECKBOXES > "Checkboxes Disappear." I hate the way computers suddenly do things on their own. I KNOW I did NOT uncheck that checkbox option at any point!

GUEST ACCOUNT – If you want to allow someone (like a baby sitter) to use your computer but not access your data, you can set up a guest account: Start > Control Panel > User Account and Family Safety > click green "User Accounts" > Manage another account > Guest > Turn ON.

HARD DRIVE – A hard drive is the basic data storage device in a computer. A disk rotates within a protective enclosure. Data is magnetically read by a head that floats on a film of air above the disk.

Hard Drives – Life

A knowledgeable geek guy told me hard drives last maybe 5

years, then start to have problems. Not something I've experienced myself. My old laptop was working fine after 8 years; my next one was fine after 5 years (still OK).

HARD SPACE – A "hard space" is what you get when you press the spacebar, the Shift key, and the CTRL key ALL at the same time. You get a set space.

In modern word processing, when you get near the end of a line, a spacebar entry (a "soft" space) makes the text automatically go to the next line down. A "hard space" between words keeps that from happening at that point. You can keep two words together, as though they are one word, instead of having them separated into different lines.

A fairly useless function for the most part. But, say you have a movie title of "Top Gun" and you want to keep those two words together, in the same line; put a "hard space" between the words "Top" and "Gun" and they'll stay on the same line together.

Think of a "hard space" as a set space entry, rather than the usual "soft" space entry that triggers the text to automatically jump to the next line when it gets near the end of the current line.

More useful, I find, are these two operations:

1) In a table, under "Autofit to contents", you can move a cell border to the right, by entering hard spaces.

2) If you want to make a shaded line with no letters in it, like this: , a series of "hard spaces" will do that. Block your hard spaces and order up your shade.

HEADERS AND FOOTERS – Headers and footers are short texts at the very top or bottom of the page, outside your normal text. Like a title at the top, or footnotes or page numbers at the bottom.

To insert a header or footer: Insert tab at top > Header & Footer box > click either Header, Footer, or Page Number, and then make your choice > type in what you want (or click on a page number position and style) > click "Close Header or Footer." A title, for example, then appears on every page of that document.

To adjust the header or footer: Double-click on the header or footer itself as it shows on your screen above or below your normal text. Make your adjustments using the toolbar at top, or using other normal commands (CTRL+R will move the number to the right; blocking the number and CTRL+[will decrease its size, etc., etc.)

I usually use only the Page Number feature, to number my pages. See "NUMBERING PAGES." Note the difference between Footer and Page Number: If you use Footer for the page numbers it will show the same page number for every page, whereas the Page Number selection will give you successive numbers.

HEADINGS – To make a heading or title within your text, you can type the title, block it, and then increase its size, bold it, center it, whatever, using Home tab, Font box.

Or, if you want a big, fancy, colored title, you can go to Insert tab > Text box > "A" WordArt. They have a nice selection there. Click on the one you want, type in the word(s), click OK. That inserts that title into your text wherever your cursor was.

You can also manipulate that title by right-clicking on the title, selecting Edit Text, or Format WordArt. [W7 – Click the heading, then click on "WordArt Tools" tab at top for a toolbar] You can change size, fonts, colors, stretch things in different directions, etc.

HEADING

HEADING

HELP – OVERVIEW – Simply call this number – 1 800 TORTURE – or visit this website – "frustrationbeyondbelief.com" – and you will get a satisfactory answer almost immediately. It's just that simple!

Hah, right! Think again, my friend. If you ever find an answer to a computer problem easily, you have struck gold that day.

Website Help

Look for the words "Contact us" somewhere, usually at the bottom of a site page. Writes Stokes: "If, at any time, you see a customer service number, jot it down. Websites are notorious for concealing their contact numbers. For reasons of cost, most sites prefer all correspondence be by email."

Phone Tip

If you seek help over the phone, make sure your cell phone is fully charged before calling. Nothing worse than being cut off, after half an hour on the phone and right on the verge of a solution.

Note that phone numbers and websites change over the years.

My Help Source Preferences

For me, despite the preference order below, for each new problem, I decide anew which help source to pursue. And ninety percent of the time, the experience ends up being a major hassle. (That's the reason I decided to write this manual – to help myself and other non-Geek people solve problems without the aggravation, or at least that degree of it.)

It depends somewhat on the type of problem, but here's roughly the order of my preferred resources for help:

1. My own notes, i.e., this very manual. (Often I forget I already went thru a particular problem before, and I already have solution notes on it.)

   Also helpful: The book *Vista [or Windows 7] for Dummies* by Andy Rathbone. (Pretty comprehensive.) And *Is This Thing On?* by Abby Stokes (Very good basic explanations of the computer world, geared to people who have an aversion to computers.)
2. Question mark icon at upper right (seldom helpful, but sometimes good for a quick answer).
3. "eHow" website, under their "Computer" category (quite good with clarity of answers and percentage of times I get a solution, maybe 60%, which is very good).
4. Google search (requires hunting around, but good for odd problems).
5. Sony online help thru emailing (for me anyway, since I have a

Sony laptop).
6. Best Buy (the best "final resort" resource for sticky problems!)
7. Program manuals (if you can find one).
8. Microsoft phone or online help (my least favorite; decent help only maybe once in 25 tries).

1. HELP – USING THIS MANUAL – Obviously, for myself, I find referring to my own notes the most helpful for any old problems. I can get to topics quickly because I have everything alphabetical. For new problems, I go to the resources below.

2. HELP – USING THE QUESTION MARK ICON – Click on the question mark icon at the upper right (or press the F1 key, the keyboard equivalent of the question mark icon – gives exact same info) and that brings up a help window. When in Word, the question mark icon is for Word problems. When on the internet, the question mark is for Internet Explorer.

Type your topic or question into the search box and click the spyglass. That brings up related topics and info. (When you are not online, Word help still has info, but not as much as when online.)

I have had some luck typing words in and eventually getting some kind of answer, but usually it's just frustrating; They invariably have everything in the world, but the simple thing you need. You type in "Hide Toolbars," and it shows you how to hide everything you can think of... except toolbars. I typed in "hard space" and it gave me info on CDs! I typed in "Permanent Deletion" and it lists "Tabs" at the top and 7 other topics totally unrelated to deletions. I typed in "Battery" and it lists nothing! Ridiculous!

Every once in a while I find a decent answer.

Procedural tip

I find a good technique is to block the help text you find, and print it out, so you can refer to it right in front of you while working on the problem, without having to constantly go back to the help text on the screen.

Help from Programs

Whatever Windows program you are in, click on either the question mark icon or press the F1 key, and it brings up info on that program. I find Windows help on other programs better than its help on its Word program or its help on Internet Explorer.

Programs other than Windows ones often have a "Help" tab at top; click it, and maybe "Help Topics" and it should give you info on the left, including an Index tab. The Index tab will have a long list of topics; you can scroll down the list, click on one, click Display, and it will give you info on that topic. Of course, many times that long list includes everything but the one simple thing you're looking for!

Troubleshooting Feature

Start > Control Panel > System and Security > "Find and fix problems" > click on one of the green font categories > narrow your choices down, keep clicking buttons, and it tries to diagnose the problem and offers suggestions to fix it.

I haven't used this feature for any real problem yet. Might be somewhat hit or miss. I tried it for my printer (intentionally leaving it turned off, to see what kind of response I'd get), and it indicated instead that the printer was not my default printer. Not quite correct. But, this feature may be worth exploring.

3. HELP – USING "eHOW" WEBSITE

The website "eHow.com"> "Computers" category, can be quite helpful. Unlike Microsoft, when you type a topic into the eHow search box, the articles that come up are definitely related to your topic, most often right on the money, and contain succinct, clear, step-by-step answers.

On the list of articles that come up, the first 2 or 3 are articles from sponsored links. I usually skip those and check out the ones following, which are not trying to sell you something.

Checked other sites, but I usually just keep going in circles, getting nowhere. Almost every other help site was either impossible to navigate to any direct help (needed to sign up, choose a username, set up a password, jump thru hoops, etc., etc.), or you had to sign up and pay for help.

4. HELP – USING GOOGLE – One of the best ways to get help is simply to google your question or topic. I've seen Geek guys/gals do this if they are stumped. Most likely someone else on the internet has also had your specific problem. Of course you may have to search around quite a bit among sites to find a good answer.

5. HELP – SONY

When you're on the internet, to the right of the question mark, is a dropdown arrow. You can click Online Support there. But, it just gives you a Windows website predominantly trying to sell you stuff!

Instead, go to Start > "Help and Support" > Sony Vaio support (and I assume that if you have another brand of laptop, it should have a similar selection), where you can find, if you look hard enough, "Vaio Tutorials," which are actually pretty good. Basic procedures on a dozen features, like Windows Media Center, Windows Movie Maker, etc. You need to be online to access these. [To reach these tutorials thru Windows 7: Start > Help and Support > "Use my Vaio" > "What is new in Windows 7", "Windows 7 Tutorials".]

Also under "Help and Support," you can find the Sony User Guide, basic info for computer operations.

Sony and Windows material is intermixed here; there's Sony information under "Windows Help and Support" and Windows information under Sony headings.

Sony Help

Phone: 1 888 476-6970. VAIO – 1 888 476-6972; 11-8 EST M-Sa. Or, 1-239-768-7669. Sony Camcorder: 1 800 222-7669

Online: "esupport.sony.com," for online tech support > Contact support > Tech Support > Computers – Vaio > email box, fill out email form to send the problem to them. Include the error message. At support.sony.com/LMI you can do a setup that allows them to see your screen, helping them solve the problem. That worked nicely for me a couple of times.

6. HELP – BEST BUY STORE "GEEK SQUAD" – Nothing is 100%, and you may have to pay, but, I find your best bet for sticky problems, or even basic ones, is Best Buy. Call them, ask for the Geek Squad, tell them your problem, and ask what you should do. They are there primarily to help solve problems, as opposed to websites, especially Microsoft, who are there to sell you more stuff.

Phone: 1 800 433-5778 (I 800 GEEK SQU/AD) Takes a while, but eventually you can get to talk to a human.

Paid advice over phone: 1 888 274-4335. ($2/min)

Best Buy (Salem, NH): 1 603 890-9002.

Hour Help Sessions

You can have a GEEK person come out to your place for $159/hour. Costs, but it can be very helpful. Save up a bunch of questions and have them typed out, and prioritized, ahead of time, so you don't forget anything. Expect only a percentage of questions answered satisfactorily, but I think anything over 60%, especially on your big questions, makes it well worth it. (I also have a tape recorder going, with the person's permission, so I can check back on a procedure. It's so easy to forget some of the key steps the Geek person told you.)

Yearly Tech Support Contract

They have a yearly support contract (direct help at store, as well as email and phone help) that costs $100 for the year. I have it; well worth it, ONCE you've finally navigated your way to a human being.

To Get Geek Squad Help, under Your Support Contract:

Not as easy as one would think. There's the tendency to go around in circles getting you nowhere. (Click "Chat with an agent" at top of page, it sends you only to the bottom of the page, where you click "Chat with an agent" and it sends you back to the top of the page! The site advises a phone number, the phone number advises the site. Etc.) And, you're kinda steered towards buying a support contract, which you already have!

But, this is how to do it:

Google "Geeksquad.com/chat-with-an-agent" (click on the "Chat with an agent - Geek Squad - Geek Squad" site) > under "How We Can Help," click "Computers" at right > dropdown arrow, pick "pc/mac" > yes, that you already have one of those "protection plans" > Continue (wait as it establishes the connection > enter name, password, phone number, uncheck notify of discounts > need to scroll down a bit to get "Already a member", "Sign In Here" (Or, once signed in, the typing dialogue box with agent welcoming you, opens up directly) > Start Session Now (didn't need my orange Tech Support card number, though originally I think I did; number starts with SPA) > Typing dialogue box shows with agent welcoming message > Start typing your question (or, better, type the question beforehand, copy it, and just paste it in at this point) > click the orange arrow to send it > shows "agent typing" and soon his or her text shows up there > then you type in your response, and you go back and forth like that, till you get the issue resolved.

If you want to just regular-email an agent (as opposed to the above "live" email "chat-with-an-agent") to resolve a problem, after you click "Continue" in the procedure above, the bottom lists "Featured agents" > click on the agent's name > then on the left, click on Leave Message > type in your question > Send.

That worked pretty well once for me. May take a day or two as you email back and forth, and I needed to remember that my login name is my email address and my password is my usual one; but this help source is a good "go-to" one.

Phone – Chat with an Agent

I had a bunch of questions, but every time I tried to use the Best Buy "Chat with an agent" feature, I kept getting a "Technical difficulties" message. Decided to go to Best Buy store in person for help.

You present your orange "tech support" card, and they help you right at the counter. Key is going during off hours (weekday days, not weekends) so you don't have to wait in line. They don't have appointments (unless you pay for a session); it's first come first served. And they may well be backed up. For example, if I wanted to have a program installed, I may have to leave my computer for a couple of days.

Was worried at first, but with no line that afternoon, Geek gal spent 35 minutes with me, and I got pretty much all my questions answered satisfactorily! She was very helpful, knowledgeable. In my experience, Best Buy Geek people tend to get you the answers quickly and understand the problems, whereas other help sources tend to send you in circles.

Turns out the "technical difficulties" message came up because I needed to use 32-bit, not 64-bit Internet Explorer. Once we did switch, the "Chat with an agent" feature worked fine.

I also realized a mistake I had been making when I wanted to watch Yahoo sports clips, which would only work on 32-bit Internet Explorer. I knew how to get 32-bit by just clicking on "Internet Explorer", instead of "Internet Explorer (64-bit)" (under Start, All Programs), but it would switch to 32-bit just for that time, and then revert back to 64-bit subsequently. No wonder: I would click on my Internet Explorer icon on the desktop for next time, and forget that that shortcut icon was the 64-bit one! I deleted that icon and right-clicked the 32-bit Internet program and sent that one to the desktop as a shortcut. Now when I click on the icon, it's the 32-bit program, and most video clips play for me.

"Chat" needed Adobe Flash, which only works in 32-bit. Geek gal said most people at this point still use the 32-bit one, because a lot of stuff, like Adobe Flash, won't run on 64-bit program, yet.

7. HELP – MICROSOFT

Help – Online

Microsoft's Help on Vista's built-in help program, is not as up-to-date as online help. AR says the built-in help database was frozen in 2006.

You can click Start > "Help and Support" at right > dropdown arrow at Ask Options > Settings > check Online Help > OK. Then in the window you're already in, click, "Windows Help and How-to." I don't like this route. My usual experience is that I get nowhere. But I suppose it can be useful.

Another Microsoft help route: support.microsoft.com. MS Help and Support site > Self Help > Search the Knowledge Base, For: type in problem > Search. This might be helpful. You have to give them your name, your OS (operating system), which for me is Windows Vista, your version of Vista (mine, and I think most people's, is Windows Vista Home Premium). I got some free help here once or twice, but the last time I tried it, it was no longer free, but $59/hr.

I think free service is no longer available, unless you bought VISTA separate from your computer. A few times in the past I got through and got free emailed help, but that no longer seems available.

"AskMicrosoftSupportNow" site – No. Costs money. Although, if you're desperate, it might be worth it to you.

This URL was helpful once: windowshelp.micro-soft.com/Windows/en-US/ techsupport.

Update May 2011

Got some reasonable email help here at: http://www.supportspace.com (877) 551-9924.

I think this is Microsoft tech support. (I asked about the auto tab (indent) feature for first lines of new paragraphs. They referred to a specific MS support link on the subject (rather than simply giving me an answer.) But, I was able to figure out the answer from there.

They send you a password, for future interactions with them "for your SupportSpace account."

Windows 7

I googled "Windows 7 help" and got the site "Windows 7 Help and How-to – MS." They offer help IF you bought your Windows 7 separately from your computer. But if it came already installed in your computer, they tell you to check with your manufacturer. (I guess MS made a deal with computer companies, that if people got Windows 7 free with the computer, then that company has to deal with questions rather than MS.)

In my case, it's Sony, so I clicked on the word "Sony" there > eSupport at bottom > Contact support > Product support > Product: Computer Notebook > Email, email your question > filled out info > wrote question and submitted it.

Typically they read your email superficially and give you links to the same MS help page you just read and already found useless before you emailed! So you have to keep the email dialogue going for a few days to get any satisfaction. But, I have gotten answers this way.

Microsoft Phone Help

Main support number: 1 866 452-4755. Monday through Friday – 5:00 am - 9:00 pm Pacific, Saturday and Sunday, 6:00 am - 3:00 pm Pacific. Another number: 1 866 612-2310. Also 1 800 696-5700. I think 887-696-7786 is their store number.

Vista Help – 1 800 936-5700 (no charge) Another number: 1 877 316-0736.

It's a guessing game as to which number is most helpful. (Or, should I say "least unhelpful"?) Also it seems numbers change over time. But, usually if you try one number, they will direct you to a better number for your problem. I once was sent thru about 5 different numbers to finally reach the ultimate "expert"... who ended up referring me to the website page I originally got nowhere with before I made the first call!! Is it any wonder I hate Bill Gates' guts?

Survey Response

At one point I filled out an online survey on their phone help and wrote: "You just don't get it! Voice response systems rot! We want to talk to a human being, not machines! And even then we don't want to answer ten questions before we can even ask our question! Stop gathering useless marketing info from us, and answer our questions right off the bat. And do something about that horrible, broken up music when we're on hold. We're already frustrated. Don't add to our frustration!"

8. HELP – MANUALS – Manuals can be helpful, if there is one and you can find it. Many programs do have a manual. Go to Start > All Programs > click on the program folder and usually under that folder they have a manual listed to click onto. (Or, open the program and start looking for a manual somewhere – maybe under the question mark icon, or Help tab.) Once on a manual, I use the word search feature at top to find the topic, if the table of contents is not specific enough.

My Sony manual is listed under All Programs as "Vaio Manual." Sometimes programs use the word "Guide." My Canon camera manual is under Canon Utilities > DCSD Software Guide." Other times, like for Windows there is no manual per se, just information on how to do stuff in programs: Start > All Programs > click on the program and then click the question mark icon at upper right. Check the topics they offer or type your topic into the search box, and good luck.

Some manuals you can find on the internet by entering the program name and the word "manual" in your search engine search box. But, typically, the search is harder than what one would think. I typed in "Window Media Player manual", and I got a site called "Windows Media Player Manual," but it was a monkey trying to sell me red underwear... well, not exactly that, but that's how equally and utterly irrelevant the material there was.

These days I think that physical manuals are rarely provided; they are either found under the program in your computer, or online.

HELP – "VIDEO PROFESSOR" (AD ON TV) – Has tutorial how-to disks on all kinds of programs.

Update 8/09: Ho ho! Slimeball! He sounds sincere, but it's a scam! Or at least a deceptive offer. He offers a disk free, you fill out the form, but if you happen to skip the "How it works" info (which I ALMOST did), they'll get you. You think you're getting a free instruction disk for only S&H of $8 or so. But no. You get three disks, which are a free trial, for a number of days. But if you don't return them in time, you owe $190! That's what the three cost.

Not sure I got all the details right, but basically I am sure it's a ruse to pull you in without your knowing exactly what you're getting into, namely that you have to return the stuff in time or else you owe $190, which is a lot more than $8.

HIBERNATION – See "SLEEP MODE" and "COMPUTER ON / OFF – SIMPLIFY"

HIDDEN FILES – SHOW – I'm not even sure what "hidden files" consist of. Temporary files, "rescued" files, I guess. By default, hidden files are hidden. If you want them shown: Double-click Computer > Tools at top left > Folder Options > View tab > Show Hidden Files > Apply, OK. I don't know if it makes much difference. As usual, it you click the "Restore Defaults," you'll be fine.

HIGHLIGHTING (BLOCKING) – Highlighting (or "blocking") means selecting a text, or some chunk of material, in order to make some adjustment to it, like changing the font, the typestyle, the size, the color, etc.

See "BLOCKING"

"Highlighting" – Double-Meaning

Note that the term "highlighting" can refer to either blocking a text, or, shading a text. See immediately below.

HIGHLIGHTING (SHADING) – Highlighting is the crayon icon in the Font box at top and has only 15 color choices; shading is the paint can icon in the paragraph box at top, and you have many more color choices. Because it has more color choices and shades, I usually use Shading.

To do either: Block text you want highlighted, click on the icon, choose your color.

The highlighting and shading functions are pretty much the same thing, except that highlighting covers only the text you block, whereas shading can color a whole line or whole paragraph, including the space right out to the right-hand margin.

But you can also use shading to cover just the text blocked, and not all the way out to the right margin, by stopping your blocked section at the exact end of the text desired, rather than one spot past that, which blocks the whole line to the end.

See also "COLORS"

Shading Refuses to be Deleted

If you have several paragraphs shaded, often the shading refuses to be deleted. What you need to do is delete the shading paragraph by paragraph, taking care to block only that paragraph and then backspace that block by one spot. Then it should delete OK. Unblocking that final space beyond the end of the last character of the paragraph, is a key factor.

HISTORY – WEBSITES – See "BROWSING HISTORY"

HOME PAGE – Your home page is the website that immediately opens up when you click on Internet Explorer (or whatever browser you have). Logically, it seems to me that you would want your home page website to be the one that carries your email. So, for me, since I have Yahoo carrying my email, I have "Yahoo.com" as my home page. And, since I prefer Google as a default search engine to Yahoo, I keep Google as a Favorite on the toolbar at top (the one with the yellow star and green arrow at the left).

To select a home page: Go to the website you prefer > click the dropdown arrow of the Home icon at top right (the house) > "Add or change home page" > "Use this webpage as your only home page" > Yes. By this same route, you can also add more home pages, but I prefer to keep one home page and put others I visit a lot under Favorites (see "FAVORITES – WEBSITES").

When a website refers to its home page, it means its initial page, or home base, from which you can navigate to sub-categories. Like Walmart has a home page, from which you can go to its electronics dept., its household dept., etc. If you get lost in a website, look for "Home" somewhere, click that, and you return to its initial home page.

HORIZONTAL LINE – You can quickly get a horizontal line going across the page at the spot of your cursor: Home tab > Paragraph box > dropdown arrow of the "border" icon at the lower right > click on "Horizontal Line" (located towards the bottom of the list).

HTML – Hyper Text Markup Language. This is the computer language (behind the scenes) that marks up a web page, providing instructions for how it should look. It's like embedded instructions. Your web browser reads the HTML documents and interprets the info, for how to display the web page to you.

HYPHENATION – The automatic hyphenation feature of modern computers is a great feature. I remember the old days when I would have to look up in the dictionary every word I wanted to hyphenate, to make sure I was hyphenating at the right letter! That used to be such an annoying time-waster for me!

Also, computer hyphens today are *"soft"* – if you add words to your text and the hyphenated word is no longer at the end of that line, the hyphen will automatically disappear. (Unlike my old word processor, which often kept the hyphen embedded even though the word was now in the middle of the line.)

I believe automatic hyphenation is on as the default position, but if you see it is not (you don't see any words hyphenated), this is how you turn it on:

Page Layout tab at top > Page Setup box > Hyphenation > click "Automatic."

Further Hyphenation Options

Click Hyphenation, Hyphenation Options for more detailed features. I like to have:

– "Automatically Hyphenate Document" checked. (I think this gets checked automatically once you've already clicked "Automatic.")

– "Hyphenate Capitalized Words" checked. (If I find I don't like a capitalized word – someone's name, a state – hyphenated, I can adjust it manually later.)

– The hyphenation zone at .25. A smaller zone means, slightly more text on a line (saving space), less space between words, but more hyphens overall. A bigger zone means, less text on a line, more space between words, but less hyphens overall, since it will hyphenate only longish words.

I like .25, a happy medium. Usually means I save space, don't get too many hyphens, and usually do not get a single letter hyphenated from the rest of a word and put by itself on a separate line.

Not sure of this, but I think a one-inch zone order means that the computer will hyphenate at the first syllable it can within that last inch; a .25 inch order means that the computer will wait to reach the last .25 of an inch to hyphenate (unless there are no syllables to separate within the small range, and then it hyphenates at the nearest spot it can before that).

– I select the consecutive hyphens at "1". Having hyphens at the end of two consecutive lines doesn't look that great, I think, for any formal presentation.

Click OK after your selections. Sometimes, using the hyphenation feature can save a few lines and get a 10-plus page document to fit on 10 pages.

Hyphenation Not Available

Occasionally I get a message that hyphenation is not available for a particular document. Yet, when I check, the hyphenation is fine. Haven't figured this out yet.

A "Hard" Hyphen

If, for some reason, you want a hyphen to stay in a particular word, press CTRL+Shift+hyphen. Now the hyphen will act as a "hard" hyphen, and stay there.

Keeping a Word UN-Hyphenated

If the automatic hyphenation hyphenates a word you don't want hyphenated, like a person's name, you can correct that by placing the cursor right before, or after, the word, pressing the Shift key down, and pressing Enter. That forces the line to end at the spot you hit Enter, instead of putting any hyphen in.

And, if you are typing justified text, it makes that line justify at the point where your cursor was.

"I" – THE LETTER – The letter "I" gets capitalized automatically if typed by itself. It jumps to a capital "I" as soon as you press the spacebar after it. To get a small "I" by itself (for example, if you want to type the Roman numeral "i"), type the i, hit the space bar, then do CTRL+Z once, and that will put the now capital "I" back down to a non-cap letter.

Within a grid table, an "I" jumps up into caps sometimes even if you only move the cursor through it later on.

ICONS – Computer "icons" are small "pushbutton" pictures or symbols that represent any number of things – a file, an application, a program, a device, etc. For example, on your desktop, the trash bin represents your Recycle Bin; a musical note represents the iTunes program, etc. In the Word program, at the top in the Font box, the "U" icon represents the underlining function; in the Paragraph box, the paint can icon represents the shading function, etc.

Double left-click on an icon and the item opens up for you to use. Think of icons as opening buttons.

ICONS – IDENTIFYING WHAT THEY REPRESENT – Almost all icons that represent functions, will have an explanation pop up, if you have the pointer hover over them. For example, if you place the pointer over the underlined A in the Font box, it will show "Font Color".

ICONS – MIGRATING – See "MIGRATING ICONS" for what to do with icons that move on their own on your desktop.

ICONS ON DESKTOP – DISAPPEARED – If icons suddenly disappear from the desktop (Vista trying to be too helpful, "clearing up" things), then, to get the icons back: Right click on empty section of desktop > View > Show Desktop Icons.

IM – INSTANT MESSAGING – A women from Match.com invited me to IM, which is like live emailing, or texting; you write stuff back and forth, in real time. It's very fast-paced, kind of "stream of consciousness" communication. You don't have time to think things thru. Don't really like it. Also, it sucks you in. To do it, you have to keep doing it, and hang around your computer. My overall feeling was that it tends to entrap you into endless trivia.

Here's a bunch of info on how to get on it. This is very garbled; I just jotted down notes as I went. It may not be too helpful; it's not a clear step-by-step process I went thru; I just kept going places and, hooray, ended up actually doing IM.

Google "messenger.yahoo.com", Download Now, Download Now, Run, Run, Continue, have everything checked, Next, check "Yes" box, Next, Install, wait 5 minutes as it installs, Finish. Then I went all over the place – typical computer stuff; it bombards you with one feature after another, but doesn't show or tell you how to do the basic thing you need to do – IM messaging.

Home, More Information, watched video demo... "Yahoo! Messenger" clicked on it to establish my Yahoo ID and password... turned out I needed to use my Yahoo email ID and password... New Viewer... on Messenger Home Page... Start Adding friends... Address Book, Continue, Next... the lady had given me her IM name, so I entered that into the search box above "Address Book," clicked on the new window at right, Add User, Next, Next, and boom, I got a message from her – "Hooray, you made it!"

We are now happily married... just kidding. She's going to call me tonight, and when she finds out how much I do not believe in astrology, things will go downhill from there. Ha ha. It's happened to me before.

Got rid of the Yahoo IM program after a couple of days. I detest this kind of stuff, absolutely detest it: automatic stuff popping up, demanding my attention when I'm trying to do something else. Hate it! I'm trying to do something that's important to me and I'm forced to interrupt my progress to learn that somebody I hardly know just finished brushing his teeth, or forced to decline some additional feature being offered.

IMAGES NOT SHOWING – SHOWS RED "X" – I forget the details, but at one point, messing with the computer settings, I suddenly lost images and had red "x's" instead.

To fix it, this is what I did (after googling "Enabling Java Script," which apparently is what is needed): While on the internet, Tools > Internet Options > Security tab > Custom Level > scroll way down to "Scripting" > under Active Scripting, select Enable > OK. Now I got my Yahoo maps back instead of red x's. Hooray.

INDENTING – Indenting moves a whole paragraph to the right or left. Place the cursor inside a paragraph > Home tab > Paragraph box > click on one of the top middle icons – "Increase Indent" or "Decrease Indent" if you want to get it back to where it was if you don't like the distance it indented (which is just a little bit each click).

To get exact indents on left side, right side, or both sides: Click the dropdown arrow at the lower right of the box > Indents and Spacing tab > and set the exact distance you want, for both left and right > click OK.

> In books that quote a long passage from another book, the text is usually indented both left side and right side, like this very paragraph is.

If you pick a minus number for Indentation, right or left, it allows you to type beyond the margin limits, like these very three lines (–.2 for both left and right.)

Indents of Scanned or Internet Material

A lot of problems come from scanned in, or internet, material. You most likely are importing odd embedded indents. After you get the material into a Word document, CTRL+A it, and then set your indents to what you want, usually "0" at both left and right.

I once had a text coming out ONE letter per line. Turns out I had accidentally ordered a huge right indent (7 instead of .7).

INDEX – UPDATING THE START SEARCH BOX – One of the most useful functions under Start is its search box. However, its index of files deteriorates over time, and you need to rebuild (refresh, update) it to make it work more accurately:

Start > Control Panel > System Maintenance (or Indexing Options if it has that) [W7 – Couldn't find it, but typing "Indexing Options" into the Start search box brought it up, to click on] > Advanced > Rebuild > OK. Takes a while. Good to do overnight. Mine took a few hours. It shows progress at top with number of "Items Indexed." When it's done, it shows "Indexing complete." For me, it DID seem work better after updating. I typed the word "whoops" into the search box and it showed every document in which I had that word.

INK CARTRIDGES – Be aware that this is where the printer companies drain money from you, big time. They keep the printers fairly cheap, because they know once you've bought one, they're guaranteed a steady income from you, for the next few years, as you keep buying replacement ink cartridges.

Prices

My Epson black cartridges cost about $19 each; the five-color pack, about $84.

I tried recycled cartridges at one point from some website, to save money, but they did not work well at all. The copy came out lousy, not clean at all. Returned them; got my money back.

I checked ordering new ones from an internet site, to save money. Not worth it. Price was no better than at Staples, plus you have the shipping and handling cost.

I've found prices to be quite fluid. A good plan is to check 1) Staples, 2) the website of the company that makes your printer, to order directly, and 3) Amazon.com. Then go for the best price. I usually settle for Staples. There's one close to where I live, and I like getting them right away, instead of waiting for them in the mail.

Staples gives you $3 credit for each empty cartridge you turn in. Can't use the credit right away; the credit goes into your "rewards" account, and then, a couple times a year you get a check in the mail.

Ink Low

Don't try to squeeze as much ink out the cartridges as you can; it's bad for something, I read. Replace a cartridge as soon as you know it's quite low. Most printers automatically have something pop up to tell you you're low. I usually go just a few pages more. If a printer does not tell you when ink is low, you can tell as soon as yellow starts to become white and red, pinkish.

Keep your printer off when you are not using it. Not that it uses much electricity, but its heat tends to dry out the ink cartridges sooner, I read.

Brands

I like to stick to the major brands of printers, so that replacement cartridges are easy to get at my local Staples. Hewett-Packard and Epson are the two printer brands I've owned, and Staples always has a selection of their ink cartridges.

When you switch brands or even models of printers, you may well be stuck with $100 of new cartridges that you can no longer use. My old Epson "78" ink cartridges don't work in my new Epson 810 printer. Called Epson, asked what to do with my unused cartridges. They didn't say, but offered to send me two free ones, which was nice.

Anyway, brought the unused ones to Staples. For partially used ones, and still unopened ones, the only thing they have is the rewards program of $3 dollars credit for them, whether empty, partially full, or still new. Oh well. Better than nothing.

Different printers have different procedures to install new cartridges. See "Printers."

INK CARTRIDGES – SAVING INK TIPS – Read in *Consumer Reports* that Arial font uses more ink than Times New Roman or other fonts; so to save ink, don't use Arial. Me, I'm going with "Arial Narrow" more often now, to save a bit on ink and paper. (A 125 page document in Times New Roman, was only 116 pages in Arial Narrow, for me.)

Also, of course, for printing out text you're working on, use the draft mode of printing. With the Epson printer, at first I didn't like the look of it – kind of a light brown. But, I very quickly got used to it; and it's fine, no problem to read. Plus, besides saving ink, it prints much faster under "Draft" mode.

Another thing you can do to save ink is to lessen the ink density. See "INK VOLUME" below.

Best Technique for Me

One good way around the dilemma of constant expensive cartridge replacement is something that just gradually evolved for me. I've written several books in my life and I have always preferred to work on rough drafts by writing them out long hand, typing them into a Word document, printing that out, revising it, then typing the changes in, then printing that out, and so on. But gradually over the years I find myself doing more and more of my editing strictly on the computer, without printing material out, until my final draft.

So I've cut down on my ink usage quite a bit this way. And now I even write first drafts directly into the computer, whereas I used to always write a first draft long hand. Many people of my generation feel they think better when writing long hand. But, I've found that making a gradual transition to "writing" directly into the computer and doing all my revisions there also, to be quite feasible.

And, of course, you also save paper, as well as time.

INK SMUDGE – If you grab the page right as it is coming out of the printer, you might smudge the ink. Wait a few seconds, or grab it carefully by the edges. Also, if you're printing a two sided sheet with heavy ink coverage, allow the first side some drying time first.

INK VOLUME – Most printers will allow you to change the ink density (beyond the Draft and Regular modes), usually under "Properties." With my Epson 810 – CTRL+P > Properties > Page Layout tab > Auto > Adjust Print Density > slide the marker to the left.

INSERTING – You can insert many different things into your text, by using the Insert tab at the top. Most common for me is inserting page numbers, symbols, and tables.

A very common procedure for me is to insert part of a document into another document, like information on fire-making into a bigger document on wilderness survival. Block the text you want to move, CTRL+C, open the document you want to insert it into, CTRL+V it at the chosen spot.

Inserting Date and Time

If you click on "Date & Time" in the Text box under the Insert tab, it inserts the current date and time (your choice of "available formats") wherever your cursor is.

INSTALL OR UNINSTALL A PROGRAM

Uninstalling a Program

Uninstalling what you already have is fairly easy: Start > Control Panel > Programs > Programs and Features > Uninstall a program > go down your list, highlight the program > click "Uninstall" at top. Does it pretty quickly.

Installing a Program

You install a program usually from a CD, or from the internet. As soon as you insert the CD (the "software" program you bought), it automatically runs and tells you how to proceed. Likewise in installing a program from the internet: once you click on the "Download" button on the website, and then "Run," it will tell you how to proceed. It usually involves "Next," "Agree," etc., etc.

If you have your computer set for automatic Sleep mode after, say, ten minutes, you need to temporarily get rid of that, because when it goes to Sleep mode, it stops the installation. Start > Control Panel > System and Security > Power Options > "Change when the computer sleeps" at left > click dropdown arrow > select "Never" > Save. Then, when you're finished downloading, you can reset it to your usual 10 minutes or whatever.

Sometimes it all goes smoothly; other times it does not. I give two examples below that did not go smoothly.

If a CD program does not automatically begin telling you to how install it, click (I think) Computer > open up the CD > browse it for its setup file, usually called Setup.exe or Install.exe., and proceed from there. Or, call the company and ask them to guide you thru the installation. Help over the phone is often not free, but installation help invariably is free.

(Keep in mind that if you've downloaded a program from the internet, that does not mean it is installed. For some programs, the downloading and installation are one operation, but for most, you need to download it, and THEN install it.)

If you downloaded the program from the internet, this is the route to follow to get it installed, or so I've read: Click on any folder > click on Downloads (at left in navigation pane, in the first bunch) > double-click the downloaded program to install it.

See also "DOWNLOAD" for discussion of "Run" versus "Save." What I do is click "Save" so that I have it permanently, but I make sure somewhere along the line I also click "Run" so that it installs and runs, and I can see it in operation.

SAMPLE DIFFICULT INSTALLATION OF A PROGRAM

I bought an OCR program (Optical Character Recognition – instead of scanning in a typed document as a set picture of it, it reads the actual letters and scans it in as text you can edit). Used to use it a lot. Haven't used it for a few years since I got a new printer that does not have a scanning function. Now that I have a newer printer, with a scanning function, I wanted to use it again.

I uninstalled the OCR program first, because I wanted to document exactly how to install it. Uninstalling it is fairly simple to do, except of course in the computer world there's always something. In this case I couldn't find this program under Start, All Programs list, at first. Turns out its name is not "OmniPage 15" as its desktop icon is labeled, but "ScanSoft OmniPage 15." So I found it in a different spot in the list.

Installation of "OmniPage 15" – an OCR program

1. Turn off any other programs running
2. Insert the CD
3. Didn't start automatically; showed "AutoPlay" window
4. Click "Open folder to view files"
5. It showed one file icon
6. Double-clicked on that to open it
7. WinZip Self-Extractor, OK
8. Unzip. ("Overwrite files without prompting" and "When done unzipping open /Autorun.exe.") Took several minutes.
9. English
10. Start Installation
11. Next
12. Check "I accept," Next
13. Typed in my name

14. Required my 18-digit serial number. Of what?! Not the OCR CD (the two numbers there are not 18 digits long), not Vista, not my laptop. I tried about 8 of them; none of them are 18 digits; they're all shorter or longer! Gave them a call. Could not reach a human being, except on a different number (1 800 654-11870), and then was waiting for a long time. Went to their website in the meantime (Nuance.com/support). And managed to get the info I needed:

a. Had to create an account for myself, otherwise, it says you cannot contact them!

b. Did that, getting an email which had a spot to click to Activate the account.

c. Did that, and hooray, it showed me the one product I had registered, my OCR CD, with its serial number, of the correct number of digits. That number is apparently registered with them and not on the package or CD. I think they are very strict about anyone using their stuff free. I vaguely remember that odd letter/number serial number when I registered it years ago.

15. Filled in the serial number, Next
16. Complete, Next
17. Install, took about 5 minutes
18. Finish
19. Success! OmniPage icon appeared on Desktop, and it works!

More Sample Installations

See "PRINTERS – INSTALLING" > "EXAMPLES OF PRINTER IN-

STALLATIONS" > "Setting Up Epson Artisan 810 Printer" for another detailed example of installing a program, this time the program for a new printer.

Also, for all the ones (11 of them) I had to install when I got a new computer, see "COMPUTER – GETTING A NEW COMPUTER" >"Installations" to see how those installations went.

See also "OCR" for adjustments when trying to connect this particular program to a new printer. I think normally a new printer makes no difference to a program, but in this case it did, because this is a scanning program and it involves the scanning capabilities of the specific printer you're using.

Recommendation

Installing is sometimes easy, sometimes a nightmare. Myself, I wanted to know how to do it, but generally I think it's much easier to simply pay Best Buy, or Staples, to do it for you. What else is your hard-earned money for, but to make your life a little easier, ay?

INTERNET – Extensive internet info is beyond the scope of this manual, but let me just mention a few key things:

1. Don't open any attachments to an email, unless you're sure it's from a source you know and trust.
2. Don't fall for any scams. You did not win any money. Be very wary of giving out any personal info, especially your social security number.
3. Navigating the internet, finding stuff, takes practice and experience. There's a tremendous tendency for it to send you in circles. Reminds me of a "Blazing Saddles" scene: *"The meeting is adjourned. Oh, I'm sorry Governor, you're supposed to say that." "Say what?" "The meeting is adjourned." "It is?" "No, you're supposed to say that." "Say what?" "The meeting is adjourned." "It is?" "No, you're supposed to say that." "Say what?" "The meeting is adjourned." "It is?"...*
4. Wikipedia is great: you can get the basic info you want, on any subject.

Closing A Website

Click red "x" at far upper right of screen.

No Response To Clicking an Icon

Sometimes nothing seems to happen, but actually a new tab (a pulsing salmon-colored one) appears at top. Click this and you get what you thought you should get from clicking the icon. Also, sometimes it takes the computer a good 5 seconds to respond.

Site Frozen

If a site gets frozen for no apparent reason, shutting everything down and starting over, usually makes things operational again. Also, every so often a site is "down" for a while. Go back to it later in the day, and usually it's back up.

INTERNET CAFÉ – A place that offers the public access to the internet. They usually charge by the amount of time you spend connected. They often provide snacks and drinks; hence the name café. Also called "hotspots."

I've never been to one, but I'm pretty sure, you can connect wirelessly. You get the name of their connection ("SSID") from them, and then, I think, click Start > Control Panel > Network and Internet > Network and Sharing Center > Set up a new connection of network > Connect to a network.

Note that most local libraries, at least in my area, offer public access to the internet, for free.

INTERNET – CONNECTING TO THE INTERNET – Each time I got home with a new computer, the internet was just there, under Internet Explorer icon. I think Best Buy makes sure you have it. I understand Windows finds the internet on its own. And, if it doesn't, you can go thru Start > Control Panel > Network and Internet > Connect to the internet. At some point, you have to enter your username and password. I don't know if these are something you already have or have to make up right then. Good luck.

Best bet is to ask the store selling you the computer what you have to do to get on the internet. As I said, I automatically had it as soon as I plugged the computer in. When Comcast, my ISP (Internet Service Provider), was at my apartment, they set up the wire, provided the modem, and had me ready to go.

Modem

You need a modem to transfer internet signals from the wall wire to your computer; the modem sits between the wall wire and your computer. I understand some computers have a built-in modem. See "MODEM" also, especially for buying your own, instead of renting one monthly from your ISP (Internet Service Provider).

INTERNET – COPYING MATERIAL FROM THE INTERNET

Usually, don't CTRL+A the article to copy it; because it will include everything on that site page. Better to block sections by the finger-scroll method and copy sections, then adjust stuff after you've landed it into a Word document.

A lot of stuff from the internet has embedded formatting, so it often takes a lot of work to fix it the way you want it. You delete a line and it deletes a whole section. You try to make double columns and it makes both columns contain identical text. Parts of lines drop out. Whole pages drop out. Etc., etc. So for internet stuff, sometimes, you have to simply print it as you got it, using more paper space than you'd like.

INTERNET EXPLORER – This is Microsoft's web browser. It comes free with Windows Vista or Windows 7. You click on its icon – a blue "e" – and it brings up the internet for you to browse. Their latest version (March 2011) is Windows Internet Explorer 9 (abbreviated as IE9).

Now, from MS's perspective, they are always looking to improve, add to, and simplify; hence the new versions. From my perspective, I am totally ripped every time they come up with something new, because it means things are now different and I have to go thru a whole process to learn the new setup! I absolutely hate it; it never ends.

I understand their perspective and I know there is a mountain of knowledge I do not have that technicians and engineers do have. I mean, just look at this Wikipedia basic description of IE9. I have no idea what they are talking about:

"Internet Explorer 9 supports several CSS 3 properties,[4] embedded ICC v2 or v4 color profiles support via Windows Color System, and has improved JavaScript performance. It also features hardware-accelerated graphics rendering using Direct2D, hardware-accelerated text rendering using DirectWrite, hardware-accelerated video rendering using Media Foun-

dation, imaging support provided by Windows Imaging Component, and high fidelity printing powered by the XPS print pipeline.[5] Internet Explorer 9 also supports the HTML5 video and audio tags and the Web Open Font Format."

I guess it means: Windows 7 shows pictures and video better.

Anyway, from a non-technical normal customer's perspective, here's the main issue that came up for me:

Homepage and Default Search Engine

Clicking on Internet Explorer opens up your default home page. It will be MSN (Microsoft). If you want to change that, bring up the company you want (for me, Yahoo.com, since I have my email with them) > in the middle at top is a Home icon, click on the dropdown arrow > click Add or Change Home Page > click "Use the webpage as your only home page", Yes. Now Internet Explorer will always open to this home page.

There should be the Microsoft default search box at upper right; their search engine is called "Bing". If you want a different default search engine, you click the dropdown arrow to the right of that box > "Find more providers" > click the one you want (I like Google) > "Add search provider" window comes up > check "Make this my default search provider" > Add.

However, this original Bing search box has disappeared for me, so I wasn't able to go thru the above procedure.

I used to have a setup I liked: Yahoo as my home page (so that when I clicked on Internet Explorer, my email opened up) and Google as my default search engine, with the Google search box at upper right on that same Yahoo page (I prefer Google to Yahoo, for searches). But, once I had downloaded Internet Explorer 9, that Google search box at right disappeared. I tried all kinds of things to get it back in the same setup. No luck.

In theory, you can set your default search engine by: Tools tab at upper right (or gear icon) > Internet Options > Programs tab > Manage add-ons > Search Provider (at left) > But Google was already my default engine and it was enabled. Bing and Ask Search (the Yahoo one?) were there also, and enabled > right-clicked on those two and removed them. No difference. Still getting Yahoo. And, next time I checked in this window, Bing was suddenly back in the list, though disabled.

Eventually, I managed to get a setup that's pretty close to what I had:

First, I made Yahoo my home page. There should be a spot ("Make Y! My Homepage") at the top center of the Yahoo home page which makes Yahoo your home page if you click it. Or, you can set it as your home page like this: Get on Yahoo site (or whichever site you want as your home page > Tools tab > Internet Options > General tab > Home page, Yahoo address shows in that box, click OK.

Then, I got the Google website up, and clicked the yellow star at upper left to put Google onto my Favorites list. Now, when I click on Internet Explorer, my computer opens up to Yahoo and my email as my homepage, and, I just need to click on Google on my Favorites bar to open a Google search box. Very close to my former setup.

("Google Chrome" incidentally, is, I think, an actual browser, like Internet Explorer, not a search engine for a browser.)

URL as the Search Box

The other significant change for IE9, is, by my understanding, that you can now use the URL address bar also as an internet search box. Well, it seemed to work sometimes, other times not, even after I had done this: Tools > Internet Options > General tab > Search defaults/settings > set Google as default, AND check "Search in the address bar" at lower left. So, I'm giving up on this; I don't want it; I don't need it; leave me alone!

Again the stupid Microsoft redundancy (more than one way to do something) intending to make things simpler, but instead causing confusion and aggravation.

Basic Icons to Use

I had never particularly noticed these icons before, but now with IE9 I find I use these three icons at upper right quite frequently: The house (home page), the star (favorites, feeds, and history), and the gear (tools). (Both the gear icon and the Tools tab have the same "Internet Options" category under them.)

Toolbars

I find it best to have all 4 internet toolbars up. Right-click on any empty spot on the toolbar area, and it will bring up a selection of the 4 toolbars. I checked them all on.

1. "Menu" bar is the second bar from top, with File, Edit, etc. options at left.

2. "Favorites" bar is the third bar from top, with Favorites at the left.

3. "Command" bar is the SAME third bar from top, with Page, Safety, Tools, etc. at the right.

4. "Status" bar is the second from bottom bar, just above the taskbar, and it simply gives you the "Change zoom level" option at the far right.

1↘
2&3↗

4→

INTERNET – FUNCTIONS

Internet – Search Box Help

If you start to type a word into the blank search box at upper right, it lists, just below the search box, the most recent websites visited that match the letters you've typed so far. Click on the one you want, and it puts it up into the box. Then click on it to open the site. Saves time on having to type the whole website name in.

Internet Website Browsing

As you visit various websites, you can go back to previous ones you visited in your current session, by clicking the "go back" (or "go forward") arrow at far upper left. Or, you can have the computer keep a tab of each site you visit across the top of your screen, and you can re-visit a site by clicking on its tab. See "TABBED WEBSITE BROWSING"

INTERNET - SERVERS – As a general point of knowledge, you should know that the internet, obviously, is not IN your computer, like your files are; internet info is stored at internet SERVERS, located all around the country. When you call up a website, it comes from those servers (or centers) – rooms with huge banks of computers, I think.

For example, your email is not in your computer, but stored in the Server's computers. You have to connect to the internet to access your email.

INTERNET - YOUR ACCOUNT – I get my internet thru Comcast. At one point, my fee went up $23 more per month, because I had been enjoying the introductory rate up to that point. KEY: Ask their rep on the phone if they have any other deals going. They often do. And are surprisingly quick to let you know about them, and sign you up. In this case, the best I could do is switch to their "economy" deal, which is $20 cheaper but slower in downloading. Still, saving $20 a month is well worth it.

Turns out the slower speed made little difference to me, except maybe when I download music, but I do that only every few months.

iPAD – This is a hand-held device, a tablet computer, that can be used wirelessly, thru local area networks. (Check with Best Buy for how it works.) You can get the internet. You can download all kinds of "apps" (applications) – books, movies, music, games, etc., etc. Its size falls between the smaller "smartphones" and the bigger laptops. Apple runs the whole thing, and you download, and pay, for apps thru Apple.

You control functions by touching the screen. It has a virtual (screen) keyboard rather than a separate physical one.

I think you can download what you want directly thru it, but I'm not sure. I don't have one. You may have to use your computer. Wikipedia says, *"The device is managed and synced by iTunes running on a personal computer via USB cable."*

iPad is by far the most popular of the tablet PCs. I think the iPad 2 can also take pictures and video.

****

iPOD - PORTABLE MUSIC PLAYER

OVERVIEW

For listening to music when you're out and about, it used to be Walkmans and portable CD players. Now it's iPods or MP3 players (iPod is a specific type of MP3 player). They are more compact. They hold many, many more songs. And you don't have to carry cassettes or disks with you; all your music is inside the device.

I finally bought an iPod, in March, 2011 – a (6th generation) iPod Nano ("nano" meaning very small), $180, 15 GB, about 2,000-2,500 songs capacity. The regular-sized ones have internet capability, but I just want music; I don't feel the need to be connected to the net all the time.

Phone help – 1 800 275-2273 ,1 800 692-7753. Internet help – "iPod Nano User Guide" / "iPod Touch User Guide".

The general procedure is this:

1. Get an iTunes account. You need a computer, and an iTunes account, to get songs onto the iPod.
2. Download desired songs to your iTunes account.
3. Attach iPod to computer USB port.
4. Set up automatic syncing or manual transfer option.
5. Do the transfer.
6. Listen to your songs on the iPod, thru earphones.

You have external On/Off and Volume buttons, but the rest of any navigation is done thru screen swipes and taps with your finger.

A neat step-by-step process to follow, is very difficult to establish, because there are so many side issues, concerns, and variations. But I'm pretty sure I have all the info you need below. You just have to have the persistence to work thru issues that come up; then, once you've got it, you'll feel it's been worth the trouble. It's like learning to drive. Maybe intimidating and confusing at first, but second nature once you're used to it.

It might be good to scan thru these notes first, to get an overall picture, but when you get down actually trying to get the thing to work, you should have your iPod in hand, so that you can see right in front of you what I'm talking about.

Also, different iPods may have different navigation controls, but, I think the two I own (I bought a regular iPod Touch also) are two of the most popular (and the latest as of late 2011), and have the controls common to most iPods.

The older "Classic" iPods have different controls, with a wheel. (I don't cover them.)

PRELIMINARY SETUP – iTUNES ACCOUNT

First problem was opening the package; there's a thin but strong ribbon of cellophane tape, which is very hard to see, that you have to peel off first. The thing itself (the "Nano" model) is very small, only 1½ inches square, like a Ritz cracker. Comes with a connection wire, and earphones.

To use an iPod, you must first have an iTunes account:

1. Though I have an iTunes account (see "iTUNES" under "MUSIC"), the instructions say to download the latest version of iTunes. So I googled "iTunes.com/download" as per instructions.
2. Clicked that site, clicked "Download Now"
3. Clicked Save, Save, waited (7-8 minutes) till showed "download complete"
4. Run, Run
5. Showed "Preparing to install"
6. Next (I assumed it was replacing my current version of iTunes)
7. Accept, Next
8. Install...? Needed to minimize the window to see the progress window underneath. Waited. Never said it was done, though the green was all the way to the right. Went back to it later, after 10 minutes and it was still installing, or doing it all over again, I don't know.
9. I connected the iPod to the computer. It showed "Installing device driver software."
10. AutoPlay window came up. Clicked on "Synchronize". "Applica-

tion not found" came up.
11. But then, after about 20 minutes, suddenly I get "Congratulations, iTunes has been successfully installed." I guess it just takes more time than I thought.
12. Finish, Restart.

I attached the iPod again and tried again to synchronize (transfer) songs that I keep on my computer. No luck. Figured I needed to register my iPod, so I tried to do that, but it kept saying I needed to fill out the entire form, which I DID. Maybe they needed the serial number, but I could not find it anywhere on the device.

And that's as far as I could get on my own, the day before a 3-hour adult education class on the iPod, which I had signed up for.

Now the class. Hah! What a nightmare! Exactly everything that's wrong with the computer world:

iPod Class

First of all, others were running into the same problem I had run into – we tried to register our iPods and it kept saying it needed full information, even though we were providing full info. Then, half a dozen different windows at different times would suddenly pop up, getting us nowhere. We would get run in circles. Windows would "time out" even though people were entering info without delay. One person was not allowed to access her iTunes account for the next 8 hours because she had tried too often. Sometimes it would do stuff on its own. Seemed that every half step in the right direction would raise several additional arbitrary obstacles or operations we needed to do. Sometimes you would finally get something to work, and then you did the exact same thing again, and then it wouldn't work. It would say click on the "XYZ" button, but there was no "XYZ" button! Etc., etc., etc.

I hate it! Would you like to access your account? Then please enter your password. Forget your password? Well, you need to access your account to get your password.... Huh? Would you like to enter a new password? Sorry that password doesn't work. Would you like to enter a new password? Yes, but you just asked me that and it didn't work! How many new passwords do I have now? Etc., etc., etc.

You would think it's easy: Just download the songs, attach your iPod to your computer, and transfer the songs! What could be easier? Hah! I'll answer that with another question – if it's that easy, then why is the online manual for my iPod 81 pages long!? (You can access manuals at apple.com/support/ipodnano. With the actual device you get only a tiny leaflet of basic instructions, which are not bad, assuming you can read 5-point size text.)

Anyway, by the end of the three hours I think I got the key operations figured out. You would think it's easy, but, as usual, you need to know a bunch of arbitrary things without which, you get nowhere:

FACTORS YOU NEED TO KNOW

– On the back of this particular model iPod is a clip for attaching to clothing. At first I couldn't get it to work. Turns out it's not a clip like a paper clip; it's a clip like a clipboard clamp. You need to squeeze it open, not slide it on!

– You need to peel off the cellophane icon picture covering your screen. I tried to at first but it seemed that that was the actual screen. Turns out it wasn't. Finally found an edge of the cellophane sticker, and peeled it off.

– Instructor didn't know why it wouldn't let us register our iPods, but one student suggested clicking "Register later" and that allowed us to go ahead. (Turns out the next day when I tried it again, it did let me register. I didn't change anything. I guess their website was temporarily not working. That happens. Confirmed by iPod guy over phone; that does happen.

– You need a computer. iPod is designed to go with the iTunes program, so you need an iTunes account on your computer, to download the songs. You do any editing for partial songs, song order, and song groupings (playlists) on your iTunes account on your computer first. Then you transfer the songs into your iPod.

– You can import non-iTunes songs, from old CDs for example, by first importing those songs into iTunes. See "To Add Non-iTunes Songs To Your itunes Library" below.

– Simply attaching your iPod to your computer, while in iTunes, brings up a "Devices" category at middle left, indicating your iPod. It may take 5-10 seconds to pop up, sometimes even longer.

– Click right on the name of your device, to bring up what is on the iPod. Since I just do music at this point, I click on just "Music." Note the distinction between the "Music" list here in the middle left of the page – showing what's on the iPod – compared to the "Music" list at the top of the page – showing what's in your iTunes library.

– Whenever you disconnect your iPod, you need to FIRST click the eject icon to the right of "Devices." Then you pull the wire out of the iPod, or the other end of it out of the USB port. The "Devices" category then disappears from your iTunes window.

– To get "Devices" back up, just plug it back in. "Devices" shows up 5-10 seconds later. And, if you've just rebooted your computer, it may take a good 15-20 seconds before it shows up.

– When attaching earphones, makes sure the plug goes ALL the way in. Need to force it in a bit.

– The connecting wire (iPod to computer) has a rectangular mark on the side that goes up as the iPod screen faces you. The wire only goes in one way, not the other. (It's just like the other end that connects to your computer USB port; you need the "trident" symbol up; it doesn't go in the other way.)

– The serial number is not on the actual iPod, but once you connect it, the serial number automatically shows under the "Summary" tab, in the window that opens up after you click the name of your device under "Devices."

– Need to practice at swiping and tapping, to get used to navigating the icons and choices. For me, it will usually be just songs and spoken books. If a song name is long, swipe it left and it moves to show the full name.

– Playlists are set lists of songs. I think of a playlist as equivalent to a CD – a set bunch of songs.

– Song and Playlist Organization:

Under the "Songs" icon (ALL your songs, hundreds or thousands), the songs get listed automatically in alphabetical order.

Under the "Playlist" icon, your playlists are listed alphabetically also, but the songs inside those playlists get played in the set order you arranged them in originally under iTunes.

Under the Artists icon, the artists are listed alphabetically, but the songs under the artists seem to be just randomly ordered, oddly enough, neither alphabetical nor chronological.

So, for me, to keep playlists in the same numerical order matching my CD disks list, I simply need to name my playlists "Disk 1", "Disk 2", etc. to keep them in the same order, with this exception: I need to name "Disk 1" "Disk 01", and likewise for the other single-digit disks, otherwise, "Disk 10" will show up in front of "Disk 2".

Obviously, you want to organize your songs within "Playlists" so you can navigate to particular songs more efficiently than scrolling thru thousands of individual songs. I plan on following a simple "Disk 01" thru "Disk 73" organization, just as my music is currently situated on CDs, so-named "1" thru "73", each with 25-35 songs per disk.

Note that if you scroll for a song under Songs, or an artist under Artists, there is a small alphabet going down the right of the screen, so you can tap one of the letters there to navigate more quickly. Also, artists are listed alphabetically, by first name. Elvis Presley is listed under E, not P. The word "The" is ignored if it comes first; "The Rolling Stones" are listed under R, not T.

– If you use the default "automatic" syncing option, and you already have a song on, then it doesn't put it on again. Which is fine, if you want your iPod music to always match your iTunes library. Myself, I've decided to go with the "manually manage" option.

If you've been using the "manually manage" option and you're dealing with thousands of songs, you don't want to be switching modes halfway thru the long process of getting all that music on the iPod, and risk losing all the work you've done so far! If you suddenly decide to use "automatic" sync, and you no longer have all your stuff in your iTunes library except a few new songs, and you click "Apply", then YOU WILL LOSE THOSE THOUSANDS OF SONGS FROM YOUR IPOD, AND ONLY GET THOSE FEW NEW ONES ON YOUR iPOD! The key is not to switch modes; pick one mode and stick to it, so you don't mess up.

Never switch options (manual vs automatic), unless you know exactly what you are doing.

– The option it gives (under Devices, device name, Options) to convert higher bit rate songs to 128 kbps is for lowering the bit rate so you can fit more songs on. Was advised to leave it unchecked, since space is not a big concern for me, but getting best quality sound is.

– How do you turn the iPod off!? You HOLD the "On/Off" ("sleep/wake") button down for three seconds. If you just click it, it just turns the screen on or off; if the music was playing, it still keeps playing! Holding that button down turns the iPod on or off. And, when you turn it back on, it continues music right from that same spot.

If you hold that button down AND the volume-down button down for 6 seconds, then the iPod resets to its default settings. The songs themselves are unaffected.

Note, however, a "Restore" of the iPod program while you are in iTunes, does erase your material! See "Restore" below.

– The battery inside gets recharged when you attach it to your computer. Takes 1½ hours to charge 80%, and 3 hours to charge fully. Lightning bolt icon means it's charging; plug icon means it is fully charged. It's supposed to last for 24 hours of play. The white portion (green for the iPod "Touch") of the battery icon at upper right corner, shows how much charge is left, dwindling to the left as it runs out.

The battery does NOT charge when the computer is in sleep or standby mode; your computer must be on.

– Not supposed to let it get wet. Regarding temperature: operates best 32 degrees to 95 degrees, though it probably still works outside that range. Supposed to store it between –4 and 113. Says not to store in a car because temperatures might exceed that range. Well, I think a glove compartment usually won't exceed that. I figure it's fine to keep in my car, except maybe the very coldest and hottest days.

I did buy, from Walmart, an iPod nano silicon case for it, to give it a layer of protection, in case I drop it.

– The clock icon always shows 10:15; when you tap on it, it shows the correct time. Left-swipe it and it gives you a stopwatch function.

– Support phone number – 1 800 275-2273, 6am–6pm Pacific time (9am–9pm Eastern), 7 days a week. I called at one point, to confirm several points, and they were actually very good.

– You can get some help from the "Help" tab of your iPod window at upper left of your computer screen, but you have to be online.

CONTROLS / NAVIGATION SUMMARY

I have 2 iPods, a regular one and a nano. The controls are somewhat different:

IPOD TOUCH 4th GEN.	IPOD NANO 6th GEN.
External controls: On/Off at top right; earplug lower right; cable port bottom; volume upper left side. You can hear iPod Touch without earbuds.	On/Off at top right; earplug bottom right; cable port bottom; volume upper left top. Can change orientation of screen by finger twist.
ON: On/Off button at upper right top > press > "slide to unlock" [OR, Press and hold > Apple icon > wait 25 seconds for it to boot up > "Slide to unlock"] > click on selected app icon.	Press and hold > Apple icon > click on selected application icon.
OFF: On/Off press and hold > "Slide to power off".	On/Off press and hold.
Screen Icons: Has up to 20 icons per page. To get back to icons, press Home. To get back to previous screen, usually tap heading at upper left.	Has up to 4 icons per page. Swipe left or right to change pages for more icons. Once in an application, to get back to icons, keep swiping left.
Dark Screen: If you want screen to wake up from black as it plays, press Home just below bottom of screen, then "Slide to unlock".	To wake up screen from black, tap the screen, or press On button.
Search: tap icon > scroll for	Tap icon > scroll for selection >

selection > tap. Or, press rounded square at bottom of screen > use keyboard to search.	tap.
Playing Music: Tap orange music icon > tap Playlists lower left > scroll playlists > tap on selection > tap on selected track, or, tap on first song to play straight thru all tracks on that playlist.	←Same
Volume: Two buttons at upper left side. Or, you can slide the volume marker at bottom of screen.	Two buttons at upper left top
To Stop a Song: Either press Pause, or turn iPod off. Otherwise, it keeps playing, one song to next till end of playlist.	←Same
To Stop a Playlist: See "Playlist Repeat Loop" under "iPod – Additional Problems".	See "Playlist Repeat Loop" under "iPod – Additional Problems".
To Delete: Tap Playlist at lower left > tap selected playlist > Delete > Playlist. To delete a song: tap song name > Edit at upper left > tap red minus sign > Delete > Done.	Tap playlist name at upper left > Edit > tap red minus sign > Delete > Done.
Audiobooks: Tap orange Music icon > tap "More" lower right > tap AudioBooks and successive categories. Once playing, you can press icon at high/upper right for chapter list. Can do three speeds – .5X, 1x, and 2X – small icon at low/upper right. Tap center of screen to bring up that option if it's not there. Can drag slider at top to fast forward or reverse faster than pressing and holding the double arrows.	Tap "Audiobooks" icon > tap choice > tap chapter. Once playing, to get controls up, tap the screen or click the On/Off button twice. Controls here include pause, reverse and fast forward by pressing and holding the double arrows, and previous or next chapter by tapping double arrows.
Other: Besides these basic functions, there are other things you can do. Most you can learn logically on your own as you spend time exploring. Or, check "iPod Touch User Guide" online.	Unlike the regular iPod at left, the Nano one does not have picture, video, or internet capability. In fact, I much prefer the regular iPod to the Nano, partly because it has these additional functions, but also because the Nano is just too small. For further specific instructions on anything, check "iPod Nano User Guide" online.
Size: 2¼ X 4¼, cracker thin	1½ X 1½, cracker thin
Battery: Claims up to 40 hours audio play, and 7 hours video play.	Claims 24 hours. Have never run out since I always have it attached to car radio, where it charges.

CONTROLS / NAVIGATION NOTES

Icons

The icons on your screen are called "applications." I think you can add to them, but generally I don't want extra "apps." I just want my iPod for music and audiobooks.

For my Nano, I re-arranged the 15 or so icons, so that on the first page I now have these 4: Playlists, Artists, Settings, Audiobooks (which only shows when you have one in your iPod). The rest of the icons are much less relevant to me.

The way to custom-set your screens is to touch and hold an icon till they all start jiggling, then you can drag an icon to where you want, either on that page or to another page. Then press Home to set them for the iPod Touch, or press "sleep/wake" button for the iPod Nano.

Dragging an icon to the right or left edge of the screen moves it to the next page. The little dots at the bottom middle represent each page, maybe 4 or 5 of them. If one is lit white, that means you are on that page. For the Nano, usually you want 4 icons per page, but you can put one on by itself if you want to.

On/Off or Screen/Wake Button

Needs to be held for 3 seconds to operate as an on/off button. Otherwise, it operates as a "Sleep/Wake" button – it just turns the screen on or off, once the device is on. If you are playing a song, and you press that button, just a quick press, the screen goes off, but the song is still playing. Hold it for 3 seconds to actually turn the device off.

Tapping and Swiping

To navigate, don't tap with fingernails or tap hard, just tap lightly with the broad part of your finger end. For screen touches and swipes, you don't have to do it heavily; just do it lightly.

If right-swiping the screen won't get you back to the music icon from your music list, you need to swipe the screen near the top at the bar, rather than from the middle of the screen. Or, just swipe it several times. Sometimes it doesn't work on the first or second swipe.

You need to spend some time practicing navigating. Can be confusing at first, but once you get used to it, it is actually quite a nice, intuitive system. There is a reason iPods are so popular and have won awards for design.

Navigating Back

1. For the Nano: To get from playing a song back to your list of songs – swipe to the right lightly. You swipe to the right to get back to original categories; you tap on items to move ahead to more specific categories.

To return "home" – your first screen of icons – you keep swiping right. Home is like the Desktop of your laptop. Or, touch and hold anywhere not on an icon and that brings you Home also.

2. For the iPod Touch: Tap white left arrow at upper left > tap Playlist at upper left, to get back to playlists. Press Home to get back to home icon page.

Settings Icon

The Settings icon on your iPod screen, gives you information about your iPod. Under "About" you can get the serial number, the number of songs you have, the amount of space you have left, etc. And under "Music" you can raise the bass, and do other adjustments, under "EQ".

The settings on the iPod itself are not that critical, especially compared to the critical nature of your "automatic" vs "manual" setting when you're in the iTunes window.

ADDING SONGS/MATERIAL TO iPOD

Setup

First, on your computer, double-click on your iTunes icon to open up the iTunes program. Here is a summary of what then shows up on your computer screen when you connect your iPod to your computer:

1. "Devices" shows up at middle left of iTunes page.
2. Click directly on the name of your device and then at the right a window comes up showing info on your iPod (name, capacity, serial #, etc.)
3. Under that it gives you 5 options
   "Open iTunes when this iPod is connected" (me, checked)
   "Sync only checked songs" (me, un-checked)
   "Convert higher bit rate to 128 kbps AAC (me, un-checked)
   "Manually manage music" (me, checked)
   "Enable disk use" (me, un-checked)
4. Click the "Music" tab at top. You get "Sync Music" page, where it gives you the options of "Entire music library" or "Selected playlists, artists, albums, and genres" (where it will show you those categories and what you have in them). If you chose "Manually manage", then this page is grayed out.

Under "Devices", if you click on the triangle arrow to the left, it opens up a list of the material currently on your iPod. Click on one of those sub-categories (Music, Books, etc.), and it shows what you have, on the right.

So, basically, on the first page, you are choosing between automatic ("Sync only checked songs") or manual ("Manually manage music and videos"), and then on the next page, if you had chosen automatic, it gives you the further option of syncing your entire iTunes library, or just selected material – categories or material within categories.

Myself, I much prefer "manual." I don't like automatic anything here.

And, I try to keep my iTunes music library as empty as possible. Otherwise, I find, it just gets horrendously confusing, with so much material to navigate thru. I keep my songs, all 2,000+ of them, in my Music folder under Owner [W7 – Libraries], not under iTunes.

If you prefer the automatic syncing method over manual, after clicking Devices, you need to click, not Summary tab at top, but Music tab at top. Then check the playlists, songs, albums, or artists you want to transfer (sync), click Apply at lower right. Then it transfers the selected material.

Or, if you have Entire Library checked under the Options window, it will put your entire library into your iPod.

I'm pretty sure that automatic syncing syncs only the changes from the last time you synced; that is, it updates your deletions and additions, from your iTunes library, and leaves, in your iPod, as is, the material that was not changed. It ignores the material already synced and already matching your iTunes library.

Adding Songs/Material to iPod

[For downloading songs to iTunes in the first place, see "MUSIC" > "iTUNES"]

Automatic Sync

1. iTunes, click Music under Library, to get your songs up
2. Connect your iPod to computer, to get "Devices" category up, at middle left
   If an "AutoPlay" window comes up, I just x it out.
3. If "Register Your iPod" comes up, register it or click Register Later
4. Check the songs you want to transfer
5. Click "Devices"
6. At lower right is "Sync"; click that, and it transfers the checked songs. Progress shows at top. (May have to click "Convert" at one point.)
7. Press Eject icon to right of "Device"
8. Disconnect your iPod.
9. Songs should now be on your iPod, ready to be listened to.

Manual Transfer

If the "Sync Music" window under Music tab, is grayed out, that means you had earlier checked "Manually manage music", and then instead of clicking "sync" to transfer songs, you must drag and drop individual songs manually from your iTunes "Music" library list to the iPod Music category at the left under Devices. Drop them right on top of "Music", the one below "Devices".

Or, use the method that I normally use for a bunch of songs: Edit > Select All > right-click on your list > Add to Playlist > click on your desired playlist target.

Also, what happens, after you change your setting from "sync" to "manual", is that the next time you go to do something, a window pops up telling you that you have changed settings, and asking if you would like to Apply the new setting. Only at that point, after you click Apply, is the new manual setting in operation!

I think the iPod assumption is that most people want their entire iTunes account library to be on their iPods. Hence the term "sync" (making things match). But, I don't. I find that keeping an entire library of iTunes songs makes things confusing and way too cluttered. Navigating thru hundreds of albums and songs, most situated way below your current screen page, is ridiculous. Not to mention, sometimes I find old material in the library that I don't even want; I bought it, didn't like it that much, deleted it, yet that material keeps showing up out of the blue! There probably are ways to make navigation easier, but I'm sticking to keeping my iTunes library empty normally, and to using the "manually manage" option.

Read somewhere another person saying that he likes "manual" also.

Transferring Old CD Music to iPod

My situation, and I suspect likewise for many people of my generation, is that I wanted to get a lot of my old CD music onto an iPod. So here is how. Pretty involved, but doable.

Mind you, the extensive instructions I give just below in the red box are NOT overkill. You have to do things exactly and in the right order, or else things may not work and you will be frustrated and eventually carted off to a mental institution.

Transferring CD Music to iPod

1. iTunes
2. Put CD in. (It's a good idea to clean your disk first.)

[If Windows Media Player, instead of iTunes, is the default music opening program, find a random song in your computer Music folder, right-click it, Open with, and under Choose Default Program, choose iTunes, OK.]

3. Import – Yes.
4. Wait, as it imports. Takes about 6 minutes per full disk. Orange circle next to track, means it's importing that track; green check, means it's done with that track.

If you want to import only certain songs, not the whole CD, check the tracks you want and uncheck the ones you don't want, then click "Import CD" at lower right.

5. Eject your CD by clicking the eject arrow under Devices, to the right of "Audio CD". [If you leave it in, you may well end up renaming songs on the disk rather than in your iTunes list... or something like that. Trust me, take the CD out now to avoid any confusion.]
6. Find the material you just imported, in your iTunes library under Music, at top.
7. If your songs are titled by simply track numbers (because they were not purchased thru iTunes) it's good to rename them:
    a. Double-click the first song, to hear what it is.
    b. Then right-click the song
    c. Get Info
    d. Info tab
    e. Type in the song name and the artist. (I leave "Album" blank.)
    f. OK

Do the same for the rest of the songs. Laborious, for sure, but it's nice to have song names and artists show on your iPod screen, instead of constantly "Unknown".

8. Click File (upper left)
9. Click New Playlist
10. Type in the name of the playlist (for me, "Disk 01", "Disk 02", "Disk 43", etc.)
11. Press Enter key
12. Under "Library", click "Music"
13. Edit (upper left), Select All
14. Right-click (with the pointer anywhere on the list of tracks)
15. Add to Playlist
16. Click on desired playlist (for me, for example, "Disk 01"). That adds the songs to that Playlist.

[It wouldn't let me re-order my songs while under Music, but once I clicked that playlist, it allowed me to drag songs to different spots in the order.]

17. Attach your iPod, to get "Devices" up at middle left of window ("x" out "AutoPlay" window if that comes up)
18. Drag "Disk 01" under Playlists (low on list at left) and drop it right onto "Music" (middle on list at left) under "Devices" and that copies it into your iPod (takes only 10-20 seconds, which is weird, because it took 6 minutes to import them in the first place...?

Be sure to accurately drop it right onto "Music", not elsewhere; if you drop it onto one of the playlists already there, it will add those songs to that playlist, rather than landing it as a separate playlist the way you want it. If iPod "Music" is located above what currently shows in that window on the left, just drag the new playlist right to the top edge of the window and the contents of the window will move down for you so you can reach iPod "Music."

If you click on that new playlist under Devices right away, you can see it copying songs, as titles go from gray to black.

19. Click "Disconnect" icon to right of your iPod name
20. Disconnect your iPod, and you should have "Disk 01" under your iPod Playlists icon, ready to listen to.

21. Lastly, you should back up your material. This is the way I have decided to do it:

    a. Click on the playlist you just added [The one in your iTunes Music, not your iPod Music. It won't allow you to copy that iPod playlist, but only your iTunes playlist. Also, unfortunately, if you've re-arranged a few songs in the iTunes playlist, even though it did it copy to your iPod in the new order, sometimes it reverts back to the original order when it copies to your computer. So you have to do some renaming to get your songs in that computer file into the order you want them.]
    b. Edit, Select All
    c. Copy
    d. Paste (CTRL+V) into a folder under Owner, Music.
    e. Then, also make a copy of that folder onto an external hard drive, as a backup.
    f. For me, since I like my iTunes Library to be empty, I go back to iTunes > Music > Edit > Select All > Delete > Remove > Move to Recycle Bin. And, also right-click that playlist and delete it (may have to press Delete twice here).

Now I have my iTunes library empty again, the way I like it, so that I don't have tons of material in there, and I'm ready to do my next CD.

And, I have 1) the music on my iPod, 2) the music backed up on my computer hard drive, and 3) the music backed up on an external hard drive, should I ever lose or break any of the three. See also "Backup" below.

Note that if, at any point, you want to delete just a single song, you need to right-click, not on the album name at left, but on the song name in the middle.

Keep in mind, this whole process is under "manually manage". If you prefer "automatic", you then do NOT want to delete any material from your iTunes library, because then it will also be deleted from your iPod the next time you attach it and it automatically syncs!

Note also that if the sound quality is particularly weak on some old tracks, they may not transfer to iTunes. I had a few very old tracks (8-track to cassette to CD) that simply would not go.

Last major wrinkle: I noticed that when I made song copies from iTunes to my regular Music folder under Owner, it indicated the name of the songs but not the artists. So, if I lose my iPod and need to make a copy of my complete collection from my computer to a new iPod, will all those artists' names now be missing?! No. Thankfully. When you open iTunes and use the "Transferring Music on Computer to iPod" procedure described below, when you click "Add Folder to Library", it automatically lists the artists also. Whew!

Note the horrible redundancy here with the iPod, just like the rest of the computer world: Besides getting the material into your iPod Playlist category, it also puts those songs under the Songs, Artists, Albums, and Genres categories. So you've got them listed all over the place! Some people may think that's wonderful; I think it rots. It's just confusing. I'm just going to focus on the Playlist category and ignore the rest, usually.

Though, I may occasionally pick "Artists" to hear all the songs of a particular artist.

One thing to keep in mind, both here with the iPod and also for a lot of other computer "storage" situations, is that if the material is available under several different categories, that does not mean that there are actual extra copies of it in all those categories, but just that those categories can access the material, which is actually stored in just one place elsewhere.

I plan to simply keep all my old CD songs organized as is, on 73 folders named "Disk 01" to "Disk 73", under my Music folder under Owner, with nothing in my iTunes Music library.

Transferring Music from Computer Hard Drive to iPod

1. Open iTunes
2. File at upper left
3. Add Folder to Library
4. "Add to Library" window opens
5. Click computer "Music" folder on left
6. Double-click desired folder (me, "Disks 1-73" folder)
7. Check the disk you want to add (me, "Disk 1")
8. Click "Select Folder" or, if that option is not there, check the folder and click "Open"
9. Click "Convert"
10. Wait (about 6 minutes per disk) [If you click "Music" under "Devices" it shows you the songs as they are being transferred.]
11. File (upper left), New Playlist
12. Then follow steps #10-20 above.

Adding Non-iTunes Songs to Your iPod / Converting Format

If you want non-iTunes songs on your iPod, you need to add them to your iTunes library first, and convert their format.

When you import songs from a CD to your iTunes library, it automatically converts the music to the iTunes "ACC" format. When you import songs from your computer (usually from your "Music" folder under "Owner"), at one point it gives you a "convert" option to click (step 9 above).

Naming Songs

No matter what you type in as the name of artist or song, on your original file, once you import it to iTunes, since these were not iTunes songs to begin with, you end up with "Unknown Album" and "Track 1, or 2", etc., i.e. no identifying names. You CAN, and probably should, rename the songs and artists to the actual names, once you have them imported into iTunes.

Of course, this means a ton of work for me, with 2,000+ songs, having to name the 80% of them that I recorded over the years before getting on iTunes. But, once I have it, I'll have it.

To Name or Rename Songs

1. iTunes
2. Right-click the song, which currently shows, for example, "Unknown Album", "Track 9" and no artist. (Or, highlight it and go to File at top.)
3. Click "Get Info"
4. Info tab. (This is grayed out if you went to File, Get Info, and did not highlight a song first; need to highlight a song first. I think just right-clicking a song is easier.)
5. Under Name, type in name of song
6. Under Artist, type in name of artist
   (I leave "Album" as is.)
7. Click OK

Now, when songs get transferred to my iPod, I have all the songs identified by song name and artist name, instead of tons of Unknown's and Track 3's. And, I can actually select an artist and hear all that person's or group's songs in a row, if I want to.

Note that whatever you name a song or artist, that is what it gets organized as. For example, if you named the artist "Elvis" even though the actual material is by "Beethoven", it will get listed under "Elvis" under the "Artist" icon on your iPod.

Also, you need to keep an artist's name consistent. If you spell it two different ways, it will provide two different lists.

PLAYING THE SONGS – NOTES

To turn the iPod on or off, press and hold the On/Off button for 3 seconds. [Note that different iPods may have different controls. Keep in mind the concept of pressing and holding, and also the concept of getting the Apple icon up and then waiting a full 25 seconds for the iPod to boot up! (Just like a computer.) It takes a few weeks of exploring and practice to get used to controls.]

When you turn the iPod on, it resumes play right from the spot it left off, unless you select something else.

If you tap on the Songs icon and tap on the first song, it will play ALL your songs in succession, as they are listed alphabetically. If you tap on the Playlist icon and on a particular playlist, it will play that list to its end, and then automatically keep repeating that whole playlist.

See "Playlist Repeat Loop" several pages below.

The usual way I like to listen to my music, is playlists in succession. I'll listen to my whole collection, in order, over the months, as I drive in my car. May go thru all of the songs in 4-6 months, then I start over. Each year I add maybe one or two new playlists. With a 4,000 song limit, I should be OK for several years. My first 2,000 songs represent over 30 years of collecting music.

DELETING SONGS / MATERIAL FROM IPOD

Was told you can't delete songs directly from iPod; you must have it attached to iTunes in your computer and delete from there.

1. Attach iPod to computer.
2. Click triangle at left of the word "Devices" and that will list the categories you have on your device.
3. Click "Music" and that shows what music you have on your iPod
4. Click a playlist to show the songs in it.
5. Right-click on the song you want deleted
6. Delete. You can do them individually, or you can use Edit tab at upper left and Select All and delete all of them at once.

An early problem – Suddenly when I right-clicked a song, the options list did NOT include "Delete"! Tried all kinds of things. Turns out that you have to, first of all, have your Options (after clicking your device name) set to "Manually manage." AND !!! then you have to click on your Music under Devices, so that a window comes up offering "Apply" to click. Click that, and THEN you can right-click a song in your iPod list, and "Delete" appears there as an option.

When you are under the automatic syncing option, I believe you need to delete the song from your iTunes library, and then the next time you click the sync order, it deletes them from your iPod.

"eHow" website says there are two ways to delete songs from your iPod. 1) Delete the songs from your iTunes account library, then sync (which brings material on the iPod to match your library. 2) Attach your iPod to your computer, click on an iPod playlist, right-click on the song you want deleted, and click Delete.

(Although, it seems to me, that if you are operating on "automatic" syncing, instead of "manually manage", the next time you sync songs, that deleted song will be right back on your iPod, since you deleted it from you iPod, not your iTunes library!)

Update: Actually, you CAN delete directly from your iPod. Or, at least you can delete items from being listed in categories, like Playlists; the songs themselves still remain in your iPod, somewhere, wherever they are actually stored. To remove songs, on your iPod, from a playlist list, see "CONTROLS / NAVIGATION SUMMARY" above.

Summary of Manually Adding and Deleting Songs

Adding: Attach iPod > drag and drop songs from your iTunes library onto the chosen iPod playlist > That's it. Click eject, disconnect, and that new song is in your chosen iPod playlist.

Deleting: Attach the iPod > click on your iPod "Music" > click on the playlist; songs show up on the right > right-click the song > Delete. Click eject, disconnect your iPod. Now your iPod playlist no longer includes that song.

MISC INFO

Audiobooks

Once you've purchased an audiobook (see iTUNES): Open iTunes > click on "Books" on the left under "LIBRARY" to get your audiobooks up > attach iPod to computer with your USB connector wire > drag and drop the selected book icon into "Books" on the left under "DEVICES."

The book is now in your iPod. To play it, see "CONTROLS / NAVIGATION SUMMARY" above.

Restore

Doing a "Restore" on your iPod while in iTunes, resets the original default settings, and also erases all the material on your iPod!

A "Restore" is also the way to change the name of your device. (I had named mine "Mickey" and I wanted to change it to "Mickey's iPod"): Under "Devices", Summary tab, click "restore", wait (may take a while), now you can set up the name again. Picked "English." Checked "Manually manage", Done.

If you originally had "Manually manage" selected, this "Restore" action also empties your whole iPod! So, DON'T do a "restore" under your iPod window, unless you DO want to erase everything in there. Though, I suppose automatic sync can put your library back in fairly quickly. But, for me, I like "manual" setting, and keeping my iTunes library empty.

Different Computer

If you've selected automatic syncing, and you attach your iPod to a different computer, it will sync THAT computer's material and erase what you had in your iPod from the first computer!

Disconnecting the iPod from Computer

Don't know if disconnecting the iPod without clicking Eject first will hurt the machine itself; I doubt it, but it may be screw up the material on it, or at least the most recent material. Anyway, it's good to get into the habit of ALWAYS clicking that "eject" spot before disconnecting.

Screen Displays

On the Nano, tap the little "i" at lower right and it brings up a window for you to rate the song. More than I care to be bothered with.

Shuffle icon – swipe Now Playing screen to the left to bring up the second screen. It has a shuffle icon (two crossed white arrows) at upper right – if you tap that, the arrows turn blue, and it plays songs randomly within that playlist. I don't do shuffle. Prefer to hear songs in the order I'm used to; brings back memories of that time period of my life.

On the Nano, you can rotate the screen by touching it with two fingers and rotating your fingers, in case you have it attached somewhere and it would be easier to see if it were rotated.

iPod Touch Screen – Screen with controls darkens after 45 seconds, and then turns black about 5 seconds later. Music continues to play though. If you touch the screen before it turns fully black, or pick up the iPod and turn it sideways and back, the controls screen comes back on. But if it has turned fully black, then you need to click the white rounded square at bottom, and swipe "slide to unlock" to get the controls screen up again.

iPod Nano Screen – Screen with controls changes to screen with musical note after 5 seconds, and that darkens after 10 seconds later, and then turns black after 45 seconds total. Music continues to play though. If you touch the screen before it turns fully black, it will come back on. But if it has turned fully black, you need to press On/Off button to get controls screen up again.

I find the simplest way to deal with turning iPods off and on, is to "Pause" what you are playing and just leave it. It goes to sleep on its own after 45 seconds. Then, just clicking the On button brings it back on quickly.

Other Functions

The iPod can do other functions – photo managing, pedometer, etc. – but I can't stand overkill. As if things weren't complicated enough. I just want to use it for my music and for audiobooks. Their online User Guide is pretty good, if you want to explore other functions.

PLAYING THE IPOD IN YOUR CAR

My plan, with the iPod, was to be able to listen to any song from my entire music collection in my car, and no longer have to shuffle half a dozen CDs to and from the car every couple of weeks.

OK, I got a Belkin "Tunecast Auto Universal" for $53, so I can play my iPod music in my car. It's fairly simple to set up: Plug the thing into your cigarette lighter/power outlet, connect your iPod to the other end, press a button and it automatically selects the best FM frequency to use; dial your radio to that frequency. Turn your iPod on and the songs play over your radio.

However, it ain't no good!!

The problems:

1) Even though the sound itself was good, there was constant minor static. Not noticeable for loud music, but very annoying for soft music.
2) You can adjust volume by radio dial, but you cannot skip songs, or replay songs (as I often like to do), or move to a different album, unless you pick up the iPod and work with it and that was not at all convenient, or safe (!); like texting as you drive!
3) Every time I was in a different location it picked a different frequency to use. That is a major pain, constantly resetting the frequency as I drive in different locations. Every time you start your iPod, you have to find a new best frequency! Spending half your life finding the best current frequency, is ridiculous. Crazy.
4) Since you are using the power outlet, you can't have a GPS plugged in at the same time!
5) The volume needed is maybe 20% higher than I normally select for CDs or radio, so that if I suddenly turn back to regular radio, it blasts my ears off.
6) On a long trip you also have to worry about your iPod battery running out. (For CDs, the way I've listened to music in my car for years, there's no battery worry.)
7) When you park, you have to put the stuff away every time; you don't want to invite theft.

These seven major factors make it clearly NOT an improvement over what I've done for years – simply playing CDs.

Plan: I'm having a new car stereo installed with full iPod functionality, so I can use the radio controls, safely, to listen to music. Now, at Best Buy, they had a number of options, but the only one that had no wires sticking out and did not require my attaching and un-attaching things every time I got into the car, was the most expensive one – Alpine CDA-117. (The iPod goes into the glove compartment and the wires run behind the scenes so to speak.) Counting labor and accessories to put in, it will run me $475. But, that is the one the Best Buy guy has in his own car; he called it the best on the market; and it looks like the only one which will do exactly what I want – minimum of hassles, good sound. (The Best Buy guy also thinks that the FM frequency gadgets, like the Belkin one I got originally... rot, in terms of sound.)

Bottom line, it's pricey, but that's fine with me. If my financial situation were different, looking back, I think keeping my car music system as is, with CDs, would have been my choice. It has always worked well. And I would have gotten an iPod mainly for beach-hiking-jogging listening, rather than car listening.

But, as it happens, I can afford a new car stereo, and it should make my car listening even better than it is now with CDs.

Another advantage is this: I can delete songs without affecting the rest of the material; with CD's, if you want to drop a song, you have to re-burn the whole CD without that song!

Yet another advantage: If I download an audiobook to my computer, I can put it onto the iPod, listen to it, then erase it from the iPod and just keep it in my iTunes library. Whereas with CDs, in order to listen to the book in my car, I have to laboriously burn several CDs with my computer, using up both time and a bit of money for the blank CDs.

OK, I bought the Alpine unit. I love it! It does exactly what I hoped. Plays radio, CDs, and iPod; controls are clear; from the dashboard you can control all the iPod functions; I can have my entire music collection in the car on my iPod in the glove compartment; the sound is also about 10-20 percent better than the sound of my old unit. It has a nice one-dial system for most navigation: you turn it to change volume; you press it to bring up menus, turn it to scroll for selections, press again to pick that selection.

Of course, does anything ever go smoothly in the electronics world? No. I had these problems at first: Whenever I turned the car itself off and then back on later, music would not continue from the stopping point but always reverted to the start of a playlist (a major pain!). And the clock would not stay current, but always reverted to an old set time. And the unit would always have to be turned on and the mode (radio/CD/iPod) selected first (a major pain!). I had expected what I had for my old unit – turn the car on and the music will automatically be on, and continue from the last stopping point.

Called Best Buy, who put the unit in, and the guy told me that for my particular car, a couple of wires needed to be reversed. So I brought it in, he fixed it in 5 minutes, and now everything is OK, and I am very happy with the unit. I turn the car on, the stereo unit is automatically on, the music continues, from either CD or iPod, from the last stopping point. Clock is working properly now also.

Now my entire music collection is with me in the glove compartment, and I can access and control it relatively easily.

The iPod battery, incidentally, is automatically charged when it is connected to the unit.

Bass

Audio hold > Sound Field > Parametric EQ > Then it has a number on the left which should be between 80 to 100, and then you can increase numbers on the right up to 6, to increase bass.

There are other bands you can go to adjust other frequencies, but that's just overkill for me.

WARNING: I am very careful when I fiddle with my car stereo/iPod unit – I park somewhere first! I do not drive and try to do anything complicated. It's very dangerous to do so. "20/20" had a piece recently about how texting (or just general multi-tasking) while driving is very dangerous. How people think it may be a problem for others... but not for them.

These people are stupid, delusional, and self-centered. Tests and statistics prove how dangerous it is to multi-task while driving. One teen on the program is now paralyzed because of her texting while driving. I feel sorry for her... but not nearly as sorry, and angry, as I would, if it were an innocent bystander.

Getting to Next Playlist Problem

Once a playlist finishes, it repeats itself, rather than going on to the next playlist. Getting to the next one is a problem. At least for me it is, because my playlists are numbers (01, 02...71, 72, 73, etc.) rather than names, so it is difficult for me to remember which number I was on and search and select the next one. The bottom line here, after being on the phone (1 800 832-4101) with Alpine tech guy for 25 minutes, is that for this model, you can't get the playlist to stop repeating with an iPod. Even though on the iPod you can order no repeating, on this unit the playlists repeat anyway.

Here is a more detailed description of the problem, and my workaround solution:

IF you selected a playlist, after starting your car, then a small icon shows at top middle and you CAN just press the single-arrow button to move it to the next playlist.

BUT, each time you get back into your car and turn it on, that single-arrow button does NOT work (the small icon at top is not there either). Your music continues where it left off, which is good, but you cannot move to the next playlist with one button. (Alpine guy on phone told me it has song memory but not playlist memory).

So what you have to do is press the big search dial, go to Playlists, and select a playlist.

And that is a problem because it does not indicate anywhere what playlist you are currently on! So you end up guessing which one is the next one – 45? 46? 47? It's hard to remember when your playlists are numbers. And that is a serious problem because you are then distracted from your driving, as you press half a dozen buttons trying to find the correct next playlist. (Not to mention the fact that 0 and 8, and 5 and 6, on the display panel are visually hard to distinguish, and impossible to distinguish if the sun is shining on the panel.)

Workaround Solution

Go back to your computer and change the name of the first song of each playlist you have to the playlist number and then the song. For example: Say your first song on playlist 43 is Hound Dog. Change the title to 43 – Hound Dog. That way when a playlist ends, and starts over at the first song, you can see on the display what disk it is and press search dial, press the 1-6 buttons at bottom to reach the proximity of that playlist (those 6 buttons break up your playlist bunch into 6ths, so you can reach them faster). Then simply select the next one in order.

Still have some experimenting to do, since changing those first song names is not quite working on my computer hard drive – they won't stay in the first spot. Making the first song of playlist 9 – "-9-01Heartbreak Hotel" puts it with song 9 despite the dash in front of it.

Solution: I put the playlist number AFTER the "01" of the song – "01-9 Heartbreak Hotel". That's for the copy of my songs in my external hard drive. For the actual iPod, I had to change all those first songs also, but it was easier. I just put the playlist number in front of the first song – 01-song – and it stayed right there.

So here's the selecting-the-next-playlist procedure: Keep the View button on the Date and Time. At end of playlist, press View three times, to show name of first song, which now includes the playlist number as part of the first song. Then press Search, Playlist, press button 1-6 to reach approximate place on playlist list, turn search dial to desired playlist, press select, and press again to start the first song of this next playlist.

A bit complex, but I'll be doing it on a regular basis, so I should get relatively used to doing it. I always make sure I'm in a calm traffic situation before I do it. It's still a 5-7 second operation, during which I glance up to the road 2 or 3 times.

There is no other easy way. If you're on a playlist and hit Search button and Playlists, it shows you the top of the list, not the one you're on (unless you've selected that playlist AFTER you started the car, in which case it will show the playlist you're on highlighted).

The single arrow at left of unit WILL take you to the next playlist, but only AFTER you have made a playlist selection, AFTER you've turned on the car; it does NOT work if you turn on the car and have NOT made a selection yet, and have just continued music from the last time you turned off the car. And, considering the fact that when you get into the car you are usually in the middle of a playlist, my workaround solution is the best solution for how to move to the next playlist when the current one finishes.

FINAL PROBLEMS

Windows Media Player Stops Working

After working with the iPod on the computer, I noticed my Windows Media Player would not work now. It would not even open up! I called iPod, suggesting maybe their Apple program is interfering with Windows Media Player (since they are competing programs). Guy thought no. What to do?

I went ahead and did a computer "System Restore" for my whole computer (see "Restore Settings" elsewhere) to last week's date, just before the Apple driver was installed. Well, now it's OK. Windows Media Player works again.

Of course, now my iTunes won't work. Had to re-install it. Then I attached my iPod, and ... hooray, now both iTunes/iPod and Windows Media Player work. I'm guessing the problem was that when I first installed latest version of iTunes, I didn't wait long enough for it to install, before attaching my iPod. You should wait for it to say "Congratulations, iTunes has been successfully installed", no matter if the green progress bar is momentarily at the right. It takes a good 15 minutes, and a restart, to install iTunes.

Alpine Unit Freezes for iPod

A month later, after things were working just fine, the iPod function froze (radio, CD, and iPod itself were fine, but the iPod function on the Alpine froze). Best Buy guy said there's a red reset button somewhere, which will fix that, usually, if you press it. Next time I went to my car, it was unfrozen, on its own, and working fine. Will press that button (I think it's the little wide red button in the middle, after you flip down the front panel, even though the manual shows it at the left) if it happens again. Also, the unit must be turned off when you press it "with a ballpoint pen or similar object."

Update: Happened again a few weeks later. I pressed that red button. The right half of it moved in; I pressed the left half then, and the whole thing got stuck in, and, made no difference. Drove right to Best Buy. That was not the reset button; he didn't know what it was. But, the reset button IS on the lower left, only you can't see it unless you take off the panel, not just flip it down. You take off the panel by not flipping it down but by just flipping it out a bit, almost still vertical, and then pulling straight out. (You put it back in the same way, same angle, almost vertical, almost closed, just push it in, it snaps in.) Pressing that actual reset button did nothing.

He checked the iPod itself. And he reset the iPod. That did the trick. He said most iPods are like that, they require resetting occasionally, out of the blue, for no reason. To reset the iPod, press and hold the On button for more than 3 seconds till the Apple icon comes on. And, I think, keep holding it down till it's off, then turn it back on. Not sure. Actually, this is what the user guide says: *"press the Sleep/Wake button and the Volume Down button for 6 seconds, until the Apple logo appears.*

Update: OK, a few weeks later it happened again. Did what the guide said. It worked. iPod unfroze upon resetting it.

Update: Happens every so often – it simply stops after a song. Lately I've just been just turning off the unit and turning it back on, and that works to get it going again... lately, anyway. If turning it off and then back on doesn't work, then I go to the reset – holding Sleep/Wake and Volume Down buttons for 6 seconds.

Update: Unit showed "No USB Unit" even though my iPod was connected. Tried everything. No go. iPod then showed low battery, which made no sense, unless some connection behind the scenes was loose. Unattached it, and attached it yet one more time. Suddenly, it worked. Very frustrating. So often in the computer world, it's so hard to pin down causes. Stuff reacts in inconsistent ways. Ugh.

Update: I haven't had a freeze for several months now.

THE RADIO APPLICATION

When I saw the Radio icon on the screen, I thought, wouldn't that be something, if it actually simply played the radio without any further complications. Holy crap... it DOES. Pretty amazing. There's an FM radio inside this Ritz cracker-sized object! (The earphones work as an antenna.)

Tap the Radio icon, tap the *"i"* on the lower right, gives list of options, at top is Local Stations. Tap that and it lists about 8 stations. Tap on the one you want, and it starts playing. Tap on right arrow for next station, left arrow for previous station. You can dial to other stations (drag the red radio bar to right or left), but these listed ones are presumably the best reception stations in your area.

Also on the options list are Favorites (stations), Tagged Songs, Recent Songs. Tap "Recent Songs" and it lists the artist and song names most recently played! So if you hear a song you like, you can get the name and artist. The star icon at lower left is for selecting a current station as one of your favorites.

Some stations show what you are listening to as they broadcast.

Of course... I hardly ever listen to the radio anyway.

I don't see a radio app on the iPod Touch, but I would think you could download one.

BACKUP

Myself, I feel the need for backups for all my songs, so that if I lose or break my iPod, I can buy another one and get my songs on easily, with all of them already properly renamed, and with the artists' names, instead of just track numbers. Yet, as I've mentioned, I can't stand having tons of material in my iTunes library. So, automatic syncing is not an option for me, since I keep my iTunes library empty.

My solution – I keep a backup copy of all my music on the computer, and also on an external hard drive. That way if I lose or break the iPod, I can use the "Transferring Music from Computer to iPod" procedure described above, to fairly easily copy my whole music collection onto a new iPod.

In theory, you can back up your iTunes library by clicking some backup option when you initially download material, but, I don't normally do that, and I don't think it covers my numerous, old, non-iTunes CD songs.

In theory, you can back up your iTunes library on disk, by File > Library > "Back up to disc," but every time I tried that, it would take forever for just 3 songs, and then the computer would freeze! Again, it might have something to do with the fact that most of my songs are non-iTunes, as well as being renamed songs. Also, this method would require 3 DVD disks to get all my material on. And, the disks are not playable, but can only be used to restore an iTunes library. But, as I said, it wouldn't work for me anyway, despite the fact that iTunes Help includes the word "easily". Yeah, right.

In theory, you can simply right-click a song, copy, and paste it into a folder, but, often that would not work, though other times, it would. Tried all kinds of variations. I think too much fiddling (moving, renaming, etc. at the wrong time) may have made some songs no longer available, and I would get a message including the words "because the original file could not be found."

Aha, yes. When I started over from scratch, I finally got it to work consistently. See "Transferring CD Music to iPod" above.

Following the "Transferring CD Music to iPod" procedure above should cover all disaster possibilities. I have a copy of all my music on 1) the iPod, 2) my computer, 3) my external hard drive.

If I lose my iPod, I have #2 or #3 for relatively easy backup.

If I lose my computer, I have #3 for back-up.

Transferring Purchased Content to Another Computer

This plan above also enables me to bypass the problem of what to do with my iPod music when I get a new computer. I can just transfer material from old computer to new computer.

Here's what the iPod Nano User Guide says about transferring material to a new computer:

Content that you purchase in iTunes on one computer can be transferred from iPod nano to an iTunes library on another computer. The other computer must be authorized to play content from your iTunes Store account.

To authorize another computer:
Open iTunes on the other computer and choose Store > Authorize Computer.

To transfer purchased content to another computer:
1 *Open iTunes on the other computer and choose Store > Authorize Computer.*
2 *Connect iPod nano to the newly authorized computer.*
3 *In iTunes, choose File > Transfer Purchases from iPod.*

Whether the above works for non-iTunes-purchased music, and just what happens to what, I don't know. I'm very wary and don't feel safe at all trying any kind of automatic procedure. I do not want to lose tons of transferring or naming work I've already done. I feel much more comfortable just using my method above – transfer song folders from old computer to new one, then transfer them to my iTunes library, then transfer them, manually, to my iPod.

Transferring Music from iPod to Computer

I have not been able to figure out how to do this. May not be able to. You can make a copy from your iTunes library to your computer, but when I click on an iPod playlist, getting the songs up at right, the same right-clicking procedures for making a copy, do not work, even though the "Copy" option is offered.

Checking the internet (I Googled "transferring iPod music to computer"), it seems you cannot do so, unless you buy separate software. For me, the backup plan I describe above – "Transferring CD Music to iPod" – should be fine.

Update: I did a little more research and you might be able to do it without separate software in the way I describe below. But, I gave up because it started doing funny things, freezing one song, allowing copies one time, not allowing copies another, etc. I did not want to sabotage hours of work so far by having random songs from my iPod suddenly disappear. My 21-step procedure above is fine for me.

But if you want to try, you might get somewhere. I don't recommend it, especially if you have tons of songs already on your iPod. I mean, it even refused to eject my iPod at one point, whereupon I gave up in abject terror that major material already on my iPod would be randomly ruined, or moved around, or hidden, or deleted, or frozen!

Nevertheless, here's the method (which I couldn't even start next time I tried it; couldn't find iPod "Control Folder"):

Computer > iPod icon > iPod Control folder > Music folder > That folder contains your iPod music, but it is very oddly arranged in numerous folders – FO1, FO2, FO3, etc. – each containing seemingly random songs. Yet the songs ARE there. So if you make a copy of all those folders into your Music folder under Owner, you've got all the songs, I think. But, randomly ordered and oddly named. > Presumably you can then import those songs to your iTunes account, and then have them automatically ordered (Edit, Preferences, Advanced tab, Keep iTunes Music Folder organized). > So, in theory, you've got your songs from your iPod to your computer and then back into your iTunes library, though not in their original order, but ordered by artist or album.

Update 4/11: I called iPod and they did not mention the above method, but they did confirm the other conclusions that I had come to, namely that, quote, *"any purchases that you've made from iTunes, when you plug your iPod into the new computer, iTunes will recognize those purchases and it will re-download those into your library."* But, *"When it comes to CD music or if you had bought music from other websites, those will not transfer. Syncing is a one way street from the computer to the iPod."*

So, to your computer, you can make a copy of songs from an iTunes playlist (right-click, Copy), but you cannot make a copy of songs from an iPod playlist.

So, again, my backup method is confirmed: If I've got all my music on an external hard drive, I can then transfer it to a new computer, and then import it to iTunes, and then transfer it to a new iPod.

When it transfers from external hard drive to iTunes, it's instantaneous, because it's already converted, and it already has all the song names and artists that I typed in during my original CD-to-iPod transfer process. So it's relatively easy and quick, especially compared to the original transfer with the typing-in-names process, which took huge time, a good half-hour or more for each disk! For me, a good 40 hours total for 73 disks/playlists.

iPOD – ADDITIONAL PROBLEMS – It's so deflating, when you think you have a handle on something, yet basic stuff is STILL problematic. It's a horrible feeling... but you work your way thru it patiently, gradually, persistently, and finally you get it.

New "iPod Touch"

I had decided to get a second iPod – a regular-sized iPod Touch – so I could leave my entire music collection on the "iPod Nano" one I have in my car, and use this second one for when I'm hiking or at the beach or whatever. I don't want to be constantly detaching the one in my car, plus I don't really like how small the Nano one is.

So I get the new iPod and still it's a struggle to learn how to get it working! Anyway, after two hours or so, I had it working OK. Here are some pieces of info in that process:

Attached iPod to computer.. it automatically installs its software.. registered it; have to register it.. needed ID and password; ID is email address.. password – couldn't find it; tried my usual one, no go; finally figured out I needed to capitalize the first letter; OK, got it.. Allows 5 laptops to sync with it.. noted my iPod serial number.. named it.. shows 6.5 GB capacity, though advertised as 8 GB.. downloaded updated version of software, which took over an hour.. didn't go at first; turned my computer automatic Sleep function off, which I realized was keeping it from downloading fully; computer needs to be on, not in Sleep mode.. OK, now I got it downloaded.. put in info so it would pick up signals from my router.. followed my notes from above.. problem: instead of seeing songs on my iPod, I was seeing iTunes store, advertisements, etc. I don't want to access iTunes wirelessly from my router; I want to transfer songs.. solution: I was pressing the wrong icon – the iTunes musical note icon, instead of the iPod musical note icon (they are virtually the same but a different color).. OK, so now I'm getting my actual songs on the iPod instead of iTunes website material.

Finally, I got it. I suppose it you grew up with an iPod, it's easy. But otherwise, what a pain! Though I have to say, once you get your setup done, all the navigating and features are quite intuitive; spend some time playing with it, and you can figure out most everything, without a user guide. Keep trying stuff, pressing items, swiping items, and so on.

Accessing the Internet with an iPod

You can access the internet with an iPod Touch, wirelessly, if you're within range of your wireless router or an internet café router (30 feet?) and have the password:

As long as I'm in my apartment, I can access the internet with this iPod. Which, to me, is kinda pointless since using my actual computer is easier. But, it's nice to know I can access the internet with my iPod if I'm by an internet café or hotspot.

Tap "Settings" icon > tap on "Wi-Fi" to get it on; wait a bit as it detects networks within range > I'm already on, so I just need to click on my own router's network, but if you need to get on, I think it asks for the password, you type it in, and click "Join", I think.

But then, from this point, I couldn't figure out how to access my email. And, for me, it's just not worth the trouble. When I'm within range of my router, I just use my computer; when I'm on vacation I normally do not want to see any email anyway.

Camera / Camcorder Function

For most of the apps, like the weather, you need to be connected to your router. But, the camera/camcorder function does not need that connection. Works great. My mood has improved greatly. Now I know how to listen to music while hiking, and to stop and maybe take video of a grizzly bear delighted to find me playing with her cubs.

Proper orientation is bottom (red on/off dot) to right, to get landscape orientation. Unless you press the self-portrait button at upper right, in which case red dot should be to the left. Note that if you film with the iPod in a vertical (portrait) position, the material comes out sideways! **So always record with the iPod in the horizontal position.** I noticed that the TV program *America's Funniest Home Videos* makes a big point to inform contributors of the proper orientation for taking footage.

Both sound and video quality are quite good, though not as good as regular camcorder quality.

There is no zoom feature that I can find.

Frame stability does not equal that of regular camcorders, though it's better than the Pocket camcorder I have. So the iPod video will not be that great for videos you take as you move or pan. There's no tripod port; just hold it as still as you can; maybe rest it on something as you shoot.

And importing pictures or video to a computer is easy: Attach iPod to computer > turn it on > "Import Pictures and Video" window comes up at lower right of screen. (If the AutoPlay window comes up instead of the Import window, click on Import Pictures and Videos choice, and then the Import window comes up at the lower right.) (If iTunes comes up, I "x" it out; I want the material in my Videos folder, not in my iTunes library.) > click "Import", which puts the material into the Videos folder (in a folder titled with the current date). So much easier than with my cell phone, as well as better quality by far.

(Note that when you click "Import," it automatically imports only new material. If you still have old, already imported clips on your iPod, it does not re-import those.)

iPod Video to DVD Disk

And of course getting your iPod video onto a DVD that plays on a DVD player is easy, isn't it? Hah! NO! I initially read that you can't do it without additional software, because the video format is different from what DVD players can read.

(Incidentally, my iPod clip originally landed in Windows Photo Gallery and I had to drag the clip to the desktop and then drop it into my Videos folder.)

– Windows Media Player – No go. (A geek guy told me you just use Windows Media Player. But, even though I selected "With a CD/DVD player", it would not play on my DVD player, but only in my computer.)

– iTunes – No go. (Another geek guy told me to use iTunes; but, that's only a data DVD, which also will not play in DVD players but only in your computer.)

To make a data DVD of iPod video material (which to me is pointless, since you've already got the file on your computer, but I suppose it makes sense if you want to give it to someone else to play in their computer): File > Add File to library > search for clip > highlight it > click Open > that puts it into your iTunes library under Movies > click Movies > shows your movie clips on the right > click File > New Playlist > name the list > drag and drop clip file into new Playlist > click on that Playlist > click File > Burn Playlist to disc > select Disk Format: "Data CD or DVD" > Burn > put in blank disk > it shows "Are you sure you wish to create a data DVD?" > OK, and it burns the clip to the disk. Once you hear "boing" sound, it's finished.

– Windows DVD Maker – No go. When I tried to import the clip from my Video folder, it showed empty, even though the clip IS there, meaning for whatever reason, it cannot import it.

So, with Windows Vista, I was not able to succeed with either Windows Media Player, Windows DVD Maker, or Windows Movie Maker. But, for whatever reason, I WAS able to succeed in Windows 7, as described below:

– SOLUTION – Even though Windows DVD Maker won't do it, if you go thru Windows Movie Maker, in Windows 7, it works! A bit odd, since Windows Movie Maker uses that very same Windows DVD Maker program to burn the material. (I'm guessing Movie Maker automatically converts the MPEG-4 (also called MP4) material to a usable format. At any rate, that's what worked for me. My iPod video played fine on my DVD player.

W7 – Windows Movie Maker > browse for the video clip in your Video folder (make sure you have the lower right dropdown arrow selected to "All Files") > highlight the clip > click Open, which puts it into your movie line > at far upper left, Movie Maker icon dropdown arrow > "Save movie" > Burn a DVD > title it > Save > after it saves it, wait a few seconds and it automatically brings up the Windows DVD Maker window, which now does have that clip in it > Next > Burn > put a blank DVD in, and it burns the disk, which now will play in a DVD player.

Note that under the "Project" tab, you can select either 16:9 (Widescreen) or 4:3 (Standard) aspect ratio.

The above solution worked every time for me, consistently, whereas all the other programs/variations consistently did not work.

If you have Vista instead of Windows 7, I suggest asking a Best Buy geek person to help you. The above Windows 7 procedure was the only solution I found for making a DVD from iPod Touch video, without third party software.

On / Off

So I had most everything figured out, how to navigate to material, etc. But, geez, I still had to struggle to figure out how to simply turn it on, and turn it off. Unbelievable! HOW TO TURN IT ON AND OFF!! Why is everything so difficult?!!

Anyway, here's the deal on that: The only external controls are the up and down volume buttons on the upper left, and the on/off button at upper right corner.

TO TURN IT ON, you press the On/Off button at upper right

corner, then slide the "slide to unlock" arrow to the right. Your icons come up. For me, I then click on the Music icon, so I can listen to music (under "Playlists") or to a book (under "More").

HOWEVER, if pressing the On/Off button did not give you the "slide to unlock" arrow (since the iPod was fully off rather than just sleeping), then press and HOLD the On/Off button, and a single apple icon shows up in the middle, and then WAIT twenty-five seconds!! for the "slide to unlock" arrow to appear.

You see how confusing it is? For twenty-five seconds you try all kinds of things, and you finally get it, but, you can't figure what you did to get it, because it turns out everything you did was irrelevant. The waiting was the only factor that counted!

If you're not playing anything but just have the icon window up, the iPod shuts off the screen after a while and then puts the iPod to sleep. In this case, next time you press the On button, you get the "slide to unlock" arrow. But if you powered it off, like below, and try to get it back on, then you get the Apple icon, and have to wait 25 seconds for the "slide to unlock" arrow to appear.

TO TURN IT OFF, press AND HOLD the on/off button, then slide the "slide to power off" arrow to the right.

I think it's good to think of an iPod not as a music-playing device that you simply turn on and off, but as a little computer, that needs to be powered on and powered off.

Just as I do with my computer, I now usually do not power my iPod Touch off. **I "Pause" what is playing, and just leave it, to go to sleep on its own.** Quicker to turn it back on that way.

Best Buy Geek person confirmed to me that that's probably the best way to turn off an iPod.

A recent TV program on Steve Jobs related how he did not like simple "Off" buttons, because they were vaguely symbolic of death.

No Silence Break Between Songs

I had been exploring my iPod Nano. I accidentally eliminated the 3 seconds of silent space between songs, so now my songs were starting at the very instant the previous one finished – a setup I hate! To get it back to 3 seconds silence between songs: Settings icon > Music > Audio Crossfade > tap on "On" so that it now shows "Off".

Playlist Repeat Loop

I was trying to get my playlists to stop when they reach the last song, instead of repeating. Apparently you can reach such a control on older iPods thru Settings > Repeat. But, neither of my iPods has such a category under Settings.

Solution:

For iPod Touch: When a song is playing, tap on the screen to bring up controls > tap on "repeat" icon (two circular white arrows) at upper left just below the song progress bar – the arrows turn blue and now the playlist will repeat; tap again and just the current song will repeat; tap again and the arrows turn white again and the playlist will stop at the last song.

For the iPod Nano: Hah! Hah! I say "Hah"! After two hours, I finally figured it out! → Same as above, except you have to get the right screen up: When a song is playing, tap on the big-music-note screen > that brings up one screen of controls; note the two white dots at bottom which represent the number of screens available > swipe to the left to bring up the second screen, which corresponds to the iPod Touch one noted above > tap on the same "repeat" icon (circular white arrows) to select repeat playlist, or repeat song, or no repeat.

I selected no repeat.

Attaching to Car Stereo

A positive note: I find that simply replacing one iPod with the other in my car works fine. No problem. Whichever one I attach, it simply continues playing right where it left off. I don't have to reset anything, reconfigure anything, enter a product number, turn cartwheels, etc. Hooray.

Belt Clip

Got a very useful "Survivor" brand case and belt clip, so I don't have to worry about dropping and damaging it. You have to fiddle with it for a while to learn how to take it apart and get your iPod into it, how to use the clip, etc.

User Guides

You can google any number of terms for the iPod Touch Manual or Guide, and get all kinds of stuff... other than the User Guide you're looking for! It seems to me that sites deliberately hook you into their site, and prominently display those words ("iPod Touch User Guide") YET don't have any place where you can actually download it, and try to sell you THEIR stuff, whatever it is. VERY annoying!

To actually get it: I googled "iPod Touch User Guide" and the third or fourth one down seemed the most legit (a PDF file) > clicked on that site > it immediately said it was downloading, so I waited a few minutes > and hooray, I got the correct official guide up on my screen > to make a copy, I clicked File at upper left > Save As > Save > got it onto my desktop > moved it into a folder I set up and named "iPod".

iPOD vs MP3 – These are the two main competing music management systems these days – for PMPs (Portable Music Players). It seems iPod can do more. But, it's more expensive, and it is tied to iTunes software. For me, since I get almost all of my music from iTunes, I went with the iPod. Can't tell you much about MP3, but I think it may be more versatile, since it is not tied to the iTunes program.

****

ISP – Internet Service Provider. A company that provides access to the internet. Mine is Comcast. The other big one is Verizon. They hook you up, you pay a monthly fee, and they send you the signals.

iTUNES – See under "MUSIC"

JUSTIFYING TEXT – "Justifying" text means having the text margin at the right, flush. Instead of having words end at different spots for each line ("ragged"), the ends of words all line up evenly at the right, like this very text you're reading. Of course, this means the computer calculates and automatically puts in the proper amount of space between all the words of that line to space them out evenly from margin to margin.

To get your text justified: Block it > CTRL+J (or click on the fourth icon from the left bottom in the Paragraph box at top).

Words Suddenly Spread Out on a Line

This happens when you accidentally press the SHIFT and ENTER keys.

Here's an example of words spread out. Very annoying. What hitting Shift and Enter does, is order the line to end, and justify as is, at whatever point your cursor is. That's why you see big spaces between words. You haven't really reached the end of the line, yet you ordered it to justify immediately.

To get rid of this spread-out formation of words, position the cursor at the end of that spread-out line, and press the Delete key at upper right of keyboard. That should do it.

Every so often you get spacing between words that is not consistent for a line. The first half of a line has fairly narrow spaces, the second half fairly wide spaces. Sometimes blocking the line, CTRL+L and then CTRL+J fixes it. Other times you just have to fiddle around with it, like pressing Enter, making both parts aligned left with no spacing, maybe knock out any tabs, then press Backspace key at the right spot to put the line parts back together. That has worked for me to make the spacing even.

Update 2011 – Yes, knocking out any tabs in the line usually fixes the problem. If you accidentally left a tab in the middle of the line, that will produce a line with two different spacing widths, the first half being different from the second.

Sometimes you can't knock out a tab in the middle of a line but need to separate lines so that the tab is at the start of a line, and then you can delete it, and then rejoin the lines with proper spacing.

Keeping Two Words Together

Hitting Shift and Enter is a good way to keep two words together. For example, if you have a movie title "Top Gun" near the end of a line, and "Gun" gets sent to the next line, hit Shift + Enter just before "Top" to end the line there and keep the two words together in the next line.

KERNING – See "SPACING BETWEEN LETTERS"

Wikipedia: *"In typography, **kerning** (less commonly **mortising**) is the process of adjusting the spacing between characters in a proportional font, usually to achieve a visually pleasing result."* Not sure, but I think kerning has to do with visually pleasing spacing between particular pairs of letters, as opposed to just proportional spacing.

KEYBOARD – Outside of the normal typing keys, here are some of the keys I find most useful:

Along the top

- Esc key get out of some applications.
- F1 for help.
- F4, for repeating the last function you did.
- Prt Sc, the print screen key – copies whatever is on the screen onto the clipboard; you can then paste it into a document.
- Delete – erases the letter immediately to the right of the cursor, or, deletes a blocked section of text.

Down the Right Side

- Home, to get to the start of a line.
- CTRL+Home, to get to the start of a document.
- End, to get to the end of a line.
- CTRL+End, to get to the end of a document.
- Page Up and Page Down, for medium-quick scrolling thru a document

Function of Each Key

Here's a website that has good information on what each key on the keyboard does: seoconsultants.com/windows/keyboard

Scroll down past the ads and it gives the info for every key, including CTRL+key functions.

KEYBOARD SHORTCUTS – See "SHORTCUT KEYS"

LABELS – You can buy 8½ x 11 sheets of labels, print on them, peel them off the backing, and stick them onto whatever. But, getting your text positioned exactly correctly on each label, can be a lot of work, a lot of trial and error. And, if you want to print directly onto envelopes, setting your printer tray to accommodate letters can also be a hassle.

Instead, I find using "Avery" label sheets and their free templates available online for downloading, is the best route. Each label spot on their template (instead of a blank page, you get a page of positioned label spots on your screen) is already perfectly positioned. Type in what you want, print out the sheet, peel the label off, and stick it onto the envelope or whatever.

For details on how to do this, see "BUSINESS CARDS". The process for making your own business cards using Avery label products and templates, is the same as the one you use for making labels.

Label Sheets – Repeated Use of Same Sheet

Note your two basic circumstances for labels: 1) Printing many labels of the same address or text. Here you only need to run the sheet thru once, to get a bunch of labels. 2) Printing labels or addresses, each of which is different. Here you need to run the same sheet thru numerous times.

Surprisingly, I've found that this second circumstance is not a problem. The fact that some labels are already peeled off and others are still there, making the sheet of uneven thickness, does not seem to affect the feeding, or the printing! Surprising, since normally I find successive sheets of different thicknesses do cause misfeeds. It seems a single sheet of varying thickness is OK though.

Labels for Disks

They do sell sheets with round labels that you can type on, print, and then peel off and stick onto a CD or DVD. But, if you do disk labels on a regular basis (as I do), my conclusion is that it is better to go with a printer with disk-printing capability and print directly onto printable disks. Paper labels can be problematic. Positioning might be inconsistent. The paper may eventually shrink, causing the disk to warp. Glue and label deterioration over time may make a disk unplayable.

You can label disks directly, freehand, with a marker (non-professional-looking of course). Note that "Flair" pens do not work; the ink rubs off very easily. Instead, use "Sharpie" brand; their ink stays on. (CVS has them, many colors.) If you prefer heavy, bold writing, you can use the MarksALot brand markers.

LANDSCAPE ORIENTATION – To get a page, either text or picture, printed horizontally, you need to put your document into "Landscape" orientation: Page Layout tab at top > Page Setup > Orientation > Landscape. To get it back to normal "Portrait" orientation, do the same but click "Portrait".

Note that putting the actual paper sideways into your printer is not the way to do it.

Backing Up Landscape Page

Printers may vary, but for my printer, a Landscape document comes out head to the left. To back up that sheet and get the second side oriented properly (head to head), it should be loaded in the tray – head to the left, printed side up.

Experiment with your printer till you get the correct setup for landscape page backing up; then make a note of the setup, so you don't have to go thru wasted copies getting it wrong next time. (Note that if the head came out to the left, the head should be at the left for feeding also; you just have to figure out if the printed first side goes face up or face down.)

LAPTOP – QUICK SHUTDOWN – By changing your "lid" setting to "Sleep" mode, you can have your laptop shut down quickly and automatically when you close the lid. And you can have it power up quickly by just opening the lid and pressing the On button. Both operations take only three seconds, as opposed to the standard on/off procedure, which takes a good two or three minutes! After years of using the normal procedure of Start, arrow, Shut down, I found that the lid method is a MAJOR improvement in user-friendliness. You don't have to wait for the computer to power up!

> Quick Shutdown – "Sleep" Mode
>
> Start > Control Panel > System and Maintenance [W7 – System and Security] > Power Options > Changing what closing the lid does > select > Save Changes.
>
> I recommend selecting (for both "On battery" and "Plugged in"):
>
> **For the power button, select "Sleep"**
> **For the lid closing, select "Sleep"**
>
> **That way closing the lid shuts it off; opening the lid and pressing the On button turns it on, quickly.**
>
> I also selected "Don't Require a Password."
>
> Why the power button wakes up the computer even though at one point I had selected "Do nothing" for it, I don't know. Does Vista ever make sense?

See also – "COMPUTER ON / OFF – SIMPLIFY"

Battery Drain

A computer in "sleep" mode uses very little energy. Microsoft recommends that you normally put your computer, either laptop or desktop, into "sleep" mode when you are not using it. And, if your laptop is not plugged in and the battery happens to be very low, the computer automatically saves your work to the hard drive and shuts itself off when the battery runs out.

LAPTOP BED DESK – This is a big thing, in my opinion. If you use your laptop daily, to be able to use it comfortably, while sitting or lying in bed, is a big thing!

I've had a "Laptop Lounger" for years and find it great for watching movies while in bed. Only costs $40, the height and angle are adjustable. (407 341-1789, "Laptoplounger.com")

I recently bought another laptop bed desk, the "Laptop Laidback," $80, 1 888 867-2225, "Sitincomfort.com." This one is even better. While the "Laptop Lounger" is excellent, it is not as readily adjustable, plus it's a bit awkward when transporting, with its parts sticking out kinda like a frozen octopus. The Laptop Laidback is more convenient, sturdier, easier to adjust, easier to fold up, and more stable (wider base).

"Laptop Lounger"

"Laptop Laidback"

You have to work a bit to get the exact setting that is comfortable for both watching movies and typing. The settings I like: Laptop Lounger at 8" clearance, 25° angle, for watching movies. With the "Lounger," I never got a comfortable angle for both movies and typing in bed. My preference is the "Laptop Laidback," at 9" clearance (full extension), 50° angle (2nd bottom notch), good for both movies and typing.

The "Laptop Laidback" has instructions diagrammed on it, but no written instructions, because they sell internationally. They recently improved their diagrammed instructions, and they are quite good now.

LETTER CASE – You can change the letter case of any section of text by blocking the section and clicking Home tab at top > Font box > "Aa" icon. Gives you choice of several options. Occasionally it doesn't respond; usually, putting the section into lower case first, and then ordering what you want, makes it work.

If you choose all caps, for a title, remember to make "a" and "the" smaller case, manually, afterwards.

LIGHTS AT FRONT EDGE OF COMPUTER – Laptops differ, but I have four small lights going across in front of the mouse touchpad: First one is power on or off, second is battery charging, third is active hard drive activity, fourth one is something to do with SONY.

LINE – DRAWING – See "DRAWING"

LINE – HORIZONTAL – See "HORIZONTAL LINE"

LINE SPACING – Like most functions that you order up, line spacing applies to your text from the point of your cursor forward, or, if you block a section, it applies to that blocked section.

Basic Line Spacing
– Single line spacing: press CTRL+1.
– Double spacing: press CTRL+2.
– One and a half line spacing: press CTRL+5.

Specific Line Spacing
Home tab at top > Paragraph box > Line Spacing icon dropdown arrow (to the left of the paint can) > Line Spacing Options > Spacing > make your selections.

More specifically: "Line Spacing:" go down to "Exactly" > At: > pick one and look in the preview window at the bottom, to see what is happening to your line spacing, till you get what you want > OK.

Website Text
I find I frequently change the line spacing (to single line spacing) of material I've imported from the internet, which invariably has embedded extra line spaces. After blocking the material, click the line spacing icon dropdown arrow > Line Spacing Options > Indents and Spacing tab > under "Spacing" I select "0" for Before and After, and "Single" for "Line spacing". That gets rid of those extra line spaces. And also usually clears up other odd stuff that occasionally shows up, like tops of lines missing.

Note that if you get rid of line spacing and don't like the results (because it presents as just one big chunk of text), you can block the whole thing, click the dropdown arrow of the line spacing icon, and click "Add Space Before Paragraph" so that you get a single space between all paragraphs. That gives you a nice intermediate level of formatting between the overkill of the original and no formatting at all.

Variable Line Spacing between Paragraphs
In that same window, you can select any number of specific line spacing settings. Or, you can change line spacing by pressing CTRL+[key, or CTRL+] key.

Say you have a text of 11-point font and you want some separation, between paragraphs, but, not a full-sized line space, but just a smaller line space. Press Enter to make a line space and then CTRL+[that line down to maybe 4-point size. Like the line above shaded in blue.

This is a good way to separate paragraphs yet save some space.

Unwanted Blank Space at Page Bottom
Sometimes you get unwanted empty space at the bottom of a page. To get the text to close up, usually this is what to do: CTRL+A your text pages first > Home tab > Paragraph box dropdown arrow > Line and Page Break tab > uncheck "Widow and Orphan control" > OK > and, I'm pretty sure, uncheck the other five boxes also, so that Vista doesn't keep paragraphs as set chunks but allows them to be split up from one page to the next, thereby avoiding those large empty spaces at bottoms of pages.

If you still have some pages not fixed by those actions, you can cut and move lines from the top of the next page to the empty space at the bottom of the previous page.

The other way to fix this problem – and perhaps the better way – is to make your bottom margin smaller. For example, when I order up Narrow margins, it's supposed to be .5 inches all around, yet with bottom page numbers, the bottom margin sets up NOT at .5 inch, but at one inch instead. So I just order up a .2 inch margin for the bottom, AND a "0" position for my page numbers at bottom. Then it gives me lower margins, and lower page numbers, and usually cuts out that empty space.

If you order lower bottom margins without also ordering lower page numbers at bottom, it may not have any effect. Need to do both, lowering the page number position first, to allow the text margin to get lower.

If you have trouble with this, start over, fresh. Select ¶ in the Paragraph box at top, to show all commands, and get rid of all section breaks, then get rid of your page numbers, select a common margin setting, like Narrow, then position your page numbers at "0", then reduce your bottom margin to .2. Starting over from scratch often fixes problems.

LINED PAPER – To make yourself some lined paper, press Shift and underline key (upper right, next to "0"), and hold them down while the line crawls across the page. Do that for several lines. Then block those lines, say five of them, and then press CTRL+ V repeatedly to enter blocks of 5 lines, till the end of the page, to get a full page on lines.

My particular printer has a nice lined paper feature. Just a press a button on it and it spits out a lined sheet of paper.

LINE – HORIZONTAL – To get a horizontal line across the page, press and hold the underline key at upper right. You can make it bold, not by ordering "bold" but by blocking it and ordering "underline."

You can also put in a quick horizontal line this way: Home > Paragraph box > border icon dropdown arrow (next to the paint can) > Horizontal Line. You can click on it to highlight it > right-click > Format Horizontal Line, for variations, like a fat, green line.

LINKS – A "link" is an underlined word, which, if you click on it, immediately sends you to some other designated place. Most websites have links, which send you either to another spot in that website, or, to another related website. When you hover your pointer over such an underlined word, the pointer turns into a white hand icon, indicating this is a link. If no hand appears, it's just an underlined word, not a link.

[Incidentally, if you want to match the blue font color of most links, the exact match is: Font Color icon dropdown arrow > More Colors > Custom tab > Red 0, Green 0, blue 255.]

Making A Link
If you have your own website, making a link is relatively easy – you pick your source word and your target word, and click the "Link" icon. That's it; the link is made.

Making a link inside a Word document is significantly more complex. But it can be a very useful feature. If, for example, you have ten chapters in a document, you can make ten links, so that when someone clicks on a chapter heading in your table of contents, it sends the person immediately down to the chapter text, instead of making the person laboriously scroll all the way down to the text.

To Make a Link in a Word Document:

1. Locate the target spot in your text down below, for example: "Chapter 13 – Lions."
2. Put the cursor just before the first word (just before "Chapter").
3. Click Insert tab at top, Links box, Bookmark.
4. Type in an identifying word or phrase.

Note that the link is made to the cursor spot, not the actual phrase you type in. So if you have "Chapter 13 – Lions" as your text target link, you can simply type in "Lions" to identify that link; the actual link will be made to the cursor spot. When you type in the target link word or phrase, you are not matching the actual text, but simply labeling it for identification when you select it LATER from the list under Hyperlink.

Note also that bookmark names must begin with a letter, not a number or quote mark. And, if you want to include more than one word, you must use the underscore character to separate words, for example – Chapter_13. If you don't, then the "Add" box will gray out and not be usable.

5. Click "Add"
6. That window disappears, but you now have the word identifying that target spot, in a list, under Hyperlink.

THEN:

7. Bring the cursor up to your source phrase (usually early in your text or on the first page), here for example, the chapter title "Chapter 13 – Lions" in your table of contents. Block those words.
8. Click Hyperlink. (Think of the prefix "hyper" literally – the overword, the word at the top.)
9. That brings up the "Insert Hyperlink" window.
10. Click "Place in This Document."
11. In the bigger box below is a list of your target words. Click on the desired one – "Lions" in our example.
12. That puts the word into the "Text to Display" box.
13. Click OK
14. That puts the phrase you blocked, into underlined blue.
15. That does it. Now when you press "CTRL+Click" (left-click) on that underlined blue word, it sends you down to the target spot below. (Internet links are a simple click only; for Word documents you have to use CTRL+Click.)
16. Final wrinkle. It kept working for me only on a second try, and then only intermittently thereafter! Solution: You must position the cursor exactly on the underlined source phrase, so that a small window pops up saying "CTRL+Click to follow link." If that window doesn't pop up first, you weren't exact and it won't work. But, if it does pop up, and it stays there as you press CTRL+click, it works.

Also, it changes the color of the source phrase from blue to purple after the first time you use it.

Summary:

To Make a Link in a Word Document

1. Click Bookmark, position the cursor
2. Type in your identifying word
3. Add
4. Block your Hyperlink word or phrase, click Hyperlink
5. Click on your identifying word
6. OK

To Send an Email with a Link to a Website

See "E-MAIL – OVERVIEW AND BASIC OPERATIONS" > "To Send an Email with a Link to a Website" (actually much easier than the Word Document link deal above).

LOCATION OF FILE – DETERMINING – First of all, when you create folders and documents, place them logically – all your pictures under "Pictures" folder, all your documents under "My Documents," all your financial documents under one folder, medical documents under one folder, etc. Good organization pays off in the long run.

If you're careless about where you stick documents, you'll pay the price later, when you have trouble finding them.

If you're in a folder, the address bar at the top shows you the succession of folders or locations, from left to right, that brought you to your current location. Like for me, it might be the succession "Owner ▶ Documents ▶ Religion ▶ Current Religion ▶ Rev. Smith ▶ September Letter," as locations get narrowed down.

If you don't remember where a file is, to find its location, use the Start search box. Enter the document or folder name, as best as you can remember, or even a word or phrase you know is in the folder or document you're looking for. Hopefully it will put the one you want, up into the list up top. Click on it to access it.

Now, usually you want to know where it is located for future reference, not just open it up. So, you can right-click on its icon, and click on "Open File Location." Or, click on Properties, then under the General tab; it shows you its location. Sometimes the location shown is long and goes off to the right beyond the box, so put your cursor on it, and move the cursor to the right to see the rest of the info.

See also "DOCUMENT FINDING"

LOGIN – NO PLACE TO CLICK – I forget details, but once I was trying to login at a place where it said "Login here," but after I put my info in, there was nothing else to press or click. So it did nothing! Solution: Put the info in, then press the Enter key!

LOGIN BOX – HARD TO SEE – Visually, the boxes into which you type your username, password, whatever, are often a bit tricky to see accurately. If you're not looking at them at the right angle, it's easy to mistake the area just above or below them as the place to type. Move your laptop screen/lid to a slightly different angle, and you can see better the actual box/bar into which you should type.

LYRICS OF SONGS – I like the website: LyricsMania.com. They have the lyrics to literally a million songs. Put your artist into the search box, click the spyglass. It lists all the artist's albums in reverse chronological order, with all the songs. Click on your song choice for lyrics.

It's also great for seeing if an artist has a recent album out.

MAINTENANCE TASKS – There are three maintenance tasks that should be done regularly. They don't have to be done, but they make things run more smoothly, and save space.

1. Disk Cleanup

This gets rid of unnecessary files, stuff you don't need any more, like temporary internet files.

At one point, I hadn't done it for a year, and it cleaned up 2½ GB of space. Start > Control Panel > Systems and Maintenance > Performance Information and Tools (at bottom) > Open Disk Cleanup (at left). (If a small "Disk Cleanup" window doesn't pop up, click on its icon in your taskbar at bottom. Or, easier, just type in "Disk Cleanup" in the Start search box, then click on it when it shows up at top. Click OK > it takes a minute or two to check your computer, then a window opens showing what can be deleted and how much space is saved. Check the categories you want deleted. Keep in mind that it deletes the Recycle Bin contents if you have that checked! So, uncheck that choice if you want to keep the Bin contents. Then click OK > it asks if you're sure > then click Delete Files, which it proceeds to do.

Note that any video material you have takes up a lot of space. If you have a program that allows you to record TV, be sure to delete material you no longer need. Owner > Links > Public > Recorded TV.

When I work with my movie-editing program, Studio, I need to click "Delete All Auxiliary Files" in that program every so often. One time it saved me 22 GB!

2. Defragging

This re-organizes where things are stored so that it is accessed more easily by the computer. Defragging doesn't clear up space, just makes things go faster.

Double-click Computer > right-click Local Disk C > Properties > Tools tab > "Defragment now".

I think Vista has automatic defragging. I have it set up to do it automatically every Wednesday 1 AM. Start > Programs > Accessories > System Tools > "dfrgui" > check "Run on a schedule" > select > OK.

3. Scan Disk

This repairs errors and problems in files and folders. It's a little more involved:

1. Double-click on Computer
2. Right-click on your main hard drive – for me, Local Disk (C)
3. Properties
4. Tools tab
5. Error-checking, Check Now
6. Click "Automatically fix file system errors"
7. Also click "Scan for and attempt recovery of bad sectors" for a more complete check
8. Start (don't use computer for other tasks while computer checks)
9. Shows "Windows cannot check the disk while it is in use"
10. Click "Schedule disk check"
11. Re-start computer
12. Upon restarting, the computer automatically goes thru the scan disk process.

I had never done this (at least the recovery of bad sectors part) and it took 2 and half hours.

13. Screen remains black with white text on it, telling you what it is checking. The bottom line shows what percent is done. At times it seems like it's not doing anything, but it is. Note how the number for files done out of how many, changes every so often. That check on files is followed by a check on "clusters." I had 239,000 files it went thru, and over 14 million clusters!

When you read some of the white text, you get an appreciation of how complex computers are.

14. I suppose I should go thru this process, both files and clusters, every so often, even though I didn't particularly see any difference in my computer performance afterwards.

"Cleanup" at Best Buy

If you've done the above 3 maintenance tasks, and your computer still seems to run slowly, I recommend taking it to Best Buy to get it checked out.

Recently it seemed to me that my computer was running slower than it used to (opening up documents, etc.). I took it to Best Buy (weekday afternoon, less crowded). Guy checked it right there. He said it wasn't bad. But he found my Network Sharing feature was on and using up whatever. (He had put "Event" into the Start search box to find an error list. Brought up Action Center under Control Panel, I think.) He turned that feature off. Now my computer runs a bit better, and, I'm no longer getting a "High CPU Usage" message from Norton popping up.

Guy also confirmed for me that just x'ing out that high CPU usage message was OK.

Uninstalling Programs to Save Space

In trying to save space, be careful about uninstalling programs. If you're not sure that you don't need it, leave it alone. It may be necessary to things you do, without your even knowing it. Of course, any new program that you happened to have downloaded and don't like after all, is safe to uninstall.

Cleaning Up Browsing History – See "BROWSING HISTORY – WEBSITES"

MACINTOSH vs MICROSOFT – From what I have heard, the MacIntosh operating system is set up more logically and is more user-friendly, for the normal, non-geek person, because its operating system was designed for its own hardware. But, Microsoft is more compatible with a wider range of computer companies and programs, making it more popular (91% of the market vs 5% for Mac). Myself, I'll stick with Microsoft, because that's what I'm used to, despite all its aggravations.

This manual does NOT cover how to do operations under the Macintosh system.

MAGNETS NEAR YOUR COMPUTER – You occasionally read warnings not to keep a magnet near the computer. But, from the reading I've done, a small magnet is very unlikely to do any damage to your computer. (They could damage floppy disks back in the days when those were used.) Says eHow.com: *"But modern-day computing has nothing to fear from household magnets."* (Though I think running magnets across your screen can mess up your colors, at least temporarily.)

Also read that flash drives and memory cards are not affected by minor magnetic fields.

Static electricity, however, IS a cause for concern. It can mess up computer components. If you have a deep pile carpet, discharge any build-up first by touching a metal door knob.

MAGNIFYING GLASS – See "EASE OF ACCESS"

MAPS – You can buy software that has maps, including street maps. Before I was on the internet I used to have a Rand McNally CD. It had a lot of confusing features, but straightforward finding of streets was simple enough.

If you're on the internet, there's all kinds of options. For me, when I click on Internet Explorer, the Yahoo window for my email opens up. I usually can find Yahoo "Maps" somewhere. Latest setup: Click "Yahoo!" at upper right > Yahoo Sites at left, More Yahoo! Sites > Maps.

You can type in your home address and then your target address, and it will give you directions, and an estimate of time and distance. Very useful (though the written directions are kinda suspect, often containing too many turns, instead of the direct route).

It shows the map on the right. At the upper left, it has a Plus and Minus scale which you can click on to zoom in or out. Click plus to get right down to the streets in your immediate neighborhood; click minus to zoom out to the whole country. You can also "grab" the map with your pointer and move it left, right, up, down.

Can also use Satellite, or Hybrid versions of the map, clicking on one of three icons on upper right. Satellite is good, though it doesn't get as close as Google-Earth. Hybrid is good; shows satellite view, with key streets indicated also.

Rand McNally has a nice, similar program on their website.

Saving a Location

It's good to save your home location (the start of any trip), so that you don't have to retype it in every time. Unfortunately, the way to do this has recently by revised by Yahoo. (Damn them; I hate the way so many internet sites constantly confuse and annoy you by changing formats and setups, under the assumption that they are making things better.) Keep fiddling with logical places to click and eventually you should be able to set a default "Home" location. Used to be:

1. Under "Get Map and Directions" at left, click the dropdown arrow to the right of the box "A"
2. Click "Add New Location"
3. Window comes up; fill in the address info
4. Click "Save"
5. Click "Finished"
6. Open up Maps again, click the dropdown arrow of box "A"
7. Click on your address
8. Check the "Make this my default location for Yahoo!" And, also, just to be sure, check "Default" right next to the actual address lower down. Close the window with the "x".
9. From that point on, you just need to click on the dropdown arrow and click on your home default address for your start-trip address. And, in the actual map at the right, it shows the immediate area of your default location, with a "+" sign right at your address.

Problems

Upon opening Maps, it seemed to keep putting up my old address map as the default location, instead of my new one. But, upon closer examination, it was really just putting up a local quadrant, which includes both my old and new addresses (they are only 2 miles apart). I finally noticed that the "+" sign was NOT actually on my old address, but just in the center of that quadrant. Once I clicked on the dropdown arrow and on my current "Home" address, the "+" sign relocated itself right on my current address.

Usually they have a purple line showing your route on the map. This line suddenly disappeared one day. Then, at some point a popup offered latest Mozilla Firefox free upload for making things better. I uploaded it (clicking both Run and Save). And now I have the purple line back! Hooray.

MARGINS – To set text margins in a document: Page Layout tab at top > Page Setup box > Margins, make your selection (wide, narrow, etc.). If you want custom margins, then under Margin choices, select "Custom Margins" at bottom, a window opens, put in your top, bottom, left, and right margins, then click OK. That sets the margins for your current document (blocking the whole document is not necessary). For variable margins within a document, see below.

I often like to have a 3½ inch margin on the right for editing notes, as I'm writing a paper, rather than the traditional skipping lines format. I like to do my revising on the right, rather than in between lines.

For stuff I'm working on, I prefer Narrow margins (.5 inch all around), so that I use the whole sheet of paper. For more formal stuff, like a letter, Normal or Wide is good.

Margin Limits

Printers vary, but my Epson 810 will do this: For top and side margins it can go virtually to the edge of the paper. Setting those margins at .2 inch worked fine. The bottom margin, however, is a little hinky. Regardless of what you order and what it shows on your screen, once you print it, it comes out wider than you ordered. .4 inch came out around one inch. But, if you fiddle around with it, you can get it pretty low. I ordered .1; a window came up saying "One or more margins are set outside the printable area of the page"; I clicked on "Fix"; it showed .12 as a fix, and then it ended up printing about .4 from the bottom.

Footers / Page Numbers

You'd have to experiment to see what position you like for your page numbers at the bottom of the page, and for how low you can go.

For me, I like Narrow text margins all around (.5 inches) and the page numbers set at .4. Insert tab at top > Header and Footer box > Page Number > Bottom of Page > Plain Number 2 > Position box, at top > Footer from Bottom > .4 > Close Header and Footer. Of course, the bottom doesn't really come out as ordered; it's more like a one-inch margin with the page number at half an inch, even though the top, left, and right margins ARE at .5 inch. But, that setup actually looks nice.

If you really do want to get the bottom margin lower, and keep a bottom page number, double-click on the page number to bring up page number options at top > Position box > Footer from Bottom > select a number lower than .4 > Close Header and Footer. You can go as low a "0" for the position of the footer (page number). Then it comes out with a ½ inch margin at bottom and the page number below the text, ⅜ of an inch from the bottom of the page. That's as low as you can go.

Margins – Variable

Usually it's easier to simply use indents (see "INDENTING") to get a portion of your text into a different margin setup. But, you can vary your margins within a text this way: Block the portion of text you want with different margins > Insert > Page Setup > Margins > Custom Margins > Margins tab, set your margins > Apply To: (at bottom left), select "This section" instead of "Whole document" > OK.

Default Margins

Under "Custom Margins", set your desired margins, then click the "Default" box at lower left, OK. Then, for every time you do CTRL+N for a new document, it will have those margins already. See also "DEFAULT 'WORD DOCUMENT' FORMAT"

MARGIN PROBLEMS

Extra Space at Bottom of Page

See "LINE SPACING" > "Unwanted Blank Space at Page Bottom"

Margins – Refuses to Change:

If your computer doesn't let you change your margins (most likely because of many changes you've made – scanning in, multiple columns, cobbling together, different margins, etc.), CTRL+A and put it ALL back to a single column first, then it usually allows you to change margins. If that doesn't work, what should work is this: Click ¶ in the Paragraph box at top (to show all your commands), and delete any section breaks, then make your margin change.

Margin Won't Stay at Top

At one point, my top margin would refuse to stay at the top and kept moving down. Turned out I had accidentally ordered "Vertical Centering." Page Layout > Page Setup > Margins > Custom Margins > Layout tab > Vertical alignment... changed it to "Top." Normally it's "Top"; I had ordered "Center" by mistake, which centers the text vertically (top to bottom), and that's why my top margin kept automatically dropping down from the top. I'd start typing and the text would come out at the center of the page.

Margin Stuck

At one point, whenever I tried to start a new document, my top margin was stuck at .1, right at the very top. Changing margins or selecting default margins, did NOT change it. That changed the side margins but not the one at the top. I also noticed the bottom margin was likewise stuck. Tried all kinds of things. No luck.

Update: Well, I got it fixed, but it's kind of a two wrongs make a right deal: Even though I did not want a "gutter" margin (extra space for a margin to allow for binding not to interfere with the text), I ordered up a .5 top gutter margin, and that fixed it. Now when I do CTRL+N, the new document has both a top and bottom .5 margin. Or if I order up Narrow Margins, I get .5 margins all around, the way I like it.

Page Layout tab > Page Setup box > Margins > Custom Margins > Margin tab > Gutter .5 > Gutter position "Top" > OK.

Hey, guess what? That temporary fix turned out to be a permanent fix. The next time I did CTRL+N and viewed the margin settings, it did not show any gutter margin order (the setting was back to "0"), YET the margins were all at .5. Those stuck top and bottom .1 margins were now fixed.

Margins Won't Change for the WHOLE Document

This is usually due to either of two things:

1. You have "This section" selected under Custom Margins, Apply to:, instead of "Whole document."
2. You have section breaks in your document. Need to get rid of those section breaks so that margin changes apply to the whole document rather than just to that section. You do that by clicking on the ¶ icon in the Paragraph box at top (to show all your commands), and then deleting any section breaks, with either the Backspace or Delete keys. The section breaks show as dotted lines going across the page, literally labeled "Section Break." See also "SECTION BREAKS."

MAXIMIZE / MINIMIZE – WINDOWS – Click the white square icon at far upper right (between the minus and the x) to toggle between full-screen size and smaller size for a window.

If you hover you pointer over that icon, it shows either "Maximize" or "Restore Down." (The label toggles between the two depending on which size you're in.) And that's how you change window sizes.

Note that the icon actually labeled "Minimize" is the third on the left, the white minus icon. And it does not make the item on screen smaller, but takes it off-screen and puts it into temporary storage on your taskbar at bottom.

So, on a computer, "Minimize" is not the opposite of "Maximize"; "Restore Down" is.

I suspect many people use the term "minimize" to mean making a window smaller, but technically, "minimize" means removing the window from the screen down to the taskbar.

Opening in Unwanted Size

In theory, windows, under the categories of folder, document, or internet, will open in the same size you closed the last one of their category in.

If you want windows to open full-screen, close the last one out in full-screen. If you want less than full-screen, manually drag the current one to the size and position you want, and then the next item you open under that category will open in that same size and that same position.

If it doesn't work, then hold down both the CTRL and Shift key as you click on the close-out x. That, I've read, should do it. BUT, I've experimented a lot with this and found that holding those two keys sometimes makes the difference but other times it doesn't. And that closing down a small window a second or third time or more, sometimes makes it take effect.

It's unpredictable!

My recommendation: Once you get a reduced size you like, leave it; don't fiddle with it any more. That way you have your two choices – full size and that reduced size.

Update

Oh, it's just so crazy. All the things I said above work sometimes YET not other times. Lately my Word document windows keep opening up at small size instead of the full-screen size I closed them out in... contrary to what it was doing before.

As successful as Microsoft is, they are STUPID. They think "more and more and new and more" gets people to buy... which it does. But they think use-friendly doesn't really tangibly bring in money... but it WOULD, in the long run, it WOULD, even though it's not tangibly quantifiable. Like a small business that has no clue how much better they would do if only they had friendly service.

So MS does its marketing research, finds out they need to be more user-friendly; they make some minor changes, and put out TV ads about how user-friendly they are now. Absolute horse manure. They still don't get it.

Case in point, the glitch described above – Windows won't even stay at the size you want them. Or how about migrating desktop icons? They won't even stay where you put them! How much more basic can you get!? And MS thinks it's user-friendly. Hah!

The "Show Desktop" Icon

There is also a "Show desktop" icon (a translucent empty vertical rectangle), on the taskbar (at the absolute bottom and right of your screen, to the right of the time). Click on it to minimize all open windows to the taskbar. Click it again to put the windows back up.

MEMORY CARDS – These are storage device cards that function very much like flash drives. You can store digital info on them, from your computer, or camera, etc. They are small, re-recordable, and they can retain data without power. I think they are most often used with cameras, to transfer pictures to a computer. I don't have much experience with them, but I think it's important to make sure your computer has a proper port for the card. I'd bring both my computer and camera in to Best Buy to ask for the correct memory card. Samples:

MEMORY (RAM) – Random Access Memory. This is not something you have to know, but I think it's a key concept in how computers work. You have all your programs, files, and info on the hard drive of your computer. When you go to work with any of this info, you must pull it up from the hard drive and have it temporarily stored in memory, so you can see it and work with it.

I think of "memory" as "active material," material you are currently working with. RAM holds information that is currently being used.

Then, when you save any changes, that makes the changes permanent, back onto your hard drive. If you don't save the changes, when "memory" closes down, when you turn the computer off, you lose those changes, and retain only what you originally had.

The amount of memory you have varies by computer. I think I have 2 GB of memory. When I was working with video, I found I could make a copy of a DVD to an external hard drive if it was less than 2 GB, but it would not work for a video that was 4 GB.

You can add RAM to your computer to give it more capacity. Check with a Best Buy store.

MIGRATING ICONS – With my new computer, I find that a few of my icons on the desktop keep migrating to the left. I wake my computer and they've changed positions. It's usually ones in the middle of the screen and not set inside a neat block of other icons. Very annoying. Have to put them back each time. Asked Geek guy about it; he didn't know how to fix it. He thought it was just an anomaly.

However, I researched the issue on the web, and I see it is not an anomaly, peculiar to my particular computer. Others have the same problem.

I've read that this is the solution:

Right-click empty spot on desktop > View > "Align icons to grid" to align them > THEN uncheck "Align icons to grid", and they now stay there next time you turn computer on or wake it up. Then next time you add an icon, check Align to align it, then uncheck Align to lock it in that position.

Keeping "Align" checked was the problem... so I thought.

But, it's not. It's so frustrating. You work with something for hours, and you think you've finally, finally, got the answer... but it turns out that that isn't right either. I kept track to make sure the above solution was correct. What did I find? In over 40 plus tries – aligned, not aligned, sleep, or shut off – the icons stayed only temporarily. After you work with a document, then one, two or more icons not embedded in a bunch, keep migrating to the left to empty spots.

I think right-clicking the desktop > View > Refresh; or click F5, also sets the icon positions, but, you have do it every time you put your computer to sleep or shut it off!

Checked with Best Buy. Geek person told me shutting computer off, instead of having it go to sleep, is the only way to keep icons in the same spots. But, logically, that's no answer, since the problem is not just migrating icons upon turning it on, but migrating icons AFTER I work on a document or two.

I notice it's Word document icons migrating, not folders or programs.

Workaround Solutions

– Geek guy said there's a thing you can download free called "Fences," which enables you to corral groups of icons on your desktop.

– You could arrange your icons so that the ones that tend to migrate to the left are already at the left.

– My preferred solution:

Since it's document icons that migrate, rather than program or folder icons, I arrange all my program and folder icons so that I leave an empty couple of rows on the far left, and I place any document icons there at the left. They still move around a bit, but they do stay over at the left in those two rows.

I also put desktop documents of a similar category into their own non-migrating folders. [Right-click empty spot on desktop > New > Folder > name it > drag items into that folder.]

Internet Posts

I'll let other consumers express my frustration here on this issue. And this is on Microsoft's own website "answers.microsoft.com"!

"I can only surmise that no one at Microsoft uses Windows 7 because this minor bug is so irritating I'm ready to switch to a new OS. If I worked at Microsoft and I had to deal with this every day, the team lead responsible would be sitting at my computer putting my icons back where they belong every day until this bug is fixed."

"Does MS ever do sanity checks, or Quality Assurance???"

"We know not to get too excited by finding a workaround for Microsoft's software bugs."

"I see posts dated from 2009; we are in 2011. I don't see a single post from a Microsoft technician so it's been at least 2 years they really don't care. Windows 7 is out; we have made our billions of dollars, who cares about those stupid little users who paid big bucks for our buggy OS? Let them press F5 (refresh) while holding the shift key and their little sister's hand...that might work, huh."

Migrating Taskbar Icons

Icons on my taskbar seem to migrate arbitrarily at times. Usually not a problem though. My own website login icon is the most weird: If it's on the desktop, it doesn't work. A copy of it on the left of my taskbar doesn't work either, but if I click it, it moves to the right, and then it does work, but only after jumping into the Hidden Icons bunch.

MODEM – This is the blinking device that sits between the wall and your computer. It gets internet signals from the wall cable, then sends them to your computer thru another cable ("Ethernet" cable). You should keep it on all the time.

Modem vs Router

A modem sends signals from the wall cable to your computer.

A router is another device, which is attached to the modem. It gets signals from the modem and sends them out, wirelessly, to one or more computers or devices.

So if you have a large house and many computers, you'd probably want a router, which you attach to the modem. They do sell combination modem/routers ($100). Myself, I live in a small apartment, so for a long time I didn't think I needed a router. But, now that I have one, I find the wireless capability extremely convenient. See "ROUTER".

Direct computer connection to the modem means it is not susceptible to signal interception by computer-savvy thieves. On the other hand, direct connection to a modem makes your computer more susceptible to virus attacks. Wireless routers actually give an additional level of security.

Modems usually have only one Ethernet port, so you can only use one computer at a time. With a router you can use more than one computer.

Buying Your Own Modem

I noticed I pay $7 per month to rent my modem from Comcast. Asked about that. Yep, it's better to simply buy your own ($70). Pays for itself within a year. So I bought one. It comes with a CD, but you need the CD only if you want to connect to your computer thru a USB port, instead of the "Ethernet" port (the normal internet wire with ends that look like a rectangle with a mound, and that click in). So I didn't need the CD.

I figured you just plug the thing in, in place of my old one, and it's ready to go. Yeah, right. Nothing is easy in the computer world.

I attached my new modem: I unscrewed my old one from the wall wire (had to turn the modem itself instead of the metal collar on the wire, because the collar wouldn't turn; likewise for screwing on my new one). I plugged in the power cord and attached it to the modem, connected the Ethernet wire between modem and computer. Turned on my computer. No go. I tried all kinds of things and got nowhere.

I called Comcast. Turns out I never could have gotten anywhere – they needed to change my account from "leased modem" mode to "own modem" mode. Guy put me in touch with a person to help me here. She needed the name, model number, and three (yes, three) serial numbers from my Motorola modem. She was in the process of doing stuff on her end (after which she said I'd be all set and would not have to go thru the activation procedure), but right at that point my Verizon telephone service broke in to update me on my account balance, cutting off my connection.

Again got nowhere on my own.

I called Comcast again. (Of course they always get your phone number in case you get disconnected, but when you actually do get disconnected, do they call you? No.)

Had to go thru the whole serial number deal again. And was on the phone for close to an hour. Was put on hold at least 9 times (with of course the mandatory horrible broken-up music blaring in the meantime). She had me unplug my internet wire from the wall and then re-plug it. She had me try to press the reset button on the modem (there was none). She tried to reset it from her end. Had me re-start my computer, etc., etc. Finally we had to schedule a service person to come out tomorrow to my apartment. Of course in the meantime, I have no internet.

The modem is a major brand, sold at a major store, yet after three hours of trying, I could not use it. As Mother Theresa used to say, "This is f'ing unbelievable!"

I'm not a conspiracy theorist type, but I would not be at all surprised that the higher-ups at Comcast make no effort to make things easy for this particular operation. Because they are fully aware how much dough millions of customers leasing modems at $7 per month, brings in for them.

Tech lady said they have my modem registered with them now, but for some reason it's not online.

I note that at one point she referred to the modem "address"; what she meant by that is the modem serial number. Confusing. And she confirmed that my not using the CD that came with the modem (for USB connection) was not the problem.

So the technician should be here tomorrow between 5 and 7 pm. My "oh-so-important" ticket number is CR247482578. Reminds me of Andy Rooney, annoyed at 20-digit ID numbers when, he says, there aren't even that many people in the world!

6:30 the next day. Hooray. He fixed it in ten minutes, no charge. Turns out the lady on the phone put in the wrong serial number, the USB one instead of the regular one. Once he called in the proper number, and then clicked on a few things under Start > Control Panel > Network and Internet, my internet was up. I didn't see exactly which choices he clicked there. Anyway, I've got internet now.

By the way, guy said this particular model modem does not in fact have a reset button. The guy reset the modem thru my computer (I don't know how he did that, though.)

I suppose if you call in to Comcast, register your new modem with them, and just keep default settings, you can do this on your own. But, I would recommend this: If you're going to change from a leased modem to an owned one, pick a day or two during which you know you won't especially need internet, in case you have problems, like I did. Good luck.

Final step was to return my old modem to Comcast office so I would no longer get charged for it. Getting out of my car, I thought to myself, "Something's going to go wrong. I just know something is going to go wrong, like maybe 25 people will be ahead of me in line... Yep, exactly 25, not counting one little kid. But, luckily, it went fast, 15 minutes, all set.

MOUSE – For a desktop computer, you move the mouse across a pad or surface to move the pointer arrow and locate items or functions on your screen, and then you click it to select the item.

For a laptop, the mouse is built in at the front. You slide your finger across the touchpad to move the pointer, and then left-click it.

For Word documents, the pointer arrow becomes an "I-beam" cursor when it is located inside the text of a document. If you left-click as the pointer rests in a document, the typing cursor (a straight vertical bar) locates itself there, and if you type, your typing proceeds from that point.

A left-click on a function icon at top orders up that function. For example, placing the pointer on the Font box "B" icon, and left-clicking, orders up bold type.

For document, folder, or program icons, a double-left click opens that file. Or, you can open a file by right-clicking and selecting "Open." A right-click brings up a menu of things you can do to that file (open it, move it, rename it, delete it, etc.).

Sticky Pointer

Every so often, the pointer responds hesitantly to your finger slide. I don't know if that's static electricity or what, but usually just keep trying to move it, and eventually it responds. Sometimes moving your finger very lightly across the surface does the trick. Update: Lately I find blowing warm air on my finger first, works pretty well.

Another reason a pointer may seem sticky or erratic at times is this: You're resting your left finger a bit on the left side of the pad as you slide your right finger across the pad. You've got to get that left finger completely off the pad or else the right finger slide does not move the mouse. (And there IS a tendency to rest that left finger on the pad just above the constantly used left-click button.)

Mouse Settings

If you want to change something with the mouse: Start > Control Panel > Hardware and Sound > Devices and Printers > Mouse, select. Usually just leave it at default settings, but you might want to get rid of some features, that I, for one, can't stand. (I can't remember whether these features were default settings or not):

Tapping – See also "MOUSE – TAPPING FUNCTION" below.

Scrolling – Another annoying setting I got rid of was one-finger scrolling. It seemed that very often the cursor would jump up in my text or down in my text, suddenly, when I just slightly touched the touchpad. VERY ANNOYING. I figured maybe the one-finger scrolling function was on. Sure enough, it was. Got rid of it: Click Mouse > Function tab > uncheck Use Scroll Function > OK.

[W7 – Mouse > Device Settings > Settings > click on scrolling + sign > click on One Finger Scrolling > uncheck all the items there > OK > OK.]

Update, Pinch Zoom function is also under Scrolling; click on the + signs to reach this and other categories. Under "One-Finger Scrolling" are options for areas of the mousepad to keep sensitive; this may be why the mouse was reacting to my touching any part of the mousepad at one point.

Anyway, I use the regular scroll bar at right for the most part, because I'm so used to it.

Mouse Speed – You might want to change the pointer speed. Mouse > Pointer Options tab > slide bar to right, OK. The default is I think set near the fastest speed. I moved it all the way to the right for maximum speed. I see no point in having it move slowly. I tried it at slowest speed; saw no advantage at all to having it move limaceously (limaceous = like a slug).

Update: I scaled it back a bit from max speed. I think speed here might be tantamount to sensitivity, and it seemed like sometimes I would accidentally touch the mouse just a bit and the damned cursor would jump to an unwanted spot. Likewise for double-click speed (under the Buttons tab); I scaled it back from the fastest speed; it seemed like an unwanted website link would open up suddenly just because I grazed the mouse a tiny bit.

Mouse for Left-Handed People

If you want to switch left and right side button functions on the mouse:

For Vista, I think it's: Mouse > Buttons tab > in button selection box, click the dropdown arrow next to "Right" > scroll UP to "Click" > OK.

For Windows 7, it's: Mouse > under Buttons tab, under "Button configuration", select "Left-handed" > RIGHT-click OK (the switch takes place immediately even before you click OK; the right side is doing what the left side used to do and vice versa).

Getting back to the original right-handed setup is – surprise, surprise – confusing and tricky; you have to press the correct buttons in the correct order: First you have to RIGHT-click your way to the "Button configuration" window > right-click the "Left-handed" selection > right-click the "Cancel" button. That's it.

Notice that even when you were in left-handed mode, "Right-handed" was checked (!) next time you opened that window (by left-handed right-clicking); so you try all sorts of combinations, to order up right-handed clicking again, getting nowhere, until you think of using the "Cancel" button. So, basically, you order up left-handed by clicking left-handed, but you order up right-handed, not by clicking "right-handed," but by clicking "left-handed" and canceling it! The computer world has a knack for making the simplest things complicated.

Now, unless you, a lefty, are the only one using your computer, and, it's the only computer you use, I would think it's easier to simply get used to using regular righty mode, since most computers are set up that way.

"Mousepad" vs "Touchpad"

Note the difference here. "A mousepad" is a pad one uses for a traditional computer mouse to roll across, for better friction. Whereas a "touchpad" is the built-in rectangular section of a laptop mouse that you slide your finger across.

Spinning the Mouse

Somewhere in the AR book, he talks about spinning the wheel of the mouse to increase the size of something. I have no external mouse, but only the touchpad on my laptop, but I think you can sometimes replicate this function by sliding your right finger up or down the right side of the pad. I figure this, because my Chessmaster 9000 program includes resizing the board this way. But, it is very hinky. Usually you have to try it several times to get it to work! BUT, I found that pressing the ALT key and sliding your finger up or down, makes it work consistently. Also, more recently, I find that instead of sliding the finger back to increase the board size (with mixed results), slide it forward first, then slide it back. That makes it more consistent.

Attaching a Regular Mouse

Some people like a regular, external mouse for their laptop, instead of the touchpad. I've never done it, but I suspect attaching one is easy enough; I'm pretty sure you attach it to a USB port, and install it following the "Wizard" instructions. (Or, go to Start > Control Panel > Printers and Hardware > Mouse > click on the mouse's icon.)

Just don't disable your internal touchpad until you've got the new one working.

MOUSE – TAPPING FUNCTION – A problem I had when I first got my laptop was that just touching the pad brought up random functions. Very annoying. Turned out the "Tapping" function was on, meaning that just tapping the touchpad, functioned the same as left-clicking. Ugh. Overkill, as usual. Satisfies the Geek who loves new tricks, but just befuddles and annoys the normal user. Got rid of that: Mouse > Tapping tab > uncheck Tapping at upper left > OK.

[W7 – Mouse > Device Settings tab at top > Settings at middle right > click on the word Tapping > shows box at right > uncheck "Enable Tapping" > OK > OK.

Note that the + signs in front of the categories at left simply mean that if you click on the plus it will show subcategories under that word; the plus does not mean it is selected; you select by clicking on the word to highlight it and then enabling the category by checking the box at right.]

New computers usually come with mouse tapping functionality. In other words, touching your mousepad in certain ways makes certain operations occur. Like tapping with one finger will equal left-clicking, or swiping down with two fingers will make scrolling occur, or pinching two fingers together will decease screen size, etc., etc. How wonderful! Yes?

NO! I HATE this feature! I am constantly accidentally touching the mouse with an off finger and ordering up functions I do not want! VERY ANNOYING. I had turned this feature off for my last computer. Here's the trouble I had turning the feature off for my new computer:

Tried to do so for my new computer with Windows 7, but I could not find any "Tapping" tab.

Start > Control Panel > Hardware and Sound > Devices and Printers > Mouse > .... then what?

Figured out the "ELAN" tab was for the mouse, and I unchecked it ("Disable") figuring that might disable the tapping. No, it disabled the mouse! So now my mouse won't work and I can't move the pointer at all – it's frozen on the screen now. But I need the mouse, to enable the mouse! A catch 22.

I pressed the Start key (since I could no longer access the Start button!) and navigated selections by use of the arrow keys and the Tab key, and pressing Enter. That works, though it often got stuck and I would have to start over and alternate using the Tab key and the arrow keys. Finally got to my desired selection. And pressed Enter to enable the mouse again. That unfroze it. Whew!

OK, and then I figured out that the tapping functionality is under ELAN > Options. [Update – I can't find ELAN anymore; the proper tab is now "Device Settings".] They have a list of things it does on the left. Click on an item to highlight it, then click OK, OK, and restart computer (I think) to enable those functions.

The items have a plus sign to the left; if you click on the plus sign, it shows further options under that category. For example, under Scrolling it has Pinch Zoom. Also when you click on an item it gives a decent explanation on the right for what it does.

The stupidest thing is that they have "Buttons" listed right in among the other items, when in fact "Buttons" is not a function category but is essentially the On/Off button for the mouse!!

Anyway, I unchecked all of them including the tapping function one, all except the "Button" function. And that did it. I got rid of the tapping nonsense.

For Windows 7, the route is: Start > Control Panel > Mouse > Device Settings tab > Synaptics TouchPad > Settings > Tapping.

Except that another catch-22 came up. I accidentally unchecked the "Button" selection also, and now my mouse won't work again!

It is so frustrating how the computer world – the guys who invent this stuff – have such a distorted understanding of user-friendliness. They think having more ways to do things and more options, is user-friendliness. No! User friendliness means anticipating what the consumer's actual experience will be, providing basic info that people need to know to make things work, and having a consistent and logical way for each operation. User friendliness does not mean adding more and more bells and whistles!

I have no doubt millions of people hate this mouse tapping function. For most of us, it simply causes more problems than it solves. This is a very common issue. Yet they make it incredibly difficult to solve the problem. Type in Mouse, Tapping, or Synaptic into the Start search box, and you get no help. They keep the solution to the problem hidden away, as though only a handful of people in the world ever have this problem.

This mouse tapping issue is a microcosm of what is wrong with the computer world. It's such a straightforward issue and should have a straightforward resolution, but they make it hard, and neglect to inform the consumer of basic how-to steps.

And then again I accidentally disabled the Button function! The fact that the term "Button" means "Mouse On/Off" hadn't sunk in yet. I had to keep laboriously trying to reach the proper box by pressing the Start key, and the exact right combination of Tab key, arrow key, and Enter key. Finally I was able to get that check back in the Button "Enable" box. Geez! Then I disabled the stuff I wanted to, being very careful not to touch the Button category. All set now.

DO NOT DISABLE THE "BUTTON" FUNCTION!!

Mouse Freeze

At one point I couldn't get the mouse to do anything at all, even though other stuff was working. Restarted the computer. That fixed it.

MOVIE MAKING – See "DVD – MAKING A DVD FROM CAMCORDER VIDEO," "WINDOWS MOVIE MAKER," or "STUDIO."

MOVING MATERIAL

Moving Text

Block the text you want moved > CTRL+X > move to your target spot (either in the same document or another one) > CTRL+V. That's it. Note that the material automatically adopts the margins of the target document; it you move wide-margin material to a narrow-margin document it reformats into narrow margins.

Moving a Document or Folder

Right-click the document icon > click Cut > move to your new location > CTRL+V. You may have to left-click inside the target folder window before it lets you paste it there.

Moving More than One Document

Check the checkbox at the left of each document > then with the pointer within at least one of those checked document icons, right-click > Cut > move to your target location > CTRL+V.

You can also "lasso" them if they are adjacent documents. See "GROUP SELECT – DOCUMENTS OR FOLDERS"

Moving Programs

DON'T MOVE PROGRAMS. Windows does not like that. Shortcuts can no longer find them. Just like Studio [movie-making software, by Pinnacle/Avid], if you move where an item is stored, in Studio, it's the kiss of death; the dreaded giant blue exclamation point icon shows up and your whole movie line is screwed up, littered with blue exclamation points, until and unless, you move your stuff back to its original location with its original name. Now, for Windows I don't think it's that drastic, but the Studio experience sure taught me to be wary.

You can move or delete Shortcuts, that's OK, but in general do not move actual programs. Programs tend to be located where it's good for them to be located anyway.

Consolidating Documents

For some reason, using CTRL+A, CTRL+C, and dropping a whole document, or chapter, into a new document usually screws up the formatting to some degree – some stuff goes into a wrong size, you lose italics, you lose justification for some sections, etc., etc. HOWEVER, I found that if I do this consolidation into a previously existing document, instead of a newly opened one, it holds its formatting much better.

Now this is critical for me, because I work on chapters separately at first, then at the end try to put them all together into one big document. Being able to consolidate without the formatting getting altered is crucial. Saves me days of work!

This procedure is still not 100%. It still loses some of its formatting, but only maybe 1 or 2% – some centering, some bolding, etc. It may happen to me more than other people, because I like to use a ton of formatting for my texts.

So, basically, when I consolidate chapters, it still is a somewhat, though not horrendously, laborious procedure, as I check the formatting throughout the text and make corrections.

MULTIPLICATION SIGN / DIVISION SIGN – Insert tab at top > Symbol > More Symbols > Font at upper left ("normal text") > scroll down to find it, [10th row, 7th over for ×, and 12th row, 7th over for ÷] > click on the symbol > Insert.

They are actually hard to find. Why, instead of being with the math symbols, they are lower down right in the middle of letters, I don't know.

If you're picky and want a slightly better sign that's not slightly raised [× vs ×, ÷ vs ÷], you can click on the Font dropdown arrow and scroll the fonts all the way down to "Symbol", click on that one and find signs that are positioned lower. (Both are in the tenth row down.)

For the multiplication sign, I just use a small letter x. Or, for division, the forward slash /. Not worth the trouble finding the signs under Symbols. It's so annoying, and so typical. You have to search hard for ten minutes to find a multiplication or division sign, but you can easily find § or ∫, stuff hardly anyone uses.

MUSIC – This is a major section, about 18 pages of information. I've provided a "Contents" for it.

****

MUSIC / AUDIO TRANSFERS THRU A COMPUTER

CONTENTS

****

Overview

The most common audio procedure I do is: download music to my computer, edit it, then transfer it to either CD or iPod, so I can listen to it, usually in my car. I assume many people want to do the same thing.

Basically, it's a three-step process:

1) Downloading – Get your songs onto your computer by downloading them from iTunes or from ripping them from CDs you already have.

2) Editing – Edit the songs so you have the songs on a playlist the way you like it.

3) Transferring – Transfer the playlist of songs to a blank CD or to an iPod.

The details on how to do this are described in sections A, B, C, and D below.

> If you are satisfied with the limited editing capabilities of iTunes – song order, one trim per song, crossfades – **then the procedure is fairly easy**. But, if you're like me, and strongly prefer a greater level of editing – specifically, the ability to record several parts of a song with pleasing fades to silence between them, not jarring cuts – then it can get very complicated... but, doable.

There's a lot of information here. **I think just skipping right to the specific procedure you want to do, is your best bet**. Just get the basic procedure done once, then you can go back and learn more about it. For example, get a disk burned first, then go back and learn how to edit songs, what different programs can do what, what end result suits you best, etc. And then burn another disk. Don't try to learn everything at once.

And don't try to learn just by reading; you have to actually be doing the procedures to see what I'm talking about.

A. PRELIMINARY INFORMATION

1. Burning vs Ripping

"Burning" refers to transferring material from computer to disk.

"Ripping" refers to transferring material from disk to computer.

Both the Windows Media Player and iTunes programs can do either operation.

2. Music File Formats

There are different music file formats. If you hover your pointer over an audio file, it will show you which format it is. Don't worry about them here; I'll tell you what you need to know below, when these formats show up. A brief summary of the ones that normally show up for me when I deal with music files:

MP3 – The most compatible format. Not the best sound quality, but I've read that usually people can't tell the difference.

WAV – Best sound quality. Doesn't lose anything when transferred.

WMA – (Windows Media Audio) Good sound quality. Needs to be converted to AAC to play in iTunes.

AAC – (Apple/iTunes) format. Shows as "MPEG-4" when you hover your pointer over such a file. I've read that it is Apple's equivalent of MP3; not sure on sound quality of material converted to it. I don't hear any difference. I've read one place that AAC has better quality than MP3, but MP3 has greater compatibility.

Note that you can convert formats:

When you rip CD songs onto the computer into your Music folder, using Windows Media Player, you can, at that point, convert the material to a different format. (In my experience, getting everything into WAV format is best, because it keeps the sound quality, and, it works with both Windows and iTunes programs, whereas WMA tends to work with Windows only, and AAC (MPEG-4) tends work with iTunes only. Not sure of my conclusion here, but that's what it seems like to me).

Likewise, when you rip songs into your iTunes library from a CD it can convert material to a different format. Open iTunes, insert a CD and an iTunes window shows a message asking if you'd like to import these CD songs to your iTunes library. Just x out that message window and go to the lower right and click on "Import Settings" and choose "WAV encoder". Also check the "Use Error Correction" box, which automatically slows down the speed of transfer, if necessary, for shaky CD material. Click OK, and that sets those settings. Then you click "Import CD" at lower right.

Note also that when you import material from your Music folder, to your iTunes library, it will offer you automatic conversion to AAC (MPEG-4), the normal iTunes format.

3. Disks – Information

CD "Speed"

Not sure how it works, but from what I've been told by tech people, when you see 8X, 16X, 52X, or whatever, on the CD itself, that refers to the speed rate up to which it can be burned. And, from what I have read, for music, slower speed is better for stability. It's the burning instrument (the computer) on which you can set the speed, so that 52X disks can be burned at 8X (though I think 8X disks cannot be burned at 52 speed).

Now, the term "kbps" is also a unit of data transfer rate. Yet here, I understand the higher the rate, the better the quality of the sound. How one sorts that out logically, I don't know. Maybe it's that the first is just speed, the second is amount of info transferred per second.

Ejecting a Disk

When you're in Drive E, there's an eject icon at upper left. Or, you can right-click Drive E, Eject. When in Windows Media Player,

CTRL+J makes it eject. Otherwise, you can always physically repeatedly press in and release the disk bay, till it pops open. Or, better, press it once and wait a few seconds for it to open.

"Computer" vs "Music" CDs

A stand-alone CD recorder usually needs, specifically, a "Music" CD–R disk to record on; computer "data" disks do not work.

A computer, however, can burn music onto either type of disk, which can then be played on most CD players.

Most electronics stores sell both types. You can usually get either type at CVS or Walgreen stores.

I found this info on the internet: *The computer CD-R can be read by most computers and CD players; however, the music CD-R is optimized for playback in the widest range of computers and audio systems, which makes it superior for storing and playing back audio.*

While both the computer CD-R and music CD-R are very similar in most facets, the computer CD-R has a faster write speed and the music CD-R has a superior playback compatibility.

I have found that Music CDs do work a bit better in my car. On very cold days, my player won't work till the interior of my car warms up; music CDs seem to respond quicker than computer data ones.

CDs vs DVDs

I've found that CDs are much more stable than DVDs. Once in a great while something will go wrong with a CD for me. But with DVDs, things go wrong more often. Maybe one in 50 plays, something will go wrong. They suddenly won't work in my player, or start to stall at spots, for no apparent reason. If you're lucky, cleaning the disk, fixes it. If not, you try all kinds of things, and nothing works. Sometimes using a different player works.

I try to handle disks always by the edges without touching the underside, where recording takes place. I note that both CD and DVD recording starts, I believe, at the center, then works its way out to the edges. That would explain why my CDs tend to occasionally skip on songs near the end of the disk because that's where I have to grip them with my fingers to pull them out of my case, near the edge of the disk. So they get some interfering fingerprints on them near the edges.

RW Disks for Non-permanent Material

"RW" means re-writable; you can use this kind of disk over and over. They won't play in my car, but they do play in my walkman CD player. Good for stuff I want to listen to only once, then erase, like a downloaded podcast.

Disk Compatibility

Usually you can import material to the computer from a CD–R, a CD–RW, or a CD–Music disk; they all work. The computer can then burn the material back to ANY one of those three types of disks. So you can transfer material from one type of disk to another. My Long's duplicator (described elsewhere) can also transfer material from ANY of the three types to ANY of the three types.

A couple of limitations to keep in mind though: 1) CD-RW disks are not compatible with some players. I found that a CD-RW plays in my computer, walkman, and boombox, but not in my Sony player or in my car. 2) If you use a CD recorder, most of them require a "Music" type CD, and will not work with a "Data" type CD.

4. CD vs iPod

A couple of significant differences here in transferring music. 1) Some editing adjustments – volumes and fades – that you make to songs under the iTunes program, hold when you transfer the songs to an iPod, but do NOT hold when you transfer them to a CD. 2) iPods hold much more material than a CD.

The information here applies to audio going either to a CD, or to an iPod. For the CD, you click "Burn" for your final step; for the iPod, under the iTunes program, you drag and drop songs onto your "Music" category under "Device," to transfer them to the iPod. (For full information on iPod procedures, see "iPOD".)

B. GETTING MUSIC ONTO THE COMPUTER

1. iTunes Overview

After years of buying CDs, I now download music from the internet. It's a significant improvement. 1) You buy only songs you like, individually. You don't have to buy a whole album which may contain many songs you don't like. 2) You get to hear 30 seconds of each song before you buy it, so you're pretty sure to like the full song.

There is no monthly fee. You just download songs at $.99 or $1.29 per song. (I think the $1.29 versions give you unlimited play, whereas the $.99 versions only give you 7 plays before you have to buy them again. This 7-play-limit setup makes burning a CD of your songs very important so that you can listen to them without limit.)

Great article in *Time* magazine (12/6/10) concerning iTunes. Page 59: *"It turns out that there is something than can compete with free: easy. Napster, Gnutella and Bit Torrent never attained the user-friendliness that Apple products* [iTunes] *have, and nobody vets the content on file-sharing networks, so while the number of files on offer is enormous, the files are rotten with ads, porn, spyware and other garbage."*

So that's why iTunes succeeds in the face of free music: it's easier to use, more dependable, without embedded junk, and it's reasonably priced.

You need the iTunes program on your computer to download iTunes songs, and then you use the iTunes program to burn songs to a CD. And, you need to have your full playlist of songs ready to go. Can't just do one song at a time. Or, if you do, that's all you'll have on that CD – one song. (You can transfer just one song at a time to an iPod.)

Account Notes

I forget exactly how I signed up. Google "iTunes" to sign up. Involves giving them your email address, a password for your account, your credit card info, etc. The songs get charged to your credit card automatically after you click "Buy." And you get sent an email receipt within two days. [I recently bought a new computer. See under "COMPUTER – GETTING A NEW COMPUTER" > "14. iTunes" for exactly how I downloaded the iTunes program.]

Note that when your credit card expires, it won't allow purchases until you enter the new credit card info (new expiration date, new ID number in back of card). Forget how I did it, but once I did, it immediately did allow new purchases (or maybe as soon as I re-opened iTunes, I don't remember).

To check your account: Open iTunes Store > click your account (your email address at upper right just below the search oval) > enter password > View Account. Under "Purchase History" it also has a "Report a Problem" box at bottom.

However, once you've got an account, you rarely need to check it. You're set to go and start downloading songs. (I've checked mine only once in the last three years.)

Browsing for Songs

This is the basic procedure I use in browsing for songs: Keep a list of my favorite artists. Go thru each one's entire catalogue; download the songs I like. Check off that artist. Make a CD once I get 79 minutes of material (CDs are 80 minutes). Then, revisit each artist's catalogue periodically for their latest albums. (I have about 200 artists on my list; so far, after three years, I've gone thru only about two thirds of them. Takes time, but it's well worth it.)

Very often I've found that the couple of songs I've liked from an artist, are the only ones I like! Because those are their big hits, the ones everybody liked. So it's disappointing to discover that there is not much else I like from them. But, other times, you get lucky, and find a dozen more you like a lot.

Catalogue of Songs

They have a huge selection.

Note that a few artists, like the Beatles, or AC/DC, have hardly any songs on iTunes. They don't sell their music online. (Update 2010: The Beatles finally worked out an agreement and they now have their songs on iTunes.)

iTunes – Store – Won't Open

One time, for me, the Store suddenly wouldn't open. Emailed their email "help" address below. They sent me info that worked: Start > Control Panel > Internet Options > Internet Properties > Lan Settings, uncheck the "Use a proxy server..." That did it. Now I get the store instead of a limited store with lots of blue question marks on each line.

Why that did it, who the proxy server is, what the address is, etc., I have no idea! But just unchecking that box made it work.

iTunes Help

Phone help: 1 866 712-7753... actually no good. Just gives what you owe. No human being there. Instead, go to: 1 800 MY APPLE (1 800 676-2775), although I don't think they're open on weekends; when I called on a holiday, they were closed.

Internet help, website: http://www.apple.com/support/itunes /store

Email help: iTunesStoreSupport@apple.com

Of course, the reason I've typed up these notes is that, in the computer world, usually HELP ROTS. Companies are far more interested in selling you more stuff than in helping you. Contacting a human being who can help you is always a struggle, starting with the fact that simply finding a viable phone number to call takes half an hour.

2. Downloading Procedure

From Downloading to Disk – The Procedure I Use

1. Click iTunes icon on desktop (or find iTunes program under Start > All Programs). Note that iTunes usually takes a good 5-10 seconds to open up.

2. Click "iTunes Store" at left

3. Browse or Power Search at right under Quick Links

4. Type in the artist (or title if you're looking for a particular song) at top. Click Search. It then lists the artist's top hits. (Note that spelling must be exact; if you're not sure, go to Google and they give suggestions for correct spelling of a name.) Can click "More Results" at bottom for next 150 songs.

5. Best for me is to click "See all" next to songs (in the middle) Then click "Name" at upper left. This gives all the songs alphabetically, rather than by popularity, so that duplicates and alternative versions of a song are bunched together.

6. Double-click on a song to listen to a sample of it. Click "Buy Song" if you want it.

7. That downloads it to your hard drive. Takes maybe 30 seconds. (The songs are not just in your account somewhere on the internet; they are actually on your hard drive, usually under Owner > Music.)

8. Start a Playlist by clicking File > New Playlist > name it. (I name each new playlist as "Disk 62," "Disk 63," etc.)

9. Click "Recently Added" at left to bring up those songs and right-click each song > Copy > CTRL+V each song into that new Playlist. Or, easier, just drag and drop songs from the right directly onto your new Playlist on the left.

10. In your new Playlist, drag and drop the songs into the order you want.

11. The playlist list keeps a running total of time, at the bottom. When you get to about 80 minutes, or 1.3 hours, you can then burn that playlist to a CD.

At this point, if you want to do any editing of songs before burning a CD, see "2. EDITING, AND GETTING MATERIAL ONTO A CD" below before going to step 12. Myself, I do edit; I prefer a lot of partial songs with fades to silence between them.

12. Put in a blank disk. Click File > Burn Playlist to Disc" > "Burn Settings" window comes up > I change the default "Gap Between Songs" from 2 seconds to 3, and I also check the "Use Sound Check," which evens out the volumes of the whole group of songs. Songs often DO get imported from the iTunes store at different vol-

umes, so it's good to have this checked.

13. Takes about 10 minutes to burn one CD (about 25 songs).

14. After it stops whirring, it takes another minute or so, as it shows "Burning Disc...finishing" at top; then it makes a "boing" sound, which signals that it's done.

15. All set. Disk is ready to play, in stereo, car, and most players.

16. Using iTunes, print out a list of songs on that disk: File at upper left > Print > Song Listing. (For me, I choose the simple one-page song list, not the jewel case list.)

17. Use a Sharpie pen to label the disk. [Using stick-on paper labels is not a good idea; they tend to cause problems over time. See "LABELS"]

3. Procedural Tips

– They list the songs of an artist in order of popularity. So, if you want, just check out an artist's top 10 or 20. But I like to check their entire catalogue... which means: Click "Power Search" > "Songs – See all" > then click the word "Name" at top left so that it puts the songs in alphabetical order, instead of popularity order. (Takes about 3-5 seconds.) That way multiple versions of a song are bunched together and you don't end up re-listening to 6 different versions of the same song at various stages of your search.

(Re-click the word "Name" and it puts the list in reverse alphabetical order. Click the word "Popularity" at top right, and it reverts back to popularity order.)

– Note, as in so many computer operations, things sometimes change or get revised by a company over time. It also takes some practice to get efficient at operations. Typically, the first time you try something, you'll be quite slow. If you do the same operation constantly, you'll get very good at it, and it will seem like it's always been a snap.

If I do a music downloading session one month after my previous one, I'm OK. But if it's 6 months later, I tend to forget how to do things.

– You can go to the previous page by clicking upper left arrow of dialogue box.

– Once you click "Buy," it takes about half a minute for the song to get downloaded (you can continue browsing other songs as it downloads the current one). It puts the song automatically under "Recently Purchased" at left. From there you can right-click a song and move it to the playlist you want.

– Once bought, you can then listen to WHOLE song. BUT, only 7 times, then you need to buy it again. Thus, getting them onto a CD (or iPod) is critical, so you can listen to them as often as you want. I rarely listen to music from my computer anyway; I like to listen to music in my car.

– Every so often, as you listen to song samples, it "times out" to reconnect. It just stalls for a couple of seconds, but then it continues.

– DOUBLE-CLICK the song you want to hear. Do that and it also immediately cuts off the previous song (if you've played only a few seconds of the previous song and already know you don't want it), and starts the one you want to listen to next.

– Note that when typing an artist's name into the search box, it has to be spelled correctly, or else you get nothing. I was getting nothing for Jacob Dylan. I googled the name on the internet (where they give you spelling suggestions), and found it was Jakob Dylan. Then I was able to find his songs.

– I buy all the songs I want from one artist at the same browsing session, because by next session, maybe months later, song positions might change and I might miss something. That's why I like to do one artist completely, then periodically check his or her catalogue in the future for a latest album. You want to avoid the trap of checking an artist's songs partially or superficially; you end up going over the same stuff again in the future because you can't remember what's new, what's old, what you checked already, what you didn't. I think meticulousness pays off in the long run.

On the other hand, for an artist I'm lukewarm about, I may just check his or her top ten. Going thru lists of songs, 100, 300, 500 songs sometimes, is quite time-consuming.

– The Playlist (at bottom) shows time total of current playlist. When you go to burn a disk, it automatically lets you know if it's too much for one CD. Since CDs are 80 minutes, shoot for about 79 minutes, which is 1.3 hours (they show time in tenths of hours).

But also note that if you edit songs to partial songs (say you only like the first half of several songs), it will show the time total as though those were full songs. Myself, I usually need two hours of material, which I edit down to 79 minutes of material I like.

– To make a new Playlist, click File at upper left > New Playlist > a new one shows up under Playlists > type in the name you want for that playlist > then drag songs from your "Recently Added" list to it. Just literally drag a song from the list, over to the left and drop it onto your current playlist. It stays in both your Recently Added list and your current playlist.

– They have a few playlists already there – like Top 25, Recently Played, etc. Worthless to me. I deleted them. The Party Shuffle one is also worthless to me, but it won't delete.

– Finding a song you've got: Regardless of what you've selected, moved, or deleted in other areas, it keeps a long list of ALL the songs you've purchased under "Purchased." So to find a song you know you've got somewhere, go to "Purchased" and use the Search function at top right. Though, for me, once I have a disk made, I rarely have any need to find a song on my original "Purchased" list.

– After you click "File" and "Burn Playlist to Disc," the "Burn Settings" window offers you burning speed options. Tried 24X and then 8X, but I couldn't tell any difference in sound quality. Like for so many operations, usually you won't go wrong with the default option that was already in there to start with (24X). It's the default option because that's what's best for most people for most situations. But, slower burn speed is more stable and is best for old or shaky-sound CD's.

– For the oval search box at the very upper right which says "Search Store": Instead of typing in a song and then clicking something to start the search, you just type in a song and it automatically lists below any possible matches.

Transferring All Songs from One Playlist to Another Playlist

File > New Playlist > name it > go to "source" old playlist > Edit > Select All > Edit > Copy > go back to "target" new playlist > Edit > Paste

Transferring a Bunch of Songs

Use the same procedure as above, except instead of "Select All", check each one or "lasso" a bunch, and then paste them in the new playlist. Actually I can't seem to lasso them (I thought I did once); may have to simply move them individually by right-clicking each one and using "Add to Playlist". Or, if you want to move all but a few, move all of them, then delete the few you don't want in the new playlist.

Update: Aha, you can "lasso" them by clicking the song at the top of the list, holding down the Shift key, and then clicking the song at the bottom of the list. That highlights all the songs in between. (Usually to lasso files, I press the left of the mouse and drag the cursor from a little to the right of the list, back left, up thru the group of items to lasso them. But in iTunes, if you try this, you end up just moving one item. Need to use the Shift key method.)

Whatever you do, note carefully which songs are checked before you do something. Sometimes you forget you have 5 or 6 songs checked, and you want to move only one. It can get very complicated keeping track of what you've done, what you haven't, which songs are where, etc.

If you accidentally move a bunch of songs when you meant to move only one, you can, just like for normal computer operations, undo that operation with CTRL+Z.

Song Order

You can adjust the order of songs by simply dragging them up or down, not as they show in your iTunes Music library, but once you've dropped them into a playlist. Then you can move them.

Playlist List Included on Disk

When I moved all my songs from my iTunes library to an external hard drive (at one point, to clear up space on my computer), I forgot to print out the playlist for my latest music Disk #72. But, when I put the disk in, iTunes showed an option to display the list that worked! So all I had to do was print it. In other words, when you burn an iTunes disk, it INCLUDES all the names of the songs on the playlist! So that was nice.

4. Saving a Podcast to a Disk

Besides songs, you can download what are called "podcasts" from websites – radio programs, lectures, interviews, presentations, etc. My experience with podcasts is limited, so I will just show here what I did to get material on disks from three particular websites – Skeptic, Freethought Today, and The Bible Answer Man. Procedures seems to vary quite a bit; just try to follow what seems to be the most logical next step; usually you can get it.

Note that sometimes, I think, you can only get a podcast if you subscribe to it on a website.

– Often material is in MP3 format. If you don't have a player for MP3, you can simply play it on your computer and run a 1/8 inch wire from the ear phone outlet to a CD recorder (to make a CD of the material), or to a voice recorder (the modern digital equivalent of the traditional "tape recorder") to record it there for listening to later, away from your computer.

– If you can't seem to download a podcast, you can play it, and send it with a 1/8 inch wire in the earphone outlet, directly to a tape/voice recorder, and listen it there.

If you want a disk but have no stand-alone CD recorder, but only your computer, then after you get the material on a voice recorder, you need to use the "Sound Recorder" program to rip the material back into the computer, and then you can make a disk thru Windows Media Player. (Of course this procedure is not good for music because you lose sound quality, but it's OK for spoken-word material.) But, that's how you can get a podcast on a disk when you can't rip the download directly to your computer.

Note that sometimes this doesn't work. I tried it once with some material of pretty shaky quality, and it did record on a CD–RW and it would play in my computer, but not in my walkman player, which normally does play CD–RWs. Then I tried the same thing with a CD–R, and it DID work in my walkman. Which suggests to me that CD–Rs are more "stable" than CD–RWs.

– Some podcast selections may not be available. You'll get only the introduction to it. Or you can listen to it but not download it. Although, by using the above procedure (recording from the ear phone outlet to a recorder), you should be able to get it on a disk.

Skeptic

SKEPTIC website > podcast tab at top > past episodes > browse past episodes (2008) > click "DOWNLOAD" under selection > Save > pick folder to send it to (for me, Desktop, Owner, Music) > Save took about 4 minutes (41MB) > click "Close" when download is complete > then go to folder where you sent it. It's there as an audio file (blue music note icon). > double-click it to get it playing in Windows Media Player > then click the Burn tab to burn it to a disk. (See "Burning a Disk Thru Windows Media Player."

FreeThought Today

Freethought Today website > News tab at top > Freethought Radio in dropdown list (or at right on the actual page) > Archives and Podcasts at right > Browse by year > make selection and click on "Download Podcast" > Save > rest is same as above for Skeptic website.

Bible Answer Man

Bible Answer Man website > Bible Answer Man tab at top > Podcasts > select a program (listed chronologically) > click "View in iTunes" at right > "Allow" > iTunes opens up > same list opens up, except now it has "Free" at right > click "Free" > takes about 8 minutes to download (a one hour program) > click "Podcasts" at left of iTunes (that's where it's stored, not in the Music library) > I don't know if you can directly record it to a disk from there, but you can use the procedure under "Notes" above – play it on your computer and record it directly from the earphone outlet onto a CD recorder, or voice recorder.

5. Downloading Audiobooks

You can download audiobooks from iTunes.

If you have an iPod (or iPad or iPhone): iTunes > iStore > wait > Audiobooks tab at top > type title into search oval at upper right > click on the title when it comes up < click "Buy." It downloads and sends it to your iTunes library under Podcasts. Then you transfer the material to your iPod.

See "AUDIOBOOK DOWNLOAD" for full information.

Make sure you don't buy the "Apps" version (which I did by mistake at first), which gets you the readable version, instead of the audiobook version you want. Audiobook version cost a bit more ($21 instead of $16) and took much longer to download (20 minutes for a 7 hour book, instead of just a couple minutes).

To burn the material to CDs: File > New Playlist > title it > Books (upper left) > drag book to the new playlist and drop it there > click on File again > "Burn Playlist to disc" > insert blank disk. It burns one disk after another for you, about 10 minutes per disk. You should do this in one sitting, because you can't continue where you left off at one of the middle disks; it burns them first disk to last, in order. If you do two disks and want to continue later, it starts with the first disk all over again.

Took 5½ disks to do the 7-hour book I bought. Labor intensive, but oh well. I want to listen to it in my car, not in my computer.

Actually, it probably would be easier for me to simply buy the physical audiobook off Amazon.com, and get the CDs sent to my address, so I don't have to do all that transferring of material. I'll simply have the disks, with its chapter breaks. (Don't underestimate how annoying one long single track for a disk can be. If you listen to something else before finishing the whole disk, fast-forwarding to the spot you left off is a pain.)

Of course, now (2011) that I have an iPod (See "iPOD"), transferring material to an iPod is simpler, because you don't have to burn all those disks; the whole audiobook gets transferred in one operation. And, you get the chapter breaks.

Note that in my iPod-compatible car stereo, I can advance/rewind a book by chapters by pressing the double-arrow buttons, but, the tracks don't display as numbers. Instead, the total accumulated time shows. I could be 132 minutes in, press a reverse double-arrow, and it does jump to the start of the chapter again, showing maybe 119 minutes in. Or I could press the forward double-arrow, and it jumps to the next chapter, at maybe 146 minutes in. But the actual track numbers do not display anywhere.

Downloading from Amazon.com

There's a great Roy Orbison song called "Walk On" that iTunes did not have. Googled it, found it at Amazon.com, clicked a bunch of logical buttons, including downloading an MP3 downloading program, and, the song itself (for 99¢). Hooray; it landed in my Music folder under its own folder ("Amazon MP3"). Opened that up to reach the actual song file. Then I right-clicked that file, copy, and pasted it into my latest iTunes playlist, never expecting that action to actually work. Hah! It worked! I can hardly believe it. I now have the song on my latest iTunes playlist, set to transfer to either CD or iPod. What a great day! A computer procedure went easily without complications!

MP3 Format

MP3 is audio material in a compressed format; I think you can get 100-150 songs on a disk instead of 20-25. My car plays MP3. It's the same physical CD (I believe), but just holds more info. My one experiment here:

I wondered if I could get, by converting material to MP3 format, several CDs of songs onto one CD, thereby reducing the number of disks I had to deal with. Since I got an iPod, the question has become moot for me, since I no longer deal with disks. But, you can do so:

Windows Media Player > insert disk with the songs > put Rip Settings to MP3 > Rip CD > lands songs into Music folder under "Unknown Artist" > do the same with more disks. (I note the original disk was about 700 MB, and the landed material was reduced to 182 MB; so you can get maybe 3 or 4 disks onto one disk.) > Gotta fiddle around to get all the songs together under one folder; may have to re-number or name them and/or move them around. Otherwise, you get multiple tracks 1, 2, 3, etc., and end up getting all the first songs on, followed by all the second songs, etc., instead of songs 1-25 of the first disk, then 1-25 of the second disk, etc. > at any rate, get them all under one folder, in the order you want them > open Windows Media Player again > put in a blank disk > click "Start Burn" > and it burns all those songs onto one disk.

I tried the disk in my car and it played just like regular disk, and the sound was fine. So basically, it worked. (Though I suspect some car stereos would not play it.) You can make your own decision as to whether the sound quality is up to what you like. (As I said, for me, it's now irrelevant, since I use an iPod instead of disks.)

C. EDITING, AND GETTING MUSIC ONTO DISKS

Overview

All the information below on editing, applies to material to be transferred to either a CD or an iPod. It's just the final transfer step that's different. (See "iPOD" for the final step of transferring material to an iPod.) One significant factor to keep in mind is that iTunes-edited material does not hold volume and fade adjustments when burned to a CD; it does when transferred to an iPod, but not to a CD.

I'm sure a lot to people have the iTunes program on their computer. If you're fine with relatively simple editing, I would recommend iTunes. And then... most of the information below becomes irrelevant.

BUT, if you're like me, and like more extensive editing – specifically being able to include parts of songs with fades to silence between them – then things get very complicated. (Part of the difficulty is the fact that Windows (Microsoft) and iTunes (Apple) are competitors and don't necessarily want to make it easy to switch between programs.)

I used to experiment for hours, trying to find a feasible way to edit songs or audio material thru the computer, without third party software. I consulted several Best Buy Geek people. One emailed: "I do not know of a way to do so without third party software." And this guy had had over 3,000 cases, had a top 5-star rating and five years experience as a Geek Squad Agent.

But, lo and behold, there is a way, not with Windows 7, but with Windows Vista: Edit each song in Windows Movie Maker, save each as an audio file, then make a playlist in Windows Media Player, and burn it to a CD. See below under "DETAILED PROCEDURES" > "3) WINDOWS MOVIE MAKER (VISTA VERSION)" for the details.

SUMMARY OF PROGRAMS

Here's a summary of what I found, or concluded, about the key programs, followed by detailed procedures for each:

1) WINDOWS MEDIA PLAYER

Good for ripping selected CD material to the computer, and for burning material from the computer to a CD. But, it has no editing features, other than song order.

2) ITUNES

This, of course, is third party software, but many people have it. (It's *my* main source for obtaining music.) It can both rip stuff to the computer, and burn stuff to a CD, as well as transfer it to an iPod.

It does have editing features, but I find them limited in a couple of key categories (partial songs, and fades to silence). Not only that, but the editing that you do – except for partial song length settings – does not hold when you transfer to a CD! They only hold if you transfer them to an iPod.

3) WINDOWS MOVIE MAKER (VISTA VERSION)

This is the way to go if you want extensive editing without third party software. You edit in Windows Movie Maker, then burn a CD in Windows Media Player.

4) WINDOWS MOVIE MAKER (WINDOWS 7 VERSION)

You can edit the audio material on the movie line, but the Windows 7 version of Movie Maker has reduced functionality compared to the Vista version: You cannot burn a CD separate from the video material, like you can with the Vista version. (Though, you can burn the audio portion to a stand-alone CD recorder, analog, if you want to. First generation analog copy may not be bad.)

5) AUDACITY

This is an audio-editing program you can download for free. I recommend it. It's my go-to program for audio editing. Its features are excellent. It's not like most other free programs that try to dupe you into buying stuff. And, you don't have to sign up, get an account, establish a password, or any of that crap.

6) STUDIO (PINNACLE STUDIO)

This is third party software for video-editing, but it allows audio-editing and burning CDs of the audio portion. Costs about $100. Tricky to learn. Used to be my go-to program for audio-editing, before Audacity. Still is my go-to program for video.

7) ROXIO

Don't really know anything about this program, other than the fact that people mention it often. Might be good. Costs about $80.

8) STAND-ALONE CD RECORDER

You can edit thru a stand-alone CD recorder and not use a computer, other than burning an initial "working" disk (thru iTunes or thru Windows Media Player). This is the way I originally edited audio, but, it's very tricky. You make one mistake, you have to start all over again.

PROGRAMS / PROCEDURES

Note that this entire section is about editing ONCE you already have your material in your computer (see section "B. GETTING MUSIC ONTO THE COMPUTER" above for how to do that.) In some situations below, you may have to re-import material in order to get it into a compatible format.

---

1) WINDOWS MEDIA PLAYER

If you don't need to do any editing except for song order, and don't have iTunes, use Windows Media Player.

RIPPING Songs to Computer Thru Windows Media Player

1. Open Windows Media Player (If you don't have its icon on your desktop, click Start > All Programs > Windows Media Player)
2. Put your pointer over the Rip tab at top and a dropdown arrow shows up; click on the dropdown arrow, to choose settings. [W7 – Inserting the CD puts "Rip CD" tab up at top; there is no "Rip CD" tab until you put a disk in! Also, the window needs to be at maximized size to see the tab; it's over on the top-middle-left); then click "Rip Settings" dropdown arrow.
3. Format – I prefer "WAV Lossless" (keeps sound quality and works in both Windows and iTunes) (Automatically sets the "bit rate" at the best rate.)
4. Click "Rip CD automatically when inserted" and pick "Never." (Otherwise, it rips all the songs instead of just the ones you want.) Also check box for automatic ejection after ripping.

Now you have your settings, which stay as selected unless you change them in the future.

5. Insert your disk of songs you want to rip to the computer.
6. Click "Rip" tab at top [W7 – "Rip CD"]. It shows you all your tracks and you can uncheck the ones you don't want to rip.
7. Click "Start Rip" at lower right. Shows progress for each song in green. Takes maybe 5 minutes for a full 79-minute CD of songs.
8. It sends the songs to your Music folder, inside folders "Unknown Artist" > "Unknown Album."

That's it. The material from that CD is now on your hard drive as an audio file (blue note icon), in your Music folder.

It's a good idea to right-click each actual song file and name it.

Notes

– Regarding audio formats, I don't see the point of saving space. I note that when I ripped the same song to my computer under the different categories, the file size showed significant differences (MP3→10MB; WMA→26MB; and WAV→43MB. So, I like to stick with the best quality sound throughout any process. A favorite song may distort for me at louder volumes if I go with the lower levels.

I note that the original of that song was 9MB. I understand the principle of not being able to make a song sound better than the original, but maybe the extra MB size of the file copy may keep it from distorting at loud levels. I don't know. I was told by a tech guy that the bigger size of a file does not necessarily mean it's better quality

– You may need to wait a bit as it says it is ripping, before it starts to show progress (10%, 20%, etc.) under Rip Status.

– Don't use computer for other stuff while it is ripping. AR says, "Running other programs may distract it."

BURNING a CD Thru Windows Media Player

1. Open Windows Media Player, reduce the size of the window and drag it to the right.
2. Open your Music folder, reduce the size of the window and drag it to the left.

3. Click "Burn" tab at top of Windows Media Player window. Be sure to do this, otherwise, the "Play" tab is on, and you won't get the "Start burn" option later on.
4. Put your pointer over the Burn tab to bring up the dropdown arrow > check "Apply volume leveling across tracks" [W7 – click on the "Organize" dropdown arrow at upper left > Options > Burn tab > under Audio CDs, check "Apply volume leveling across tracks" > OK.
4. Put in a blank disk. (If AutoPlay comes up, just x it out.)
5. Drag (in the order you want) each individual song file from the left onto the Panel at the right of the Windows Media Player window where it says "Drag items here" under "Burn List".
6. Click red "Start burn" at bottom [W7 – at top]. (If "Start burn" is not there, that means you didn't click "Burn" tab at top first, and you just put in a Play list rather than a Burn list. If you click the "Burn" tab at this point, your list disappears and you have to click "Import Unsaved List," right where your burn list was, to get the material you dragged there in the first place to show up again, now ready to be burned.)
7. It starts burning and shows progress as each song shows "Writing to disc" or "Pending." Then it shows "Complete."
8. Disk usually ejects itself after it stops whirring. Disk should now be ready to play in any player.
9. X out your burn list from Windows Media Player window, now that you're done.

You can also go to your Music folder directly and order a burn from there (I had to do this once when my WMP burn panel at right showed "Data Disc" instead of "Audio CD"):

Music folder > highlight your selection > click Burn tab at top > insert a blank disk > "Prepare this blank disc" comes up > title it > very important, you click the down arrow at left for "Show formatting options" > pick the "Mastered" option, not the "Live File System" [in Windows 7, they now call these two choices "With a CD/DVD player" and "Like a USB flash drive"] > Next > window comes up showing the files ready to be burned to disk > click the Burn to Disc tab at top > title it, pick your speed (slower is more stable) > Next > Make an Audio CD > Next > that brings you to Windows Media Player window (step #6 above) > Start burn, and it burns your CD.

Notes

(If you're using CD–RW disks, then once you have recorded something in "Mastered" format, instead of "Erase Disc," delete the material, and that disk is still set in the "Mastered" format for any subsequent burns.)

I spent hours trying to find out how to set the default to "Mastered" format. Finally came upon this on an internet Vista help site:

> Question:
> *I haven't met a single person in a business environment that wants their Vista to default to the "Live File System", rather they would like a CD format that works on a multitude of platforms. Is there a way to default Vista's burning functions to "Mastered Mode"?*
>
> Answer:
> *I have been doing a bit of research on this topic and as far as I am aware there is NO WAY to change the default behavior. Of course, if the default was the other way round, i.e. 'Mastered Mode' as opposed to 'Live File System' then some people would want it the other way round. There is no way to please everyone, and it just so happens that the programmers at Microsoft chose the 'Live File System' as the default.*

Note that if you wanted to save a playlist, somewhere along the line before burning, you'd have to click "Playlist" or "Create Playlist", and/or "Save Playlist, at either bottom, top, or left, depending on whether you're using Vista or Windows 7. Title the playlist and press Enter key. It's maddening how different options pop up at different times. Usually you just keep clicking logical things and you get it, but it's annoying how hard it is to establish a set order of steps.

I found, logically enough, that Windows Media Player, Vista version, would not import an iTunes song (MPEG-4 format). But then, surprisingly, I found that Windows Media Player, Windows 7 version, DID burn that very same iTunes song that Vista would not burn... (?) See what works for you. Every time I tried it, I came up with that same result.

Sometimes the song's name gets changed as you drag it over; "Pretty Woman" suddenly becomes "Track 12".

---

2) iTUNES

If you have the iTunes program, and don't want to do any editing other than trimming songs, then iTunes is the way to go.

RIPPING Songs to Computer Thru iTunes

Normally you already have your songs in your iTunes library after downloading them, as well as in your Music folder (Owner [W7 – Libraries] > Music folder > iTunes folder > iTunes Media > Music folder > artist name folder > album name > and finally, there's the actual song file, a blue musical note icon).

But if you want to rip a song from a CD you already have, into iTunes, you do this: Open iTunes (often takes a good 5-10 seconds to open) > insert the disk of songs you want ripped to your computer > up pops a window that asks if you'd like to import the CD into your iTunes library > x that out and check the song list that it put up, so you can uncheck the ones you don't want imported > then click "Import Settings" at lower right > pick "WAV encoder" and check the "Error correction when reading audio CDs" box > OK > "Import CD" > it starts importing, showing progress at top > it lands the songs in your Music folder as well as your iTunes library.

Note that those places are connected; if you delete a song from your Music folder it also deletes in your iTunes library (the name stays on your list, but when you click on it, it says the song can't be found). Basically, the songs are actually stored in your Music folder, and iTunes merely accesses them and lists them for you in your iTunes window. If you go to delete a song from your iTunes window, then it asks if you want it deleted only from your iTunes library or also from your computer. (I like to keep my iTunes library as empty as possible, and keep all my songs in my Music folder until I need them.)

And, again, to find those actual songs in your Music folder, you have to dig deep into folders, following the route noted above.

BURNING a CD Thru iTunes

1. Open iTunes program
2. Click "File" at upper left
3. Click "New Playlist", which brings up a new one in the left panel at bottom.
4. Title the playlist, press Enter key to set that title.
5. Click "Music" category at top under LIBRARY, to get your available music to show at right.

6. Drag and drop your choices directly onto the new playlist in the left panel.

7. If you want songs that are not in your iTunes library, but are in your Music folder, you need to import them to iTunes: Click File at upper left > Add File to Library > browse your Music folder to get to the actual audio file of the song > click on it > click "Open" at lower right > that imports it to your iTunes library. If songs are in Microsoft format (WMA), a window pops up saying iTunes will automatically convert them "to Apple Lossless format so they can be added to your iTunes library." Click "Convert" and it converts it right away as you import it. > click "Music" under LIBRARY to open what you now have there > drag the new song also into your playlist at left.

8. Click your new playlist to open it up to show the songs you have there.

9. Edit the order of songs by dragging them to desired positions of order, and trim any songs you want to trim.

You can trim songs by right-clicking each song > Get Info > Options tab > type in the exact start and stop time. Note that you can get only one part of a song; you cannot get two or more sections of a song. * See note below.

Key point: Any other editing you do takes effect immediately on those songs when you play them in iTunes, in your computer, BUT, the editing adjustments will NOT hold when you burn them on a CD. Any volume, fading, or equalizer adjustments you made will disappear. Only the song order and trim settings you made will hold. Likewise, if you drag an edited song to your Music folder, your editing will disappear, except for the trim size. ** See note below.

For iPods, on the other hand, all your editing does hold.

If you do want to do further editing, just for playing on iTunes, you can adjust volume and equalizer settings for individual songs under that same Options tab. You can do crossfades between songs under Edit > Preferences > Playback icon at top > check Crossfade Songs box > drag slide to your number-of-seconds choice > OK.

10. Click File > "Burn Playlist to Disc"

11. Options Window comes up. I like to go for 3 seconds instead of 2, for the silence gap between songs. Also, I check "Use Sound Check" which evens out the volumes of the whole group of songs. Songs often DO get imported from the iTunes store at different volumes, so it's good to have this checked.

12. Click "Burn". Insert blank disk. And it burns your disk.

Notes

* Note that in iTunes when you set any song to a partial length, that sets the length for that song no matter where it is in iTunes, whether in your library or in a particular playlist, or several times in that same playlist. You cannot establish 3 different sections of that song by putting it in your playlist 3 times with different start and stop times; all 3 will come out the same, because it always reverts to your latest length setting. You can only set ONE part of a song, not several parts.

** When you adjust individual song volumes, they play in iTunes, or on an iPod, at those adjusted volumes, but, once you burn a CD, they all come out at the same volume. I pursued this issue without success at iTunes help number. Downloaded newest version of iTunes. No difference.

Update: Long story short, after talking to a third tech person at iTunes: You can change song volumes to listen to in iTunes (you can hear the difference immediately), but when you burn the songs onto a CD, the songs get sent at the original set volume. Likewise, when I transfer a song from iTunes to my Music folder – the song reverts back to its original volume.

I have to go thru the Audacity program first (see below), to get volume adjustments to stay when I burn songs to a CD. However, this issue is usually not a big deal, because you normally want all your songs at the same volume. Sometimes they don't get imported at the same volume, but once burned to a disk, they should land at the same volume.

Reminder: On your playlists with your TRIMMED songs, at bottom, it shows total FULL song time, rather than total PARTIAL (trimmed) time. When you go to burn a disk, what the playlist shows as maybe 2 hours time is actually maybe only 1.3 hours of actual disk space needed. It will tell you automatically if you need a second disk. If so, what I do is drop songs one by one till it lets me record on one disk. (And I put my dropped songs into my next playlist.)

You can fade a song – Edit > Preferences > Playback tab > check Crossfade Songs box > slide seconds choice > OK – but I tried all kinds of things and I can't get it to fade the normal way I like it. Instead of fading to silence and then back up for the next song or segment, it "dissolves" with one song fading out as the next one already fades in ("crossfades"), in other words, no silence between songs. I nut like ziss, eh! I suppose a long 12-second crossfade isn't too bad, but I don't like it. Especially because it was not stable, and would often do weird things, like playing one song in the middle of another song. And, of course, crossfade settings do not hold when you burn the songs to a CD, only when you transfer them to an iPod.

You can adjust bass, treble, etc. if you want, by right-clicking song (the song name, not the album) > Get Info > Options tab > select choices under Equalizer Preset. Usually I prefer to keep this at "None."

To delete a Playlist, right-click > Delete > Delete.

Sometimes, when you import a song to iTunes from your Music folder, the title reverts back to an older title (like "Track 7" instead of the song's current name).

If you right-click a song and you don't get "Get Info," usually you can click File, and find "Get Info" under there.

If you try to delete a song by right-clicking and Delete, and no option panel shows up, you can highlight the song and press the Delete key on your keyboard. Then click "Remove" in the window that comes up.

Note that in searching for iTunes songs in your Music folder (if they are not in your iTunes library), you often have to go deep into the iTunes folders to get at the actual song file. Need to open two or three folders to get there. I try to avoid both the iTunes library and the Windows Media Player library as much as possible, and try to keep my music organized under my Music folder. I hate the libraries of those two programs. Trying to find material there is hard; you have to search through tons of material, organized by their anal-retentive, overkill system; they put tons of extra material in. They list items repeatedly in different categories. They do stuff automatically contrary to what you want. Windows Media Player even seems to import random songs you might want, further clogging everything up. I hate their systems. And I don't want to spend half my life trying to figure it all out. As I said, I try to organize my music essentially only in my Music folder.

When importing songs from your Music folder, if you click on Add Folder to Library, instead of Add File to Library, you just highlight the folder and click on Import Folder at bottom right to import that whole folder. If you were to double-click on that folder where it is located, to open it, it would show as empty, because you had selected adding a folder, not a file. If you had selected adding a file and double-clicked that same folder, then it does show the files inside there.

You CAN export an iTunes song directly to your Music folder, by right-clicking > Copy > paste into music folder. It lands as an MPEG-4 file (iTunes format).

If you set up iTunes and the Music folder side-by-side, you can just drag and drop songs either way. [Dragging and dropping here makes copies, not cuts-and-moves them.] But no matter what format your song is in, once inside iTunes and then back out, it is now in the iTunes "AAC" format (which shows as "MPEG-4" when you hover your pointer over such a file).

Anything you drag to iTunes, if it's not the right format, brings up a window to click "Convert" to AAC ("MPEG-4").

Somewhere in iTunes info, it describes formats like this: "...of an uncompressed song file such as AIFF or WAV to a compressed format like MP3, AAC, or Apple Lossless Encoder." So it's good to keep in mind that WAV is uncompressed, but MP3 and AAC are compressed formats. And, oddly, Apple Lossless Encoder is also a compressed format despite the word "lossless." Again, it seems my best bet is to stick with WAV as much as possible to retain sound quality.

Like Windows Media Player, when you put a CD in, then the window automatically changes to show the songs on the CD and give you a Rip tab to click on. Otherwise, you have just the regular iTunes window, with no "Rip" option.

iTunes can import video clips (they land in "Movie" category), but not any clip that went thru Windows Movie Maker. Whenever something won't go, remember that iTunes and Windows are competing systems.

---

3) WINDOWS MOVIE MAKER **(VISTA VERSION)**

This is the one feasible way I found to do the kind of editing I prefer – many partial songs and fades to silence between segments – without third party software. It works on the Vista version of Windows Movie Maker, because this version allows making an audio CD off a movie project (whereas the Windows 7 version of Movie Maker, does not).

Burning a CD Thru Windows Movie Maker **(Vista Version)**

1. Open Windows Movie Maker; work station comes up. Note that Windows Movie Maker and Windows Media Player are two different programs.

2. Under "Import" at left, click on the blue "Audio or Music". That brings up your Music folder and the stuff you have stored there.

3. Find and click on the track/folder you want; click "Import". That imports it up onto the imported media area, upper left.

Note that copyright protection may prevent some maverick songs from being transferred ("No burn permission" comes up). You may have to use analog transferring – see first ▮ note below. Though, I have to say, I have rarely had that message come up. Virtually every song I've tried to burn – old CD copies, iTunes songs, even original commercial CDs, allowed me to burn them.

4. From there, you can drag material down to the audio timeline below to edit it. Now, you could work on all your songs there as one project, but that's no good because you'll end up with a single long track for, say, 25 songs. Instead, to get separate tracks, you should work on only ONE song at a time and then save it as a separate file to your Music folder (under a folder you label for this whole bunch of 25 songs). That way you'll get 25 separate tracks. Not quite as much work as you might think, because most of the songs are probably fine as they are, as full songs. It's only a few of the 25 songs you'll want to chop up into only the sections you like.

Note that you can expand or contract the timeline by clicking on the + or – spyglass at left. At very top left, you have the Undo icon, if you want to undo your last operation. There's a slide bar at bottom to navigate forward or back.

5. The editing techniques:

a. Trimming – Click play icon till you get to desired spot > pause it there > go over to the right and click the razor split icon to split the track at that spot. Use this technique to divide the song into however many sections you want, and then highlight the sections you don't want, and press the Delete key at upper right of your keyboard, to get rid of those sections. Then drag your remaining sections together on the timeline.

b. Fades – Highlight desired section > click "Clip" tab at top > Audio > Fade In. Then, to get a Fade Out for the section, repeat the process, picking "Fade Out" this time. Now that section will fade in at the beginning and fade out at its end. Fades are set at only about 2 seconds, but, if you have a section fade out and the next one fade in, that adds up to a decent 4-second fading. And it's real fades to silence, not the damn iTunes "crossfades."

c. Volumes – Same as for fades but select "Volume" and slide the marker. Unfortunately, you can only decrease sound, not increase it. I find fiddling with volumes is usually not worth it anyway.

Rather, what you should do is: When you get to Windows Media Player (step 7 below) to burn it, put your pointer over the Burn tab to bring up the dropdown arrow > check "Apply Volume Leveling Across Tracks"

6. After editing, after each song, go to top where is says "Publish Movie" and click on that > highlight "This Computer" (NOT "Recordable CD") (Typical Vista logic: You want the material on a "Recordable CD," so the key is NOT to select "Recordable CD"!) > Next > name it (send it to your Music folder) > Next > song lands as an audio file in your Music folder. You want to end up with your full list of 25 songs, maybe 18 full ones already there and 7 edited songs.

7. Use Windows Media Player to burn a disk of those songs → See "Burning a CD Thru Windows Media Player" above. Now you have songs on a CD, edited the way you like it, listening to sections of songs you like without the parts you don't like, and with pleasing fades between parts instead of jarring cuts.

Notes

▮ If you have a CD recorder, you can use analog transferring to get around a "No burn permission" and get that song into your Music folder: Play the CD from a CD player, run a 1/8" wire from its earphone outlet to a CD recorder input port, and record it analog onto a disk, pressing Stop after each song, to get individual tracks; then rip that disk to computer (Music folder), then import the material to Windows Movie Maker for a burn. Quality will not hold as well as digital. But, try it; it may be fine.

Sometimes when you go to check the small box to the left of an audio file in your Music folder, there is no small box. If you put your pointer over it, the small box might show up. If it doesn't, then just click on the file, to get it highlighted. Checking a box to the left of a file, or highlighting it, amounts to the same thing.

Windows Movie Maker accepts all the audio formats that I usually deal with – MP3, WMA, and WAV – and, surprisingly, also the iTunes format, MPEG-4.

You can only adjust the volume DOWN, not up. So if you want to raise the volume on one song, you can only do so by lowering the volume on all the rest of the songs by comparison and leave the selected one as is. It's rarely a problem though. (At least for songs; for me, for interviews I record, being able to raise the sound IS important.)

You can't use iTunes to burn a disk here, since, once an audio file is part of a Windows Movie Maker movie, then iTunes will not accept it; you have to use Windows Media Player here. Remember, Windows and iTunes are competing systems.

Sometimes the computer wouldn't let me delete a file from my Music folder. After I did the delete, it was still there (usually with a "couldn't find" message). But, next time I opened the Music folder, it WAS gone.

Try to get the names of your songs, and their location, in a folder SET before you start importing them to Windows Movie Maker. Otherwise, Windows Movie Maker can't find them. If you're in the middle of a project and then change names or location of the files, it usually can't find the files and you can get into an unholy mess.

Key reminder: When done with a song, click "Publish Movie" NOT to "Recordable CD" (!) but to "This Computer."

---

4) WINDOWS MOVIE MAKER **(WINDOWS 7 VERSION)**

You can edit audio in the Windows 7 version of Movie Maker, but the setup is quite different (the "wave" timeline at bottom is gone, etc). And, it has reduced functionality; it won't let you burn a CD from the movie file, with your computer, like the Vista version will. You have to use a stand-alone CD recorder.

Burning a CD Thru Windows Movie Maker **(Windows 7 Version)**

1. Open Windows Live Movie Maker (Windows sticks the word "Live" in.)
2. Click on center of screen to import video (or "Add Videos... " icon at upper left.)
3. Browse your Videos folder and click on any random video file that is at least as long as your song will be. Note that operations here are like Word operations – you can highlight and delete sections, you can use CTRL+C, etc. If you make a mistake, you can CTRL+Z it out.
4. In the Windows 7 version of Movie Maker, you can't just import audio; you must attach it to video first. Note how the "Add Music" icon at upper left is grayed out until you get some video material in there.
5. That puts the video clip into a movie line (at right going across in rows.)
6. You can expand or contract that movie line by clicking on the + or – at the lower right corner.
7. Click on any spot in the clip > click on the yellow Video Tools tab that comes up at the top.
8. Click on Video Volume at upper left.
9. Drag the volume bar all the way to the left.
10. Now the audio portion of the video clip is off, and you can essentially forget about the video bar. It's just there as a necessary silent base. Just note that to move the movie line cursor to a spot, you can click inside the video bar to land the cursor there, or at least close to the spot.

11. Click on Home tab, and then on Add Music dropdown arrow > Add Music (At one point, "Location is not available" window came up. I x'd it out and went ahead; no problem.)
12. Browse for your song > highlight it > click Open
13. That brings that song onto the top of the existing video bar, as a green audio bar.
14. Trimming – Play the movie cursor line to the spot you want to split the audio > click Pause > click on the green music bar > click green "Music Tools" icon at top > click Edit tab > click the Split icon to split the audio at that point. Do the same for other desired splits, and then highlight each section you don't want, and press the Delete key on your keyboard. Drag the remaining clips together.
15. Fades – Highlight desired section of green audio bar and under the Music Tools tab, select any fades you want (none, slow, medium, fast) for each section. If you play your project, you can see the fades indicated at upper left as the movie line cursor moves along.
16. Volume – Do the same procedure (clicking on green sections to highlight them with a black frame, clicking on Music Volume at left, moving the slider for any volume adjustments you want to make for any section. Keep in mind that you need to be under the green Music Tools tab.
17. At this point, you've got the song edited the way you want, but, you're stuck, because under the Home tab, at right, even though you can now Save the "movie", you can't separate the audio from the video and burn it to a CD.

18. But, if you have a CD recorder, you can proceed to simply play this "movie" on your computer, run a 1/8" wire (male/male, Radio Shack) from the computer earphone outlet to a CD recorder input port, and record it analog onto a disk. (If I remember right, I needed a female/female connector piece (Radio Shack) for the male wire out of my computer ear outlet, to connect to the male wire attached to the input at the back of my Sony CD recorder.) You'd have to use earphones on the recorder to hear where you are, sit there thru the full real-time recording, and press stop after each song before going on to edit the next song under Windows Live Movie Maker.

A bit of work, and the sound quality won't be as good as a digital transfer, but first generation analog copy is not bad. You may find it perfectly fine. I made one of my old CDs by analog transfer, and I can't tell much difference.

That's it. Of course, if you don't have a CD recorder, you're out of luck. I would recommend using the Audacity program instead anyway.

---

5) AUDACITY

A Best Buy geek guy told me that this program is surprisingly good for a free program. I agree. When I asked another geek "Agent" for a recommendation, he immediately said many people like Audacity. It does all the basic things a normal person would want to do with audio material. It has a nice big visual sound line, and you don't have to deal with video, only audio.

Some drawbacks: It is in the so-called "beta" stage, i.e., still being worked on. Internet quote: *"Before a commercial software program is released to the public, it usually goes through a "beta" phase. During this stage, the software is tested for bugs, crashes, errors, inconsistencies, and any other problems."* (Best Buy Geek squad usually won't offer support for products still in the formation stage.)

Audacity does not import songs from a CD, or burn them to a CD; but, you can do that with Windows Media Player.

And, it seems you can only work on ONE file (or song) at a time; you can't add files to a project you're working on. But, that's OK, since, for songs, I edit them and export them to my Music folder one by one anyway, before burning them in Windows Media Player.

I find these drawbacks not a problem. I highly recommend the program. It's ideal for editing songs or spoken-word material. It's my go-to program for audio-editing. Of course, you do have to spend some time learning the features, but if you're a person who wants to edit audio on a regular basis, this program is the way to go.

Downloading the Audacity Program

Google: audacity.sourceforge.net/download. Click "Audacity: Download" to open the site.

At the top of the page, it has Download, a 1.2 series at the left, a 1.3 series at the right. For Windows 7 or Vista, use the one at the right.

Under "1.3 Series (Beta)", under "Windows" > click "Windows 7" or "Vista" > click "Audacity Beta" in the box at top > under "Recommended Download" click "Audacity 1.3:13 Installer".

At bottom, click Save > shows "downloading..." showing percent progress > click Run > allow? Yes > English > OK > Next, Next, Next, Next > check option for having icon on Desktop > Install > starts to install > Next > Finish > up comes a window with the program open, showing all the controls. (Click OK if a welcome window comes up.)

Help Tab

Under their Help tab, they have good instructions and tutorials. The controls can be intimidating if you haven't worked with anything like this before. (Myself, I happen to be fairly used to most of the features, because of the Windows Movie Maker and Studio programs I've worked with before.) But if you start off with an easy project, as described in their initial tutorial, you'll be on your way and eager to go full bore editing songs, etc. The good thing is that the features and controls are sensible and logical, not weird, inconsistent and all over the place like so much of the computer world.

In theory, the program cannot open copy-protected music files, like from a commercial CD. Good luck. I don't really know the limits here, but I find pretty much everything does work after you rip it to your computer.

If selections under File are grayed out, that means your project is still on Pause; you need to press Stop first, then the options under File will be available.

Editing Audio Material Thru Audacity

1. Open Audacity program, click OK on the preliminary window that comes up.
2. File at upper left > "Import" (halfway down the options list) > Audio > browse for file > click on it > Open at lower right
3. Keep the default setting of "Make a copy..." > OK
4. That lands the file into your Audacity work station, IF it's a compatible format.
5. If it's not a compatible format, they have a thing called "FFmpeg" thru which you can apparently convert files. You can find out how to use it thru their Help info, but, it seemed complex and I didn't want to struggle to learn how to use it. I prefer to use this workaround solution:

Use Windows Media Player to burn those incompatibly formatted files onto a disk, then rip that disk back into the computer selecting the "WAV (lossless)" format: "Rip Settings" dropdown arrow > Format > WAV (Lossless) > then click "Rip CD" tab. That lands those songs, now all in the compatible WAV format, into your Music folder, under "Unknown artist" folder. Then start the Audacity import process again, selecting the file you want and clicking Open at lower right.

[The four formats I usually find my material in are 1. MP3 (OK), 2. WAV (OK), 3. MPEG-4 (needs converting), and 4. WMA (needs converting).]

So, basically you collect your desired songs, burn them onto a CD using Windows Media Player, rip them back into your computer, all in WAV format, then start your importing into Audacity and do your editing.

6. After you import your first song into Audacity, you edit it. (The controls are at left-top, Play, Pause, Stop, etc.)

a. Trimming – By default your pointer should be an I-beam when it rests on the sound wave bar. (If not, you can click the I-beam icon at top to get it. You highlight a section you don't want, by dragging that I-beam across (making a shaded area). Then click the Delete key on your keyboard to delete that section. Remove other sections you don't want in this way. (You can expand the audio bar by clicking the plus spyglass at upper right, in order to make your selections more accurate.) Then click on the double arrow "Time Shift Tool" icon at top, to drag the remaining sections together.

You can also move sections around by the normal Word commands of CTRL+X and CTRL+V.

Note that joining sections usually leaves a little click sound where they join. Expand the wave > highlight that click (you can see it clearly on the sound wave) > click Edit tab at top > Silence Audio. That gets rid of the "click" sound.

To get the wave cursor back to the start of the project, click Stop button at top. If you only clicked your pointer into that spot in the first place, then you need to click on the double-left-arrow to get back to the beginning. Also note that clicking the Stop button, or the double-left-arrow button, undoes highlighting. If your highlighting is still on, then when you press Play, it plays only that section.

You can expand a highlighted section by dragging the edges out. But, to reduce the highlighted section, you have to delete it and start over.

b. Fades – Highlight the section you want to fade. (The nice feature here is that you can make your fades as short or long as you want by how much you highlight). Then click on Effect tab at top > click either Fade in, or Fade out. Remember that expanding the wave out makes accuracy easier.

c. Volumes – Highlight section > Effect tab at top > Amplify > move the slider > OK. Note that you can raise the volume, though you have to click the "Allow Clipping" box first. After you click OK, you can see the change in the height of the sound wave.

Reminder – if you left it in Pause, stuff won't work. Need to click "Stop" button first.

7. Once your song is edited to your desire, click File > Export > choose the file format you want it exported as from "Save As Type" dropdown arrow > pick WAV > title it > Save.
8. Edit Data window comes up; can fill in artist name, track title, etc.

9. That lands it into your Music folder. Do the rest of your songs the same way.
10. Burn them to a CD, using Windows Media Player or iTunes, as described above. Now you've got a CD of songs edited the way you like them, and with good retention of sound quality.

Notes

When Audacity refers to "tracks" it usually means layers of audio for the same section; it doesn't mean another song track. As described above, I think the way to go with music, is to set up, say, 25 separately-edited tracks first, then combine them on a playlist, for burning in Windows Media Player, or iTunes.

That's what I do for editing music and burning it to a CD.

If you want to divide a long project into separate tracks, you do this: Put the vertical cursor at the spot you want to set a track start > Tracks tab at top > Add Label at Selection > that puts a track start there > type in its name or number in the little square that shows up there > do that for each track you want, working your way across > when finished setting all the tracks, then click File > Export Multiple > pick WAV under "Export format" dropdown arrow > Export at lower right > enter names if you want > OK, for each track as it pops us > OK again > lands them to your Music folder, as individual tracks. Ready for importing into Windows Media Player for burning to a CD.

I do likewise for editing interview material (one long recording from my voice recorder) and burning it to a CD. (Though I use MP3 instead on WAV.)

The point, in either case, is that you don't want to end up with one long single track. That makes navigating thru the material a pain, rewinding and fastforwarding instead of pushing track buttons.

Note that even though you can undo operations with CTRL+Z, CTRL+Z doesn't seem to work with the track setting operation. So you've got to be pretty careful here not to make a mistake. I would say make a copy of your whole project first before putting in separate tracks; that way you don't have to do your whole project over, if you mess up with the tracks.

Several key things to note: 1. To carry out operations on the material, you can't have the project playing or paused; it needs to be stopped (otherwise, you'll see most options grayed out). 2. Often operations take several seconds to take effect; so wait a bit before you decide nothing is happening.

Use WAV format rather than MP3, in order to keep sound quality high.

Now, when I burned 5 varied bits and songs to a disk, and then ripped them back in under WAV format, I note these file size comparisons between the versions I burned and the versions ripped back into my Music folder:

1) MP3, 5MB →29MB
2) WAV 45MB→45MB
3) WMA, 3MB→18MB
4) MPEG-4, 7MB→38MB
5) WMA, 396KB→4MB

In other words, they lost no sound quality. (By my logic, anyway. A tech guy did tell me that bigger file size does not necessarily mean better sound.)

This is where Windows Media Player is very useful – it can convert formats for you.

Very useful is the icon to the right of the + and – spyglasses, the "Fit Project" icon. Click it and the wave bar expands exactly to fill the screen with that project.

Unlike Windows Movie Maker, you can't play the project, pause at your desired split spot, and split it there. Because stuff is grayed out if the project is in Pause mode. Need to stop it (which returns the cursor to the beginning) and then move the cursor back to the spot. For accuracy here, you can play it at first and when it reaches the spot, note the time ("Audio Position") below, stop the project, move the cursor close to there, and expand the wave so you can see the sound wave of each separate word, then move the cursor to the exact spot, and then go under Edit and click Split.

You can adjust the accuracy of your highlighting by expanding the wave bar. As you move your I-beam cursor to a section edge, the I-beam turns into a white hand pointing. And you can drag your highlighting to the edge of a section. Also, it has an automatic snapping-into-place feature when you get close to an edge.

The effects under Effects tab are pretty neat. You can change the pitch of a voice, or do an echo, etc.

The Help tab at top leads to some pretty decent instructions, a quick one and a longer one.

---

6) STUDIO

Pinnacle Studio is a third party movie-making program. Costs about $100. Takes a while to learn. See "STUDIO". Its latest versions (I have "Studio 14") allow editing on just audio and allow you to burn the audio section to a CD, not directly, but thru iTunes. Studio also has a "iPod Compatible" (iTunes) option.

If you import all your songs for one disk, say 25 of them, and edit them, when you save that project to the computer, it's saved as a single long track, all songs under "Track 1", which is not good, because navigating to a particular song or repeating one is a hassle. That's why I do each song separately as one whole project and THEN combine them for burning under Windows Media Player, so that I get a separate track for each song.

Editing Audio Material Thru Studio

1. Open Studio.
2. In theory you should be able to click the music icon (bottom of vertical list of icons at left) to browse for your choices from your Music folder; but, it doesn't work for me. Half the stuff is missing, and the stuff I am able to import doesn't work. So, what I do instead is first make a CD of the songs I want, thru Windows Media Player, then import this music from the CD to Studio, because the procedure of importing music from a CD, does work consistently:
3. Click "Toolbox" tab at top of the Studio window > click Add CD Music > insert the CD and check the track you want to add. (Remember, you're doing a separate project for each song, otherwise, you'd get a single long track for a bunch of songs.)
4. Add to Movie. That automatically puts it into the music bar of your movie line. Unlike Windows Movie Maker, you don't need to already have video material for it to attach to. It goes into the music bar by itself fine.
5. Edit it the way you want. (Remember, you don't have to do any editing for the songs you like as is, only for the songs you want to trim, or to split into segments with fades between segments.)

Trimming – Move the movie cursor to the spots you want and click on the razor "trim" icon at the right. Highlight and delete the sections you don't want, by pressing your Delete key on your keyboard. Then drag sections together.

Fades and volume changes – Inside the Music bar is an orange volume line which you can drag up or down to make fades, as well as volume changes. You can click the + or – icons at lower left to expand or contract the movie line, for greater accuracy.

6. Click "Make Movie" tab, select "to File", pick "Audio". Click "Settings" > pick WAV.
7. Click "Create File" and it makes an audio file and sends it to your Music folder, as a WAV audio file. Don't have to be concerned with Video at all.
8. Do that for each song.

9. Then burn that group of songs onto a CD thru Windows Media Player, as described earlier.

Notes

Actually, I would not recommend Studio for audio editing, because it is so unstable. Stuff so often just doesn't work. I much prefer Audacity for audio editing; things don't go wrong all the time like with Studio. So much computer stuff will not work unless you press the right buttons in exactly the correct order, and even then suddenly things won't work.

For example, for this Studio program, some of the files in my Music folder don't show, even though they ARE there, and, Studio DOES accept the format. Yet, I can't import them, except... sometimes. At one point I found if I go to my Music folder separately (not thru Studio) and make a copy of the files in question into the Downloads folder, THEN, I CAN find them thru Studio, and import them into Studio to use... as long as they were in WAV format, not MPEG-4 (which makes some sense, since MPEG-4 is Apple/iTunes, which tries to keep everything "in house").

Making a CD from the Audio Portion of a DVD

If you have a CD recorder, you can play the movie on your computer and record the audio portion on your CD recorder, as in step 18 above. It will be analog recording instead of digital. But the sound quality may be fine; it's a first generation copy.

If you have the Studio program you can record it digitally: Open Studio > if you have the video clip already in your computer (under Videos folder), under the Edit tab, import them to your movie; [if it is on a DVD, click the Import tab at upper left > under Import From, have "DVD" highlighted > insert your DVD > shows your clips on the DVD > select the one you want > click Start Import at lower right, that puts it at top of your work station] > Drag desired video clip to the music line at the bottom of the movie line > "Make Movie" tab ("File" type should show "audio") > At far left, click "File," not "Disc" (it won't allow you to directly make a disk from this point; you need to Create File first to your computer hard drive > Create File > Type in name, select folder destination (Music folder) > Save, which gives you an audio file in your Music folder > THEN, you can use Windows Media Player to burn a CD.

Works well. I got a nice Bill O'Reilly vs Bill Maher segment on religion this way, from "The O'Reilly Factor" TV program to a CD.

---

7) ROXIO

Might be a good program. But, since I already have Studio, I'm not about to buy another program. I started to download a free trial for it, but felt like I was getting entrapped in an underhanded plot to make me buy something, unless I followed a "simple" 43-step process to get out of it. I just hate that kind of stuff. Again, as I've said, most of these companies are less interested in helping you, than in getting you to buy things. The irony is that if they were more interested in helping you, they would, in the long run, sell you more stuff! (Like Audacity; I would be glad to buy stuff from them in the future.)

Incidentally, at one point I took a look at another program, but it was very intimidating; I think it was designed for professional musicians. It had a ton of terms I never heard of.

---

8) STAND-ALONE CD RECORDER

Just some general notes here. I have detailed notes for myself, but it's all for my particular Sony CD recorder.

I used to use my CD recorder extensively to edit interviews and produce final CDs, and my notes reflect procedures for transferring spoken-word audio rather than music, for the most part. Now, I no longer use my CD recorder to work with audio; for both interviews and music, I use Audacity to edit, and Windows Media Player to burn a final CD. But, if you want to incorporate a CD recorder into your audio editing, here are some concepts to keep in mind:

– You have to use a Music CD, not a data CD if you're going to use a CD recorder. The computer will burn music on either type of disk, but usually a CD recorder requires a Music CD.

– Transferring material from a voice recorder is tricky. It involves avoiding buzzing sounds and beeps. And any extensive editing is very tough, because if you make one mistake in your timing or button pushing, you have to start all over again!

– If you want to transfer material from a voice recorder to the computer, rather than transferring material directly from the voice recorder to the computer thru its "Sound Recorder" feature, you are better off transferring it to the CD recorder first, getting it on a disk, THEN ripping that disk onto the computer. Because the sound is better; the CD recorder is a better quality recorder than the computer "Sound Recorder" one.

– It's my understanding that when you use analog recording mode, sound gets transferred in a literal way (think iron oxide particles on a cassette tape getting arranged a certain way), whereas for digital recording mode, sound gets transferred into a series of 1's and 0's (digits) to represent that sound and then gets transferred back to reproduce that sound. Thus the analog sound gets worse and worse with each succeeding copy, whereas the digital sound stays at the same quality.

I've experimented and found that even though analog songs on a first generation copy (digital source, analog copy) are generally just fine (maybe because listening to music in my car is something of a compromised environment anyway, with traffic noise, etc.). BUT, certain key songs I love, will distort with analog at loud spots, yet will hold their sound with digital. Therefore, my final decision on how to get songs on a CD is to stick with digital, all the way thru even though analog recording might be easier.

– Any extensive editing with the Sony stand-alone recorder – left playing compartment to right recording compartment – is tricky, because when you do 100 starts and stops, if you screw up just once with your timing, you have to do the whole disk over again! Therefore, in the future, I plan to do ALL my audio editing thru the computer (Audacity for editing, then Windows Media Player for burning the disk). That way I can adjust everything until I get no mistakes and everything properly timed, at proper volume, etc., and THEN, I make the disk.

– Myself, for interview material, I need to remember that only after I am ALL done, with a final fully edited disk, only then should I erase the original material from the Olympus voice recorder.

Additional Notes

– Can make up to limit of 99 tracks per disk.

– When recording from disk on left to disk on right, record level is auto set.

– You cannot use Sony analog to edit (from left/play to right/record compartments).

You CAN use Sony digital to edit left to right (hooray), but, you cannot put the disk you just recorded in digital, into the left compartment, to make another digital disk in the right compartment.

It's a one-time digital recording system. Once you record a digital disk on the right, you cannot make another (L-R) from it digitally. Must use analog at that point, and, since you can't edit left to right now, analog, you must use a separate player to send signals to the Sony input at the back, and adjust volume that way.

– You cannot adjust the volume (at individual separate spots) when doing L-R digital copy, though I believe you can adjust the entire disk transfer volume under Menu, "Deck A Lvl."

You can adjust volume as you record if you use a separate player and run it into the back of the Sony. You adjust the volume of that player. BUT, since this is analog, there's a tendency for it to distort on loud segments, whereas digital does much better on loud segments, with little distortion.
– Syncro-Dubbing – This feature on the Sony copies the whole disk from the left to the right, with no edits.
– You can separate tracks on an incoming one-long-track source, by listening to the feed with earphones on the CD recorder, and just pressing REC at each spot for a new track, as the disk records straight thru; you don't need to stop the recording; it puts those tracks in "on the fly" so to speak.

D. OTHER PROCEDURES

1. Digital Voice Recorders

The new digital recorders (the modern "tape recorder") are great! No more tapes to mess with! I had gotten a Sony one some years ago but the sound was chintzy and the controls awkward. But the Olympus ones (Radio Shack) I now have are great. The mono one ($70) has decent sound and convenient controls that you can use easily (even without looking). I keep it in my car and find it very useful for reminder notes for myself.

My stereo one ($250, DS–50 model) has excellent sound. I use it for my interviews.

Olympus phone support (very good) – 1-888-553-4448, Mon-Fri 9am-9pm ET.

If I record an interview on my voice recorder, this is how I get the material onto a disk:

Making a CD from Digital Voice Recorder Material

1. Turn off other programs
2. Connect the recorder to the computer (wire with a trapezoid end and a USB end). Turn the recorder on.
3. AutoPlay should come up, click "Open folder to view files." (If AutoPlay does not come up, you can access the recorder files thru opening "Computer," which should show you an icon for the recorder, which you double-click to show the files there. For me, the icon is called "DS_50".)
4. It shows about 10 folders, none of which you need except those that correspond to your recorder folders A, B, C, etc. on which you actually have material. ("DSS_FLDA" = Folder A, "DSS_FLDB" = Folder B, etc.) Myself, I usually only use Folder A.
5. Set up your Music folder at reduced size.
6. Go inside folder A of your recorder window and select the audio file (blue musical note) you want, and drag and drop it into your "Music" folder.
7. You now have an audio (blue note) file of the material.
8. From there you can use one of the editing programs above to edit it, and then burn the final result to a CD. (My preference, Audacity to edit, Windows Media Player to burn to a CD.)

At some point I did download a free driver first for my DS_50, from the Olympus website. I think that made a difference, I don't know. Actually I think it's supposed to simply install itself automatically when you first connect it to the computer. Not sure. [Update: Yeah, I'm pretty sure it does.]

Monaural Recorder

The above worked with my stereo voice recorder, but not my mono one. I needed to download software from the company for that, but, long story short, that's no longer the case with their newer model. Just bought another one, $60. It includes the connection cable and you essentially just drag and drop files from recorder to computer, just like with the stereo one. So, their 20 pages of directions in microscopic font size notwithstanding, it's pretty straightforward. A terrific item! Hours of good quality recording with no tapes to mess with. (Note that spoken-word material does not demand as high quality sound as music does.) And batteries last a long time, not like with cameras which eat up batteries very quickly. Gives you the choice of either MP3 or WMA type audio files.

I can even end up with "stereo" by playing the mono one onto my stereo one (1/8" wire), and then importing that result to my computer. I end up with the exact same material on both left and right channels, but I get both channels producing sound.

Olympus Recorder Controls and Notes

– Each folder allows 100 entries. When Folder A is filled, you can press FOLDER/INDEX to get to Folder B for another 100 entries. So with 4 folders (A, B, C, D), that gives you up to 400 entries. (Myself, I only use Folder A, but the other folders are useful in case the topic is different. For example, Folder A may have a dozen notes to myself, Folder B my entire session with an astrologer, Folder C my discussion with an atheist.

If your material suddenly disappears and you don't know how that happened, most likely you pressed a FOLDER/INDEX by mistake and moved to folder B; your material is still on folder A. That's happened to me several times. Scary, till you realize what happened.

– When you do "erase-all," it erases all the tracks in THAT folder, not in the next folder. So you can erase all of folder A by pressing "erase-all" but you'd have to go to Folder B to do an "erase-all" there.

– Be careful that when you go thru your tracks, that you don't accidentally use "erase-all" when you only wanted to erase that one track. Major blunder if you do. You LOSE all your tracks, before you've finished working with them .

I find the best procedure is NOT to erase individually ANY tracks as you go – too many clicks, too easy to screw up – but to go thru ALL your tracks first, then do an "erase-all," when, and only when, you've gotten your final disk, and a copy, made.

– Also, important: For the mono one, the button for Lock is on the left side, but for the stereo one, the button in that exact same position is for mic sensitivity, not lock! I am very used to shutting off the mono and then locking it with that left button. Don't accidentally by habit, click that left button on the stereo one to lock it, because that's not what that button does; it changes mic sensitivity.

– My stereo Olympus has 3 payback speeds – Regular, slow (S), and fast (F), which you toggle to by simply pressing the play button repeatedly.

Note that with the stereo one, you can pause playback by pressing the Play button again, whereas with the mono one, you have to press Stop each time you want to pause a playback.

– You get the Menu up by pressing and holding Menu (same with mono one). Use left arrow to get back to Menu. Use stop button to exit Menu.

– I've set Noise Cancel to high (makes surroundings less noisy), Low Cut Filter on (reduces AC and low frequency noise), and Voice Filter off (cuts high and low voice, but can't be used when Noise Cancel is on.

[Was trying, like I used to with my old excellent Panasonic tape recorder, to use a "Y" splitter so I can record sound from two different people, each with a mic, both sound sources going into the recorder. Good for recording, for example, in a noisy restaurant, using the Dictation mode to lower the background noise.

On both mono and stereo recorders, the splitter wouldn't work (both mono and stereo mics worked by themselves in either side of the splitter, but not when BOTH were inserted into the splitter. Radio Shack guy thought they sold a dual mic input recorder.

Result: Dual input mic recorders are very expensive, it seems, like $400. Solution, after talking to "The Sound Professionals" 800 213-3021 (guy was excellent): Need to have the recorder be the stereo one, not the mono one, and have BOTH mics either mono or both stereo. Tried that, using my old Panasonic stereo lapel mic, and my Sony lapel mic. That worked! Hooray.

Bought two new mono lapel mics from Olympus. They work excellently. If I do a conversation in a restaurant or noisy place, use Dictation mode. Otherwise, use Conference mode. For normal quiet location, you don't need mics (which are kinda intrusive).

Note that when you change batteries, that does not affect the material you've recorded on the recorder; it will still be there in the recorder and ready to go once you get the new batteries in. You don't have to worry about stuff disappearing because the device has no batteries.

2. Transferring Cassette Material to Disk

They do sell converter machines that play cassettes and record the material onto a CD. But, here is the way to do it thru the computer:

Cassette Material to Disk Thru "Sound Recorder"

1. Windows "Sound Recorder". (To get the shortcut icon onto your desktop: Start > All Programs > Accessories > right-click "Sound Recorder" > Send To > Desktop)
2. Attach connection wire (1/8" standard, can get at Radio Shack) from cassette player earphone outlet to laptop red mic input in front of laptop.
3. Play cassette at normal (maybe slightly louder) volume.
4. Press "Start Recording" on the Windows "Sound Recorder". (Volume level green indicator band should pulse according to the volume to no more than ½" across.)
5. Click "Stop Recording" when done.
6. "Save As" comes up. Title the material.
7. Save As Type is default "Windows Media Audio File."
8. Pick a target folder (usually Music folder, for me).
9. Click Save. Now you have the material as an audio file on your computer.
10. Then you can edit the material and burn to a CD using one of the programs described above.

Note: The sound quality recording directly to the computer this way is not as good as the sound quality you get when recording to a CD recorder and then ripping that CD to the computer. (My old McKinsey tapes came out much better on the stand-alone recorder. Other tapes – which were better sound quality originals – came out OK recorded directly to the computer.)

– Can use EITHER "computer" or "music" CDs on computer to make copies. But on a stand-alone CD recorder, you need to use blank "music" CDs. (Though I believe they do sell some CD recorders that can do both.)

Editing Cassette Material to Fit on Disks

Since material on cassettes go maybe 30-45 minutes per side (podcasts can go over 80 minutes), you often need to do some editing and combining to get material to properly fit onto disks. It's up to you whether you want to edit out sections or songs as you rip it into the computer (stopping and starting the playing and the recording), or to do all your editing after ripping the whole deal in. I prefer the latter. Easier to keep track of things and visually see what you have.

3. Recording Directly into Computer

A. Without a Mic

1. "Sound Recorder" > small window comes up with "Start Recording" (To get the shortcut icon onto your desktop: Start > All Programs > Accessories > right-click "Sound Recorder" > Send To > Desktop).
2. Click "Start Recording" and start talking near the front of the computer.
3. "Stop Recording" when finished.
4. Send to desired folder.
5. You now have an audio file of what you said.
7. Edit and burn using programs describe above.

Sound is only fair; retains a background whinny sound. Using a mic is better:

B. Using a Mic

1. "Sound Recorder," small window comes up with "Start Recording"
2. Plug in a mic at front (I like my Panasonic stereo one)
3. Click "Start Recording" and start talking
4. "Stop Recording" when finished
5. Send to desired folder
6. You now have an audio file of what you said
7. Edit and burn using programs describe above.

Notes

– If you don't like the sound level you're getting, you can adjust the recording level by: Start > Control Panel > Hardware and Sound > Manage audio devices > Recording tab > click on Microphone > Properties > Levels tab > drag the volume slider > OK. Actually, if I remember right, I needed to adjust the recording level. I was getting barely a sound at first. So, I upped the mic volume setting (somewhere between 55 and 80 seems best). THEN, both my Sony and Panasonic mics worked well.

– You can also record material from a digital voice recorder this way (1/8" wire between recorder and computer, instead of your own live voice thru a mic). HOWEVER, my experience is that the sound quality of material recorded directly to the computer thru this "Sound Recorder" feature is not as good as material imported from a CD, or drag and dropped from a digital voice recorder. It stands to reason that a computer's recording ability is not as good as a CD recorder's ability. And I find I get much better quality sound by narrating something onto my voice recorder, then transferring it to the computer, instead of recording directly to the computer.

So, "Sound Recorder" sound quality is not the best, but it's a nice feature to have for impromptu situations – your three-year old is saying funny things, a friend needs to give you directions to someplace, etc. You just click the icon, click "Start Recording," and start talking.

– For whatever reason, my excellent Olympus stereo mic does not work with

"Sound Recorder." My old Panasonic stereo mic works well. My old Sony one works OK, but it's mono. I want stereo, so I'll go with the Panasonic mic.

– Incidentally, I tried recording directly into my CD recorder with a mic. No go.

4. Backing Up Material

The Procedure I Use

I want to have a back-up for all my songs, in case a disk, or my iPod, gets lost or damaged. I'm not too concerned with keeping the iTunes original songs. Much more important for me is a copy of my edited songs, so that I don't have to find and re-edit all those songs again.

I do not use my iTunes library, or my Windows Media Player library. I hate those places for storing stuff; way too confusing, and interfering, for me. Rather, I make sure I have all my songs, as edited, in my Music folder, each disk/playlist in its own folder, numbered #1 to #73 or whatever my current disk/playlist number is. I make a copy of that whole deal onto an external hard drive.

Thus, I have them in three places: 1) computer Music folder, 2) external hard drive, 3) actual CD, or iPod. If something happens to any of the three places, I have the other two.

Now, somewhere along the line, when you buy iTunes songs, it asks you if you want to back up your purchases now or later (with them, I guess, at a server somewhere). I always pick "Later". The songs already land automatically in my Music folder, as well as my iTunes library. I delete them from my iTunes library. I don't want even more storage places. My mantra is: Redundancy leads to confusion.

Copy Protection

Though it has never happened to me, if, for some reason, your computer won't let you copy music that you've already bought from iTunes, you may have to remove the protection option in Windows Media Player: Windows Media Player > ALT key to bring up menu > Tools > Options > Rip Music tab > uncheck Copy Protect Music. I think it's usually unchecked by default.

I think it's mostly regular, commercially sold CDs that have embedded copy protection. I tried copying one on my CD recorder, digitally, and it let me copy it, but not "Finalize" it, which means essentially that I could NOT copy it. (Though one can always copy a disk, analog, I'm pretty sure.)

But when I tried to rip that same commercial disk to the computer and then burn a copy, it DID let me! So I don't know. I'm guessing it's a case by case scenario: Some disks will or won't copy on a CD recorder, some will or won't thru a computer. And the computer route seems to be the more likely way to succeed.

Shaky Sound / Old Disks

Had problems with some of my early CDs with shaky sound (I think I had originally transferred the material from 8-track tapes, around the time of the Civil War). Some of the tracks would not copy ("error"). Tried to make new copies in Long's duplicator. No go. Also showed "defective." Tried to make a copy in Sony CD recorder, digitally. No go. Tried to make copies, analog. Even that, no go. (Would not "finalize," showed "Check disk.")

I was finally able to make a disk copy, analog, from a separate player into the back of my Sony CD recorder. I then ripped the disk to the computer, and moved songs to appropriate spots.

Long's Duplicator

I have a stand-alone duplicator machine that makes copies of either CDs or DVDs in about 6 minutes per 1-hour disk. I call it "Long's," but that's just the name of the company I bought it from. The actual name is Microboards or UltraSpin.

It can do all kinds of combinations of source disks and target disks. Whether your source disk, or your target disk, is CD–R, CD–RW, or CD–Music, it will make a copy. Likewise for DVDs. Whether source or target, DVD–R or DVD–RW, it will make a copy.

Long's will not transfer audio from a video disk. If you want just the audio portion of a DVD on a CD, see "Making a CD from the Audio Portion of a DVD" under "Studio" above.

If source disk is much more than 79 minutes, it won't copy – too much material.

Note that 79:05 minutes of material worked, but 79:57 minutes did NOT work ("Target Overload"). Absolutely key factor, since you don't want a master that won't reproduce because there is slightly too much material on it!! It needs that extra bit of space to embed info on the target disk besides the actual material.

For CDs I don't really save that much time compared to burning one thru the computer, but it certainly saves time for DVDs – 6 minutes versus a good hour or more thru Windows DVD Maker. Plus, burning a DVD on the computer ties up the computer. For most things you can multi-task on the computer, but for burning a DVD it's best to let the computer use all its power on that task alone, to ensure a smooth job.

5. Sending Audio Material Thru Email

Final tidbit. You can send audio, as well as video, by email, as long as, in my case, it's less than 25 MB. You just attach the file like any regular document attachment. The receiver clicks on it, clicks on Play, and Windows Media Player plays it.

So, that's what I know about audio transfers thru a computer, from the perspective of a normal person, not a computer expert. They do have other third party audio-editing programs, but when I looked into them, it was intimidating – seems like it's for professional musicians, with terminology I never heard of. As if the procedures above aren't complex enough! I'm going to get an ice cream. My brain hurts.

****

NAMING A DOCUMENT – You end up naming a document a little differently, depending on whether you created the document 1) while in a document, or 2) while in a folder:

1) When in a document (created by doing a CTRL+N to get a blank page up to work on): when done, CTRL+S > that brings up a "Save As" window > type in the name, pick a destination folder, and click Save. That sends the document to the chosen folder, as named. Note that you named the document after you worked on it.

2) When in a folder (you created the document by clicking File (upper left) [W7 – press Tab key if File tab is not up there, to get it up

there] > New > Microsoft Word Document [W7 – "Create" under "Blank Document" at right], which immediately puts a new document icon into that folder called "New Microsoft Office Word Document"): Type in the name over that > press Enter key. Note that you named the document before you worked on it.

When creating a document under a folder and naming it, you don't have to go thru the "Save As" window; it's just "Save". (I think a good way to understand the "Save As" window is to think of it as the "Send To" window; here, you don't have to "Send To" because you're already there, already in your chosen folder.)

See also, "SAVE vs SAVE AS" and "DEFAULT 'WORD DOCUMENT' FORMAT" for related info.

Renaming a Document or Folder

Right-click the document or folder icon > Rename > then just start typing the new name and the old one is written over > press Enter key.

NARRATOR – COMPUTER TALKS TO YOU – Narration would be for vision-impaired people. Start > Control Panel > Ease of Access > Ease of Access Center > "Let Windows suggest settings" > check "I am blind" > Next, Next, Next, Next > Done > check "Turn on Narrator," Save.

It does NOT narrate out loud the text you type; what it does, is narrate the headings on screen or the functions you click on. To get it to narrate the stuff you type in, you have to use third party software (like "naturalreaders.com").

Narrator – Won't Shut Off

Once I had it on, I couldn't get it to turn off!

When I emailed Microsoft for help, they were, as usual, no help. Instead of directly answering my simple question, they sent me a full page of general information, suggesting four different help websites, which I could visit and spend hours going in circles in, and get nowhere also.

Finally figured it out: Go thru the above process for turning it on, (keep "I am blind" checked so you can get to the "Turn on Narrator" box, otherwise that box doesn't show for you) > uncheck "Turn on Narrator" > Save > THEN restart your computer to have it take effect!

NAVIGATION PANE – At the left of every folder window, it shows you the major locations you have (Desktop, Libraries, Computer, etc.) and you can click on them to get there.

"NEW" – TWO NEW'S IN THE SAME OPTION LIST – When you are in a folder, and click "File" at upper left to create a new document, an option list comes up which sometimes has two "New" options listed. The first one is the same as CTRL+N; it immediately opens a new document in your chosen format. The second one is for opening a new document (or folder or other options) in Vista's default format... Or so it seemed to me at one point; right now I can't even get that "New"s option list. See also DEFAULT "WORD DOCUMENT" FORMAT.

NETFLIX – This is a DVD movies rental company. They have various packages – one, two, or more movies at a time. They send the DVDs in the mail. No late fee; they just send you the next one on your list once you've returned the last one. The DVDs come in red envelopes, which are also used to return the DVDs to them, postage-free.

They have a huge selection, which you choose from on their website, after you get an account.

I've had it for years. Very satisfied. They do very well in getting the next movie to you quickly. I have the one-at-a-time deal. If you watch the movie the day you get it, and mail it back the next day, you basically get two movies a week. That's 8 or 9 movies a month, for about $11. (Good deal, though, just recently, fall 2011, they upped their prices; it's now $16.)

They also have a setup where you can get movies streamed to your computer, or TV, or other device, but I haven't tried that yet.

NETWORKING – This is when you have a setup where a collection of computers share information and resources, as in a company sharing computers in a building, or as in a home sharing several computers. I have no experience here. Sorry, can't help you. Check Andy Rathbone's book *Windows 7 for Dummies, Chapter 14, Connecting Computers with a Network* for basic info. Options should appear under Start > Control Panel > Network and Internet. Or, give Best Buy a call and have someone come out to set it up. Probably the most common situation calling for networking is a home where there are several computers but only one printer. You want all the computers to have access to that printer.

NOTEPAD – Is a simple plain-text-only word processing program. Comes with Windows. Is located under Start > All Programs > Accessories. Drop a complex web page into it and you get all images and formatting stripped away. From there you can copy it to a regular Word document and edit it to your desire. (Though, I find it very inconsistent; chunks get left out.)

NOTE-TAKING – ORGANIZATION TECHNIQUE – If you have dozens of pages of notes and you want to organize them, under proper headings or topics, it is a pain moving hundreds of notes to their proper topic location. I find the following an excellent technique for organizing notes:

1. Add an underlined topic word before each note.
2. Make sure each note consists of only ONE paragraph. If it's a long one, then separate paragraphs by two tab spaces instead of the "Enter" key. That way the note will stay in the same paragraph, and you can separate it into paragraphs later.
3. Block the whole deal and use the **A/Z↓** alphabetizing icon under the Paragraph box at top. That will alphabetize every paragraph by topic. All paragraphs on the same topic will now be bunched together, and you have avoided the tedious consolidating of notes piece by piece.
4. Then make final adjustments (separating long paragraphs into two, line spacing, etc.).

NTUSER – I got about a dozen files that showed up somewhere named "Ntuser." Best to just leave them alone, according to Geek gal, and guy. Might need it. Though I had deleted them before without an apparent problem. Of course, now I can't even find these files. But, as a general rule, you do not want to mess with files when you don't know what they are. They may be data files that have some association with other files. Maybe something to do with "OneNote" program use, I don't know.

NUMBER LOCK – There are two types of standard keyboards – regular, and a wider one, with an extra bank of keys at the right, which includes number keys. If you have a regular keyboard, as I do, those number keys are actually available as an alternative in the middle of your keyboard: If you press the Num Lk key, that makes a bunch of letter keys act like a "numeric keypad," namely, the 7-8-9, U-I-O, J-K-L, and M keys will produce instead: 7-8-9, 4-5-6, 1-2-3, and 0). You can see those numbers printed on the lower right corner of each of those keys. You might find this function convenient, if you use numbers a lot. Myself, I never use it.

At one point I had accidentally pressed the "Num Lk" key and was getting numbers instead of letters. I pressed Num Lk and got those letters back. The Num Lk key is a toggle one, switching the function back and forth each time you press it, between numbers and letters. Also, if you have Num Lk on, your CTRL+letter functions won't work; if you press CTRL+U, for example, nothing happens.

NUMBERING WITHIN THE TEXT – AUTOMATIC – Home tab at top > Paragraph box, upper left, center icon (1,2,3 with lines); the dropdown arrow gives you different styles of numbering to choose from. Clicking on the icon or one of the style choices, starts automatic numbering from your cursor spot, or, if you've blocked a text, it numbers each paragraph in that block.

Note that automatic numbering applies itself to paragraphs, adding a new number each time you press the Enter key, as you go down the page. It doesn't number items going across a line; if you want that, you have to do it manually.

Any line space with no text in it will not get a number, which is good, because you generally don't want an empty line numbered.

Automatic Indentation of Numbers

Numbers that result from automatic numbering are automatically entered indented. If you want your numbers with no indent, flush with the left margin, click on one of the numbers (which highlights the whole column of numbers), then, in the Paragraph box, click the left "Decrease Indent" icon (upper row) one or more times to move them over to the left. Or, you can place your I-beam cursor on the numbers and literally drag the whole deal to the left, or right.

Getting Rid of Automatic Numbering

Rather than deleting numbers individually with the Backspace key, and having to adjust your indents, it's usually easier to block the whole numbered text, click the dropdown arrow, and select "None." Note that the "None" selection won't work if you blocked an extra non-numbered line; you have to block the numbered lines exactly. On the other hand, you can "un-number" just selected lines.

As with automatic bulleting, press Enter key twice to end that automatic action.

Getting Rid of AUTOMATIC Automatic Numbering

If you type in the number 1 at the start of a paragraph, and the computer automatically then numbers your next paragraph #2, that means you have that kind of automatic setting in effect for any time you type in a number at the start of a paragraph! (Or, if you type a * at the start of a paragraph, it automatically inserts bullets for the succeeding paragraphs.)

If you don't want that: click Review tab at top > Spelling & Grammar at far left > Options at lower left > Auto Correct Options > "Autocorrect As You Type" tab > Apply as you type > uncheck "Automatic numbered lists" and "Automatic bulleted lists" > OK > OK.

(Sometimes when you click on Spelling & Grammar it won't give you an option window; it just checks your spelling and that's all. Press F7 key at top; that usually gives you the option window. Or, keep fiddling around, switching documents, go to the bathroom and come back, and usually, suddenly, that window is back.)

Interrupted Sequence

If you have a list of 20 items but numbers 11-20 are under a different heading than the first ten, to avoid having the heading for the second bunch labeled #11 and ending up with 21 items: Type your list of 20 first, including 3 empty line spaces between #10 and #11, then block the bunch, then click the numbering icon to number the 20 items, then go back and manually type in the heading for the second bunch in the middle of those three empty lines. That way, the heading you type in, does not itself get numbered.

NUMBERING – MULTI-LEVEL – You can get multi-level numbering, that is, automatic labeling of subcategories with letters or numbers. Home tab at top > Paragraph box > click on "Multilevel List" icon (third from left) dropdown arrow > pick choice of style under "List Library." Then, as you type, each time you press Enter, it enters your main category; each time you press Enter and then the Tab key, it automatically enters your next subcategory. For example:

1) Animals
    a) Cats
    b) Dogs
        i) Collie
        ii) Labrador
            (1) Black
            (2) Yellow

If you make a list like the one above without the numbers and letters, but tabbed over as shown, you can block it, select the multi-level numbering style, and it will automatically put in the numbers and letters as shown.

But, like so many features, this isn't worth using, unless you do it a lot. Normally I just do something like this manually, not automatically. Update: Now it won't work! Blocking a tabbed list still works, but typing a list and then pressing tab after Enter, doesn't work. Told you it wasn't worth it. Maybe I'm doing something wrong, but I do not think so. At any rate, it's more trouble than it's worth to try to figure it out.

NUMBERING PAGES – Insert tab at top > Header & Footer box > Page Number > select position (I usually like "Bottom of Page," select style (I usually like plain, centered) > click on it, then at upper right, click on the red "x for "Close Header & Footer." That numbers all the pages of your document, from 1 to whatever.

Note that a double-left click, with the I-beam on the page, also closes Header & Footer, and brings you back to your regular text.

Adjusting Page Number Appearance

Double-click directly on any of the page numbers to bring up the function (the regular text grays out), block the number, and apply changes. For example, you can CTRL+L to move it to the left, or you can bold it, or change its size, etc. Then click on the red "x" to close Header & Footer, setting that appearance.

Note that adjusting that one page number, adjusts all of them. If you made it smaller, then all the page numbers for that whole document are now smaller.

Formatting the Page Numbers

You can make other changes by: Insert tab > Header & Footer box > Page Number > Format Page Numbers. You can choose, for example, small Roman numerals. Or, you can start your numbering with some other number than 1.

Note that if you start a document with page 3 and order page 1 to print, nothing will happen.

Deleting Numbering

Double-click on one of the numbers > block/highlight the number > press Delete button > click on red "x" to close Header & Footer. Deleting that one page number deletes all of them throughout that document.

Numbering Pages for a Booklet or Book

See "PAGINATION – BOOK FOLD"

Pagination Problems

If pages repeat themselves, or there is some other problem, it's usually because you've cobbled together various sections of text from different places. To fix it, start over: Delete your page numbering. Then delete any section breaks (click ¶ in the Paragraph box at top, to show where the breaks are – see "Section Breaks"). Then, insert your page numbering anew.

To check if your page numbering is OK, look at the far lower left of your screen. It should tell you what page, out of how many total, you are currently on. If it says you are on page 6 of 23, yet your page on the screen tells you that you are on page 3, then – unless you intend your document to have more than one type numbered section (see below) – your numbering is messed up, and you need to go thru the procedure described in the previous paragraph.

Sample Complex Pagination Setup

Say you want:

– No numbers for a title page, with a blank back side
– Small Roman numerals for a table of contents and an introduction, for the next four pages
– Then, traditional numbering from the 7th page on

Now, that's a very typical start to any book or document. And, the easiest way to produce that kind of varied numbering is simply to break it up into three different documents. But, if you want that numbering setup in ONE document (a book/essay/article) you're writing, it is VERY tough to set that up.

It took me hours of experimenting. Here's how to I managed to do it:

1. Delete any pagination you have to this point, so that you start fresh.
2. Click on ¶ symbol in the Paragraph box, to show commands.
3. You need to replace page breaks, at the bottom of 2nd and 6th pages, with "Section Break (Next Page)" – click Page Layout tab, Breaks, under Section Breaks click Next Page to get "Section Break (Next Page)" at those two spots (where your number format changes).
4. Put cursor at start of third page.
5. Insert tab, Header & Footer box, Page Number, Format Page Numbers, select small Roman numerals style, Start at 1.
6. Again, Insert tab, Header & Footer box, Page Number, Bottom of Page, make selection. That should put i, ii, iii, iv, at bottom of third thru sixth pages.
7. Put cursor at start of 7th page.
8. Insert tab, Header & Footer box, Page Number, Format Page Numbers, select regular numerals style, Start at 1.
9. Again, Insert tab, Header & Footer box, Page Number Page, Bottom of Page, make selection. That should put 1, 2, 3, etc. from the 7th page onward.

10. OK, except for this: Regular numbers consistently somehow get automatically put onto the first two pages (Title page and back)! Deleting does no good, since deleting any, deletes ALL. Changing them to white (so they don't show up), does no good, since that changes ALL the numbers to white. "Remove Page Numbers" does no good, since that removes ALL of them.

Different first page (Page Layout, Page Setup dropdown arrow, Layout tab, check Different first page) does little good, because it just starts the numbering on the back of the first page, rather than on the third page (the front of sheet two).

So how do I get page numbers deleted from the first two pages without deleting all the page numbers in the other sections?

Spent hours working on this. Internet searching only gave the same simplistic answers again and again, as though no one EVER wants to do what to me is a VERY logical setup – start numbering on the THIRD side in, so that that first sheet, front and back, has NO numbering.

Aha, I came up with a solution (a "workaround"); then later found one person in the internet with the same solution:

11. Put a white rectangle over the page numbers on the title sheet, front and back.

a. Insert > b. Illustrations box > c. Shapes > d. Pick a rectangle > e. Drag the "+" sign to the first page, left click it onto the page > f. Drag the rectangle on top of the page number > g. Right-click it > h. Format Auto Shape > i. Line, color, select white, OK; that blocks out the page number. > j. Right-click on rectangle, Copy > k. Drag the second rectangle on top of the second page number.

Now, finally, you've got two pages with no numbers, 4 with Roman numerals, and the rest with regular numerals.

And that, my children, is the story of how the evil monster, Vista, was finally defeated this time, in the ongoing saga of good versus evil.

Note that ordering up these early pages to print, can be tricky – you have three different versions of "page 2"! You have to experiment for a long time to get what you want, if you ever do.

Note also that if you have trouble and fiddle around with it too long, things tend to get hopelessly complex – you order "start at I" but it starts at ii, you order 1 and it gives you 6, stuff comes and goes, your order one format and it gives you another, sometimes you can get pages with no numbers, etc. ,etc., all kinds of weird results.

It is way, way easier to simply do this setup in three different documents!

Page Numbers – On Internet Material

If you block and print a section of a website text, you don't need to enter pagination. Usually it automatically has page numbers ("1 of 6", "2 of 6", etc., usually at upper right).

NUMBERS – GETTING NUMBERS INSTEAD OF LETTERS – See "NUMBER LOCK"

OCR – "OPTICAL CHARACTER RECOGNITION" – Refers to a program that will scan in a typed document, not as a set picture, but as editable text. It reads the actual individual letters and scans them in so you end up with text you can edit.

I think some printers have an elementary OCR program in them. My current one doesn't. I bought an OCR program years ago (ScanSoft OmniPage 15, Nuance company (1-800 654-11870, M-F, 9-8 EST). I wanted to use it again, so I clicked on the program icon, and the program came up, but it wouldn't work. To get it to work – my particular program – I had to do this:

I checked with the program's Help, Quick Start, Setting up your scanner. I think I needed to set up the connection to my new printer (scanner), or scanner driver, first. Followed their instructions as best I could:

a. Start, Programs, ScanSoft OmniPage 15, Scanner Setup Wizard (I think what the Scanner Wizard does is match OmniPage to the particular scanner you have, i.e., sets up a driver for it.)

b. The Wizard window showed, Next

c. Checked "Select and test scanner or digital camera," Next

d. Picked from a list of scanners (think I had the wrong Epson one at first); there's a note at bottom that says "Avoid using a driver presented as "TWAIN:WIA..." So, I selected the TWAIN one without the WIA, namely, "TWAIN Epson 810...", the one at the top of the list.

e. OK, Next

f. Says this scanner is not in the database. (Makes sense, since my OmniPage 15 is from 2007, and the Epson 810 is a new (2010?) scanner/printer.)

g. So, I need to run thru some diagnostic tests to match my Epson 810 scanner/printer, to use with OmniPage 15

i. Yes, Next, Next

j. 5 of the 6 boxes are already checked as the default choices, Next

k. Put a text document into the scanner (already did that), Next.

l. Epson scan window appears at left, click Scan. It starts scanning.

m. Scanned image of document appears at left.

n. Basic scan passed, Next

o. Next, Next

p. Take the document out, Next, Next

q. Put the document back in, Next [For me – remember the Epson printer lid slips easily from your fingers when you hold it by the edge; be careful, never get careless and let it drop several inches; may well damage it! The lid is NOT neutrally balanced; it's heavy and will drop down heavily!]

r. Scanned image shows, Next

s. Insert a B&W photo, Next, scanned image shows.

t. Insert a color photo, Next, scanned image shows.

u. "Successfully configured," Finish. My OCR program now works.

There's all kinds of things to learn, but below is the basic procedure that got me a decent result – the page scanned in accurately, with just a few adjustments that needed to be made (a few words came out bold, instead of regular, a couple of words were positioned one spot over, etc.)

If you have just straightforward text, it can make a 100% accurate copy. Though, it does tend to make certain mistakes, like interpreting "½" as "A".

Here are factors that contribute to accuracy:

– Cleaner, clearer, bigger, original is better.
– As little formatting (underlining, shading, colors, different font sizes, etc.) as possible is better
– Single column is better.
– Also, I think straightforward fonts, like Arial or Calibri, do better than fancier "seriffed" fonts, like Times New Roman. (With Arial the word "finally" came out correct, whereas with Times New Roman, it came out "fmally.")

OCR Scanning Procedure, For Me

1. Load text page onto the scanner flatbed glass, face down, head to the left.
2. Double-click OmniPage 15 icon on desktop. ("Tip of the Day," close)
3. The window that opened up has four boxes at top, going left to right: "1–2–3", "Load Files", "Recognize Images", and "Export Results." That's the order it does things.
4. Make a selection from the dropdown arrow of each box.

I chose "1–2–3", "Scan", "Automatic", and "Copy to Clipboard."

("Automatic" selection above, reads multiple columns and puts them into a single column.)

5. Click the upper part of the first box, on the "1–2–3" blue arrow. Initializes, and brings up the Epson scanning window.

[Actually, the last time I tried it, it wouldn't go. Had to go thru whole setup procedure again, and then I got stuck; it kept saying the ADF (Automatic Document Feeder) option was wrong (i.e. I had no page in it to feed, I had the page on the flatbed), but I couldn't figure out how to change that option. Under Tools tab at top > Options > Scanner tab > Source, it had ONLY the ADF (automatic document feeder) option there, not the flatbed one, which is the one I normally prefer since I usually do parts of magazine articles, not whole sheets; I don't want to have to tear out a full page and feed it thru the ADF!

Anyway, I went thru the setup again and this time picked a different Printer (Epson 810 but with "WIA" in the name), figuring maybe the one I had it set to, only did ADF feeds. Well, it worked. Who knows why. Some of the things to click are a bit different, but relatively straightforward. But basically the numbered procedures here, now work.]

6. Before you press Scan, click Preview at lower left and, if you want less than the full page, drag the handles on the preview picture to limit the rectangular area of text it will scan in.
7. Click "Scan" in that window. It scans the text page you have on the flatbed.
8. Window comes up for "Stop Loading Pages" or "Add More Pages." Click on the "Stop" one, if you want just that one document.
9. Next box ("Recognize Images") runs automatically, putting your documents onto the screen. (If a "Proofreader" window comes up, I skip it by clicking "Document ready" or "Ignore," since I like to do corrections on the document only AFTER landing it into a Word document.)
10. "Copy to Clipboard" window comes up, check Plain Text (I find "Plain Text" comes out more accurately than "Formatted Text"), OK. Note that the clipboard does not show anywhere, but the scanned material is now in there.
11. Minimize the OCR window. Find your destination folder or document and CTRL+V it there. (I prefer pasting into an empty Word document.) There it is, your original document now in EDITABLE type.
12. Check it for corrections. Fix the errors. Re-format it to your tastes, to a different font, size, columns, whatever.

Note that if you're saving it to a File, or Folder, I think it sends it as a document with an icon, whereas if you save it to the clipboard, it sends it as text into the document you open for it to land into.

Now, there's all kinds of options, features, and fine-tuning you can do, but I don't do too much OCR scanning at present, so I'll just stick with the basics. If you do a lot of it, then you should spend major time experimenting and learning the program to get the most out of it.

I scanned in a Newsweek article (3 columns, title, pictures), and it came out pretty decent. Some to the formatting changed, some positions changed, and the three columns became one column, but, all the info was there.

As a general rule, reformatting scanned-in text causes more odd adjustments to deal with than does ordinary text. For example, scanned in text often has embedded tabs for paragraphs and changing them is not simply a matter of deleting them (they refuse to get deleted).

If you want a copy of an article, in most cases, you're better off simply scanning it in regularly, as a picture, rather than with OCR. People have all kinds of purposes, but, for me, I'm realizing OCR-scanning of articles is too much work; you have to correct all kinds of formatting. Easier to just regular-scan it so that an article keeps its formatting and pictures, AS IS.

TIPS

Embedded Commands

If you use OCR-scanning to scan in something with a lot of formatting, once you've landed it into a Word document, change it to ONE column, click ¶ to show all the formatting commands, and knock out as much of them as you can, especially page and section breaks, to simplify the whole deal. THEN, put it into the format you want. (Sometimes, the "¶" show command feature doesn't even show some of the embedded information.)

Changing Margins

The more complex the stuff you scan in, the less likely it will let you change margins. Usually, putting the text to one column first helps. (Then switch it back to your desired multiple columns after you've changed the margins.)

Another key for changing margins (for multiple-page text) is this: Click ¶, and delete page and section breaks.

Preview

If you click "Preview" in the Epson scanning window, you can use the pointer "+" marker on the preview of your material on the right, to frame a section of text, then click Scan to scan just that section of the page. Often it's better to do it this way rather than scan in the whole page at once.

Line Spacing

It helps to CTRL+A and put all your line spacing to single spaced lines, to get rid of embedded, varied, or extra line spaces: Home > Paragraph > Line Spacing > Line Spacing Options > Before and After at "0" > Single.

Embedded Indents

Here's an old note I made that might be applicable: "If the first word of the next line is indented and you can't get rid of that unwanted indent, then instead of pressing Backspace at the start of that word, press Enter. That fixes it, oddly enough. Gets rid of that embedded indent." Sometimes.

Checking it today, a better method is to position the cursor at the indent, and click the "Decrease Indent" icon in the Paragraph box up top under the Home tab.

Sometimes, pressing the Enter key, splits the line up and often reveals an embedded space you need to knock out.

Bottom Line

For me, OCR scanning is, in most cases, more trouble than it's worth – involves too much adjusting. But, it's nice to have for simple jobs with straightforward text.

"OK" vs "APPLY" – Here's another perfect example of Vista adding unnecessary options, trying to make things "easier," but ending up just confusing people.

"OK" makes the desired change take place, and closes the dialogue window. (Think of "OK" as "OK, I'm done.") "Apply" also makes the desired change take place, but keeps the dialogue window open for any further changes you want to make. So, in theory, you do not have to click both; just click one or the other. But there are some programs, like Norton Antivirus, where you DO have to click both. So, I always click both just to make sure, Apply, then OK.

OLD COMPUTER – ERASING INFO – AR: Old computer hard drives "can be a thief's delight." You may well have financial records, passwords, etc. still in there. There are data-destruction programs you can buy, but, I think your best bet is to give your old computer to Best Buy. They simply take out your hard drive and give it to you.

OLDER PROGRAMS – COMPATIBILITY MODE – Some programs were designed for older version of Windows, and run better with the older versions. Vista has a compatibility mode to let you run them under the old programs!

Right-click program > Properties > Compatibility tab > check "Run this program in compatibility mode for:" > select desired Windows version from dropdown menu > OK. That old program might run better now. Tried it with my old Chess (2003) program. Didn't see any difference. Actually, turns out the chess program was already in the old Windows XP version, so no wonder I saw no difference.

ON / OFF – QUICK SHUT-DOWN, TURN-ON – For years I had been shutting my laptop off by clicking the Start button, the arrow to the right of the lock icon, and Shut Down. A process that takes a good three minutes; likewise for turning it back on, using the actual power button at the upper right of the computer.

I finally realized that putting the computer into "Sleep" mode is much better than shutting it down. The turning on and off process become a matter of only seconds, not minutes.

I now have my laptop set up to go into "sleep" mode by simply closing the lid. So much more convenient! See "Laptop Lid Closing Setting."

OPTICAL CHARACTER RECOGNITION – See "OCR"

OPTIONS LIST – MISSING "CUT" AND "COPY" – If you right-click on a file and the options list is missing "Cut" and "Copy", what you did was right-click on an empty spot in the file's line. You need to click directly on the file's name or date, not the space in between.

ORGANIZATION OF ITEMS – When you open any folder, a panel at the left shows you all the items on your computer – Desktop, Owner/Libraries, Documents, Music, Pictures, Videos, etc. If you click on one of those items, it opens them and shows you what's inside, over on the right of the window.

ORGANIZING NOTES – See "NOTE-TAKING – ORGANIZATION TECHNIQUE"

OPENING – DOCUMENTS, FOLDERS, PROGRAMS – Generally, you open items by either double-left-clicking on it, or, right-clicking the icon and then clicking "Open."

Opening an Icon on Desktop

Sometimes, if it doesn't open, it's because you need to click on the top part of the icon, not the bottom part.

Opening a File with a Program

Generally, you can view or play a file (document, audio, picture, video) by either of two routes: 1) Double-click on the file and the default program automatically opens it. 2) Open a program first, and then drag or import a file into that program. For example, if you double-click on a video file, it opens up and plays, using your default player (for me, Windows Media Player). Or, if you open Windows Media Player first, you can drag a video file into it, and then play it.

See "DEFAULT PROGRAMS" for selecting which program you want to use to open files of a certain type.

Opening Problems

If your computer won't or can't open something and gives you an error window saying so, then choose the second option it shows – "Select a program from a list...," OK. It might open up then. If it doesn't, try selecting the first option to search the internet for an appropriate program to open it with, and download it to use.

At one point, for a period of several months, my computer always required two tries to open a document, giving this error message first: "Windows cannot find [x document]. Make sure you typed the name correctly, and then try again."

Always, I just did it a second time and then it opened fine. But, of course, it's annoying to have to do it twice every time. Geek guy (Brian) figured it was because I had made my own "My Documents" folder and stored it where Vista is not used to looking for it. He moved things around, renamed folder, or whatever, and now it's fine.

Update: No; it's still doing the same thing.

Update 8/09: Suddenly, it's no longer doing it. Maybe one of the Windows automatic updates fixed it – ?? That happens sometimes; problems go away without your doing anything. General advice: Do not move major folders, like "My Documents"; Windows has trouble finding them if you do.

ORPHANS – To get rid of "orphans" – a single line of a paragraph by itself at the bottom of a page – CTRL+A your text pages first > Home tab > Paragraph box dropdown arrow > Line and Page Break tab > check "Widows and Orphans." Or, for me, since I prefer to keep them, uncheck that box. (I don't mind single lines at bottoms, unless it's a heading.)

Note that this function, like most, applies "from this point forward." So you have to CTRL+A to get it to apply to the whole document.

See also, "LINE SPACING" > "Line Spacing – Blank Space at Page Bottom"

OS (OPERATING SYSTEM) – Refers to an overall software system that runs a computer. An OS manages the computer hardware and its software applications, acting as an intermediary between them. Microsoft Windows is by far the most popular operating system. Macintosh and Linux are other examples. If a tech person on the phone wants to know what operating system you have, they usually want to know which version of Windows you have – Windows XP, Vista, Windows 7.

OUTDOORS – SCREEN BRIGHTNESS – If you're using your laptop outdoors and the sun is out, it's very hard to see the screen. You can increase the brightness of your screen by pressing the Fn key at lower left and simultaneously pressing the F6 key (but, I have the screen at maximum brightness all the time anyway).

I was hoping my new computer might be better outdoors, but no. Same deal: In the sun, no matter what angle, it's barely readable. In the shade, it's OK, with full screen brightness and correct angle.

OVERTYPE MODE – Instead of the normal process of pushing forward what you already have in your text, "overtyping" replaces that material as you type. Each time you press a key, it types over the next spot, replacing what was there.

I hate this function! I used to order it up accidentally on my old computer every so often, and then I couldn't remember how to get rid of it! This is how: MS Office Button (big colored one at far upper left) [W7 – "File"] > Word Options (at bottom) [W7 – "Options"] > Advanced (at left) > Editing Options, uncheck Use Overtype Mode (9th one down) > OK.

Typical computer problem: You suddenly start getting something out of the blue that totally screws things up and you cannot logically figure out how to get rid of it. I mean, that MS icon at upper left is one I never even knew was there, for years. Had never used it. For this problem, luckily, MS gave me the above straightforward solution, under the question mark help icon, after I typed in "Overtype" into the Word Help search box.

I don't know what the default setting was, but in that dialogue window, just above "Use Overtype Mode" is "Use the Insert key to control overtype mode", which means you can switch this overtype mode off and on by pressing the Insert key at upper right of the keyboard.

"OWNER LOCKED" – STUCK – At one point I started getting "Owner Locked" every time I left my computer for more than 5 minutes. If I just clicked on it, it would return to the desktop. Fine. But, that takes three seconds, and it was very annoying to have to go thru that extra step every time I returned to my computer.

To get rid of it: Right-click any empty space on Desktop > Personalize > Screen Saver > uncheck "On Resume Display LogOn Screen" > OK. Now, you're no longer displaying LogOn screen, i.e., "Owner Locked," every time you leave the computer for 5 minutes.

That should do it, but if I remember right, this didn't work for me the first time. I also had to do these operations:

Right-click Desktop > Personalize > Screen Saver > Change Power Settings (at lower left) > User Accounts (at lower left) > Turn User Account Control On/Off > uncheck Use User Account Control > OK > restart computer.

AND, while on the internet, Tools tab at upper right > Internet Options > Security tab > Settings > click Internet > Custom level > Security Settings > scroll all the way down to the bottom to User Authentication > I checked Anonymous Logon > OK. That (along with the very first operation described above) seemed to make the difference for me in getting rid of "Owner Locked," but, I can't be sure. It could be I had to re-start the computer on one of those operations and I didn't.

PAGE BREAK – If you're typing text and want to go immediately to the next page, leaving the rest of your current page blank (as you would for the end of a chapter), you should insert a "page break": Press CTRL+Enter keys. Or, click Insert tab at top, Page Break.

To get rid of a page break, you can use the delete key but you have to position the cursor exactly at the end of that page break. To make sure you have positioned the cursor in the right spot, you can click the ¶ icon in the Paragraph box at top to show you where your commands are. A dotted line with the words "Page Break" in the middle, is your page break command. Put your cursor at the start of that dotted line, and press the Delete key. That will close up your text, so that text continues from that spot instead of having a blank space from there to the bottom of the page.

PAGE FORMAT – To set what you want your page to look like: Page Layout tab at top > Page Setup > select your choices (margins, orientation, paper size, etc.) Selecting "Landscape" under "Orientation" sets your page horizontally so it's 11 inches wide instead of 11 inches tall.

Size

Setting a size, puts that size on the screen for you to type into. If you set, for example, under More Paper Sizes, a 3 by 5 card size, it puts a 3 by 5 card on screen for you to type into.

If you want a half-page size (5½ by 8½) or some other small size, like card size, and you plan to print on paper of that size feeding thru your printer, make sure the paper or cards are cut exactly, and are stacked very neatly, otherwise you'll tend to get feeding problems.

Three-Hole Punch Paper

Left and right margins should be at least .6, so that the text doesn't go right over a hole.

Default Page Setup

See "DEFAULT 'WORD DOCUMENT' FORMAT' and "PAPER SIZE"

PAGINATION – See "NUMBERING PAGES"

PAGE NUMBERS – Whatever page you're on, in a Word document, the page numbers show at far lower left, right above the colored flag Start icon. It tells you what number page you are on, out of how many total. Like "7 of 12."

Re-Pagination Time Delay

If you change the margins or font size of your document, Vista automatically re-paginates, but, it often takes a minute or two to complete. If the little page-turning book icon at the bottom left is still moving a pencil across the pages, it's not done yet. You can, however, check to see how many pages the new format is, immediately, by pressing CTRL+End key to get to the last page right away.

PAGE – NUMBERS AND MARGINS DISAPPEAR FROM SCREEN

If you suddenly get only a horizontal gray line between your text from one page to the next, and the normal page number and margins do not show on screen, it's because you accidentally ordered that particular page-display format – just text, no margins or page numbers shown. (It still prints out correctly with page numbers and margins, but does not show them onscreen.)

To get back to normal, put the pointer right on that gray line, an icon showing an arrow up and an arrow down pops up along with a message "Double-click to show/hide white space," double-click.

Or, if you DO prefer the white space and page numbers hidden, position the pointer on the space between the pages (those two arrows then pop up) and double-click.

Each time you click on that double-arrow icon in the space between pages, it toggles back and forth between the two types of page displays. I personally don't like the no-space format; I like to see margins, page numbers, and some separation between pages, on the screen.

PAGINATION – FOR A BOOKLET – If you want to print a leaflet of one horizontal 8½ by 11 sheet, folded in the middle, i.e., 4 pages of text, you can do so if your printer has two-sided printing and the "Folded Booklet" feature:

Keep your paper size at 8½ x11 > keep your paper orientation at Portrait > set your top and bottom margins as narrow as possible > CTRL+P > Properties > Page Layout > Auto (for 2-sided printing) > check Folded Booklet > OK > then OK to print.

(The "Folded Booklet" function is grayed out unless you choose two-sided printing.)

BUT, I found this feature is pretty worthless. Because 1) the pagination only works for ONE sheet (4 text pages); more than that and it does not paginate correctly. 2) The top and bottom margins come out way too big; the setup is no better, or different, than what you get when you select in your Print window – "Pages per sheet: 2 pages."

Instead, if you want more than just a one-sheet folded leaflet, the best answer, I found, is to ignore the printer's "Folded Booklet" feature, and instead use the computer's "Book Fold" feature as described below:

PAGINATION – BOOK FOLD

I would say that with anything more than 16 sheets, i.e. 64 text pages, your booklet starts to get too bulky to fold, and then you're better off cutting your stack down the middle and using some kind of binding, rather than folding the sheets down the middle.

The difficulty with booklets, or a book of many pages, of course, since you are printing two pages on each side of a sheet, is the tricky pagination. For example, for a 16-page booklet, you need 16-1-2-15, 14-3-4-13, 12-5-6-11, 10-7-8-9.

Ideally, you want automatic pagination so that, for a booklet, when you fold a bunch of sheets and staple them in the middle, the pages come out right. Or, for a book of many pages, you want to be able to make one cut down the middle after printing and simply put one stack on top of the other, with the pages properly paginated.

THIS YOU CAN DO! After a long journey thru mathematical conundrums and paltry help from Vista and the internet, and being initially convinced my only options were complex printing versus laborious collating, and that there simply was no easy way... it turns out there IS a way, a simple way, provided you get your steps right:

Pagination for a Booklet or Book

1. Type your text in regular 8½ x 11 page size, and keep it in that format.
2. Keep your page orientation in the normal "portrait" (vertical) orientation.
3. Click the Page Layout tab at top.
4. Click the dropdown arrow at lower right of box.
5. In the Margins tab, under Pages, Multiple Pages, click on the dropdown arrow and select "Book Fold."
6. Once you order Book Fold, it automatically puts your text from 8½ x 11 size into 5½ x 8 ½ size, and into landscape orientation (that is, landscape when it prints; on screen it will show as 5½ x 8 portrait orientation pages.)

Note how the Preview in that window to the lower left, shows you how your setup actually looks – like a book.

7. CTRL+P, (Page range – All). Select 2-Sided printing (on my printer that means clicking on "Auto" under Properties, Page Layout tab). [See below for printers that print only one side at a time.]
8. It should print out your whole job, properly paginated.

Vista, of course, typically, doesn't bother to tell you about steps #1 and #2, or much about step #6, without which information you'll be frustrated no end with an array of weird and unusable results.

Now you have both proper positioning and proper pagination. And, no sorting, uncollating, and collating problems. If you have 16 or less numbered pages, fold the bunch in the middle and staple it there; and you have your booklet. If you have more pages, then go to your local print shop or a Staples store, to get a nice clean cut down the middle, one step collating (the left stack folded on top of the right stack), and binding of some sort; and you have your book.

Note that once you've selected "Book Fold," the document stays in that format until you go back and select "Normal" again. And if you do go back to "Normal," you also at this point have to change your page orientation back to Portrait, manually.

Also, do not have BOTH "Book Fold" for your document AND "Folded Booklet" for your printing, selected at the same time. You'll get weird results, like 4 pages per side and upside down backup. Stick to "Book Fold" only. In fact I think the "Folded Booklet" printing function should be totally ignored.

Must Do in One Operation

Note that you have to do the operation in one action, rather than in sections. If you're a math whiz, maybe you can figure out how to do it in sections. But when I experimented with a 16-page booklet in sections, I got all kinds of inconsistent, weird stuff – wrong pages, skipped pages, duplicate pages, etc.

But, any time I ordered the whole job to be printed, it came out good. A 400-page book means only 100 sheets of paper, so it's not an abnormally big job. Just make sure the paper in your feeding tray is set up just right; you don't want misfeeds on a big two-sided job.

For Printers That Print Only One Side at a Time

1. – 6. Same as above for "Pagination for a Booklet or Book"
7. CTRL+P
8. Check "Manual Duplex" at upper right. "Duplex" means two-sided printing; "manual" means you're going to turn the sheets over yourself instead of the printer.
9. Click OK ("Page range – All"), to print, and it prints the first sides of your sheets, two pages per side, properly paginated (For example, for a 16-page booklet – it puts page 1 with 16, 3 with 14, etc.).

Note that once you've chosen "Book Fold," your odd and even pages option at lower left is automatically grayed out.

10. On my printer the sheets come out – printed side up, head to left.
11. A message comes up saying "Please remove the printout of first side from tray and place it in the input tray. Then press OK to continue printing."
12. Before you do that, you must reverse the order of the sheets in your stack! Page 1 must be on top.
13. Then, go ahead and put the stack back into the feeding tray. For me, again – printed side up, head to the left.
14. Click the "OK" in that message window, and it prints the second sides, properly paginated. That's it.

Lastly, don't forget to uncheck "Manual Duplex" when you're done. And if that option suddenly disappears on you, then in your printing window, click Properties, Page Layout, 2-sided printing off... or something. I fiddled around with things and the "Manual Duplex" option suddenly showed up again, and I unchecked it.

Printing on 5½ x 8½ Sized Paper

Another option for a book setup, is to simply print on 5½ x 8½ paper. Just be sure the paper is cut EXACTLY, to avoid misfeeds. Misfeeds on two-sided jobs is a killer; one mistake engenders a bunch of mistakes, as you get successive wrong pages backing up pages. Also, of course, it will take you twice as long to print, because you are printing "one-up" not "two-up" (pages per sheet side). But, printing on half-sized paper is a viable option.

PAINT – MS "PAINT" PROGRAM – I've hardly used this program at all, but it's kind of neat. You can make drawings, just like you would with a crayon or paintbrush.

Start > All Programs > Accessories > Paint. Make your drawing using the features at left and color choices at top. You can draw lines by dragging the pencil icon. You can fill in or paint enclosed areas. Here's an example of a rudimentary drawing:

Once done, this is how I saved it to a Word Document: File > Save As > named it "Sample Drawing" > target – my Pictures folder > Save. Then, to get to it, Owner [W7 – Libraries] > Pictures > double-click "Sample Drawing" icon > Edit > Copy > CTRL+V it into a Word Document.

One mother told me her child loves MS Paint, and it's the only thing he does on the computer. I might use it more in the future. You can add text to a drawing or a picture, though I haven't figured out how to do that yet; the "Text" icon is always grayed out.

If you click on Help at the top of the Paint window, click Help Topics, and type in "Using Paint" in the search box, it will show you more information on how to use "Paint."

Adding Text Update

Oh, this is just so typical of Vista! In order to use the text icon, you have to have your drawing or picture at exactly 100% size. Otherwise, it's grayed out and not available. Do they say that anywhere? NO! Can you figure that out logically? NO! They put your drawing in at such a small size, you naturally zoom it out to a bigger size to work with it, negating the text feature.

I had to Google "MS Paint text icon grayed out" to find an answer.

Anyway, here's how to add text to a drawing or picture, thru Paint:

1. Start, Accessories, Paint.
2. File at upper left, Open.
3. That opens a window showing all your folders, most likely the Pictures folder, where you normally keep your pictures and drawings.
4. Click on the file of your choice, click Open at lower right.
5. That puts your item into the Paint window.
6. Click on the A icon on the left. That icon is available if your picture is at 100% size.
7. That opens up two new icons at the bottom left [W7 – at top].
8. Click on the top one if you want your text inside a white box.
9. Click on the bottom one if you want your text inside a transparent box.
10. Draw this box by putting the cursor at desired spot and dragging it to make a box.
11. That brings up a font toolbar (if it doesn't, right-click the rectangle and select Text Toolbar).
12. Choose your font and style.
13. With the cursor inside the box, start typing your text.
14. Then File [W7 – upper left corner Paint icon] and Save As, as described above.

Myself, I've always added text to a picture by landing the picture in a Word document and simply typing in text. Right-clicking the picture gives you options (under the Layout tab) for text on top of a picture.

Working with Photos in Paint

I don't think you can adjust the photo itself, other than its size. Pictures folder > Open With > Paint. It lands the photo inside Paint. For me, it lands it usually 5-10 times too big. Sometimes you think nothing is there because only an upper blank corner of the photo is viewable. So you click Image tab and Resize, to get it smaller.

Another way to import photos to Paint is to open Paint first, then click on the dropdown arrow of the Paste icon at upper left, click Paste From, browse for your photo, highlight it, open.

As I say, editing features for the photo itself are limited, but you can draw on top of it, or add text, or add shapes like cartoon bubbles (and then stick text inside).

PAPER

Size

Default size is 8½ by 11". To order up a different size paper to work with on your computer: Page Layout tab > Page Setup > Size > select. If you're changing the paper size for text you've already typed, note how the computer shows your new page size and automatically fits your text into the new size. For example, if you select 4x6 size, a document of 4 pages, 8½x11 size, becomes a document of 14 pages, 4x6 size, retaining the same margins, font, etc.

Then, when done, when you go to print your documents, after adjusting the size of the printer's paper trays, specify to your printer what size paper you are using, matching the printing size to your computer document size: CTRL+P > Properties > Main tab > size > select > OK > OK again to print it.

Feeding Problems

Some printers are better than others. I've had two Epson printers. My old one was terrific for feeding; hardly ever had a misfeed. And the reason, I'm pretty sure, is that it fed from a slanted vertical tray from the back, where sheets are fed largely by gravity. My new one doesn't do nearly as well; it feeds from a horizontal tray from the bottom, and sheets have to be picked up, I guess, by suction. Something to keep in mind when buying a printer.

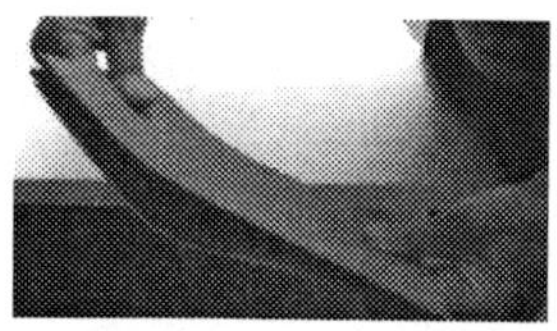

I always fan a new bunch of sheets out by holding each end and wiggling the stack back and forth a bit, to get air in between sheets. Helps keep sheets from binding to each other.

I found printing smaller than regular 8½ x11 paper, or printing envelopes, are problematic. I mean, it works, but unless you have trays and paper set up just right – not too tight, not too loose, not too many, jogged perfectly, etc. – misfeeds occur. If you want to print both sides of 3x5 index cards, don't do a whole bunch at once, but only, say, 10 at a time, because one misfeed will throw all the ensuing back sides off. You can live with doing a few over, but doing 50 over, because of one early misfeed, will cause cursing.

Paper Jams

Usually printers will specifically indicate to you if it has stopped because of a paper jam. Usually you have to lift the lid and search for a jammed sheet of paper, grab an edge of it, and pull slowly and steadily to get it out. Then put the lid back down and maybe also press a Start button on the printer, to get it going again. If paper jams occur repeatedly, then you have to make some adjustment, most likely re-stacking the pile carefully and/or loosening the side or top/bottom tray guides.

Scrap Paper

Invariably you end up with sheets printed on one side that you're not going to use. I save those for scrap paper.

Curled Paper

Never store paper vertically; lay it flat; otherwise it tends to curl.

A neat trick I learned when I worked in a print shop: to uncurl a single sheet of paper, hold it down (curl side up) at the edge of a desk with one hand, and pull it down while applying pressure. The harder the pressure, the greater degree of curl or uncurl. Also, the sharper the edge of the desk, the greater the curl effect.

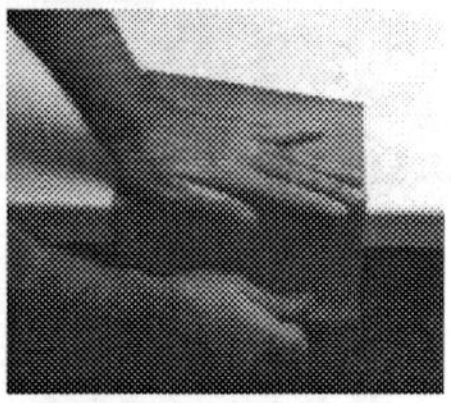

PAPER TYPE – Use paper specifically made for your type printer (for me, "ink jet" paper.) I have an old note saying not to use copy paper, because tiny fibers come off the sheets, eventually sticking to your printer rollers, and causing misfeeds. But, I don't know how relevant that is anymore; I don't know if my new printer even has rubber rollers. However, I do know, from a Staples store person, that you should use inkjet or multipurpose paper for inkjet printers, and laser paper for laser printers. If you mix them up, you won't get as good quality. Something to do with absorbency.

The brighter the paper, the cleaner the printing and color. I use Staples, 98 bright, 22 lb., 8½ x11, multipurpose paper. Very satisfied with it.

If you have heavy printing and are concerned the back side of sheets will show thru too much, use heavier paper – 24 lb. I measured a ream (500 sheets) of 24 lb., and it was about ¼" thicker than a ream of 22 lb. Weight was pretty much the same – 5.6 lb. So it may not be literally heavier, but rather thicker, and maybe treated with different chemicals to make it more opaque (nontransparent).

Use photo paper for printing photographs. Makes a difference. And, also, make sure, when doing CTRL+P on your printer, to select – under Properties, Paper Options, Type – the category of paper that matches what you are actually using. Makes a difference! The printer uses less, or more, ink for different types of paper.

PARAGRAPH FORMAT – To format your paragraphs, go to Home tab at top, Paragraph box, and select your options. Rather than clicking on those icons, I much prefer using the keyboard shortcuts here, namely:

Left align – CTRL+L.
Center – CTRL+E.
Justify – CTRL+J.
Right align – CTRL+R.

See also DEFAULT "WORD DOCUMENT FORMAT" > "Getting the Page Format You Want"

Formatting Information

You can get instant formatting information on your document by pressing Shift+F1. A window pops up on the right showing the font and paragraph information of the text you are currently in. Press Shift+F1 again to get rid of it. Not that useful, I find, since, if I ever forget what font or size I'm using, all I need to do is look at the Font box at top; it shows you.

Words Suddenly Spread Out on a Line

This happens when you are working with justified text and you accidentally press SHIFT and ENTER.

Here's an example of words spread out:
I hate when this happens.

To get rid of this spread-out formation of words, you can CTRL+Z and start over, or, put your cursor right at the end of that line and press the Delete key.

See also "JUSTIFYING TEXT"

PARAGRAPH SYMBOL – ¶ – In the paragraph box at top, at the upper right of the box is the paragraph symbol – ¶. If you click on it, it shows paragraph symbols and other hidden formatting/command symbols that you've used throughout your text – indents, spaces, page breaks, etc. Click on ¶ again, the command marks go back to being hidden, as they normally are.

Main use for me is to find and knock out "section breaks" (they show as dotted lines) to fix inconsistent formatting.

PARENTAL CONTROLS – I don't have any experience here, but I think it's fairly straightforward: Start > Control Panel > User Accounts and Family Safety > Set Parental Controls for Any User > click the user account you want to restrict > turn Parental Controls on or off > choose options and limits > OK. [W7 – AR says Windows 7 parental controls are not as comprehensive as Vista's.]

PASSWORD BOX – HARD TO SEE – On most websites, the box into which you're supposed to type a password, or name, or address, is usually hard to see. It's a white empty box and there's a tendency to want to type above or below it. You have to look at it at the right angle to see it properly, to make sure you're typing inside the box.

PASSWORDS – They say you should make your passwords – for whatever – hard to guess but easy for you to remember. And to change them every so often. However, the problem is that it becomes a nightmare to keep track of all of them! My solution: I use only two passwords. 1. A simple one for unimportant stuff (90% of situations). 2. A more complex one for sensitive, important stuff. That way, I can remember them easily and not have to go search who knows where to retrieve one. Of course, reality makes things a bit more complex; sometimes you have to use a company's password given to you (a 25-digit number, a squiggly word you cannot read, etc.). But, I try to stick to my plan as much as I can.

Now, with regard to passwords for your computer, I think you can have one for the computer and another one for Windows. I'm the only one that uses my computer, so I'm not even going to try to put one in for my computer... for fear of something going wrong... like having to generate a new password to get my old one back thru an ambiguous one they give me, for which if I copy a O for an 0 accidentally, they will require a simple 7-step process for me to call a person in India who will send me email instructions on what to do next (a simple 9-step process that eventually will inform me that that process does not apply to my version of Windows), and someone else will tell me they will be glad to retrieve my password, all I need is a PIN number, but in order to get a PIN number first they need my password... catch-22 computer hell!

But, I can see the value having a Windows password, so a casual friend can use my computer, but can't get at my material. Doing this is relatively straightforward. Just remember that letters are case sensitive here, and you need to have an Administrator account, not a standard or guest account:

Start > Control Panel > User Accounts and Family Security > User Accounts (click on green) > click on "Create [or Change or Remove] your Password" > Type in the password > type it in again in the box (hard to see) right below the first one [if changing it, there are three boxes – old, new, new one repeat] > click Create [or Change or Remove]. That should do it. It takes effect once you shut your computer off and turn it on again. In the center of the screen is a place to type in your password to open up Windows.

I do not like to type in my password each time, so I personally keep no password on my computer, except when I anticipate the need for it in some unusual situation (shaky acquaintances over, computer in a repair shop, etc.) Plus, I don't keep sensitive info on my computer anyway.

Guest User

If you don't have a password, you can let a trusted friend use your computer, no problem.

If you do have a password – I haven't actually done this, since no one else normally uses my computer – I'm pretty sure you can allow a friend to open up and use your computer by going under Start > Control Panel > User Accounts > Manage another account [W7 – "Add or remove user accounts"] > Guest > Turn on. The friend can then use Windows, yet does not have access to your material. In fact, this is what I plan to do next time I have my computer at Best Buy for any adjustments, so that the tech person there can work with my computer, yet not have access to my material. I feel safer that way. You never know who might have access to your computer data when it's sitting somewhere else.

PASSWORDS FOR WEBSITES – SAVE – The computer (Internet Explorer) can save your log-on information – user name/email address and password – for chosen websites, so that you don't have to enter the info each time you want to access your account. For me, that would be three sites: Yahoo.com for my email, Netflix.com account, and Match.com account. (I tried all kinds of things to preserve this log-on data under Start > Control Panel > User Accounts... but I think that's for computer network passwords, not website log-on info to your account).

The "Delete Browsing History" window gives you a password saving option (Internet Explorer > Tools > Safety > Delete Browsing History > options)... but I got mixed results, checking/unchecking, deleting/not deleting various options. This "Delete Browsing History" window had always been very confusing to me, but I think I finally figured it out:

A. The "Delete Browsing History" Window

– If you check a category, the information is saved. (There is no "OK" or "Save" button to push. Just check the category, close the window, and it's set; it saves the info for each checked category.)

– If you click on the Delete button, it deletes all the past info under each category you had checked.

– The top category refers to info for websites that you have in your Favorites list.

[This top category was confusing to me for the longest time. I thought it was a major heading for all the categories below, because it is separated from them by a horizontal line. And I couldn't figure out if clicking the Delete button included it or not, or what, because of the separating line. But then I finally registered in my brain the key word "Favorites" (sites you have on your Favorites list); this category is NOT a heading for the others, but simply a separate category from the others. It's separated by a horizontal line, because it's a category one might logically want separate from the others; you might want none of the categories below to save info for average websites, but do want info saved for your favorite websites.]

The Delete Button

– When you click on the Delete button at lower right, it deletes all the data for the categories checked. It does not uncheck those categories; it just deletes their data accumulated up to the current time.

Thus, after you've clicked on "Delete," all the checks remain the same; Internet Explorer will at that point start again to accumulate data for the checked categories. It's just that their past history data, up to when you clicked Delete, is gone.

OK, with the above in mind I checked the top box ("Preserve Favorites website data"), and ALL the ones below (including "Passwords"). Result: It worked; I don't have to enter my logon info to open up my Yahoo (email), Netflix, and Match.com accounts... with this exception – I still have to enter my info for Yahoo every two weeks, as per their setup.

To make sure this feature works the way I think it does, with all 8 categories checked, including the top one, I clicked Delete, to remove all the data. Then, when I tried immediately to open any of the three accounts, I saw that I DID need to put my log-on info back into all three of my accounts to open them. After I entered my info for all three accounts, from that point on, I did not have to re-enter my info, because all the categories were still checked. It had started to again keep info.

When I had put my info in, I got the message: "Do you want Internet Explorer to remember the password for Yahoo.com?" I checked Yes. Does this option automatically check the "Passwords" option in the "Delete Browsing History" window? I don't know. At any rate, keeping all of the categories checked works for me; I can access my accounts without having to enter username and password each time.

The Window Choices

I suggest leaving the default settings as is, and then changing them only if you find you don't like one or two, as you use your computer over time.

In fact, as a general rule of thumb, rather than looking at any unfamiliar window and making a bunch of logical choices in it, I say leave things in their default settings, and make specific individual changes only as you find the need to. Otherwise, you may select something that messes you up royally! And often you have to struggle to remember how to undo what you did. The default choices represent what most normal people normally prefer anyway.]

See also "WEBSITE – BROWSING HISTORY"

PASTE BUTTON POP-UP ICON – In Windows 7, a new feature is a small rectangular icon (yellow border, with a dropdown arrow) that pops up to give you pasting options. I hate the thing; it keeps popping up, covering my text. When you start typing again, it automatically disappears, but it's annoying to have it pop up each time..

To get rid of it: File at upper left > Options (near bottom of list) > Advanced at left > "Cut, copy, and paste" section > uncheck "Show Paste Options button when content is pasted" > OK.

PASTING – Refers to inserting an item into another location. Usually a word, or block of text, into another spot in the text. This function is accomplished by blocking the text first, then cutting (CTRL+X) or copying (CTRL+C) it, then moving to the new desired location, then pasting it there (CTRL+V).

The pasting function also applies to whole documents, files, and folders. Common examples are moving a document to a different folder, or copying a music file into a particular program. You highlight the file, CTRL+X or CTRL+C it, and then paste (CTRL+V) it into your new location. (Or, you can also right-click the item and select Cut or Copy, then paste it.)

PDF – PDF ("Portable Document Format") is a document file format that is compatible with different software, hardware, and operating systems. So, it's a more universal format. I understand it's being used more and more. Lots of internet material is in PDF format.

Like most internet text, you can land it into an MS Word document by simply blocking it, CTRL+C, and then CTRL+V into a Word document. Though, some formatting tends to get embedded and you have to work, to get it the way you want it, if you ever can. For example, justified text from my website that I imported to a Word document ended up no longer justified, and, it lost line spaces.

Also, sometimes it only lets you copy stuff one page at a time. I suggest doing a CTRL+A (which tends to work OK) and then landing the whole thing into a Word document. That way, you have for example, a manual or user guide readily available for yourself, rather than having to revisit the website each time to refer to a manual.

Note that sometimes you cannot make a copy of a section of PDF text for yourself. Adobe Reader Help page says, *"PDF authors can allow recipients to save a document by enabling the local save capability. Often, PDF form authors do not enable the local save capability."* What I do to work around this is: Do a Prt Sc (Print Screen key at upper right) and copy to a Word document.

To open a PDF file, you do need Adobe Reader, which I think most computers have these days.

RS says PDF looks better on the internet (plus intended more to be read, than to be edited, like MS documents). For my website I converted my MS documents to PDF.

To Convert an MS Document to PDF format:

1. Get doc into the final format you want under MS Word
2. Google "doc2PDF Online"
3. Doc 2PDF Online tab
4. Browse, select doc, check it, Open
5. Name the file/doc. NOTE: ONE word, no spaces
6. Put in your email address
7. Click "Convert to PDF (click once, wait)
8. In a couple minutes, they send the converted doc to your email address, as an attachment [For me, sent to Spam!]
9. Open it, download it, Save, pick destination folder.
10. Minor loss of formatting for me (one section didn't do italics, fairly subtle, no big deal).

PERMISSION – Haven't had this happen for a while, but if I'm trying to do something, like change settings, I might get a window that says "Windows needs your permission to continue." Since I am the owner with the "Administrator" account, I just click "Continue" and it lets me continue.

PHISHING – Refers to email activity by scammers, trying to get valuable information from you. They invariably disguise themselves as legitimate companies. Be wary, especially any email requesting username, password, account number; usually you enter that info when YOU are initiating some action, not when THEY contact you out of the blue.

Be wary of any email supposedly from your bank, requesting updates on your bank account; if you think it might be legit, call them, so you know you are in fact dealing with them, not a scammer. I had an email once requesting info on my Yahoo account, in order "to prevent scammers"; but, they were the scammers; I could tell they weren't really Yahoo, because the request looked very unprofessional – bad spelling, bad sentence construction, etc.

Internet Explorer, under the Safety tab at right, has a Smart Screen Filter that filters out a lot of these phishing sites. It's on by default.

PHOTOS / PICTURES – BASIC OPERATIONS – I'm sure there's plenty I don't know, but here is how I manage my pictures:

IMPORTING PICTURES TO THE COMPUTER

Most cameras today are digital and come with a USB cord that attaches to the camera at one end and your computer USB port at the other. Once attached, turn the camera on and pictures should automatically get imported, to your Pictures folder AND Windows Photo Gallery. See also "CAMERA."

Pictures come in different file types. I understand JPEG is very common, very versatile, and good for sharing. And TIFF is good for high quality larger size photos.

Storing Pictures

I think it's a good idea to store all your photos under Owner, Pictures folder, where they automatically go anyway. Then, copy them to any other program, like Word, to edit or print them. That way you still have the originals in your Pictures folder, in their original format. I remember Match.com could not accept a picture from me from a Word document because it was no longer in its original JPEG format.

When I import pictures, I get a copy in both my Pictures folder and Windows Photo Gallery automatically. Or, more accurately, one copy that appears in both places. Note that if you delete a picture in either place, it is deleted in both places, and you've lost it to your Recycle Bin!

You can make a copy from either of these two places, into a Word document, and then later delete that picture from the Word document, and you still have the original in both your Pictures folder and Windows Photo Gallery. But these two particular locations – Pictures folder and Window Photo Gallery – are connected and deleting material from either place puts it into your Recycle Bin.

I think of my Pictures folder as the place my material is stored, and Windows Photo Gallery as a place where the same material is also presented.

Organizing Photos

Windows Photo Gallery has all kinds of options for storing and arranging material. And, as usual, it's overkill. They are always giving you umpteen options. [W7 – seems less cluttered] I don't do that much with pictures, so I just let Windows Photo Gallery do its thing, which is, by default, to store pictures according to date taken. Currently I can see all my photos going from latest, to oldest. If you right-click an empty spot and click Sort By, you can also sort by other categories, such as "File name."

It IS a good idea, as soon as you get your photos imported, to name them something other than the serial numbers that they arrive with. Name a bunch of pictures "Washington Trip 1", "Washington Trip 2", etc., instead of 007, 008, 009, etc. That way, they are much easier to identify. Also, create a folder called "Washington Trip" and put all of them in there.

Erasing Camera After Importing

Usually, as you import from your camera, the importing window gives you the option of "Erase After Importing" from the camera. I prefer NOT to erase just in case something goes wrong. Then, after I KNOW the pictures are in the computer, I manually erase them from the camera. However, other people, who take many pictures, may prefer "Erase After Importing" so that they don't forget and end up cluttering up their camera. I'm pretty sure that Windows Photo Gallery automatically does not import pictures it already has.

Backing Up Photos

Once you get your photos into your computer, it's a good idea to make copies to an external storage device like a flash drive, DVD disk, or external hard drive, because one day eventually your computer hard drive will die, and you'll lose those pictures! Myself, I have my favorite photos in my computer, and on an external hard drive, as well as, of course, the "hard copies" (the actual physical photos).

Pictures From the Internet

To import a picture from the internet, or some software program, highlight the picture by pressing the left of the mouse and dragging thru the picture. It should show a shadowing over it, indicating it is highlighted. Right click, CTRL+C, and CTRL+V it to the file of your choice.

Scanning in Your Photos

See "SCANNING" for how to import an actual photo by scanning it into your computer.

EDITING THE PICTURES

I usually copy pictures to a Word document to edit them, and I print them from there. Put the pointer on the picture and then right-click for a menu of the following editing options:

Cut, Copy, and Paste

Allows you to move the picture by selecting Cut or Copy. Then use CTRL+V to paste the picture to whatever other page or other document you want.

Or, to move it to another spot on the same page, you can simply drag the picture and drop it to your desired spot. Left-click on the picture, press the left of the mouse and drag the picture by sliding your finger across the right side of the mouse. Then release the left at your desired spot. However, to move pictures by dragging and dropping, you should first right-click them, and under Text Wrapping (or Format Picture), click on "Behind Text" or "In Front of Text." That allows them to be dragged much more consistently. See "TEXT WRAPPING OPTIONS" just below.

Besides dragging and dropping, you can also left-click the picture and then press the arrow keys at bottom right of your keyboard to move the picture in small increments.

Text Wrapping Options

If you right-click an image, then click Format Picture, under the Layout tab, you have these 5 options:

1. In Line With Text – It makes empty lines where the image is:

In line with text. In line with text. In line with text. In line with text. In line with text. In line with  text. In line with text. In line with text. In line with text. In line with text. In line with text. In line with

[Why it's sticking partway into a line, I don't know.]

2. Square – It puts text around the image in a square:

This is square layout. This is square layout. This is square layout. This is square layout. This is square layout. This is square layout. This is square layout. This is square layout. This is square layout. This is square layout. This is square layout. This is square layout. This is This is square layout. This is square

3. Tight – It puts text around the image just like "Square." (Note that this function wraps around the rectangle of the picture edges, not any oddly shaped subject matter itself.) Same as "Square" above, except it can accommodate your picture as tilted.

This is tight text wrapping. This is tight text wrapping. This is tight text wrapping. This is tight text wrapping. This is tight text wrapping. This is tight text wrapping. This is tight text wrapping. This is tight text wrapping. This is tight text wrapping. This is tight text wrapping. This is tight text wrapping. This is tight text wrapping. This is tight text wrapping. This is tight text

4. Behind Text – It puts the image behind the text:

This is behind text. This is behind text. This is behind text. This is behind text. This is behind text. This is behind text. This is behind text. This is behind text. This is behind text. This is behind text. This is behind text. This is behind text. This is behind text. This is behind

Note that to access the image and click on it in this layout, is hard. You usually have to press the Enter key several times to temporarily separate text lines and make the image available for clicking, Otherwise, you end up being able to click only the text, not the image!

5. In Front of Text – It puts the image in front of the text, hiding the text:

This is in front of text. This is i... of text. This is in front of text. This is in front of text. This is... f text. This is in front of text. This is in front of text. This is in ... text. This is in front of text

I find it's usually best to type your text first, then drag the image over to the text. These functions often do all kinds of odd things when you work with them. Usually the "Behind the Text" and "In Front of Text" ones are pretty stable though.

Note that all five selections activate the rotation function, as well as make it easier to drag images to different spots in the text.

Rotating a Picture

Note that the rotating feature in Windows Photo Gallery refers to simply changing the orientation of the image from vertical to horizontal or vice versa, not straightening out a crooked picture. Under Windows Photo Gallery, or Windows Paint, you can't rotate by small increments. Although I see on the internet that with Paint Shop Pro, or other separate software, like Irfanview, you can. However...

You CAN do degree rotating by simply right-clicking your image once it's in Word document > Format Picture > Layout tab > In Front of Text (or one of the other 4 Layout selections) (this is the key, it allows the picture to slide, and to rotate; otherwise the Rotation feature Is grayed out!!) > right-click the image again > Size tab > Rotation > select degrees.

You can also rotate it by clicking on the picture and dragging the green handle at top, but this method is less accurate than the degree-by-degree rotation available in that window.

Of course, the problem with rotating a photo to correct its tilt, is that, while the subject is now straight, the rectangular frame of the picture is now crooked! You can, however, use the "workaround" solution below. [Or, if you have Windows 7, it has a nice new feature that allows you to straighten and adjust the frame automatically with one click.] (A third option is buying some separate photo-editing software, but I'm keeping this manual limited to just Microsoft programs as much as possible.)

Straightening a Picture – "Workaround" Solution

In Windows 7, your Windows Live Photo Gallery (they added the word "Live") now has a "Straighten" button, under Edit. It does a great job of automatically adjusting both the subject matter of a picture, and its frame, so that you get the best overall result – a straight subject matter, with the frame cropped strategically so that it is also as straight as feasible, given the limitations of the space in the photo that it can work with. See "Windows 7 Straightening Feature" below.

With Vista, however, you have the rotating feature but not the straightening one. But, there is a complex "workaround" way to straighten a picture; it involves using the Windows drawing feature to put a heavy white frame around the picture:

1. Click Insert tab at the top of your normal toolbar at top, Illustrations, Shapes, and paste a rectangle into your document.

2. Right-click the rectangle, Format AutoShape, Colors and Lines tab, put the lines up to a fairly heavy weight. Click Layout tab, In Front of Text.

3. Put the rectangle onto your crooked picture. Right-click it and under Format AutoShape, Colors and Lines, pick No Color, so the picture shows thru.

4. Right-click your rectangle and drag the handles till you have a larger rectangle

5. Increase the line width all the way up to maybe 20 points

6. Then change the line color to white.

Takes some doing, but if you want that picture straight, that's one way to do it.

Windows 7 Straightening Feature

Instead of being able to only rotate a picture, AS IS, in Windows 7, under Windows Live Photo Gallery, you can actually straighten subject matter itself, with automatically adjusted new borders: Windows Live Photo Gallery > Edit > Straighten.

Vista – subject rotated to straight, but frame is now tilted:

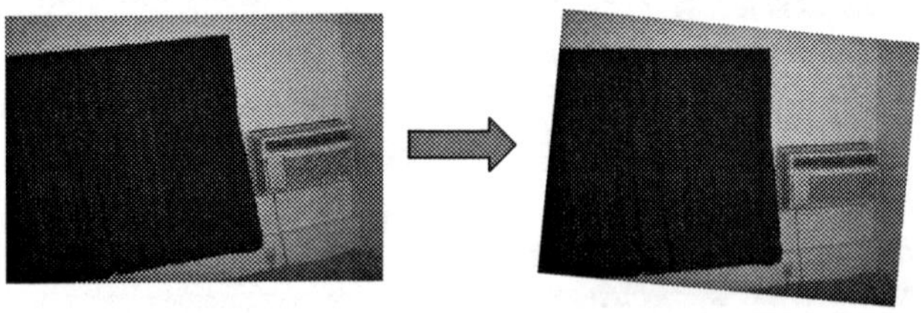

Windows 7 – both subject and frame are straight:

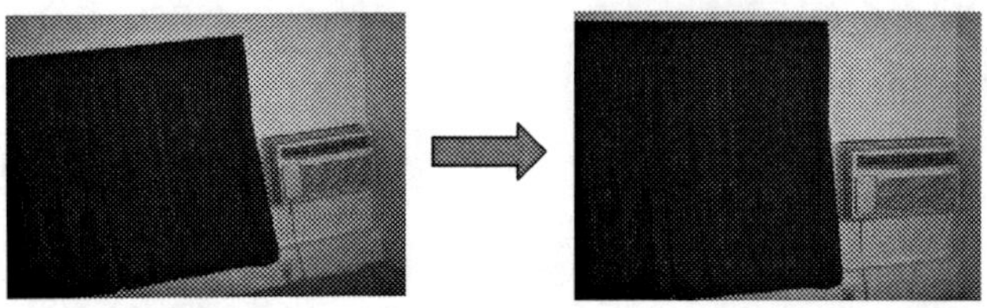

Not surprisingly there are limitations to this feature. Parts of the picture are necessarily cropped. Also I took a crooked picture of my face crooked, and it wouldn't straighten it. Don't know if the key element is background mix, or size of primary subject, or what. Good luck.

Aha, you can do it manually also! Instead of clicking Gallery's "Edit" at top, double-click the chosen photo and it opens another "straightness" button over at the right, which, when clicked, shows you a sliding bar that you can adjust manually to set the picture to whatever straightness looks best to you, all the while maintaining a properly straight frame instead of a tilted one.

Update: Oh pooh, now I can't find it... wait, I got it. Gotta follow this sequence: Double-click on the picture > Edit > "Fine tune" at top > that opens up the manual straighten feature on the right.

Size & Cropping

You can increase, or decrease, a picture's size by clicking on it and dragging one of the corner handles in, or out. When you change the size of a picture, the picture's actual subject matter stays the same.

However, when you want to crop a picture, to remove extraneous material from sides, top, or bottom, you can't just drag an edge in, or you'll get a squeezed, distorted picture. Even with "Lock aspect ratio" checked under Format Picture > Size tab, dragging an edge in, will distort the picture. Instead, with Vista, you need to right-click > Format Picture > Picture tab > set values under "Crop from" > OK. And then see what you got. Adjust some more if necessary.

In Windows 7, you can crop more easily; you can drag edges in: Right-click the picture, and above (or below) the list of options, there is a new double-plus-looking icon to click on, which allows you to crop edges manually, by dragging the edge handles in or out. You can see exactly what is happening to the picture, as you move edges till you get what you want.

Also next to that cropping icon, are arrows for increasing and decreasing picture size (a little more convenient than going to the "Format Picture" window and Size tab, to adjust size).

Format Picture

Right-clicking a picture brings up a Format Picture option, which allows you to change the picture's brightness and contrast, as well as other features.

Windows Photo Gallery Editing

Windows Photo Gallery offers more extensive editing features than Word Document. Double-click the photo to open it, click Edit tab at top. You can adjust for "red eye," etc. Under the Fix tab, click Auto Adjust at the right, and it optimizes the picture in all respects, saving you a lot of time. And the picture usually ends up better than if you had done it all yourself manually.

Also, under the Crop feature, you can crop by dragging the handles. Whereas with Word (Vista), if you drag handles, it elongates or squeezes the picture, rather than cropping the picture. In Word, you have to crop in increments under a right-click window (more tedious).

Under Fix, Adjust Color, Saturation, move the slider all the way to the left and you get a black and white photograph. [Windows 7 setup is a bit different, but the same features can be found. (Here, for B&W, you can just click on one of the Effects options at top; or, go thru Edit > Fine tune > Color).]

For Windows 7, at one point, I had to download and install a "Microsoft camera codec pack" to help open a picture that wouldn't open for editing in Windows Photo Gallery... it still wouldn't. I hate the computer world. Luckily it was not an important picture. And, if it were, I could still make a copy of it into a Word document and edit it in there.

Changing the File Type

Here's something I think can be quite useful: You can change a picture's file type. Given the fact that most pictures are in JPEG, and that TIFF is the file format that keeps its quality the best, if you have a precious picture, change it to TIFF. (Actually you are making a copy of it in TIFF; you end up with two copies of that picture, one in the original format, the other in the TIFF format.)

1. Paint program (under Start > All Programs > Accessories)
2. File [W7 – Paint dropdown arrow at upper left]
3. Open
4. Click on the picture, Open
5. File, Save As
6. Click the Save As Type list, click on your choice
7. Pick your destination from the folders on the left (Pictures folder usually)
8. Save

That sends your picture to your Pictures folder, now in the new format, in addition to the one you have still there in the old format.

I recently used this feature under Paint to grab a picture I had embedded in a Word document and to change it to a JPEG picture file: Opened Word document > right-clicked on the picture I had in there > Copy > opened Paint > CTRL+V'ed the picture into there > Paint dropdown arrow at upper left > Save As > "Save as type: JPEG..." > clicked Pictures folder on left as destination > Save. Now you have the picture as a separate JPEG picture file.

Note that if you try to use Paint, File, Open to find an embedded picture in a Word document, Word documents won't even show in your pictures folder. Paint only opens picture files. Usually when you want to work with pictures outside of a Word document they are embedded in, you have to change them to a picture type file, like JPEG, by the method described in the previous paragraph.

PRINTING THE PICTURES

If you have your picture in a Word document, just print it as you would a normal document.

To print a picture directly from your "Pictures" folder, right-click the photo > click Print > choose your options (paper, size, printer, etc.) > Print.

To print directly from Windows Photo Gallery: Check the picture > CTRL+P > make selections from print window > Print.

Keep in in mind two key factors: 1) use good photo paper, not regular paper, 2) in the printing dialogue box, check Selection, click Properties, and select the paper type that matches what you have loaded into your printer. Makes a big difference.

Also note, if you want the best quality, you might want to go thru a CVS drugstore. They probably have better paper and better printers. Just make sure you have the original, in case something goes wrong.

Paper

Though printing on plain white paper is not bad, you get a much better quality picture if you print on photo paper. I like to use Staples Photo Supreme, double-sided matte paper. Of 1,000 plus family photos, I chose 250 favorites, scanned them in, and then made a family photo album of one to six photos on each side of sheets. I put the sheets in a three-hole binder. Came out neat; the album is not too bulky and the pictures won't fall off. Plus, having scanned them in, I now have a record of my favorite photos on my hard drive.

Note that having regular sheets of paper stacked beneath one sheet of photo paper, sometimes leads to the printer pulling that regular sheet thru also. Therefore, if you use photo paper, use several sheets of it, so it doesn't pull extra sheets.

I got some Epson ultra supreme matte paper, and I found it was not as good as the regular Supreme. I plan to do some experimenting – printing out the same picture using each of the different paper choices of the printer, and comparing them. Better to believe my own eyes than their recommended choices.

PICTURE FROM A DVD – You CAN produce a still-shot picture from video material. See "DVD – STILL CAPTURE"

PICTURES – BURNING ONTO A DVD – Burning your pictures onto a DVD disk is a great way to save pictures. A DVD disk can hold a ton of photos. My "Pictures" folder (about 1,000 photos) is 270 MB; I copied them on a standard DVD of 4.38 GB and had 4.05 GB of space left. The actual copying took only 4 minutes. (You can save them on a CD also, but a DVD holds 5 times as much material.)

METHOD A – Video DVD (Slide Show)

This method is good if you have a large number of set pictures you want to keep on a disk, and watch on TV as a slide show. But, you can't add pictures to that disk without re-doing the whole thing, nor can you print out the pictures on paper.

1. Insert a blank disk – either R or RW (re-writable). Remember that R's are a one-time burn and cannot be changed.
2. Windows Photo Gallery
3. Click "All Pictures and Videos", "Pictures" at upper left [W7 – Have your items checked first, then click File icon dropdown arrow at upper left > Burn > Burn a DVD]
4. Check the items you want burned
5. Burn tab at top
6. Video DVD
7. That brings up Windows DVD Maker window with those items listed
8. Click Next
9. Click Burn (if necessary, click Yes to overwriting content already on disk). It starts to burn.
10. Wait. May take a good hour for 100 pix. (The "Video" DVD mode takes much longer to record than the "Data Disc" mode.) You can play the result on TV as a slide show.

METHOD B – Data DVD

This method is good if you want to keep adding pictures to a disk over time, and you like to be able to print them out on paper.

I prefer this method, because: 1) I don't usually look at pictures on a TV. 2) This method allows you to copy pictures of ANY file type, whether they are in their original format or embedded in a Word document (as most of my pictures are). And 3) I can simply add material to the disk, keeping the material that's already on the disk.

Drag and drop your pictures from your computer (either "Pictures" folder or "Windows Photo Gallery, either folders or documents) to your disk, as described below. (Or, if you prefer, at step 7, CTRL+C the files and CTRL+V them onto the disk.)

1. Insert a blank (new or erased) DVD–RW Disk
2. AutoPlay window comes up. Click "Burn files to disc". (If dialogue window did not automatically come up, double-click on Computer, double-click on DVD-RW Drive)
3. "Prepare this blank disc" window opens
4. Under the "Show formatting options" dropdown arrow, "Live File System" should be checked. (The other one – "Mastered" format is for making a DVD for playing on a DVD player. [W7 – "Like a USB flash drive" should be checked, not "With a CD/DVD player".]
5. Click Next and it formats the disk. If it doesn't go, make sure you have a brand new disk; sometimes an old one won't go.
6. "AutoPlay" window comes up, click "Open folder to view files"
7. That opens the disk window
8. Make the window smaller by clicking the Restore Down icon at upper right.
9. Drag that window to one side (by dragging the top part of the window)
10. Find the folder that has your picture files
11. Make that window smaller, and drag it to the other side
12. Now you have the two windows side by side (computer window, disk window)
13. Drag and drop items from the computer window to the disk window
14. That's it. It makes copies, not cuts. The material is now on that data DVD disk.
15. With a Sharpie marker, label your disk.

You could, of course, also use a regular DVD-R if you just want a SET copy of your pictures to date.

An extra backup of precious pictures is always a good idea. You never know when you're accidentally going to press a wrong button, or something gets stolen.

When I tried to copy the whole "Pictures" folder, or to copy all the folders in the "Pictures" folder, by clicking "Burn" at top, it did nothing. So, I find the Drag and Drop technique described here in Method B, to be the best way to copy pictures to a DVD disk.

You can now print out those pictures from your disk to paper, and, you can ADD new pictures to the disk in the future, using the same procedure. (When you insert that disk, an "importing" window may come up; just "x" it out; that's for copying what you have on the disk to your computer. And that is not what you want to do here. You want to copy new pictures from your computer to the disk.)

PICTURES – FROM CELL PHONE – See under "CELL PHONE"

PLUG-INS – These are additions to programs that help run them. [See also "ADD-ONS"] This is how Wikipedia defines them: *"A **plug-in** is a set of software components that adds specific abilities to a larger software application. If supported, plug-ins enable customizing the functionality of an application. For example, plug-ins are commonly used in web browsers to play video, scan for viruses, and display new file types. Well-known plug-ins examples include Adobe Flash Player and QuickTime. Add-on is often considered the general term comprising snap-ins, plug-ins, extensions, and themes."*

See "ADD-ONS" for enabling or disabling them. At one point I needed to enable Flash Player to play internet video clips.

Rathbone says the following are both free and trustworthy: QuickTime, RealPlayer, Adobe Flash, Microsoft Silverlight, and Adobe Acrobat Reader.

POINTER – The pointer is the arrow that moves on the screen as you slide your finger across the mouse touchpad. While on the internet, the arrow turns into a hand if you hover over a word that leads you to more info if you click on it (a "link"). While in a Word document, the arrow turns to an I-beam once it enters the text area. If you position the I-beam on a spot in the text and left-click, the typing cursor (a simple vertical beam) gets put at that spot and typing proceeds from that point.

See also "MOUSE"

POP-UPS – I forget what the default setting is, but if you don't want as many pop-ups (advertising): Internet Explorer > Tools > Pop-up Blocker > Turn On Pop-up Blocker if it isn't already on. If you want to allow certain ones, click on the second choice – Pop-up Blocker Settings, and fill in the info on sites you want to allow pop-ups from.

PORTS – Ports are outlets on a computer where you can plug things in. Like the USB cord from your printer to your computer, or the internet cable into your computer. Usually it's the USB ports (my laptop has three on the right side) that get used – for inserting a flash drive, or a camera to import pictures, etc. Signals get transferred between the device and the computer.

POWER CORD – Provides your computer with electricity. See "CORD – POWER CORD" for tips.

POWER – SAVING – AR says he leaves his computer on 24 hours a day, that most PCs use less power than a light bulb. But, you should (if it's not a laptop) turn off your monitor. And, you should turn off your printer, because the heat dries out your ink cartridges faster.

See "Laptop Lid Closing Setting" also.

PREVIEW PANE – In Windows 7, when you are in a folder, there is a "Hide/Show preview pane" icon at upper right, next to the question mark. Check a document, and that preview pane shows what's in your document at the right. When on, the pane can also be dragged by an edge to a smaller or bigger size. (I keep it hidden, I don't like it.)

PRINTING

Overview

Modern printers can do quite a lot – print text, pictures, make copies, scan in material, fax, etc. For what they can do, their cost is quite reasonable, but, that's mainly because the companies make their money on the ink cartridges that you constantly have to replace. Once you own their printer, they're guaranteed a steady income from you! A decent average printer may cost only $150-200. Cartridges cost maybe $20 each, and you need several of them, black and colors. I estimate I buy a new bunch of cartridges maybe 4 times a year. And that easily exceeds the cost of my printer.

(A laser jet printer is more expensive, but if you do a huge volume (like businesses), it's cheaper in the long run, because it uses toner cartridges which last longer than ink-jet cartridges.)

It's almost always better to buy a new printer than to get an old one repaired (assuming it's not just a minor problem). Companies are eager to sell you their new models, and will often have specials on them. It's a good deal. The newer ones also tend to be better.

I've had 4 printers over the last 12 years, two HP and two Epson. I recommend going with one of the major brands, if only because you want your local Staples or Best Buy to carry their replacement cartridges.

My HP ones were pretty good, but didn't feed all that great. My third one – an Epson R280 – was fantastic. It hardly ever had a misfeed. (I'm pretty sure that was basically because it fed from a slanted vertical tray from the back, so that gravity always sent paper in nicely.) You could feed different thicknesses of paper in one stack; you could even add paper as it printed, by slipping a new bunch behind the current stack in the process of feeding.

It could also print directly on CD or DVD disks, which is a priority for me. Drawbacks – it had no scanning feature, and was bit slow. It started having trouble producing correct color after a few years. (Maintenance operations did no good; re-inserting cartridges helped only temporarily.)

My latest one is an Epson 810. It has scanning and disk printing. Pretty happy with it. It does everything, including 2-sided printing, and is faster than my old Epson. But, because its feeding system is from a horizontal tray instead of a slanted vertical one, it does not feed nearly as well as my old Epson. You gotta stack that paper just right, to avoid misfeeds.

Basic Printing Operations

There are several ways to order your printer to carry out a print job. Print icons appear at top for various programs. But I find the easiest is to simply consistently use the CTRL+P order; that way I don't have to search for any icon. And CTRL+P works equally well for internet printing as it does for document printing.

1. Press CTRL+P and your print window comes up.
2. Click OK, to print all the pages of your document on the front sides of sheets, at "normal" quality.

Printers vary, but they all should have these additional options and features:

a. You can print just a section of text you've blocked by picking "Selection."

b. Under "Page range" you can pick all the pages, just the current page, or pages you specifically enter, like "1, 2, 3, 7-10."

c. Under the lower left "Print" dropdown arrow, you can pick just the odd pages or just the even pages [W7 – Under Settings > "Print all pages" dropdown arrow, way down at the bottom > pick Odd or Even]. This is what you would do to print 2-sided copies – run the odd pages thru, then reload the stack to print your even pages.

d. Somewhere there will be a choice for how many copies of a document you want to print.

e. Under "Properties" you can select the quality level of the printing – draft, regular, picture, etc. Higher quality means slower speed; lower quality means faster speed.

f. Under "Properties" you can select the type of paper that goes best with your job – plain white for regular jobs, photo paper for pictures, etc.

Multiple Jobs

As the printer is printing your current job, just click on the "Minimize" icon ("–") at upper right of the printing window, bring up the next job, CTRL+P it, again minimize the window, go to the next job, and so on. The printer just chugs along printing one job after another in order.

Or, select a bunch of document icons, right-click with the pointer on at least one of those document icons, click "Print," and the printer will print all of them.

Cancelling a Print Job

Most printers these days have a button on them to push, to immediately cancel a print job, if you suddenly decide you don't want it printed yet.

If your printer has no such button, then you need to find a printer icon somewhere (often at right of taskbar at bottom) and click or double-click on it for options, which should include cancelling. Or, you can go Start > Control Panel > Hardware and Sound > Printer > double-click (not right-click) on your current printer [W7 – you can right-click and then click on "See what's printing"] > click the job, then click on "Cancel." [W7 – right-click > Cancel]

Actually, the last option sometimes would not work for me; maybe having the cancel function in the printer, makes the cancel function in the computer not operable; I don't know. But, cancelling a job is an important feature (you don't want to print out 30 pages of stuff you realized at page 2 that you don't really want). Call the printer company, if none of the above procedures work... though I'm reasonably sure most modern printers DO have a "Cancel" button right on them.

Typical computer world mentality – brilliant technology, but it takes them years to figure out that consumers would like a simple "Cancel" button. (My first printer didn't have one.) See also "CANCEL PRINTING"

Print Preview

There should be a Print Preview option somewhere under "Properties," but I think it's easier to simply click the minus icon at lower right of the screen to reduce the size of what you see on screen, in order to see what your pages look like, before you go to print them.

To Set "Draft" Quality as Your Default Print Quality

"Draft" quality is the lowest quality setting, which means it doesn't look that great, BUT, it prints much faster. Plus it saves on ink. So, for many people, myself included, I like that setting as the one I use most often, as I work on drafts of my documents.

To set "Draft" quality as the default setting: Start > Control Panel > Hardware and Sound > Printer > right-click on your printer icon > select Printing Preferences > Quality Option > Draft > OK. Now when you open a document and print it, it will automatically print in "Draft" print quality, instead of your having to select "Draft" each time for each job. If you want to up the quality to "regular" or "photo" for a current print job, select those manually, under Properties.

Note that the print quality selection goes back to your default setting automatically, when you go on to another job.

When you go to print a job, the dialogue window that opens is the very same one that you get when going thru the Control Panel and Printer, but, to change your default setting, you have to go thru the Control Panel route.

(Actually, the first time I did that, it didn't work, but on my second try, and subsequently, it worked. I now have "Draft" as my default print quality.)

Checking Ink Levels

Usually, when you get low, a message pops up that it's time to replace one or more cartridges. To check your levels: CTRL+P > print window shows up > click Properties > Main tab shows levels. When you order your first print job of the day, the cartridge icons take a good ten seconds before they show the ink levels.

Don't try to squeeze ink out to the last drop, or go way past your first "low ink" warning. I've read that it's not good for the printer. It needs some ink left to lubricate things and to keep some ink in the print heads. Similar to not letting the oil in your car run out.

HOWEVER, I cannot help but suspect companies are trying to rip us off by encouraging us to replace cartridges before it's really necessary. Well, guess what, a recent "PC World" video on the net confirms this. They did some careful testing, by weight, to determine just how much ink was really left at the "low ink" warning. Sure enough, in many cases there was plenty left. On average – Kodak 43%, Canon 24%, Epson 8%. (HP works differently, with results just getting fainter as it runs out.)

That's actually good news for me. I figure 8% for my Epson printer is pretty good. And it matches what I have been instinctively doing – going maybe 10-15 sheets past first warning. (For me, as a matter of principle, I plan to avoid Kodak and Canon in the future, based on this simple evidence of dishonesty and greed.)

Anecdotal tip – taking a cartridge out and shaking it, putting it back in, may give it more life.

Buying Ink Cartridges

2/08 – Buying at Staples, is better than over the internet (direct from Epson). It's significantly cheaper. 5-color-pack was $67 at Staples, $89 on the internet. Single black cartridge was a couple bucks cheaper too. Plus, from online it's $3 (4-6 days), $6 (2 days), or $18 (overnight) for shipping.

Update 1/11 – I guess prices have changed. I just got a 5-pack at Staples for $84, and a black cartridge for $19. From Epson online, it's now $80 and $17. But, with shipping added, the difference is moot. Actually I should go to the NH Staples, to save on tax – $6.42 savings, for 5-pack and a black one. (And yes, I am proud to have used the word "moot" in a sentence.)

Staples has a cartridge recycling program. Give them your empty cartridges and you get $2-3 credit on future purchases.

Ink Volume

On some printers, if you're very picky about just how heavy your ink is, you can, besides selecting one of the basic print quality options, fine-tune your ink volume by finding an option under the print window that allows you to adjust your ink volume. For my current Epson 810, it only allows this when you are printing 2-sided copy, so that pages don't stick or the ink offset: CTRL+P > Properties > Page Layout tab > Auto (for 2-sided) > Adjust Print Density > drag marker to desire spot > OK.

You can always do 2-sided copy manually, if you want to keep your ink density the same as your usual. Let the first side stack sit for a few minutes, to dry, then do the second side.

Grayscale

Another way to save (color) ink is to print your color material under the "grayscale" option, for your draft copies. Your pictures, and any color text, come out in black and white: CTRL+P > Properties > Advanced tab > check "Black/Grayscale" > OK. Then, when you're finally ready for your final copy in color, uncheck "Black/Grayscale" to print in regular mode.

Landscape Printing

For 2-sided manual copy, landscape orientation, on my printer, the head of the first side comes out to the left. For second side reloading, keep head again to the left, printed side up. (My Epson 810 printer prints on the bottom side of the top sheet in the stack.)

Sharing a Printer

This would be a typical situation in a home where several people have a computer, but need only one printer. That is not my situation, so I don't have experience here. But, I'm pretty sure you need to follow this route to get what you want: Start > Control Panel > Network and Internet > HomeGroup. See also "NETWORKING"

Old HP Notes (2005) and Related Issues

– Had to switch cartridges for photos. (Not so for Epson printers I've had.)

– Needed to reverse the order of sheets before putting the stack in for second side printing. For my current Epson 810, sheets are printed on the underside of the feeding sheets, and they come out "printed side" up, page one on the bottom of the printed stack. So, for second sides, I need to reverse the order of the sheets to get page one on top, and reload that stack, printed side up.

My old Epson printed on the top side of sheets and came out print side up, so that all I needed to do was turn the whole stack of printed sheets over and reload, no need to reverse sheets. Page one, print side up, on the bottom, was now page one, print side down, on the top, ready to be printed on its second (top, blank) side. All the rest of the stack was also ready to go, in order, print side down.

– Feeding problems: Didn't feed well on hot, muggy days. I avoided big, 2-sided jobs on those days.

Especially on a muggy day, heavy black ink coverage will make the paper a bit wavy and subject to jamming when doing a reverse side. You might want to wait a while to let the ink dry fully and the paper even out some. Or, a good solution for one side with heavy ink coverage – do the heavy-ink side second, not first, so the sheets do not have to go thru the printer in a wrinkly/wavey state.

– Can order up more than one job to print at a time. That way you don't have to wait, you can leave the room, come back later and it's all done. For 2-sided jobs, you can order all your odd pages for each job, return to your computer, and then order all your even pages. However, I've never been comfortable doing more than one job at a time. Too easy to screw up, especially with two-sided jobs. One screwup means all subsequent pages are screwed up.

– If you order a job but your printer is not on, nothing happens. But, the job is queued up so when you do turn the printer on, it will then print (after it warms up). Computer of course needs to be on.

– You can work on another job, while it is printing the current job. (Under Options, "Background Printing.") For my current printer, just minimize the print window (the "–" icon at upper right of window) to continue work on another project, or even on the one that is currently printing.

– If you see you're going to run out of paper before a job finishes, don't try to add paper while it's printing. Will most likely cause a misfeed. Instead, just let it run out of paper; the printer stops; add paper, press the flashing amber button (or "Start" or "Continue" button on your printer), and it will continue printing.

– If everything seems normal but the printer won't print, it may well be that you are ordering a page number that the document does not contain. If you order page 10 of a 9-page document, nothing happens. Especially when using section breaks, check your pagination to make sure it's correct. Also, make sure that under CTRL+P > Printer > Type, the printer you are currently using is the one checked.

– If you did multiple copies of a job, check that you don't still have multiple copies ordered ("Number of copies" in the print window) for your next job. Most times it automatically resets itself to one copy, but not always.

If you want many copies, it's easier, instead of scrolling up to 10 copies in that little box, to just type in "10."

– Sometimes I got text that had white streaks within each line. I took the cartridge out, wiped those two lines where the ink comes out with a paper towel. Replaced cartridge, and that fixed it. Got clean copy after that.

– I used to have to clean the rubber wheels every few months, with alcohol and a Q-tip, to remove tiny pieces of paper (I call it "paper dust") that collects on the rollers and makes misfeeds more likely. Don't need to do so on my current printer.

PRINTING WEBSITE MATERIAL – Block the section you want, press CTRL+P. See also "BLOCKING" > "More Consistent INTERNET Blocking – Caret Browsing"

You can also print website material by clicking on the Print icon on the toolbar at upper right. But, it will print all the pages showing for that website, not just the section you blocked.

PRINTERS – INSTALLING – Some printers can be installed relatively easily; Windows recognizes them. Follow the instructions of its manual > Install the ink cartridge > load the paper > plug the printer into the computer > turn on the printer > Start > Devices and Printers > that brings up window showing the devices you have connected; it should have an icon for your particular printer model > right-click that icon > Printer Properties, which opens a window with a Print Test Page button at lower right > click on that, and it if works, you're all set. If not, you'll have put in the printer's CD to install the program, or go to the manufacturer's website to download the program.

I think the norm is a CD that comes with the printer, which you use to install their bundled software. Put the CD in and follow the instructions.

Two Printers

If you have more than one printer, in the Devices and Printers window, right-click the one you use most often, click "Set as default printer." And if you want to use the other one, do the same thing just for that instance, and then change back afterwards. However, in Windows 7 you can do a CTRL+P and in the window the comes up, there's a dropdown arrow for "Printer", from which you can select the printer you want, for just that single printing instance, without changing default printers.

Two Computers – Adding the Same Printer to a Second Computer

After I turned on my wireless switch on my old computer and added it to my router network, so I could get the internet on either computer, I realized I'd like to add the printer also to my second computer:

Make sure your computer is connected to the printer by an ethernet cable or by a router (my situation) > turn the printer on > Start > Control Panel > Hardware and Sound > Printers > Add a Printer (at top) > that opens a window with two choices. The first is "Add a local printer", and you use this if you don't have a USB printer. But most printers these days ARE USB printers, including mine. It says "Windows automatically installs USB printers when you plug them in." However, since I have a router (wireless connection) I clicked the second choice, which is "Add a network, wireless, or Bluetooth printer" > Next > it starts searching for available printers, and those printers show up in a box in that window; I saw my correct printer up there (it also showed other icons for the same printer, one for fax, one for ethernet cable) > click on that printer > Next > says "installing printer..." > takes a minute > then it shows the name of the printer with a box checked for it as your default printer > Next > shows "successfully added..." > click "Print a test page > it did > click Finish. All set. Now my old computer can also print on my printer.

Disturbing Thought

What if, when it was searching for available printers, it found my neighbor's printer, and I end up printing my stuff on his printer!? After I thought about it, I decided that would not happen, since his printer only responds to his router and network, not mine.

EXAMPLES OF PRINTER INSTALLATIONS

Printers vary in many respects, but they are also similar in many respects. Here are descriptions of how I installed my last three printers:

1) NEW HP 6840 PRINTER TO REPLACE OLD HP 840C PRINTER (2005)

As I remember it, installing this particular printer was fairly easy.

1. Uninstall old one first. Start, Programs, HP 840C, right-click that icon, Uninstall (Easy.)
2. Turn computer off. Unhook the old printer.
3. Put all old stuff away – wires, instructions.
4. Plug in new printer – wall outlet, to box, to printer.
5. Turn on printer. (Far left button.)
6. Load paper.
7. Put in ink cartridges – (included: 94 B&W, 95 Color)
8. Connect printer to laptop with USB cable.
9. Turn on computer.
10. Wait for Wizard (click a few "Next's")
11. Insert new printer CD.
12. Follow instructions. Easy. Takes 5 minutes.
13. Push HP Report Page button. Gives you great sample picture of fruit.

2) NEW EPSON R280 PRINTER TO REPLACE OLD HP 6840 PRINTER (2007)

1. Unwrap the printer.
2. Connect the power cable (back), press ON button (front).
3. It buzzes for a while, then the orange flame button goes on, meaning the printer needs ink cartridges.
4. Install ink cartridges. Open big cover, then open the ink cartridge cover (just lift up, don't push down).
5. Unpack the ink cartridges (two packs of three) removing only the yellow tapes. Recent discovery (2010): There is also cellophane covering the round hole; the cellophane does NOT come off; it is supposed to stay there! I never noticed it before. I tried to peal if off at first, but then checked my old cartridges; they all had the cellophane still on!
6. Cartridges are vacuum-packed; don't open them till you're ready to insert them. They have a nice little notch you can use to tear them open by hand; don't need to use scissors.
7. Insert all 6 cartridges, with the little tab in the back, so you can read the cartridges as you look at them, with each matching the color it shows just behind them, left to right – yellow, black, light blue, pink, red, and blue. [The Epson 810 also shows proper colors where you insert the cartridges, only it has a different order for the six.]
8. Close the ink cartridge cover, and the printer cover.
9. Press the ink button (the middle orange "flame" one), to charge the ink, which takes about two minutes.
10. Open up the paper support in the back (the feeder), pulling out the extension to make it higher.
11. Open up front cover, pull out the front tray extensions.
12. Load the paper in the back. Slide the gray edge guide from left to make the paper snug.
13. Never load the paper sideways. Even though you may be doing "landscape" orientation, load the paper in "portrait" orientation always.
14. Put the software disk in. (So far do not yet connect the computer to the printer!)
15. Click "continue," "install," "agree." (Select "Install Driver USB," not "Network Connection." "Next.")
16. Above step takes several minutes.
17. Plug the USB cable into the printer, one end, and the computer, the other end. Turn printer on (left button in front, green).
18. USB cable in back goes in sidewards – with the rounded edge to the side, not the top.
19. The installation continues for a few moments.
20. After a bit, click "Yes," to the license agreement.
21. Above takes a few minutes, as dialogue box shows "driver," "print CD," "PhotoImpression," "User's Guide," in succession.
22. Actually doesn't show you when you're done; it just stops making noises.
23. The "(Acr) Soft Photo Impression" is made yellow, and I think that is when you are done.
24. Take out CD. You're ready to print.

It doesn't put any icon on the desktop, except the "Epson Print CD" one, which is for printing directly on disks, which is what I bought it for. When you press CTRL+P, the print dialogue box shows up with the Epson printer as your default printer. I think Vista automatically shows and uses the printer you have connected.

But, if it doesn't work and still has your old printer as the default printer, press Start, Control Panel, Hardware and Sound, Printer, window showing your printers opens up, check the one you want as your default printer, click on "Set as Default" at top. If the printer checked is already the default printer, the "Set as Default" option does not show; it only shows when the printer you check is currently not the default printer.

Note that when you press CTRL+P, the window tells you which printer is being used ("Printer", "Type" upper left). And, of course, if you no longer have that printer attached, nothing happens when you press OK to print.

NOTES

– Print window (dialogue box) is similar to HP one, except, under Properties, you have five print quality options, named a bit different than HP.
– Also shows your current level of ink remaining in each of your cartridges.
– To replace ink cartridges – press the middle button on the left (between the start button and the "waste basket" button); open the printer cover; that will move the cartridge carrier to the correct spot so you can replace the cartridge.

Printing on Disks

Obviously you need "Printable" (white) disks, not regular ones. Printing on regular "non-printable" disks seems to work, but it actually doesn't, because the ink smudges off very easily, even after several days of drying.

I used a Memorex ExPressit program originally, but found that printing on paper labels and then sticking them on the disks, was problematic (sometimes not playing, due to extra thickness of disk, or label deterioration, or warping of disks). Printing directly on disks, I think, is the way to go.

I won't go into detail, but the CD printing program takes some practice. Key thing was that you couldn't change text size or color within a "box"; you had to click "Create New" for a new box with a different size or color, and then drag it to a spot. Also, you had to set up the disk tray attachment just right.

Epson R280 Printer vs Old HP Printer

– Epson feeds great! Hardly ever misfeeds.
– You don't need to reverse the order of first sides of a job, just reload the stack, as is, head at bottom feeding in, blank side up. With HP – it was reverse order of sheets, reload, head feeding in, printed side up.
– Can print directly on disks.
– Can load more paper. 125 sheets rather than 50, approximately.
– Prints faster (though this is probably because it's a newer machine, rather than the brand difference).
– Don't have to change ink cartridges for photos.
– Turns on and off more quickly.

Only real minus is that the Epson has no scanner. Also, at first I didn't like the "Draft" mode; it produces a light brownish color of text. But, I soon got used to it.

Note that, even though you can get what you want, the HP text was generally darker or heavier than Epson text if you used comparable settings. Something to keep in mind if you're in the middle of a big project and need to switch printers, yet want text appearance to be consistent.

Ink Cartridge Replacement

Middle orange button will light up when you are due to replace a cartridge. Use this blinking orange light as the indicator that you need to replace a cartridge, rather than the ink level graphics that come up.

1. Lift lid > 2. Press the orange button; cartridges will line up automatically to small tab at middle back of machine. > 3. Press orange button again and it will send the cartridge bank over to the right for correct access position. (Do not try to use force to move the cartridge bank over.) > 4. Open new cartridge pack. > 5. Squeeze tab at top of old cartridge to remove, and put in new one. > 6. Close lid and press orange button again. > 7. Takes a minute or two to settle in and be ready. > 8. When green left button has stopped blinking, it's all set.

3) NEW EPSON ARTISAN 810 TO REPLACE OLD EPSON R280 (2010)

Bought a new printer. Went to Best Buy; they no longer carried this model. They had a newer one, which does not do disk printing. Guy said apparently there was not that much demand for this feature.

Went to Ultimate Electronics (new store in the old Circuit City building). They had it. Bought one, having resolved these key issues:

1) Was a bit heavier and bigger than my old one. But, it fits on my desk fine.

2) A bit pricey at $300 compared to other ones. But, it included 7 (2 black) ink cartridges, which is a good $100 savings right there.

3) Can do double-sided printing, saving me time.

4) Now I can do scanning (my old one did not do scanning).

5) And, it does print on printable disks.

OK, here's the exact, detailed procedure to set it up. Turned out to be a pretty involved procedure. But the Quick Start instructions were pretty good:

Setting Up Epson Artisan 810 Printer

SETTING UP THE PRINTER

1. Unpack it, remove all the securing tapes. > 2. Raise the scanner (push up on the right side, right where is says "EPSON") and remove the transportation lock (little green plastic thing) and store it, as shown, at the end of the arrow. > 3. Lower the scanner – VERY GENTLY; IT TENDS TO DROP FAST THE LAST TWO INCHES! It is NOT neutrally balanced! > 4. Connect the power cord, at rear left. > 5. Press the On button, lift out the control panel from the silver runner bottom to a readable angle. > 6. Select settings (language, time, etc.) > 7. Install the ink cartridges.

a. Lift up scanner. > b. Put in all six (plastic packaging has a small notch for easier tearing). > c. The cartridges look the same as my old ones, but they are "99", not "78" cartridges. > d. Lower the control panel by pressing the yellow "Unlock" button at top left. > e. It "initializes" on its own. Wait 5 minutes; do not touch it in the meantime as it's going thru this process. > f. When it's done, the printer screen shows your options of Print, Copy, Scan, etc. > 8. Pull out the paper tray (reach under the very bottom, front, pull out). The tray comes completely out. > 9. Remove the securing tapes. > 10. Lift up the lid from the front and slide it back (the top of the lid actually constitutes the smaller photo tray). > 11. Slide the gray edge guard from the left all the way to the left edge of the tray, to make an area for 8½ by 11 paper. Also slide the bottom edge guard up, so that the paper is snug against the back of the tray, yet not crawling up the inclined edge there, for proper feeding. Tray holds up to about 100 sheets. > 12. Load paper with side to be printed on down. In other words, it's the bottom side of the top sheet that gets printed on. > 13. Close the lid. > 14. Put the tray back into the printer. > 15. Pull out the paper receiver "stopper" (the extending plastic shelves that the printed paper lands on). > 16. Do not connect the printer to the computer with a USB cable yet! (USB cable not provided.)

INSTALLING THE PROGRAM

17. Insert into your computer the Artisan 810 software CD that came with the unit. > 18. Click "Install." > 19. Click "Accept" to agreement. > 20. Click "Install driver" to direct USB connection. > 21. Next. Wait as it goes all its stuff, which takes 10-20 minutes! > 22. THEN, when prompted (blue screen), connect a USB cable from computer to printer (at rear of printer, rounded squarish outlet). Wait. > 23. Follow any instructions. > 24. At lower right you should eventually get "Your devices are ready to use." > 25. Should register the printer (though I didn't see that option come up anywhere). > 26. Take out CD.

PRINTING

27. You're ready to go. Pick a document, CTRL+P, print it.

Two-Sided Printing (See also "DUPLEX PRINTING")

The 810 has 2-sided printing capability. In the print window, under Properties, Page Layout, check "Auto", OK. Worked great. Paper comes partway out, then gets sent back in for the second side.

Note that 2-sided printing involves sending the paper thru twice, not printing on both sides at the same time. And it's a bit slow. So if you really want to print both sides as fast as possible, you should do it manually. The machine's turning-the-paper-around procedure takes some time. But, it's very useful; you can do something else while it prints the whole job, both sides, on its own.

Interesting – when you order up 7 pages, two-sided, the printer still turns that last page around and runs it thru, even though it's blank. Why? Answer: To get all odd-numbered sides facing the same way.

Goes back to regular one-sided printing when you open up another document, and you have to order up double-sided again. However, if you switch among documents already open, the "Auto" 2-sided feature stays in effect.

NOTES

You order your printing from the computer just like my old Epson (CTRL+P), with virtually the same dialogue box. The control panel on the printer itself, is for direct copies (just like a copy machine), and for scanning.

It can do fax (sending an image over the phone line), but I don't do fax. I only have a cell phone, no land line. Faxing is probably becoming less popular these days as internet-based alternatives appear, but a lot of businesses still do fax.

Actually, first drawback: it doesn't feed as well as my old one, which fed by gravity down the back. This one doesn't always feed straight unless the paper is exactly set in the horizontal tray. And reloading the tray for a second side is a bit messy – you have to pull out the tray, lift and move a lid, and put paper in exactly. The old one, you just stuck the paper in and gravity settled it nicely into a straight position.

Pictures so far, print much faster than on my old Epson. Same good quality.

I think it's best to wait till the printer is on before ordering up a print job, rather than ordering it and then turning the printer on. Not sure, but one time when I ordered up a job first, it simply wouldn't print. I had to restart the computer to get it to print. (Update: Lately every time I order a job, THEN turn on the printer, it still works fine.)

Feeding Issues

Actually, the fact that it does double-sided sheets means that I don't have to take out the feeding tray and reload for the second side. Which means that, generally, once you've loaded a bunch, correctly, you're all set and you don't need to deal with reloading paper till you run out.

At first it was not feeding card (photo) stock, getting jammed. Finally realized that my side guide was too tight. It looked like it was all the way out, but it wasn't. Moved it two more clicks out; now it's fine. Update: Still a bit hinky on card stock. Needed to loosen, tighten, move paper. I found it seems to feed better if I move the foot of the paper up a bit from the 11" click, so that the head of the sheets goes a bit up the back of the tray incline, and paper gets picked up a bit easier. Another time, it seemed putting the sheets in, curved slightly up instead of down, made the difference. I think that may be my main problem: my current stack of photo sheets is a bit curled. (I had stored them vertically because they were inside a stiff package, but I realize now I should NEVER store paper vertically. Always store paper flat, to help keep it from curling.)

It doesn't do two-sided for thick photo paper. When I order "Matte" for paper, the "Auto" selection becomes unavailable. Makes sense; paper is too thick to turn around easily.

Feeding is good as long as: 1) Your side guides are not too tight, or loose. 2) You fan sheets (provides air, less stickiness), stack them very neatly, jog them to the bottom of the tray, then put the tray in carefully. 3) You don't use papers of different thicknesses. If you're going to do card stock, make the whole pile card stock. (My old Epson one could mix thicknesses nicely, but not this one.)

Help

Epson has some decent online help at "Epson.custhelp.com." Their general help is the usual no help at all. As is usual in the computer world, they have every topic except the one a normal person would want. But, once you get to their email help page, they finally provide good, specific help on your topic, just before you submit your email. At that point, their help topics that show up are geared specifically to what you typed in as your problem.

Ink Cartridge Replacement

To check your ink levels, CTRL+P, Properties, window shows ink levels. Or, on my printer, on the Control Panel of the printer itself, Press "Setup," Ink Levels."

To replace cartridges, lift the cover, pushing up on the right corner of the printer; the ink cartridges are there at the front, right. Squeeze the top and bottom to pull them out. Click the new ones in. Remember to lower the cover carefully; it's heavy and will bang down if you don't pay attention.

Maintenance

If your printing starts to show white lines thru the text, or gaps, or has faded areas, use the maintenance features, which most likely will fix the problem, unless your printer is getting too old.

I have an old note that says for maintenance, go to Start > Control Panel > Hardware and Sound > Printer > right-click printer icon, and use the maintenance features. However, for my Epson 810, there are no options for maintenance on that menu after right-clicking. Instead, if I want to do maintenance I have to go thru the printer control panel: Home > Setup > Maintenance, and click on Nozzle Check, or Head Cleaning, or Head Alignment, and follow directions.

Update: I found I can access the maintenance options by right-clicking the Printer icon at the bottom right of my taskbar, as opposed to the Printer icon under Control Panel and Printer.

Options on the Printer Itself

Using the printer as a copier, you can do all kinds of things – print in color or B&W, reduce the size, crop photos, print out lined paper or graph paper, etc.

Printing Photos

My printer has a nice upper part to the feeding tray, where it has places for 5x7, 4x6, and 3.5x5 paper. Works great for photos. Just order that size as you print from Windows Photo Gallery. Very convenient because you don't have to spend time adjusting tray edges for photos; the standard sizes are already there in the upper tray.

Printing Index Cards

Can't print on 3x5 index cards; feeding trays do not accommodate that small size. I used to print 3x5 vocabulary cards (word on front, definition on back). If I have to do it again, I'll probably print on bigger sheets and then cut... which is a lot of work, because, with, say "4 up" per page, horizontal orientation, you have to arrange your back sides in proper reversed order. I would probably do this instead: Print 3 up, going down the center of the paper, vertical orientation. Then cut sides off afterwards. This way it's easier to back up your cards; 1, 2, 3 backs for 1, 2, 3 fronts, each page.

DISK Printing

The CD tray button is at left bottom of control panel. (Oddly enough CD printing is nowhere mentioned in the full instruction booklet.)

Printing on Disks

1. Press "CD Tray" button at left of printer. A gray tray with "teeth" comes out a little bit, after 10-15 seconds. > 2. Position your blank disk, side to be printed UP, into that tray, in the middle at the edge, where there is a spot for the disk to snuggle into, so that you only see about 1/3 of the disk sticking out. > 3. Press "CD Tray" again; it goes back in. > 4. Bring up your label document, click "Print" at left (or CTRL+P), OK. > 5. Prints it in about 30 seconds, much faster than old Epson. Excellent quality. > 6. Remove your ready disk; press "CD Tray" again to retract tray back into the machine.

If you want to add text to a disk that already has text on it, you insert the disk foot in, not head in. And try to get the text on the disk as horizontal as possible, so that your addition does not come out looking crooked.

In the printing window, under Properties, Paper Options, Type, you have a CD/DVD option. Never noticed it before. But, that's because under my labeling program, when I do CTRL+P, it automatically selects that option.

PRINTER – ON / OFF – AR says it's actually good to turn the printer off when not using it because, even though it uses very little energy, the heat of the printer tends to dry out your ink cartridges faster!

PRINT SCREEN – The "Prt Sc" key at upper right of your keyboard, allows you to make a copy of whatever is currently on your screen. Pretty neat. Just press Prt Sc; that puts the material onto your clipboard (which you don't see, unless you click the dropdown arrow of the Clipboard box under the Home tab). Then find a target document and CTRL+V it there. At that point, you can resize it if you want to, move it around, whatever, just like a picture.

If you want it to make a copy of just the open window, rather than the whole screen, hold down the ALT key as you press Prt Sc key. For example, if you're playing a video clip in a small window on your desktop, you'll get a still shot of that video only, not the entire desktop. (Though this does not work with You Tube clips; you get the whole screen.)

PRODUCT KEY – When you buy a significant program, like Vista, it's good to make a note of the "product key." For Vista, it is located on the package the CD came in. It's a 25 character key, and, if I remember right, I needed to have it to install Vista.

Vista is an OS (an operating system, of programs) rather than a program itself, so I couldn't right-click on an icon and find that 25 figure key on my computer. Had to store the figure the old-fashioned way – I wrote it down right on the CD front.

PROGRAMS

Finding, and Accessing Them

Click Start, All Programs, look all the way down the list to find it. Double-click on it to open it. A program may be hard to find because some programs are inside other folders. For example, the "Sticky Notes" and "Sound Recorder" programs are under the Accessories folder. So when you're having trouble finding a program, usually your best bet is to type its name into the Start search box, and that brings up a panel with the program listed at top, where you can click it open.

Another problem is that sometimes a program is listed by a different name than you thought. For example, my "Chessmaster" program is listed under "Ubi Soft," a company name for it. But if I type in "Chessmaster" into the Start search box, it will list it for me.

To get that program icon up on the desktop as a shortcut: Right-click it, Send To, Desktop (shortcut), position it where you want by dragging it there. I prefer program icons on the desktop, rather than going thru Start, Programs.

You can also keep icons for favorite websites on the desktop, but I prefer to keep those under "Favorites" in the window that opens for Internet Explorer. (See "FAVORITES – WEBSITES")

Renaming

You can also rename program shortcuts if you want, by right-clicking, Rename, type in new name. I did this with my Bible software. The original odd name was not clearly associated in my mind with a Bibles program, so I just renamed it "Bibles." (You might want to make a note of the exact original name of the program, if case you have any trouble, and need to put it back to its original name.)

Programs – Installing and Removing

Installing a program: AR – "Today, most programs install themselves automatically as soon as you slide their CD into the drive."

Usually you just follow step-by-step directions that the CD gives you, and it's not too hard. However, sometimes, it IS hard! See "INSTALL OR UNINSTALL A PROGRAM" for more details.

Note the term "software" is roughly equivalent to the term "program." "Software" or "Programs" are not physical devices (other than the CDs they are on), but rather a collection of data, telling the computer what to do and how to do it.

Removing (uninstalling) a program: Start > Control Panel > Programs > Programs and Features > Uninstall a Program > select the program > click "Uninstall." That's it. You might want to click View first to put programs into a list rather than large icons, so that you can find it more easily. And remember that you can't uninstall a program by simply right-clicking and deleting; that will just confuse your computer; you need to go thru the Control Panel.

Often, one looks under the wrong name. [I still don't see my Studio 14 program there ?? Aha, Studio 11 was listed under "Studio," but Studio 14 is listed under "Pinnacle Studio 14."] If you CAN'T find a program, use the Start search box to find out where it is.

Note also that sometimes, once you click "Uninstall," the computer seems to be doing nothing for a minute or two. Just wait; it should show the progress it's making on the progress bar soon enough. If it says "Uninstalling..." with those three periods after the word "Uninstalling," then it is doing it.

Program – Repairing

Under the same procedure above, once you click on a program, at top you have three choices – Uninstall, Change, Repair. If a program has been acting funny, you can try clicking Repair. I've never tried it, but I know some programs can do self-repair.

Program – Unwanted

At one point, some anti-virus program called "AntivirusGT" installed itself (a free trial program) on my computer and started to constantly pop up. Messages came up trying to scare me into buying their program for $80. (I could tell by their disingenuous, sneaky choice of words, that there was really nothing in fact wrong with my computer. But, I couldn't uninstall it!

Couldn't find it under Programs. Used the Start search box, and it showed it was under hard drive C. Found it there, but when I tried to uninstall it, it refused me permission. And it kept popping up.

I finally noticed that this program was now an icon on my taskbar at the bottom. I right-clicked it there, and a choice of "Uninstall" came up. I clicked that, and, hooray, it immediately got uninstalled.

Programs – Moving

DON'T! AR: "Programs wedge themselves into Windows. Moving a program may break it, and you'll have to reinstall it." (You can, however, do whatever you want with program shortcut icons.)

PROGRAMS – PREFERENCE FOR OPENING STUFF – See "DEFAULT PROGRAMS"

PROPERTIES – Properties" refers to basic information about a program or file – its size, date created, location, etc. To see this info: Right-click the program or file or folder or document, click Properties, General tab.

For example, if you want to see how much space you have left on your main hard drive C, double-click Computer, right-click Local Disk C, click Properties, and it shows you a nice pie chart of how much space you've used and how much you have left.

"Properties" also refers to categories of printing options, after you press CTRL+P.

PROPORTIONAL SPACING – Fonts are termed "proportionally spaced" if their letters take up different amounts of space ("m" takes up more space than "i"). Most typefaces are proportionally spaced these days; it looks nicer.

Non-proportional typefaces use the same width for each letter. Doesn't look as good. But if you're working with numbers, then characters line up under each other.

"Courier New" is one such typeface. Ten i's line up with ten m's:

iiiiiiiiii
mmmmmmmmmm

Recent discovery for me: Many proportional fonts today contain fixed-width (tabular) figures, so columns of numbers do stay aligned. Yeah, look at this. With Times New Roman, a proportional space font, ten i's don't line up with ten m's, but ten 1's DO line up with ten 5's:

iiiiiiiiii
mmmmmmmmmm

1111111111
5555555555

PUBLIC FOLDER – Since I am the only person using my computer, I know little of the details here. I think the basic concept is that when you are sharing a computer, you have your own account which contains your stuff, but the "Public Folder" has stuff in it that is available to any user. And you make settings here under Start > Control Panel > Network and Internet > Homegroup.

QUICKTIME – This is a program that comes with iTunes (Apple). It plays audio and video. I think QuickTime is what plays your iTunes songs. I prefer Window Media Player when it comes to playing video.

If you right-click a video file > "Open with" > QuickTime Player, it comes up to play that video. I click View at top and put it to "Half-size" in order to see the controls at bottom (otherwise they sit below the screen sometimes); then I put it up to "Full-screen" size (which is actually very nice – a full full-screen view with no junk on it). Taking the pointer off screen removes (within a few seconds) the controls showing; putting the pointer on screen makes the controls pop up again to use.

In my old computer, I found the video picture was nice, but it had frequent glitches or stalls. Yet, the same video file, when I played it on my new computer (Windows 7, instead of Vista), played very nicely.

At any rate, I still prefer playing video thru Windows Media Player or the built-in Sony Vaio video player, rather than QuickTime.

QUOTATION MARKS – STRAIGHT vs CURLY – Quotation marks and apostrophes are by default "straight" style → " ' . [W7 – quotes are by default "smart" (curly) style → " ' .]

If you want curly style as your norm: Review tab at top > Proofing box > Spelling & Grammar > Options at lower left > AutoCorrect Options > AutoFormat As You Type tab > check Replace As You Type "Straight quotes with smart quotes" > OK.

If you want curly quote marks for just a single instance: Press CTRL + apostrophe, then Shift and quote mark key. If you want a curly apostrophe for just a single instance: Press CTRL + apostrophe, then press apostrophe key by itself again.

If you keep getting quote marks instead of an apostrophe, you probably left the Caps Lock key on.

I think the curly ones are called "smart" quotes because the computer distinguishes the start quotes versus the end quotes, and puts the start ones upside-down – like "this".

RAM – See "MEMORY (RAM)"

"READ ONLY" – I do not have a certain answer for what to do when this message comes up when you're working on a text. But, there's enough information below to enable you to proceed. You might want to skip immediately to the yellow "Bottom Line" box below.

If other people do have access to your computer, and you don't want anyone to alter a document, you can use the "Read-Only" feature: Right-click a document or folder icon > Properties > General tab > Check the box that says "Read-Only" > OK.

Now, if someone makes changes to it, that person – theoretically – cannot simply "Save" it with the changes, but can only "Save As" it. The person clicks Save and the computer brings up a "Save As" window, where you need to re-name it, and then click Save. That sends the new, changed document to the same folder as the old one, with the new name. But the old document, remains the same as it was.

So you end up with two documents, which is what I hate about this feature! I may be in a rush, forget to delete the old one, and then proceed in the next months adding new stuff sometimes to one, sometimes to the other, and before long I'm in a huge editing bind, because I don't know which document has which new material. Both have some, but neither have all!

I'm the only one using my computer, so I don't need it. I theoretically have it off; but, I still get that message, and it often forces me to make that second document!

"Read Only" – Getting Rid Of

In theory, right-click the document or folder > Properties > General tab > Attributes – uncheck "Read Only" > OK.

But, I still get "Read Only" popping up occasionally when I try to Save it! I think what's happening is that the computer is slow in opening the document, I try to open it again, and then the computer figures I've already got the document open, so it puts the second opening of the document under the "Read Only" restriction, because the first was already "docked for editing," i.e. open. Or something like that.

I think when you open a document a second time when it's already open, that's OK. But, when you open it a second time when it's still in the process of opening the first time, that's when you get a "Read Only" message.

But, I'm really not sure.

Internet: Part of what a very knowledgeable guy wrote on this issue:

"I wish I could say that there's a perfect solution to this problem. There's not. Some methods work for some users and some don't. I really wish that Microsoft would address this problem since it does show up fairly often, it's been showing up since Windows XP, and it

can prove extremely troublesome in small networks. I mean, come on, this is file permissions. How hard can it be?"

One Solution for Me

At one point I was getting "read only" for a document I no longer needed, and I just could NOT delete it, even though the document did NOT have the "Read-only" box checked. I'd get a message saying I had the document open already and needed to close it, but that was not the case; I had closed it. Nor could I find a copy of the document open somewhere else.

Finally, hah, upon reading that "read only" can apply to folders as well as documents, and seeing that the folder of that document had the "Read Only" attribute on, I got rid of it like this: Right-clicked the folder it was in > Properties > General tab > Attributes: > uncheck "Read-only" > Apply > OK. Then I was finally able to delete the document.

When I tried to experiment with this setting to make sure that that was the problem, I would get inconsistent results – sometimes setting "read only" for the folder made documents "read only," sometimes not. And vice versa. Likewise for documents – sometimes ordering "read only" worked; other times, it did not, allowing me to delete it. **I hate Microsoft.**

At any rate, unchecking it for that folder basically did finally allow me to delete that document inside that folder, in this instance.

Also note that sometimes when you uncheck that box for the folder, when you click Apply, a window comes up for "Confirm Attribute Changes". Then you pick if you want the change applied to this folder only, or to this folder, subfolders, and files. I checked the second option, because I don't ever want to see "Read-only"!

"Read Only" – For Real

If you think about it, the "Read Only" feature doesn't really stop people from changing your document. 1) They can uncheck the "Read Only" box just as well as you. 2) They can make changes, "Save As" it as a new document and give it the same name. In theory, the "Read Only" feature just preserves a copy of the original as is. But even that is not the case – though they can't change it and directly save it, anyone can DELETE it to the Recycle Bin!

So, if you really DO want your document to be read only and not be able to be changed at all by anyone else: While in the document, click Review tab at top, Protect Document at far right [W7 – Restrict Editing], then check the second category down – "Editing Restrictions" – then click "Yes, Start Enforcing Protection." Enter a password, twice, and make a note of it somewhere (otherwise, you won't be able to change it either!), OK. Now, no one can made ANY changes to that document, except a person who checks "Stop Protection" in that window and can provide the correct password.

I tried this, and it works. No one can now make any changes to that document – you press the keyboard keys and nothing happens.

BUT!! Does anything make sense in the computer world? ANYONE CAN STILL DELETE SUCH A DOCUMENT!

I'm not is this type of situation, but if I wanted to seriously protect a document, I would give it an odd name, store it in an odd place known only to me, and make the entire text font WHITE, so that if someone did stumble across it, it would look like nothing was there.

Update: It occurs to me that maybe the "Read only" feature is not intended as a safeguard against deliberate mischief (because it doesn't really do that), but is intended only as a safeguard against friendly users from inadvertently changing what you don't want changed. They CAN change it, but need to go thru steps to do so, thereby bringing to their attention the fact that you do not want any changes made.

Update: From Windows question mark icon and search box, I learned this:

You get that "read-only" and "locked for editing by another user" message if 1) Word did not quit properly and that file is still open. 2) A second instance of Word is running in the background with the document already open (as I guessed, a few paragraphs ago). 3) Someone else on a shared network has it open.

So, for me, I think I should open a document and wait for it to open, rather than impatiently trying to open it a second time, which I'm guessing puts two instances of that doc up, and you end up getting the "read only" message that someone else has that document open.

In any case, to get rid of the "Read-only" document, I usually fiddle around with it and manage to get that second one deleted (never sure how I did it) and get left with the normal version of that document, but, if that's doesn't work, you can do this: First, do a CTRL+A and make a copy of the material into a new document, just in case this procedure doesn't work. Then, go back to the "read only" document and right-click an empty spot on the taskbar at bottom (or press Ctrl+Alt+Delete) > "Start Task Manager" > Processes tab > Winword.exe (near top of list) > read the warning first > "End Process" at lower right > Yes. Now you should, hopefully, be left with only the regular version of that document, not the "read only" version. If this process does not work, then you may have to simply use the new document you made.

Bottom Line for the "Read-only" Issue

1. Don't try to open a document again, as you are waiting for it to open. Just wait.

2. Make sure "Read-only" option for both the document and its folder, is unchecked for the "Read-only" option.

3. If it still does it, do the "Task Manager" procedure described above. Myself, I was afraid to try it, after reading the warning there; but, I tried under Task Manager > Applications tab > End Process, and it worked!! Was able to save my latest version of a stuck on "Read-only" document.

4. I strongly suspect another major factor in eliciting this "Read-only" message, is doing operations too quickly. Like maybe changing a few words and immediately clicking Save before it has any chance to finish changing those few words. I suggest, on important stuff, don't go too fast.

Update – Number 1 above confirmed. Since being more patient and waiting for a document to open instead of trying to open it again, I have not had the "Read-only" problem.

Or, look in the document's folder and if there is a second document there named the same but starting with ~$ *(for example, the* *owner file for Document.doc is named ~$cument.doc.*), delete that file. Logically, that could be the duplicate instance of the document causing your current one to show "Read-only."

Good luck.

Update 11/11

Here's part of my interchange with a Geek Agent as I tried to confirm my conclusions:

AGENT: *Most likely a "Read-only" message happens if the document is already opened for writing like you said. Also yes, letting the PC FULLY boot before clicking is very essential, as clicking too quickly will have multiple windows opening and can seem like its "Freezing."*

ME: It does seem that doing stuff too fast causes problems.

AGENT: *Yes it can.*

"Save As" Comes Up Instead of "Save"

Sometimes, when I work with a grid chart, especially a chart to which I add info on a weekly basis, it suddenly won't let me Save it, but only Save As it, just like the "Read Only" problem. Which is a real pain, because then I have to rename the new one, delete the old one, and then name the new one again, with the old name. So, to get around this, this is what I do: Highlight the newly added text, copy it, close the doc without saving it, re-open it and then paste in the changes I just copied onto the clipboard, into the doc. Usually, it then allows me to simply Save it.

Obviously, if the new info you entered is a lot, or all over the place, this technique is not practical. That's why, on an unstable chart, I save it every few seconds as I go. And, every so often, I am unfortunately forced to "Save As" it as a new document, and get rid of the old one.

Reminder of the "Save" vs "Save As" difference – when you "Save" something, you save it, as currently edited, and the old version no longer exists; when you "Save As" something, you are making a new file with a new name. You end up with a new file and the old one.

However, in most situations other than the "Read only" one, if you do a "Save As" yet KEEP the same name, then your new file, as currently edited, replaces the old file, which then no longer exists.

All that notwithstanding, sometimes, you can get old versions by right-clicking a file, and clicking on "Restore previous versions." See "DOCUMENTS – RETRIEVING OLDER VERSION"

RECOVERY PANE – See "SAVING – AUTOMATIC" > "Document Recovery Pane"

RECYCLE BIN

Material that you delete goes to the Recycle Bin. It stays there until it gets permanently deleted, or, you change your mind and decide to bring the material back.

You can permanently delete an individual file from the Bin by right-clicking it and deleting it. Or, you can permanently delete all the files in the Bin by clicking "Empty the Recycle Bin" tab at top. Note that if you check all items but one, and then click "Empty the Recycle Bin", it will still delete ALL the items, even the one you did not check. To get only the checked items deleted, you have to right-click while within the group, and click Delete. "Empty Recycle Bin" overrides any checks you made or didn't make!

If you just leave the Bin alone, at some point eventually down the line, it automatically self-deletes the oldest files. (Actually, I believe it's once it consumes about 10% of your hard drive space. You can decrease this amount by right-clicking the Bin > Properties > and changing the MB amount > OK.)

I recommend doing what I do: Empty the Bin every week or two, as a happy medium. You don't want to delete stuff permanently right away, just in case you change your mind. And you don't want to build up a huge amount of material in there.

Restoring Items

If you want a file back, check the file on the left, click "Restore This Item" at top. It sends it back to where it came from. Note that the check box to the left of items (when the icon View format is in "Details" format), only appears once you put your cursor there! Or click "Restore All Items" if you want everything in the Bin back to where it came from.

Don't mess up your choices. You don't want to order "Restore all items" by mistake, and then have to delete them individually again, from folders all over the place!

Note how the titles at the top change – "Restore this item" or "Restore selected items" or "Restore all items" – according to how you selected, or did not select, the items below.

Finding a File in the Bin by Date

To find something recently deleted that you want to put back: Click View (not "Views," but "View," to the left of "Tools"; there are two there), Sort By, select Date Deleted and Descending. I keep those choices selected, so that my Bin items are normally listed with the most recent items at the top. Makes it much easier to find a recently deleted item. (I think that's the default setting anyway.)

You can also go a simpler route (the icons have to be in "Details" format for Name and Date Deleted to be at the top): Ignore that setting under "View," and at the top of the Bin simply click Name, or Date Deleted, to get the items listed alphabetically, or by date. Note that a second click of those categories puts the items in reverse order, Z to A, and the most recent at bottom instead of top.

You can also simply put your pointer on top of the document icon and it will show info including the date when you specifically deleted it, under "Date Modified." It also includes the exact time you deleted it, which occasionally comes in handy in identifying it.

Windows 7 – The setup is a little different. Click the dropdown arrow to the right of the "Change your view" icon at upper right > click Details > it shows tabs including Name and Date Deleted > click the desired tab to get items listed alphabetically or listed by date.

Computer Won't Allow Deletion

You can't delete a file if it's still open. The computer will let you know with a message saying so. Go to your taskbar at bottom, right-click that file, and close it; then you can delete it.

Immediate PERMANENT Deleting

To bypass the Recycle Bin, and just get rid of stuff directly, permanently, (say, sensitive material): Select the file, hold down Shift key and press Delete key.

To make permanent deletion your normal setting: Right-click the Bin icon on the desktop > Properties > check "Do not move files to the Recycle Bin. Remove files immediately when deleted" > OK. Now, when you delete, THE ITEM IS GONE. I do not recommend this setting! Unless you are a person who never makes mistakes and never changes their mind. Do I see any hands?

The same goes for another category in that window: "Display delete confirmation dialog." I think these "Are you sure..." messages before you delete, are a nice safeguard. I keep that box checked.

(Note that if you check that "remove immediately" box, then the "Custom Size" box for your Bin size, logically grays out, since you are no longer using it. And vice versa, if you check the "Custom Sized" box, the "remove immediately" box grays out, since if you are using the Bin you are not removing material immediately. Sometimes computers do make sense.)

Remember that deleting a file from a DISK does NOT send the file to the Bin. It is permanently gone!

"REFRESH BUTTON" – This reloads the page of a website, sometimes unlocking a freeze situation. Located at end of URL line, it's the double blue arrows (or the blue semi-circle arrow), to the left of the "x." Or, just press the "Refresh" key, "F5", at top of the keyboard. If it doesn't work, close your Internet Explorer, then open it and start over.

REGISTRY CLEANER – Don't know how, but I suddenly got some program named RegClean Pro, for cleaning my registry...whatever that is [*"a hierarchical database that stores configuration settings and options on Microsoft Windows operating systems"*]. Was very wary of it. Checked the internet and apparently it is a legit program. BUT, this is what Wikipedia says about registry cleaners: *"The necessity and usefulness of registry cleaners is a controversial topic, with experts in disagreement over their benefits. The problem is further clouded by the fact that malware and scareware are often associated with utilities of this type."*

Also, *"There is a popular misconception that the value of registry cleaning lies in reducing "registry bloat". Even a neglected registry will seldom contain more than two or three thousand redundant entries. Bearing in mind that the modern registry may contain more than a million entries, the elimination of two or three thousand is not going to save any noticeable amount of scanning time."*

I also saw other internet entries saying that companies like this offer free scanning but will quickly try to get you to buy their full program, to do the full job. Forget it; my computer runs fine. I uninstalled the program.

RENAMING A DOCUMENT / FOLDER – Right-click the item > Rename > type new name > press Enter key. Note that the item must be closed, to allow renaming. Also, give it a few seconds to finish closing; if you try to rename too quickly, it may say it's still open.

If you don't get "Rename" in your options list upon right-clicking, try again, but click directly on the file's name or date, not on empty space in that line, which brings up a different set of options.

If you are saving a file that has not been saved before (for example, after pressing CTRL+N to open a new document), the "Save As" dialog box appears automatically when you click "Save," at which point you can name it.

See also: "SAVE vs SAVE AS"

REPLACING – When you want to replace a single instance of a word or letter with something else, you just delete the old, type in the new. Where the "Replace" feature becomes very useful, is when you want to change multiple instances of a word, all at once. For example, if you have a document with dozens of instances of the word "disc" and want to replace them all with the word "disk", you can do that in one operation:

CTRL+H > type in (or CTRL+V in) your info for "Find what: Disc" and "Replace with: Disk" > then click "Replace All." That replaces all instances of the old word with the new word. Note that you can also replace a word with more than one word, or a phrase, if you want. For example, you can replace all instances of "boogers" with "mucus management."

If you mess up or suddenly change your mind, you can CTRL+Z that operation out, to get it back to what it was originally.

Capitalization

Note that if the original word is capitalized, the replacement word will also be capitalized, even though you do not enter it in the replacement window as capitalized.

If you want to change capitalization, click "More" at the lower left, check "Match Case", type the "Find" word in its desired letter case, then type the "Replace with" word in its desired letter case. For example, if you want to change all your CTRL's to Ctrl's, type those two words in exactly, click Replace All.

Replacing a Word "One by One"

Click "Find Next" and then "Replace", instead of "Replace All." That way you can check the context of each instance to decide if you want a few exceptions to that replacement. (Drag the dialogue box over to the side, to get it out of the way, so you can read the text more easily.) [W7 – You do these sorts of operations in the panel at left.]

Replacing Word with Nothing

Just leave the "Replace with:" line empty, then click Replace. One wrinkle though: Make sure you type in the original word you are replacing as that word PLUS one space; otherwise, the word will drop out of the line OK, but the line will have an extra spacebar space left in it.

Replacing Small Words

For small words, you should type in a space before and after the word; otherwise, instead of replacing all "on's" with "onto's", for example, you'll replace every "on" syllable of every word!! Your 3 instances of "poison" will now be "poisonto"!

And, even when you do this properly, you still have some checking to do, because you'll probably get a few instances where the word is at the end of a sentence and does not have a space after it, but a period or some other punctuation instead. And using space-new word is no guarantee of an error-free result either, because you might have the word "Only" at the beginning of a paragraph and end up with "Ontoly". Myself, I stay away from any multiple small word replacing. Too easy for some unexpected screwup. (Replacing instances of "few" with "several", you might end up with one instance of "curfew" becoming "curseveral" without your noticing it.)

Replacing Word with Same Word (Word Count Technique)

This is a great technique for seeing how many instances of a particular word you have in your document. Type the same word in both the "Find what:" and "Replace with:" lines. It replaces all instances of that word with the same word. You end up changing nothing, but the window automatically tells you how many instances it "changed," giving you a word count.

After you get the count, I recommend doing a CTRL+Z, just in case you misspelled the word.

Replace All in Just ONE Section of a Document

Simply block the section. It will replace the chosen word or words for just the blocked section. When it asks if you want to search the remainder of the document, click No.

Replacing Typestyle or Font

If you want to change the typestyle of a word throughout your document, in that "Find and Replace" window, type your "find" word and your "replace with" word in, in the desired typestyle. For example, if you want True Grit phrases to be italicized instead of underlined, for the "Find" word, do CTRL+U, type in True Grit, then for the "Replace with" word, do CTRL+I, and type in *True Grit*, click Replace All.

Note that the typestyle you order up, gets shown right below the word you type. To change your typestyle, for example, italics back to regular, press CTRL+I again.

Once you've ordered a particular typestyle, it stays there in your order window for your next orders unless you un-order it, using CTRL+whatever. Just keep an eye just below the word box; it'll tell you what you currently have ordered – bold, italic, whatever.

Also, if you want to replace a word with a different font (say, 15 instances of "hey" with "**hey**" – i.e. replacing Times Roman with Arial Black), go under "Format" at lower left and select the font of your choice. The area just below the word will show you your currently chosen font. (This wholescale font changing was very useful for me once for a large document with four people talking. I wanted to get all their names bolder, bigger. I was able to do so in four operations, instead of hundreds.)

Replacing Double Spaces with Single Spaces

Actually this is an excellent thing to do. One of the most common typos that occur and one people rarely notice, is entering two consecutive spaces instead of only one between words. If you do a CTRL+A, then CTRL+H, enter two spaces in the "Find" line, and one space in the "Replace with" line, you'll get rid of all your two-space errors in one operation and get all your words spaced properly. Try it. You'll be amazed how often you've made this error.

Be sure your tab indents for starting a paragraph are actual tabs and not multiple spaces, or it will alter those also.

Replacement of Words with Symbols

To replace instances of a word with a symbol, or, vice versa: CTRL+C an instance of the symbol in your text (it's now on your clipboard) > then CTRL+V it into either the "Find" or "Replace with..." line > then type the word on the other line > click "Replace All".

For example, if you want to replace every instance of the word "cents" with the symbol ¢: find that symbol under Insert tab > Symbols > More Symbols > Font (normal text), 7 down, 2 across > Insert. Now you have the ¢ symbol in your text. CTRL+C the ¢ symbol you just inserted, press CTRL+H, type "cents" into the top line, and CTRL+V the ¢ symbol into the bottom line, click Replace All. All your instances of "cents" become "¢".

Note that, weirdly, instead of putting that actual symbol into the window line, it puts in some odd-looking symbol; but, after you click Replace All, the correct symbol gets inserted into your text.

You can use the same technique for setting up an ongoing "autocorrect" function (auto-replace, basically). See "AUTOCORRECT – SYMBOLS". That's one of my set auto-replacements – every time I type "cents", it automatically becomes ¢. Note that, when I ordered that automatic replacement, I entered a space before the word; otherwise, every instance of the word "percents" would become "per¢".

Replacement of Symbol with Another Symbol

Can be done, but because the replacement window only allows ONE symbol to be inserted at a time, you need to go thru an extra step, changing the symbol to a random word, and then that random word to the second symbol:

Say you want to replace each instance of ▶ with ⇨.

1. CTRL+C ▶
2. CTRL+H, and CTRL+V that copy of ▶ into the top line
3. Type into the bottom line any odd word or random bunch of letters that do not appear in your text, like mmm
4. Click Replace All. Now all your ▶ symbols have become "mmm"
5. Insert a copy of ⇨ into your text and CTRL+C it
6. CTRL+H, CTRL+V your ⇨ symbol into the bottom line
7. Type mmm into your top line
8. Click Replace All, and now all your mmm's turn to ⇨.
9. Thus, you have in effect replaced ▶ with ⇨.

REPEAT OPERATION KEY – See "F4 KEY"

RESTARTING COMPUTER – Whenever your computer freezes, the time honored way to unfreeze it, is to restart (reboot) it. Also, for many programs that you install, you have to Restart to finish the installation. Click Start button at lower left > click arrow to the right of the lock icon [W7 – arrow to the right of "Shut down"] > click Restart. Takes my laptop about 3 minutes, 10 seconds to do so [my new computer with Windows 7 – about 2 minutes, or less].

RESTORE BUTTON – See "MAXIMIZE / MINIMIZE – DOCUMENTS"

RESTORE – DELETED FILES – See "DELETING"

RESTORE SETTINGS – IF COMPUTER GOES NUTS – A "System Restore" is a valuable, last-resort technique for getting a computer to behave properly, the way it was behaving before something made it go completely awry.

Says Windows: *"Sometimes, the installation of a program or a driver can cause an unexpected change to your computer or cause Windows to behave unpredictably. Usually, uninstalling the program or driver corrects the problem. If uninstalling does not fix the problem, you can try restoring your computer's system to an earlier date when everything worked correctly."*

Note that any software you put in after that restore point date, you will have to put in again. But any files, pictures, etc. are not affected. You don't lose them, but only the newly installed programs or settings.

Close all open programs or documents > Start > [W7 – Control Panel > System and Security > Action Center > "Restore your computer to an earlier time"] All Programs > Accessories folder > System Tools folder > System Restore > wait, "Restore system files and settings" window opens up, select "Recommended restore" if problem just started, or, select "Choose different restore point" at lower left [W7 – "Show more restore points"] if you had the problem before the most recent change to your computer; you can also click on "Scan for affected programs" at lower right, to see which programs will be affected (and which you subsequently may have to re-install) > Next > Finish. Use *"the restore points created just before the date and time you started noticing problems."* And, I believe you have to restart your computer to make the restore take effect.

Restore points *"are created automatically every day, and just before significant system events, such as the installation or a program or device driver."*

I had to use this "System Restore" feature recently after I installed an iPod. And it worked; the procedure fixed the problem. See "iPOD".

After you successfully install something you might want to create your own restore point, for that point: Start > Computer > Properties > System Protection (in left panel) > Create > type a name for the new restore point > Create, to save this new restore point. (Myself, I've never felt the need to do this.)

If your computer gets a virus, you should erase ALL restore points, because they've most likely been infected also. To delete them all: Start > right-click Computer > Properties > System Protection (in the left panel) > Protection Settings area, click the drive called "C system" > Configure > Delete > Click Continue > OK; that deletes the restore points. Create a new restore point named after the virus you just disinfected so that you know that that restore point is safe. (Actually, if you've gotten a virus, I recommend taking it to Best Buy to deal with it. I would feel safer myself, having a pro do it, in case there's other stuff that needs to be done, to fully get rid of that virus.)

Windows Updates After a System Restore

According to a Sony tech guy: If you do a "system restore" and it deletes your latest automatic updates from Windows, if you have the updating feature enabled and set to automatic updating, *"it will automatically re-install the missing updates."*

"Restore Defaults" or "Reset"

On a smaller scale, whether it's settings on a toolbar, or settings for a program, or adjustments you made to a picture, right-clicking an item usually offers you the convenient options of "Restore Defaults" or "Reset" for putting the item back to its original setup.

RESUMÉS – There used to be some neat, useful templates in my old computer (Windows 98). I think with Vista, you have to download them: While in a document, click the Office icon [W7 – File] at upper left, click New, scroll down to Resumés, click that, pick one and click the download button. It gives you a template – everything is already set up – you just need to type in the specific info on yourself. Very convenient – you get a format that is known to be acceptable, and you don't have to bother figuring out how to format and arrange things.

I read somewhere that you should use a common font at 10-12 point size, and don't justify your text. Apparently, scanability is important these days. You don't want odd stuff in your resumé, like a cursive handwriting font.

RHYMING DICTIONARY – I really like "RhymeZone.com" on the internet. So much easier than looking up words in a rhyming dictionary, which often requires looking and searching in several different sections. Here, you just type in your word, and it provides all the one-syllable, two-syllable, three-syllable, etc. rhyming words.

RIBBON – See "TOOLBAR"

RIGHT ALIGNING TEXT – Place cursor anywhere in the line, CTRL+R. Or, for more than a line, block desired section of text, CTRL+R.

RIP A CD TO COMPUTER – See "RIPPING Songs to Computer Thru Windows Media Player" under "Music"

RIP A DVD TO COMPUTER – The ability to rip commercial videos to the computer is obviously a major concern to movie makers, who fear financial losses thru piracy. So, while you can watch commercial movies on your computer, usually you can't copy them. Under Windows Media Player, the "Rip" tab is only for CDs, not DVDs.

Now, for your own video material, or material recorded on DVD from TV, you CAN make a copy onto your computer. It's unbelievable the number of false paths I went down, the complexities, etc., but it turns out to be relatively simple... once you know the correct path, and realize you have to dig deep into a bunch of folders to find the actual file:

Ripping a DVD to the Computer

1. Insert the disk
2. Double-click Computer
3. Right-click Drive E (where your disk is)
4. Copy (nothing happens yet till step 6)
5. Go to your Videos folder
6. CTRL+V it there.
7. It makes a folder called "DVD Video Recording" (check the date and time to make sure it's the right folder)

8. Open the folder, then open the "Video_TS" folder
9. Inside that folder, the "VTS_01_1 file is your DVD material, now on your hard drive. Note how you need to ignore all the other associated folders to reach this one with the actual material.
10. You may want to right-click and rename the clip for easier future reference (click on its date in the middle to get the Rename option up). And, what I do, is cut that file out and paste it by itself in the Videos folder, and then delete the "DVD Video Recording" folder with all those other pointless folders in there.

Windows Media Player should be able to play it. If it doesn't right away, and a window comes up saying "Windows can't open this file," click the selection below that says, "Select a program from a list of installed programs," OK, select Windows Media Player, OK. (Or, if a window comes up saying Windows doesn't recognize the extension, do you want it to try anyway, just click "Yes" and it plays it.)

Third party software can also import video material from a DVD. My Pinnacle Studio 14 can do so: Import tab at top left > Import from DVD RW Drive E > Start Import at lower right; wait > Sends material to both your "Videos" folder under Owner, and right to your work station in Studio. You can edit the material, or just keep it in your Videos folder to play in the future.

RIP vs BURN – RIP means copying something TO the computer. BURN means copying something FROM the computer to a disk.

ROUTER – This is a device that can send data to, and from, your computer, wirelessly. Instead of your modem receiving signals and sending them to your computer thru an ethernet cable, the modem transfers signals to the router, which in turn sends them to your computer, wirelessly, over the air. Typically it has a range of 60 or more feet, depending on obstructions. (There is such a thing as an "aircard" to get wifi – wireless internet – wherever you are, but it uses phone towers and you have to subscribe to it like a cell phone line.)

Several router types:

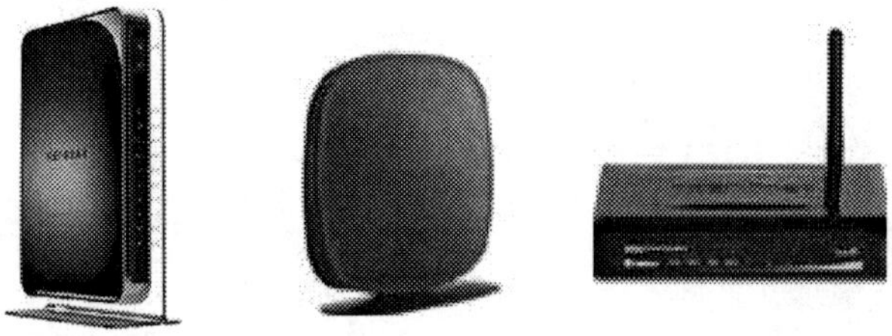

You can also configure the router to work with other wireless capacity devices, like a printer.

I recently bought one (Radio Shack $42). I think it's a Netgear model.

Summary of all the material below: It's a major pain in the butt to get working, but get a professional to help you, and once you've got it, it's great. I absolutely love it.

– Now I have two less cables cluttering up my desk (modem to computer, computer to printer). My computer-printer cable used to really get in my way; it connected to the right side of my laptop, which is right where I like to put documents to read or write on.

– My back won't get sore from a long computer session, because now I can work from my bed comfortably instead of having to sit by my desk in a chair; yet, I'm still able to use the internet or iTunes, without having to laboriously move my cable connection setup. (No wires at all attached to my laptop, till battery runs low, at which point I do have to use the power cord.)

– I see no drop-off in functions; everything works just as well as it did with the ethernet cable. It's not like certain things don't work as well, or as quickly.

That's the upside. The downside is that it was a major pain to install and get working. In theory, it's pretty simple: Take the cable that goes out of your modem to your computer and plug it into the router instead of your computer, put the router program CD in, and follow the steps.

I did that, but after the 23rd step I came to a dead end; I could not continue because I couldn't supply the proper username and password; I tried all the ones I could think of.

Called Best Buy Geek Squad to set up a home appointment ($99). He came out and we got it done in about an hour. My recommendation: Don't go it alone; it's not worth the aggravation. They know stuff that is important which you have no way of knowing.

To those who scoff and say, "Aw, c'mon, it's easy," I would ask this question: If it's so easy, how come the standard session for doing this is 90 minutes?! For a professional! I rest my case.

OK, here's the exact procedure I did before calling Best Buy, followed by direct quotes from our session (I recorded it).

1. Turn modem off (disconnect power cord) > 2. Unplug your ethernet cable from modem (leaving the other end still in your computer) > 3. Plug the now free end into the router (into any of 4 black ports).[Ultimately you no longer need this ethernet cable (but only the one between modem and router), but I think you do for now, to set up the router; not sure.] 4. Attach (yellow) ethernet wire (comes with the router package), one end to the port on your modem that you just opened up, the other end to the router port (yellow) > 5. Turn the modem back on (attach power cord) > 6. Plug in the router power cord > 7. That turns the router on > 8. For me, a modem window came up – "Set Network Location." Clicked "Home network" > Next > wrote down password they showed – a 10 number/letter deal > Finish. I don't know it this step 8 was necessary. I'm guessing it was, to reconnect my modem to my computer. >

9. Insert CD > 10. Click on "Run auto.exe" > 11. Click on Setup > 12. Next, wait 2 min. (Click on part of the current window to make it jump in front of the previous window so you can see it.) > 13. Select one of two ethernet adapter choices (I picked "Marvel Yukon" – ??) > 14. Next. Shows newer version of program is available (happens a lot – store-bought CD is somewhat out of date; the newest version is available to download from internet) > 15. Next. Wait about 6 minutes as it downloads the newest version. > 16. Enter a "Wireless Name" [This, it turns out, can be just any random name you like] > 17. Next. Enter a "Wireless Passphrase" [This, it turns out, serves as your password] > 18. Wait 2 min. > 19. Shows Register Product window. I clicked "Skip" at lower left > 20. Window shows "Congratulations... router is set up." They send a copy of your wireless name and passphrase to your Desktop (under the "Router Setup icon) > 21. Finish >

22. Another window shows, Clicked "Wirelessly Connect Your PC to the Router" > 23. Waited as it progresses (shows percent progress), a few minutes.

OK, setup is done, but now I needed to "configure the client" whatever that is → Start > Control Panel > Network and Internet Connections > Properties > select "Wireless Network Tab" > select "View Available Wireless Networks" > select the network and click on "Connect" > enter Network Key (?) > click on "Connect.

Here I got stuck. Clicked Router Login icon; wants User Name and Password; tried a bunch, no luck. Called Best Buy.

Here are selected informative quotes from our session. Geek guy's words (or a paraphrase as I understood it) are in italics.

Yeah, you've got everything connected right...

We (Geeks) *bypass the disk completely. It sometimes causes more issues, than it actually helps. We just log directly into the router itself, without actually using the software, just because it's easier and it doesn't cause issues later on...*

[Me seeing the window asking for my User Name and Password] See, now this is as far as I got, and I have no idea what to put in there.

The User Name is "Admin"; the password is "Password."

Oh... hah, hah! **The password is "password"?!!!** Geez! I thought it was something I already had in there, or that they had given me.

[That brought up a window (blue if I remember right) for setting it up. He said a lot of it can be just left at default. He did change the channel selection from "Auto" to one of the channel numbers little used, for better security.]

[He took out a smart phone or whatever it was, to check the local area signals.] *You see I pulled up all these different networks in this area that have a signal* [on his device was a list including, already, my network under the name I had given it]. [You can select it and, if you put the correct "passphrase" in, you can use it.]

[We changed my password from "Password" to one of my choice, for better security.] *Again, I'll be sending you an email with all this information* [password, etc.].

This is a lot of stuff.

A lot of it is set by default, and most of the time we don't touch it.

If I tried to go thru this on my own, 90% of it, I wouldn't know what it is.

[Then he went thru a lot of stuff on my printer display panel.] *You go to "Setup" > network settings > wireless LAN setup > wireless setup wizard > and from this point you pick the SSID* [the name I chose for my network].

What if I clicked on somebody's else's?

It's secure, it won't connect.

OK.

Put in your passkey / passphrase [he put it in, letter by letter (you have to press a button continuously to reach each letter)] *It's just a matter of learning the nuances of the printer.* [He reserved the IP address of the printer into the router, so it will still be there even if the computer loses power. (I think all devices have an "IP address.") At any rate, we ended up, under Start, Control Panel, Printers and Devices, with an icon for my printer, <u>wireless</u>, as separate from the icon for the printer <u>with a wire</u>.]

[To log on to router thru "Router Login" icon on Desktop]: *"Admin" is always the User Name, the passphrase is* (the phrase I chose).

There is a wireless switch that you would have to turn on. [Switched <u>on</u> the wireless switch on the front of my laptop.] *And, just leave it on.*

So there's this little icon down here on the taskbar (lower right), *click it and it will bring up this list* (of local networks giving signals). *Select yours, tell it to connect. Once it's in there, it will remember and connect automatically; you only have to do it once.*

"Security key"? Is that that same thing as "passphrase"?

Yep.

See, I hate that! They're talking about the <u>same</u> thing but from one paragraph to the next they don't use the <u>same</u> name or terminology!!

It's called "security key", "passphrase", "pass key", "password", heh, heh.

So "security key" is the same thing as "passphrase"?

Yep.

So I put that in there, clicked OK, it's gonna connect.

What's gonna connect? My computer to my router?

Yep. You can see these little signal bars down here [taskbar, lower right] *So, we're on the network now. Now you can access the internet from here. That's part one.*

OK, now you want to print without the connection cable to the printer.

Yeah.

But other people in this building, when they turn on their things, they'll see my particular network also?

See it, yes, but they won't be able to connect without the password.

So nobody is going to interfere, because I have that password. And, <u>I</u> don't need to put in the password either?

Only if you <u>add</u> something to the network. Like a smart phone you want to connect, you'd go into Settings, like I did with mine, wherever the settings would be, find it in the list, put in the security key and password, and go from there.

I went into Start, Devices and Printers, Add a Printer, "Add a network, wireless or bluetooth printer"... [list] *Here's the IP address of the printer.* [waited] *It's installing the networking drivers it needs.* [We hovered the pointer over the printer icon and it showed "Ready" as opposed to my old icon for the printer, which is no longer ready because it's not connected to the computer by a cable anymore. He went to the internet, picked a Google page, and printed it. In other words, now both my computer and printer are working wirelessly. My printer, wireless, is my default printer.] *If you wanted to turn the wireless off on the computer, and plug in the cable* [computer to printer cable], *then it would still work.*

Let me get that into my head: The computer talks to the router, and the router talks to the printer.

Yeah. The router is basically the brain; the computer is sending all the info to the router, and the router is telling it where to go. So it doesn't matter that the printer is connected with a wire, or wireless, it's getting the same thing. [If I went back to wired instead of wireless, I'd have to pick the <u>old</u> printer icon.] *The checkmark by the printer icon there shows it's the default one; it'll go there unless you specify otherwise.*

Some of those things, like the changing the channel, reserving the IP address, you don't necessarily have to do it, but we like to, because it eliminates some of the issues that could occur if it's not working properly.

You have 6-months phone support, and if a problem can't be resolved by phone, we'll set up a return trip.

Geez, I needed your help. I could have spent 5 more hours doing this getting nowhere!

That's why we're out there. We done it a few times. We know what to look at.

Because people say, oh, it's easy, all you gotta do is plug it in, or whatever. It didn't turn out that way.

[End of session.]

OK, so it was working fine. All set. But then I had a dream. The computer was giving me a message: "The computer would like to hit you in the head with a hammer one more time, just for the fun of it."

One of the power cords was wrapped around a desk leg, so I unplugged it, positioned it behind the leg, and plugged it back in.... now it won't work!! Does it ever end, the unexpected problems!?

The internet window came up not working. I pressed the "Diagnose" button. Showed something about the "adapter." Then showed "solved." Tried their suggestion of unplugging the modem for ten seconds and then putting it back on. Well, half a hooray. The internet was back on, but, the printer was still not working wirelessly.

Came up with message: my wireless network does not have a valid IP configuration. But then, suddenly, it did. But, still the printer was not working wirelessly. Tried the suggestion in the general Geek Squad notes emailed to me – unplugging and plugging back in, except modem first and router afterward, waiting a full minute rather than ten seconds, and waiting for the lights of each to be fully on, in succession. Then, as kind of a general principle, I turned both computer and printer off, waited a minute, then turned them back on.

When my computer opened up, it showed that the Windows firewall has blocked some feature of this program, namely, the printer! In that window at bottom was "Allow Access." I clicked that. Hooray! Now everything's working again.

Installing a router is simple? Well, then how come, in the info they emailed me it had all this stuff to keep track of: the router User Name, the router Password, the router IP, the SSID (the network name), the network authentication and data encryption type, the network key (which is actually my password), the channel number, and the IP address of my printer. That does not represent "simple" to me!

Happily, now that everything is done, I don't think I need to know any of that stuff or normally access it. My computer automatically works wirelessly now, for both the internet and my printer, and I don't have to do anything to make it work. And, it's secure.

Update

Absolutely love it. So convenient. Can use my laptop fully at any place in my apartment with no annoying wires. Well worth the trouble putting it in. I also got my old computer on it: Wireless switch on, at front of computer > Start > Control Panel > Network and Internet > Network and Sharing Center > Connect to a Network; it shows local "networks" > clicked on mine > Connect > put in my passphrase > forget exactly what, but just a couple more easy clicks, and from that point on, you're on and you don't have to do anything to get on each time. The passphrase is only for the first time you connect.

(One time, due to an odd movement of my laptop against my laptop stand, I accidentally turned off the wireless switch at the front of my computer, losing my internet connection. That's something to consider if you can't figure out why you're not connected – you accidentally turned off the wireless switch. In fact, it's happened to me several times; I think as I take my laptop off my bed stand, the front of it sometimes brushes against the ledge support and switches my wireless switch off.)

Final Wrinkles

My printer CD printing function would not work (it was trying to use the old printer name). Solution: Instead of using the Print button on the label file (which offered no printer name choices), I used CTRL+P, which gave me a dropdown list of available printers to choose from; I chose the new name. It printed. And next time I clicked the Print button, it worked.

I had added my old computer to my router network, but one day it wouldn't connect. Did this to get it back: Start > Control Panel > Network and Internet > Network and Sharing Center > Connect to a network > picked mine from the available list > Connect. In other words, I just repeated the original operation for connecting to my router. Now I have both my old and new computer working thru my router.

If you are having trouble with your home network, you can right-click the network icon in your taskbar at lower right, and click "Troubleshoot problems." Might be helpful.

Well, guess what. A month later I tried to use my printer to scan something, and it would not do so! Oh, does it ever end?!! I proceeded, in existential agony, to try different things, and, hooray, managed eventually to get it going. Did something like this: Start > All Programs > found Epson > clicked on "Epson Scan Settings" > changed option from "Local" to "Network" > Add > shows scanner address of my printer > entered that number in the box lower down > OK > window came up with "Test" option; clicked that > gave message that test was successful > OK > OK.

It's working.

Update, two months later: Again it wasn't working!! My Epson Scan icon would not open up. Worked on it for two hours. Went thru Start > All Programs > Epson > Epson Scan > Epson Scan Settings > tried to do the same as above, but no luck; the only "Select Scanner" showing was my "Epson 810"; I needed to get "Epson017F41" (the wireless version of my printer/scanner) in there; could not figure out how to do so. And, after waiting on the phone for 20 minutes and giving them all my info, I was informed by a man in India that I needed a "Plan", which costs $109, to get an answer. Yeah, right.

Final try: I went to Start > Control Panel > Hardware and Sound > Devices and Printers > Add a printer > my wireless version of my printer/scanner – the Epson 017F41 one – was in the list. I added it. Hooray, now it works! (Why it had stopped working, I do not know; I never made any adjustments to it.)

At one point a message window popped up at lower right corner of screen, telling me if my computer was currently connected to a network or not, and it stayed there; wouldn't go away. To get rid of it: Start > Control Panel > Network & Internet > Network and Sharing Center > "Change Advanced Sharing Settings" on left > turned off "Public folder sharing..." > Save Changes. That made the damn message go away. (Though when I turned Pubic Folder back on, to see if it would come back, it didn't.)

RULER AT TOP – When you are in a document, there may be a ruler at top, with sliders on either side. White indicates your text width, blue your margins. You can drag either slider over to change your side margins, for the paragraph your cursor is currently in.

I DO NOT like this feature. When you set things manually like this, you can't be exact, and you may end up with text that includes several different indents.

I much prefer setting my indents for a paragraph, under Home, Paragraph, Indents and Spacing, my margins for the whole document, under Page Layout, Page Setup, Margins, and my tabs, under Home, Paragraph, dropdown arrow, Tabs at lower left, Default tab stops (I like .2). See also "INDENTING".

To get rid of that ruler and give yourself more room for your text: Above the scroll arrow at the right, is a small icon which shows "View Ruler" when you put the cursor on it. Click it to get rid of the ruler, or click it again to get it back.

"RUN" OR "SAVE" – See DOWNLOADING A PROGRAM – "RUN" OR "SAVE"

SAFETY TIPS

– Keep magnets away from your computer. (Though small magnets are usually not a problem.)
– Use a surge protector strip. Or, at least don't use the computer during a lightning storm.
– Don't move your computer when it is booting up or shutting down.

– Don't let the screen face direct sunlight for any period of time.

SAVING – To save work you have done on a document, press CTRL+S.

In small letters at bottom center, just above taskbar, it says "Word is saving..." Only takes a second or two. Now the latest version of your material is saved, in the same folder you created the document in. (You can undo a Save, but not after you close the document. See "UNDO.")

"SAVE" vs "SAVE AS"

There are basically two ways to create and save a document – 1) Thru the File tab, where you create a document, name it first, work on it, then "Save" it, and it stays inside the folder you started in. 2) Thru CTRL+N, where you create a document, work on it, then "Save As" it (naming it and also sending it to a folder of your choosing).

1) THRU "FILE" – "Save"

1. Click "My Documents" or any folder.
2. Click File at upper left. (If you have Windows 7 and you don't see "File" at upper left, press the Tab key to bring up "File". See "FILE TAB DISAPPEARED")

   In Vista, sometimes you get different a different options list. If you get two "New"s in your list, click the second one.
3. Click "New". Pick "Microsoft Office Word Document".
4. "New Microsoft Office Word Document" shows as a new document.

   Note that this new document will be in the default format of Vista, which is 11 point size, Calibri font, one-inch margins, with an embedded skipped line after each paragraph. See "DEFAULT 'WORD DOCUMENT' FORMAT" if you want to change the default format so that each new document opens up with your own choice of format.
5. Type your desired name in, press Enter key to set that name.
6. Double click the document icon to open it.
7. Work on your document.
8. Press CTRL+S to save it.
9. The document is now saved in the folder you opened it in.

2) THRU CTRL+N – "Save As"

1. With a current document open and in front of you, press CTRL+N. (If you're in a folder and press CTRL+N, nothing happens.)

   Note that when you get the option list mentioned above, with two New's, the first New is the same as the CTRL+N order.
2. That opens up a new document in the format you yourself have set as the default format. See DEFAULT "WORD DOCUMENT" FORMAT > "Getting the Page Format You Want."
3. Work on the document.
4. CTRL+S, and instead being saved right away, a "Save As" window opens.
5. In that window, you name it, and choose the folder into which you want it sent.
6. Click Save at lower right (or, if you don't see "Save" there, click on "Open" at that lower right spot, and then "Save" shows up to click.)
7. Now your document is saved under the folder you picked. I think of the "Save As" window as essentially a "Save AND Send to" window.

Note that if you didn't pick a destination folder, the Document gets sent to whatever folder happened to be open in that "Save As" window.

"Save" means your already-named document gets saved where it already is in a folder. "Save As" means you are naming it for the first time, AND sending it to a chosen folder.

For the method I find the easiest to create a document in my chosen format, see "DEFAULT 'WORD DOCUMENT' FORMAT" > "Getting the Page Format You Want".

If "Save As" Window Comes Up for an Old Document

Usually the "Save As" window only comes up if you have not yet named your document. But sometimes – I have no idea what the conditions are that cause this – the "Save As" window comes up for an old document.

In that case, keep this key concept in mind: "Save As" saves your text under the new name that you type in, and under a new location that you select, thereby creating this new document. You now have the old version under its old name, and the new version under its new name and location. **"Save As" makes a new version!**

If you choose not to change the name, then it replaces the old version with the new version, and then you have only the one most recent version. You no longer have the old version!

This concept applies I think to other programs as well. For example, my movie-making program, Studio: When you select "Save As" and enter a new name, you now have a new project, as well as the old one.

Saving Reminder

If you attempt to close a document (CTRL+W) without having saved changes to it, an automatic message pops up: "Do you want to save the changes to...". Click Yes if you want to save them. Click No if you prefer to keep the document as it was before you made changes, And click Cancel if you want to cancel the "close document" order and go back to look at it some more.

See also "NAMING A DOCUMENT"

SAVING – AUTOMATIC

I came across this bit of advice on the internet: *"...do not ever rely on Auto Recovery feature to recover your file in case of accident. It's notorious for unreliability. The best practice is to click the* ***Save*** *button or press* ***CTRL+S*** *key sequence regularly."*

So I do that. But, I'm pretty sure, the reason my latest changes to a document get saved automatically if my battery suddenly runs out, is that I have the AutoRecover function set to every two minutes:

1. MS Office Button (colored icon at far upper left when you are in a document) [W7 – File]
2. "Word Options" at middle, at very bottom
3. Save
4. Check "Save AutoRecover information every x minutes"

5. Select location for recovered file. (My Documents is good; look there for any new oddly named documents, like "WR...". Those are the recovered versions.)
6. OK

Windows 7 – File, Options, Save, check "Keep the last autosaved version if I close without saving". It's already checked as the default setting.

RS says this may or may not work. Best to simply get in the habit of continually pressing CTRL+S. Actually it seems to be working lately. I see "Auto-Recovery" popping up a lot now at the bottom.

Note that this function does not interfere with your own manual saving as you go. In other words, it doesn't save your current document when you don't want it saved. It's an "auto recovery" feature rather than an "automatic saving" feature. It's making a backup copy somewhere else.

Document Recovery Pane

If you lose power or somehow your work didn't save, next time you open up, there usually appears a selection of recovered versions of the document at the left. Click Open on the latest version and Save As, to recover your latest version of that document.

It's kind of confusing because sometimes you get stuff over there even if there was no unexpected close of a file. Except for important stuff, I tend to simply X it out; most often my document is fine and includes my latest editing. However, if something hinky is going on and your material is important, check those recovery files carefully and save the one you want. And, check to make sure you don't end up with two different versions. You don't want to get mixed up and proceed with two different versions of a document at various times. Once you've got the version you want, delete the older unwanted one.

When I had several documents in that pane recently, all important ones, when I hovered the pointer over each one, it showed either "This is the original document" or "This is the Auto-recover version." So you want to choose the Auto-recovered version, because that's the latest one.

SAVING A PICTURE – See "PHOTOS / PICTURES – BASIC OPERATIONS"

To save a picture in a Word document, do CTRL+S, just like for text.

SAVING A WEBSITE PAGE – See "WEBSITE – PAGE SAVE"

SCANNING – Most printing machines also scan – that is, they can make a copy of something and send it into your computer. Here is how mine (Epson 810 Printer) works. Other machines work in at least a somewhat similar fashion:

A. Ordering a Scan Thru the PRINTER/SCANNER

1. Printer On
2. Lift cover
3. Put document in, face down, head to left
4. Press "Scan" on printer. (Your printer may then show differently worded options; press the most logical one that pops up.)
5. Press "Scan to PC"
6. Press "USB Connection"; it shows "Scanning..."
7. Small window pops up on computer screen, showing scanning progress. Takes about 30 seconds per page.
8. Sends image (essentially a JPEG picture) to "Pictures" folder. (The "Pictures" folder window then automatically comes up.)
9. Right-click that file, Copy
10. CTRL+V it into a Word document of your choice, for re-sizing, editing, printing.

I never order scans thru the printer; I'm used to ordering scans thru the computer:

B. Ordering a Scan Thru the COMPUTER

Using the computer to order a scan provides you with more options.

1. Printer On (desktop icon will not open the printer program unless printer is on), lift cover, put document in, face down, head to left.
2. Double-click Epson Scan icon on desktop
3. Epson Scan window comes up
4. Select Color, Grayscale, or B&W
5. Select resolution. 300 dpi (dots per inch) is the default; OK for most stuff. See "Quality Levels" below.
6. Click Preview (lower left) to see what you are scanning (in case it's crooked and in case you need to adjust "Threshold" bar to scan a document in lighter or darker.)

   At one point the Preview window was hiding down below; had to drag it up. It usually pops up to the right of your scanning window.)

   You can use your pointer to drag a rectangle around a smaller portion of the page, if you want to scan only that portion.
7. Click "Scan" at lower right, OK.
8. Sends image to Pictures folder.
9. Right-click that file, Copy
10. CTRL+V it into a Word document of your choice, for re-sizing, editing, printing.

Scanning Directly to Word Document

For this printer I don't know how to get multiple images, one after another, sent directly into the same open document, like I used to with my HP printer. Instead, I have to import them individually from the Pictures folder, or Windows Photo Gallery.

After clicking "Scan" and before clicking "OK," the window shows options for the destination of the scan – Pictures folder, Documents folder, or other. But, I have not been able to land it directly into an open Word document.

Editing

For the most part I do my editing (brightness, contrast, size, etc.) AFTER landing the image in a Word document.

If you really want to get the most out of your printer/scanner, you have to spend time experimenting with settings and options and procedures, to arrive at the quickest and best-looking results. Typically, you can get good at the particular jobs you do often, and you don't need to know that much about other kinds of jobs you normally don't do.

Using the Printer/Scanner as a Copy Machine

If you don't need a copy of the material in your computer, you can use the printer/scanner simply as a copy machine. See "COPIES."

Default Picture-Opening Program

For a while my computer was opening pictures from my Pictures folder with "Picture Viewer" (Apple, QuickTime), which I don't like. I changed it to Windows Photo Gallery, which I like much better.

To set your default picture-opening program, right-click the picture file (or the picture itself) > Open With > Choose Default Program > Windows Photo Gallery (for me) > check "Always use the selected program to open this kind of file" > OK.

I found that if the computer won't let me copy a picture from my "Pictures" folder directly (right-click, Copy) into a Word document (for whatever reason), if I open the file with Windows Photo Gallery and copy it from there, then it WILL allow direct pasting into a Word document.

I normally open a picture file, right-click on the picture itself, Copy, and then paste it inside a Word document. But, you can also simply right-click the picture file, and copy and paste it into a Word document; all the pictures inside that file get pasted into the Word document.

Framing Scan Area

When you do photos, remember to use the pointer to draw a rectangle and frame the picture as the scanning area (for example, a 4x6 rectangle rather than the whole glass document table) This makes scanning faster, plus allows you to use higher dpi. It let me do 2400 dpi, though with a warning message that it may be too big. But, it worked OK.

Descreening

The "Descreening" option helps take out moiré patterns (interfering patterns that you can get from scanning in print media documents, having to do with the fact that newspaper and magazine pictures are actually made up of tiny dots). In my experience, this feature produces a soft-focus picture. Your choice – whether you like the picture sharp but with slight interfering patterns, or, not sharp but with no interfering patterns.

You can see the pattern below.

This feature is only for use in scanning in newspaper or magazine images; don't use it for original photos. And, for your scanner program, I don't know just where that option shows up, but I'm guessing, for new scanners, it's there somewhere, before you click "Scan."

QUALITY LEVELS

My printer has three Modes – Home (for regular stuff), Office (good for many documents fed thru the ADF – Automatic Document Feeder), and Professional (good for best quality photos). Somewhere under their "Help" they recommend these selections for dpi (dots per inch): 360 for normal (though 300 is default), 400 for OCR, 300 for high quality color, 720 for high quality B&W.

BLACK AND WHITE – TEXT SCANNINGS

I experimented and found, in black and white, I could not distinguish between 300, 720, 800, and 1200. The quality was good for all. The scanning time for 300 dpi was 15 seconds; for the others it was three times as long or longer.

When I went up to 1200, things got difficult. Windows Photo Gallery would show "Image size is too large." (If I right-clicked that picture file and select Open With, and Paint, then it would allow me to copy it to a Word document. The image landed way too big in Paint. I resized it down to 10% under Image tab, then under File did a Select All and Copy, to land it into a Word document OK. But, then, the computer would often freeze at that point.

So, for black and white text scannings, because the quality is fine, I'm sticking simply to the default setting of 300 dpi, under the Home Mode. I've found, as a general principle, default settings are good; only occasionally is it worth the effort to customize settings.

Threshold

The "Threshold" option refers to how dark or light you want to scan the document in. Only applies to B&W scans. You move the sliding marker left or right and view your Preview window to see at what point it looks the best – not too dark, not too light. Note that you can make adjustments after you land an image into a Word document, but, there will be limits. If you scanned an item in too dark, no matter what you do to it afterwards, it may still be too muddied. Therefore, I think it is good to use this feature and get your original scan as good as possible.

This is analogous to sound recording – if your original recording is poor, there's only so much you can do to clean it up afterwards.

COLOR – PICTURE SCANNINGS

For color scannings, you can pick higher resolutions for pictures because they are usually 4x6 size instead of 8½x11. Interestingly, after trying numerous combinations, I found the results were the same as for B&W, namely that I could not distinguish the differences in quality! I could clearly see the difference between 50 dpi (lousy) and 300 dpi (good), but between Home 300 dpi and Pro 2400 dpi I couldn't see any difference in quality, even when I upped the 4x6 photo result to a full page! A printed out full-page picture of the 300 one, and the 2400 one, looked equally good.

So, for run-of-the-mill photos I'll use Home 300.

HOWEVER, for precious photos, I'll use Pro 2400. Even though I can't see the difference, I'm sure there is a difference technically, because I note that one Home 300 4x6 scan is 465KB in size, and the Pro 2400 one of the same photo, is 16MB! Maybe if I increased the size to a 3 foot poster, then I would see the difference.

If you plan on making a family photo album of scanned-in photos, I recommend spending many hours experimenting (settings, options, paper, etc.), to get the best picture you can. You might even try taking camera shots of your photos and importing them. And then, print out a copy of each – the scanned-in photo and the photo of the photo – to compare, and decide which one is better.

It would be a shame to assemble a family photo album, only to realize later that the pictures could have been 20% more sharp.

Paper Selection

Don't forget 1) that the type of paper you use makes a big difference – use photo paper, either glossy or matte (non-glossy). AND, 2) when you order the printing from your computer, don't forget to select the proper "Paper Type" setting in your printing window, to match the actual paper you've loaded into the printer. That also makes a huge difference in quality!

"Glossy" is for one sided pictures. "Matte" (non-glossy) is usually for double-sided; it's also more durable. (Though I recently bought some Epson premium matte paper and it's one-sided. You're supposed to print on the whiter side, but I can barely tell the difference in sides beforehand. Until I print a picture, and then I can see a huge difference.) "Satin" or "Lustre" is a nice intermediate finish.

Rotating a Scanned-In Image – For rotating photos, see "PHOTOS / PICTURES" > "EDITING THE PICTURE" > "Rotating a Picture"

Windows Photo Gallery allows changing orientation from vertical to horizontal and vice versa, under its "Fix" tab. But, to straighten out a crooked picture, by degrees: After landing image in a Word document, right-click it > Format Picture > Layout tab > Behind text > Size tab > Rotation > select degrees. The "Behind text" option is the key; otherwise the "Rotation" option stays grayed out and unusable.

Preview Window

Click Preview before scanning. That way you can drag the frame out a bit to make sure you are not cutting any text off at the edge. If you just click Scan right away, it often cuts a bit off the right or left. Preview also allows dragging a rectangle around just the section you want to scan. Saves time.

Note that in adjusting the document on the document table, to straighten it, you do the opposite of what it shows in the Preview window. If the right looks too high, lift the cover and move the right even higher. If the left looks too far from the edge in the Preview, lift the cover and move the document even farther from the left edge. (Essentially, since the document is face down, left in the Preview is right in the actual document, and vice versa.)

Also, for B&W, use the "Threshold" bar to make your original scan in the best degree of brightness or darkness, as you view it in the Preview window.

Sample Scanning Project

Here is a type of job I used to do frequently for SAT tutoring, and how I would do it today with my current machine. Let's say I wanted to make a small pack of math problems, along with a reading comprehension exercise. Three pages of math, a blank page, and then two pages of a reading comprehension passage:

1. Turned printer on.
2. Carefully cut out pages of the manual so I could lay the pages FLAT on the glass ("document table") and get a good scan. Folded-back documents (manual, book, whatever) tend to be problematic – crooked, and not clean because they are not flat against the glass. If you see in your preview window that a page is crooked, just put the original document back in straight against the borders of the document table, which should be easy enough, since your document is a single rectangular sheet.

Once you've landed it into a Word document, you can trim, move, brighten or darken it. See also "Rotating a Scanned-in Image" below.

3. Used the regular default settings – B&W, 300 dpi.
4. Scanned in the 5 pages I want. Took about 15 seconds each.
5. They landed in my Pictures folder, as JPEG images automatically named in order (img011, img012, img013, etc.)
6. Opened a blank Word document.
7. Went to my Pictures folder, right-click, Copy, CTRL+V'ed each one into a Word document.
8. They automatically landed in successive pages. (My old HP used to land scans in above the previous page, rather than below, like this Epson printer.) After page 3, I pressed CTRL+Enter to skip a page, since I wanted a blank page between Math material and Verbal material.
9. Trimmed edges a bit and a few other adjustments (brightness, contrast, and Layout "Behind text" so that I could move them easily, to center them). Note that it takes some practice to get your pages right. Trimming, or selecting "Behind text" layout, might automatically move one page underneath another, and you wonder where it went, etc. I usually make a bunch of blank pages at the start and then move ready pages to the beginning one by one, after putting all of them in "Behind text" layout. (Using F4 key is a quicker way to get all of the pages into the "Behind text" layout, after you do the first one. Put the pointer on the next page, press F4, and continue like that.)
10. Typed in a couple of headings – "MATH" and "VERBAL" – at top of appropriate pages.
11. CTRL+S, and then CTRL+P to print out a copy. Stapled the 3 sheets together.

It is time-consuming, but once you're done, you can print out a copy whenever you need it in the future. And, the more you care if a page is properly centered, trimmed, straight, readable, etc., the more time-consuming it is. If you just want to get a copy and you don't care about the quality that much, it's much easier.

TIPS

Lost Pages

Sometimes, when you click on a Layout option, like "In front of text," pages move and often hide under other pages. I found pressing CTRL+Enter key several times, to give yourself a series of blank pages at the beginning of a document, THEN importing the scans onto later pages, working on the images, then moving them to the earlier blank pages, is the way to go, to avoid pages suddenly disappearing on their own underneath other pages.

Moving Scanned Images Around in Your Document

First, right-click your scanned-in images and under Format Picture, Layout, select an option like Behind Text, so that the images will move more easily. Second, put your screen size to maybe 25% (minus icon at bottom right) so that you can see a dozen pages at once and move (drag and drop) images more easily.

Double Column

Usually, if your Word document is set to a double column format, an 8½x11 image will land intact, over the two columns; the image itself will not split up into two columns.

Faster Adjustments

When you want to adjust your images all in the same way, for example, putting all of them at 90% size, or all of them at a certain brightness, do the first one, then put the pointer on the next one and press the repeat function key – F4.

Keep in mind that the F4 key only repeats the one most recently ordered function. If you want to adjust all your pages to 90% and also trim one inch off the bottoms, you have to run thru the process two separate times.

Behind Text – Anchoring an Image

When you select Behind Text for your image and you type in text just above it, the image will sometimes keep moving ahead of your typing as you press "Enter" key for each new line. What I usually do is type a line or two, drag the image underneath the text to anchor it, then continue typing. Once you get text on top of the image, then the image tends stay put.

Garbled Scan

Once in a while a scan may come out all garbled or flawed. Just do it over; usually the second try is fine.

Thin Paper Showing Print From Other Side

Putting a white sheet of paper on the back of a thin paper document you're scanning in, doesn't really help keep the print from the other side of the document from showing through. The underside of the lid of the scanner is white anyway.

Aha, but guess what? Putting a BLACK paper on top of the original, does help a bit. You have to experiment to see what works best for your particular job.

Keep in mind this distinction: A black backing may help in keeping the scanner from recording text on the other side of a thin document. But, print showing thru on your final copy may be simply the text showing thru on your final copy, because your final paper is too thin for such heavy coverage on the back. In that case you may need thicker paper – 60# instead of 20#.

However, the difference will not be that great. I find that if I hold 60# and 20# samples up to a light, there is no difference; average text shows thru equally. However, laying samples down flat on a desk, you can see some difference; the 60# is a little better. (Nowadays, I think the term "60#" has been dropped, for the more logical "24#" or "28#" for thicker paper.)

Big Jobs

If you're doing a big job, say printing 100 pages, two-sided, you might want to work with 20 pages at a time, just in case something goes wrong. That way you don't have to do the whole project over, but just the section that got messed up since your last copy.

This is a good general principle for big jobs – setting or saving IN SEGMENTS as you work. I find it especially relevant also to movie-making, because I've occasionally had to do a whole darn project over because something went wrong. Now I do videos in ten-minute set segments, and then put them together at the end.

Highlighting Scanned-in Image Text

If you are fond of highlighting certain key passages of text, in yellow – as I am – how can you do that for a scanned-in page of text? Well, I have not been able to figure out how to get shading on top of a picture of text without its blocking out the text.

But, you can highlight a paragraph with a red frame this way:

1. Scan your page of text in.
2. Put it in a Word document
3. On a blank page, click Insert, Illustrations, Shapes, click on a rectangle, click the rectangle onto the blank page.
4. Right-click it, Format AutoShape, for Fill Color pick "No Color," for Line pick red at 2 point size.
5. That gives you a red frame with a transparent interior, which you can drag on top of the paragraph you want to highlight.
6. Then drag the handles to move the edges to fit exactly around the paragraph.

Note that, to get those handles up for your frame, you have to put the pointer exactly on top of one of its edges, otherwise, you keep getting handles up for the whole page instead of the rectangle. Remember, you essentially have one picture (the transparent frame) on top of another picture (your page of text).

If you are doing several paragraphs, instead of going thru the whole procedure for each, just click on the one red frame you've done already and make a copy of it to move to the next paragraph you want framed.

Scanning Saga

I feel I have to mention one problem I had with my old HP printer/scanner. It would absolutely refuse to import certain scanned documents to a Word document. Most were fine, but for some it just would not do it. And size did not seem to be a factor; it would do 21 MB documents, but not some 1 MB ones. Over a period of weeks, I talked to eleven different tech people on the phone; they gave me all kinds of suggestions. None made a difference! Then one day I just happened to hit upon the answer: If I reduced the literal size of these documents just a few percent, from 100% to 96%, then it would allow importing. That was the key; just reduce the size a bit. Why? Who knows?

OCR – Optical Character Recognition

This is a scanning program that allows you to scan in a printed page so that the text is editable. Instead of getting a set image, you get all the individual letters, which you can then edit, just as though you typed them into your Word document yourself. See "OCR"

SCREEN – NORMAL SETUP – Once you move from the Desktop to a Word Document, the screen usually shows the Toolbar at top (for all the different functions, under a series of tabs). It shows the Taskbar at bottom (for files, programs, or sites you're currently working on). And just above the Taskbar, the screen shows, on the left, what page you're on, and on the right, with the "–" and "+" icons, the percent of your screen text size.

For virtually all the icons on the screen, you can put your pointer over the icon, and a small window pops up telling you what the icon is for. Also very useful is the time of the day that shows on the lower right of the Taskbar. Put the pointer arrow over the time and the date pops up [W7 – also has a nice calendar pop up].

At far upper right are three key icons.

1. "–" is for minimize. Click on that and your current item on the screen gets put down onto the taskbar, from which you can bring it up again when you want to continue working on it.

2. The middle one is for restoring a previous size; it toggles back and forth between full screen and partial screen views.

3. "X" is for closing your file. (When you click "x", before it closes your file, it reminds you to save it, if you have not done so already.) Note that "x" does not mean erase; it means close.

SCREEN – BLACKOUT – If nothing is typed or there is no activity for 5 minutes, the screen goes to screen saver (a moving background – flying ribbons for me) And then, maybe ten minutes later, it goes to black automatically. To get back to an active screen from screen saver or a dark screen, just press any key. (I usually press one of the arrow keys at lower right.)

You can adjust these automatic blackout times to your preference: Start > Control Panel > System & Maintenance [W7 – Hardware & Sound], Power Options, "Choose when to turn off the display" at left > select preferences [W7 – also has a dimming option]

My preferences:

	On battery	Plugged in
Dim the display (screen)	Never	Never
Turn off display	5	10
Put the computer to sleep	10	15
Adjust plan brightness	Full	Full

Some programs will temporarily disable this blackout feature. No big deal; it goes back to working properly, once you're done with the program.

SCREEN – BRIGHTNESS – Press Fn key (lower left) and either F5 or F6 (sun icon on key) at top of keyboard, both repeatedly, to lower or raise brightness. For me, I like it always at max brightness.

SCREEN – CLEANING – I'm afraid to use any detergent of any sort. I used warm water and paper towels, and that worked fine for removing slight spots.

SCREEN – DESKTOP BACKGROUND – Right click any spot on desktop where there is no icon > Personalize > Desktop Background, check the one you want > OK. I picked one of the soft solid color ones in the dropdown list. I figure the Desktop, with all its icons, is "busy" enough.

Using Your Own Pictures as Background

Right-click any empty spot on the Desktop > Personalize > Desktop Background > Browse, to find a picture > click on desired picture > Open, which immediately makes it your Desktop background. [W7 – you can also simply find a picture, right-click it, and click on "Set as desktop background"]

[Note that for me, I have all my family pictures embedded in Word docs, so it won't do it for them. Pictures need to be picture files, not Word document files.]

To get rid of that picture [which was not easy to figure out; I hate Microsoft; instead of a simple Delete command, you have to figure out which odd buttons you have to click in what exact order]: Right-click Desktop > Personalize > Desktop Background> click the dropdown arrow next to Location [W7 – Picture Location] > pick Solid Colors > choose one of those, click "Save changes" at lower right. That makes that color your Desktop background and gets rid of the picture. In other words, you can only "delete" the picture by replacing it with something else.

SCREEN PRINT – See "PRINT SCREEN"

SCREEN RESOLUTION – I think lower resolution allows more stuff on one page, but higher resolution looks better. The default resolution is the highest one (AR says it's 1,024 X 768) but mine shows 1280 X 800 (the sliding marker is all the way to the right). I'll keep it here. It's fine. My color bit mode, by the way, is 32 bit, which is where I want it.

I suggest simply keeping the default settings. But here is how to change resolution if you want to: Start > Control Panel > Appearance and Personalization > "Adjust screen resolution", move the slider left or right, OK. I tried the lowest resolution and that made everything on the screen not nearly as sharp. I see no point in keeping the resolution at anything other than the highest.

SCREEN SAVER – The screen saver refers to a moving pattern that your screen reverts to, after a selected time, in order to prevent "burn-in." If a stationary image stays on your screen for a long time, it might affect proper presentation of colors. However, modern computers generally don't suffer from this effect any longer. So it's a moot issue.

But, if you want to get some moving pattern to show up: Right-click any spot on desktop where there is no icon > Personalize > Screen Saver > select from dropdown list; select number of minutes to wait before screen turns to this screen saver; OK. I selected "None."

> Note the box just to the right of the minutes selection box – "On resume, display logon screen." That's actually an important box. When checked, it shows the user account icons for other people who use the computer, so they can log on. When unchecked, it doesn't show, saving you that extra step of having to click on your user account icon every time you turn the computer on. (This is the preference for people like me who are the sole users of a computer.)
>
> In my humble opinion, having this box under "Screen Saver" instead of "User Accounts" is terminally stupid and annoying, on Microsoft's part.

I think sometimes, when you make other adjustments on the computer, the screen saver gets canceled on its own, so you have to set it again. (One time for me, back when I still used it, it was just plain stuck. I moved the time up to 6 minutes, then back to 5 minutes, then clicked OK. That fixed it.)

SCREEN SIZE – You can increase or decrease the appearance of your text on screen by clicking the "+" or "–" icons at lower right. It tells you the percentage. Note that these icons change the appearance of the material on screen; they don't change the actual size of the material. To change the actual size of your text, you'd have to use the Font Size icon in the Font box at top.

For internet pages, you can change screen appearance size from a "Change zoom level" dropdown arrow at lower right, usually for making it bigger so you can read the print.

Or, press CTRL and the + or – key at upper right, to change sizes. Press CTRL and 0 to return to normal size. I find I like this method – less fumbling. Also, a nice feature of some websites (like Wikipedia) is that when you increase the screen size, the site material automatically reforms itself to fit the screen, so you can still read it without having to move past the edge of the screen.

For watching movies, press the F11 key to toggle between full screen size and lesser size.

See also "WINDOW SIZE"

More Screen Space

To get more screen space for text by hiding the major toolbar at top – CTRL+F1. And again, to get it back. [W7 – Click the caret right next to the question mark.]

Or, better, (since usually you want that top toolbar) to get rid of bottom margin and space between pages, double-click on the space between pages (a double arrow shows up if you put your pointer over that area), to toggle back and forth between space and no space in that area between pages.

Full Screen Internet Videos

Most videos on the internet show up in small size, maybe 3 inches by 5 inches. But they have an icon (some variation of a rectangle) at the lower right of the material. Click on it and the screen's image expands to full-screen size. Press Esc key at upper left to get it back to small size. (Sometimes you need to put the pointer on the bottom of the material to make the icons show up there.)

In other situations, pressing the F11 key will toggle the screen back and forth between full size and partial size. And pressing Alt + Enter key will do the same thing.

SCREEN – TWO WINDOWS SIDE BY SIDE – See "VIEW DOCUMENTS SIDE BY SIDE"

SCREEN – VISIBILITY OUTDOORS – Basically, working outdoors in shade is feasible, but in sunlight, is not feasible. Even with the brightness and contrast up all the way, it's hard to see text. Putting your screen text size way up (+ icon at lower right) definitely helps. But seeing your pointer or cursor is still very hard. Maybe some of the newer laptops have screens that work better in sunlight. (Update 2011: Naw, I got a brand new laptop and it's no better in sunlight.)

SCROLL LOCK KEY – At upper right of keyboard, for making arrow keys scroll a text, instead of moving the cursor. Little used these days. In fact, on my computer, whether I press Shift+Scr Lk or Fn+Scr Lk, I don't see it doing anything differently at all. The scroll arrows still work the same. Wikipedia says, *"The Scroll Lock key is little used in almost all current programs and operating systems."*

SCROLLING – At the right of Word documents and other windows there is a scroll bar. Drag the bar up or down to scroll up or down thru your document quickly. Clicking the top or bottom arrow and holding down the left of the mouse also scrolls thru the document, but more slowly. Holding down the up or down arrow key at the lower right of your keyboard also scrolls the document at a steady speed.

I find a very nice middle ground for speed, is to use the Page Down and Page Up keys at the right of the keyboard. It moves pages right along, but not so fast you go way past the page you're looking for.

If you know the page number, just do a CTRL+G, put the page number in, click Go To, and it goes to that page.

If your page size exceeds the width size of the screen, then a horizontal scroll bar also appears at the bottom, so you can drag it left or right to see the rest of the page over at the side. Of course, in such a case you would want to use the zoom function to decrease the size of the page so that you can see the entire width of the page normally.

Usually, if there is no scroll bar, that means you are seeing all there is to see already; if there is a scroll bar, that means there is more to see in that window. You can see this feature in operation by increasing or decreasing the zoom size of a single-page document; as soon as you decrease its size so that you can see the whole page on the screen, the scroll bar disappears.

SEARCH – See "FIND..." or "FINDING..."

SEARCH BOXES – These are little boxes, usually at the upper right, into which you type a word or topic you want the computer to search for. A website search is a common example. The Google search box is amazingly useful for getting information; you type a word in and it brings up a list of websites dealing with that topic. Note that a web search box is NOT case sensitive, nor does your spelling have to be exact; Google is very good at figuring out what you actually wanted. On the other hand, spelling must be exact for a web address box, or an email address, or an iTunes selection, or else you get nothing! In fact, if I can't find an iTunes selection, I google it, to get the correct spelling, and then go back to my iTunes search box and try again.

Another typical use of a search box is for online shopping. After you've typed in a search word for a store, the store's website has its own search box, for their merchandise. Just type in the item you're looking for and it will show you what the store has. For example, under the Best Buy site, type in "iPod" and you'll get a nice display of the different iPods they have.

Remember that to get any search box functional, you need to first click inside it to get your cursor in there to start typing.

Search boxes may show up at in different windows or websites or programs. Word Help (press F1 key) has its own search box at upper left. Sometimes a box has a spyglass or arrow at the right, which you click to launch the search.

But, other times there's just an "x" there. What kind of insane logic is that, you ask? Type in a search word, then "x" it out, accomplishing nothing! Answer: 1) Sometimes it does the search as soon as you type the word in, without your clicking anything (for example, the Start search box at lower left). Or 2) You need to press the Enter key to launch the search.

Search Engine – Default Choice

For my normal search engine, I prefer Google to Yahoo, or AOL. To set your default search engine to the one of your choice:

1. Internet Explorer
2. Next to your current search engine search box at upper right, click the dropdown arrow. ▌
3. Click Manage Search Providers
4. Right-click on your choice (If it's already your default provider, then "Set as Default" is grayed out.)
5. Click "Set as Default", Close

▌ Of course, now all of a sudden my computer no longer has a dropdown arrow there by my current search engine. So, instead, click Tools dropdown arrow > Manage Add-ons > "Search Providers" over on the left > your list of search providers should be on the right >

right-click the one you want > "Set as default" and click "Close" and that makes it your default search provider > if the one you want is not there, click on "Find more search providers" at lower left > it gives you a bunch to pick from (big ones are Google, Yahoo, Bing; my strong preference is Google) > click on choice, Add to Internet Explorer, Add, to get the one you want up into your list, to right-click and set as your default search provider.

It may not show right away in your Manage Add-ons window, but if you close that window and open it again, there it is now in your list of Search Providers.

Also in this window, you can check at lower left to prevent programs from suggesting changes. Or, with a right-click on the name of your current search provider, click "Disable Suggestions," if you don't like that feature.

SEARCH BOX – "START" ICON – The search box under the Start icon at lower left, is VERY useful. In fact, that's my go-to method of finding a document when I forget where it is. It will list not only documents with names matching what you typed in, but it will list documents with text that matches, and, any program names that match. Sometimes it gives you too much, but most often you can find what you're looking for.

For example, if I can't find my chess program, I type in "chess" and it will automatically show any programs with the word "chess" in them, and under that, any files with the word "chess" in them.

Click on it to open it up. Or, right-click it, "Open file location", to find its normal location, for future reference.

Note that your spelling has to be correct. If I type in "girrafe", it will show nothing. If I type in "giraffe", it will show all my documents with the word "giraffe" in them. (However, the box is not case sensitive, so you don't have to worry about getting your capitals right.)

Very often you simply cannot remember what the name of a document was, but you can remember some particular word you used and you can use that to find the document. For example, you're looking for a letter you wrote to somebody, and you get nothing putting in that person's name, but you remember you wrote that a particular movie was "lousy". Type in the name of the movie, or just the word "lousy" and that may do the trick.

If you don't see what you're looking for, you can click "Search Everywhere" [W7 – "See More Results"] just above the search box.

If there are several user accounts on the same computer, the Start search function applies only to the current user's files, not other users' files.

Better Efficiency

In theory, if you put quotation marks around the word or phrase you entered, it will narrow its search to exactly what is inside the quotes, instead of including programs or documents with only partial matches... but, I find that this doesn't really work.

Note that the Start search box needs to be updated occasionally, to work more efficiently. See "INDEX – UPDATING THE START SEARCH BOX". After I did this, I could see a nice difference. I had put in "Elvis" and it gave me tons of stuff, including many documents on religion, which made no sense. But after updating, it listed only documents with the word "Elvis" in them.

Oddly enough, sometimes when you type in a partial match, you find what you want, yet if you type in the full match, you don't! For example, when I type in QuickTime, I don't get the QuickTime player, but if I type in just "Quick", the QuickTime Player program shows at top.

Document Text Search

If using the Start search box doesn't work (maybe it's giving you too many results), you can narrow it a bit by opening your My Documents folder and using its search box at the upper right. If I can't find my Survival Tips document, I put in "Grylls" (Bear Grylls, the host of "Man Versus Wild") and that document comes right up, because it has his name in there.

SEARCH ENGINE – Refers to a website that finds information for you on the internet. Examples are Google, Yahoo, Bing. Google is the most popular and the one I like best. Note that putting a search topic in quotes makes the search engine look for websites that contain all those words in the order you typed them. (Using quotes works better here than in the Start search box.)

SEARCH – IDENTIFYING YOUR LAST STOPPING POINT – A great method of getting back to where you left off in a long essay or text you're working on: Before closing, put "xxx" where you stopped. Then when you next open that document, press CTRL+F and put in "xxx" to find your last stopping point, from which you continue.

Also what I do when working in a huge document, is mark any section I'm still working on and need to get back to at some later point, with "kkk" (easy to recognize) so I can find these unfinished spots easily.

SEARCH – WORD SEARCH – See "FIND (WORD SEARCH)"

SECOND SIDE – PAGES – Printers vary. My previous Epson was a vertical "gravity" feeder (sheets stacked in a tray propped up at an angle, fed from the back of the machine), and the sheets to be backed up with a second side of text were fed head down, blank side up. My current Epson 810 is a "flat tray" feeder (sheets get picked up from a flat position in a tray, from the bottom of the machine), and sheets to be backed up are fed head up, printed side up.

The 810 has automatic two-sided printing, so I usually don't have to worry about how I feed a sheet in for the second side.

For Landscape (horizontal orientation) text or picture, if I have the two-sided feature turned off: First side comes out head to the left. To back up a sheet, it should be loaded in the tray – head to the left, printed side up.

Whatever way your printer feeds, make a note for yourself as to which way a printed sheet should be oriented for backing up – head up or down, printed side up or down.

SECTION BREAKS – These are breaks you can order for a text so that you can change formatting for just a section of the text. For example, if you have a page in one column but want two columns for just a small section of that page, you would click Page Layout at top > Page Setup box > Breaks dropdown arrow > Section breaks > Continuous > then, Columns, Two. Type your two-column text in. Then, select Columns, One, to continue the rest of the text back in the one-column format.

Or, easier, you could type your full text in first, block the desired section, and order up a different column number; that will change just that blocked section to a different column number.

You can also use a section break to have each chapter in a document begin page numbering at 1. [Section Break, then Insert tab at top, Header & Footer, Page Number, Format Page Numbers, Start at 1, OK.] Or you can get a different header for a section of your document. Or you can put a section break at the start and end of a paragraph, block it, and then choose different margins for just that paragraph.

Note that simply changing fonts or typestyles does not require a section break.

I would say section breaks are used mostly for column changes, especially when you have a title at the top of a page, in the middle (one column), followed by two-column text.

Different Types of Section Breaks

There are different types of breaks. The "Continuous" one starts a new section on the same page, like double columns following a centered title. The "Next Page" one starts a new section on the next page, like when you want to immediately move to the next page to start a new chapter in a document, leaving the rest of the current page blank.

Deleting a Section Break

You need to go to the Home tab at top, the Paragraph box, and click the ¶ symbol there. That will show your typing commands throughout your text. The section break command is shown as a double-dotted line with the words "Section Break" in that line. Note that if you put the section break right near the end of a line of text, then it may be reduced to just a couple of dots and you can hardly see it. But if you put the break at a blank line, you can see the double-dotted line clearly with "Section Break" in the middle of it.

To delete a section break, position the cursor right at the beginning of that dotted line, just to the right of the ¶ symbol, and press the Delete key at upper right of your keyboard. That will delete the section break. Then you can click the ¶ symbol again at top to get rid of text commands showing. Remember, you need to get those text commands showing in the first place, to delete a section break; otherwise, you won't know where to position your cursor before pressing Delete.

Note that if you have trouble locating section breaks, you can right-click the Status Bar (the ribbon at bottom where it tells you what page you are on) and in that "Customize Status Bar" window, check "Section" and then that ribbon will include at the far left what section you are on. Scroll down thru your text, and when you see the section number change, that is where the section break is.

Importance of Deleting Section Breaks

If you have moved text from another document, or from the internet, or scanned something in, into your current document, often the material retains its own formatting – margins, columns, whatever. In order to avoid having your current document become a hybrid of different formats, usually you need to delete all the section breaks first, before ordering a single consistent format.

Another example of the importance of deleting section breaks is the case where you have a double column of text but for some reason the right-hand column appears immediately on the right in the middle of the page, instead of waiting for the left-hand column to reach the bottom of the page before starting the right-hand column at the top. It's because you have a section break, or an extra section break, in there. Click ¶ and delete that section break and set it up again the way you want it.

If you try to fix the situation without deleting a section break, you are in for a nightmare of frustration.

SECURITY – See "VIRUS"

I let my anti-virus program deal with security, but it might be a good idea to occasionally use the Windows security program also: Start > Control Panel > Security > Security Center [W7 – System and Security > Action Center] > attend to what it tells you, if you want to. A red band indicates that it's important; a yellow band that you should probably do it when you get around to it.

Note that normally you do not want TWO anti-virus programs; they interfere with each other; but, I think the basic Windows security program that came with Windows, is OK to keep on.

Do not trust some program, claiming to be Windows, that suddenly appears on your computer. In the case above, where you yourself navigated to the Security/Action Center, that should be safe. I currently have a yellow message there that a multi-function printer driver is available for me, but I'm going to ignore it; things are working fine; I don't want anything new messing things up. Also they suggested doing a quick scan. Did that. Took ten minutes. Got "No unwanted or harmful software detected."

Basically, if you have a good anti-virus program, I don't think you even need to bother with Windows security.

SECURITY – ALLOW OR DON'T ALLOW – If a window pops ups asking if you want to allow something or not, my rule of thumb is that if that window popped up as a result of your doing something, allow it (so it can complete what you were trying to do), but if it just randomly comes up, without your having done anything, select "Don't Allow" or "Cancel."

SERVER – Refers to the company that carries out your internet operations. When you enter a term into your internet search box, that request goes from your computer to the server. I think of a server as a big computer center, where all the info is actually stored in many computers, where requests arrive, and information is sent out. Yahoo, for example, would be the server for my email.

SHADING – The shading function – Home tab > Paragraph box > paint can icon – is similar to the highlighting one over to the left – Home tab > Font box > crayon icon – but it is more versatile.

The highlighting function on the left gives you a choice of only 15 different, kinda garish, colors, which will highlight just the text you block. The shading function on the right has many more colors to choose from (including lighter, more pleasing shades), and it can shade either the blocked text only or an entire paragraph all the way across.

Block the text you want shaded > click the dropdown arrow at the right of either the crayon icon or the paint can icon at top > click on your color choice.

Note the two different meanings of the term "highlight" – it can mean blocking the text, or, as used here, it can mean putting a color shading over the text.

Shading All the Way Across

The highlighting function (crayon icon) highlights just the text you blocked. The shading function (paint can icon) can highlight text all the way to the margins.

Highlighting.

Shading.

If you want to use the shading function to shade just the text and not all the way across, after blocking the text, you need to backspace your blocking one spot, so that it doesn't shade all the way across. Whenever your blocking extends one space beyond the end of the text in a line, it will shade all the way across.

This blocking will extend shading to the margins. ←

This blocking will end shading at end of the text.

Note that this "one extra space" distinction also applies to a framing border (Paragraph box at top, farthest lower right icon). The extra space will give you a border around the whole line or paragraph; backspace your blocking one spot, and it will make a border only for the text or word, rather than extend the border to the margins.

Refuses to DELETE Shading or Highlighting

If you've been using shading sometimes and highlighting at other times – as I often do – when you go to delete either and it won't delete, it's usually because you're choosing the wrong one of the two to click.

Also, that extra space beyond the end of a line of text is key. To delete, you have to match not only which of the two functions (Highlighting or Shading) you used originally, but also whether you originally put that extra space in or not.

If it refuses to delete several paragraphs, it's most likely because you've included that extra space at the end of one of those paragraphs; then you have to delete each paragraph separately, usually without that extra space blocked.

If you want to replace the garish highlighting yellow with a softer shading yellow, the shading yellow won't take effect until you replace the highlighting yellow with "No Color" highlighting first.

Also, under the shading function, I always choose No Color, as opposed to the White box at upper left, just in case thru some odd combination of changes, the white stays in effect, and I end up with a single word white inside a shaded line, without noticing it.

Shading Suddenly Won't Shade a Word, but Shades the Whole Paragraph

At one point my default setting for shading got changed. How, I don't know. (I was working with borders at the time, not shading.) To get it back to normal: Block a word > Home tab at top > Paragraph box > Borders and Shading dropdown arrow > Borders and Shading (at bottom of list) > Shading tab > Apply to > "Text", not "Paragraph" > OK. Note that if you don't block a word or text chunk first, that "Apply to" dropdown arrow shows only "Paragraph"; blocking a word first gives you the other option – "Text" – which gives you back your shading feature for parts of texts rather than the whole paragraph.

Shading – Best Ones to Use

Entirely up to your tastes. The only thing I would say is to usually avoid the middle gray shades, since they tend to hide the cursor; when editing; it's hard to see where the cursor is as you run it thru a text shaded in gray.

Certain dark shades automatically put the text into reverse – **like this.**

Clicking "More Colors" at the bottom gives you more choices.

The "Recent Colors" bar is useful, so you don't have to figure out again exactly what shade you used. Also, for an older section already in a shade, if you highlight that section again, and then click on the paint can icon dropdown arrow > Theme Colors > More colors > the Custom tab will usually show, with an arrow, exactly what shade it is.

Shading a Table Cell

Block the cell or cells, then use paint can icon under Paragraph. Same deal as above: You can block just a word in that cell, or the whole cell. I find shading cells very useful; it helps make a table more clear when I shade certain rows or columns.

SHOPPING ONLINE – Ordering online is relatively straightforward, though it takes maybe 5 minutes to go thru the process once you know what you want. You pick your item(s), click "Add to cart," click "Go to checkout," create an account for yourself, fill in credit card info and address for delivery; they give you a review of your order, you click "Submit" or "Place order"; they send you an email confirmation, and your item arrives in the mail a week later.

People's preferences in shopping vary, but I like to check the websites of several different stores, to see their inventory for an item I'm looking for, and then, rather than ordering online, go to the store to buy it... because I don't like waiting, and because I want to see the actual item in front of me. So I tend to shop online, but buy at the store.

There's a website – Shopping.com – that's useful for finding items. Type the item into their main search box.

As usual, if you're brand new to online shopping, it can be confusing. Just stick with it; look for and click the logical buttons. The more you do it, the easier it gets. More and more people do shop online these days.

SHORTCUT KEYS FOR FUNCTIONS – You can execute all kinds of important functions by clicking icons on the toolbar at top. But, you can also use the "Ctrl" command key at lower left, plus a letter, as shortcuts, to do the same function. I find it is easier to use the "Ctrl" key for about twenty of the most frequent operations, namely:

CTRL+S to save
CTRL+P to print
CTRL+F to find a word
CTRL+G to go to a particular page
CTRL+H to replace a word with another
CTRL+X to cut (and move)
CTRL+C to copy
CTRL+V to paste

CTRL+Z to undo the last operation
CTRL+Y to undo the undo and get back to what you had
CTRL+L to left align the text
CTRL+R to right align the text
CTRL+E to center the text
CTRL+J to justify the text

CTRL+B = Bold
CTRL+I = Italic
CTRL+U = Underline

CTRL+1 = Single spaced lines
CTRL+2 = Double spaced lines
CTRL+5 = 1.5 spaced lines

At first it may seem a lot to remember, but I use each of these so often, they are automatic and easy to remember after a while. I like using them instead of icons, because you always have to look up to find icons.

Other Useful Shortcuts at the Top of the Keyboard

Esc = To get out of a current window
F1 = Help
F4 = Repeat last operation

The Office Button (extreme upper left) presumably can be used to order up your own shortcut keys for FUNCTIONS – click Word Options at bottom right of that window > Customize at left [W7 – "File" at upper left > Options > Customize Ribbon] > Keyboard Shortcuts Customize at lower left > – but I haven't been able to figure out how to proceed from there. Don't think it's worth it; you've already got set function shortcuts for practically everything anyway.

Though, I do think ordering your own shortcuts for a few often-used symbols is easier than using Insert and Symbol at the top. See "SHORTCUTS – CUSTOM COMMANDS FOR SYMBOLS" below.

Custom Shortcuts to PROGRAMS, FILES

You can make your own shortcut to any program, or file, or folder, by right-clicking on its name > click Properties > Shortcut tab > at Shortcut Key enter a letter > OK. BUT, I think this is kinda ridiculous. You've already got your desktop icons, Start, and My Documents for getting to items! Assigning CTRL+Alt+letter codes to them also, is typical computer-world confusing redundancy. How are you going to remember all those shortcuts and what letters you used?

SHORTCUTS – ON YOUR DESKTOP – You can put shortcut icons for frequently-used programs, files, whatever, onto your desktop. Very useful; gets you there quickly.

Whether it's a program or folder or document, right-click the name of the program (under Start) or the name of the file > click Send To > "Desktop (Create shortcut)"; that sends an icon for it onto the desktop. Look for it on your desktop, drag it to the position you like. When you double-click on it, it opens the file or program.

Deleting a Desktop Shortcut

Right-click that shortcut icon, Delete. That deletes the shortcut. But, it does NOT delete the folder or program; it just deletes the shortcut; your folder or program is safe. Note that all desktop shortcut icons have a blue arrow at their lower left corner, indicating it is just a shortcut, not the actual file or program. (If it doesn't have a blue arrow, then it's the actual file or program.)

Moving or Renaming an Item After You've Made a Shortcut

Then its shortcut may no longer work. I think that that holds true for programs, but not necessarily for documents. I find document shortcuts can still find the documents even after you move them to a different folder.

But if you rename the document, the shortcut can no longer find it. You have to make a new shortcut with the new name.

I think if you move a major folder – Documents, My Documents, Pictures, Music, Video – Windows may do all sorts of weird things. So don't do that.

And, though there is no shortcut as such involved, the same principle of not moving a file's original location applies to Windows Movie Maker program; moving the location of a stored clip after you've started to put together your movie line is a catastrophe! The clips disappear from your movie line, and you have to start over, unless you can put the clip back into its original storage location with its original name!

Shortcut – To a Website

While on a website, make the window small by clicking on the "Restore Down" button at upper right, click on the website icon at upper left (very left of website address bar, to the left of "http") and drag it to the desktop. Now you have a shortcut icon on the desktop that you can click to get to that site quickly.

SHORTCUTS – CUSTOM SHORTCUTS FOR SYMBOLS – I find using a few custom command shortcuts for symbols is easier than always using the Insert and Symbols icons.

I have these three custom shortcuts:

CTRL+/ for ✓
CTRL+> for →
CTRL+= for ⇨

To Make Your Own CTRL Key Symbol Shortcuts

Insert tab at top > Symbol box at right > Symbol dropdown arrow > More Symbols (you have to click on More Symbols to get your dialogue window up) > find and click on desired symbol to highlight it > click on Shortcut Key at lower left > put the pointer into the "Press new shortcut key" box > press CTRL key + the key of your choice > click Assign > Close.

If you can't find a particular symbol you want under "Font: (normal text)", try the "Wingdings" near the bottom of the dropdown list.

To Remove Shortcut

Say you assigned CTRL+P to give you the ¶ symbol, but then you realize now you can't use CTRL+P for printing! To remove that order: Symbol > More Symbols > click on the symbol > click on Shortcut Key > highlight Current Key > click Remove.

Autocorrect – Symbols

You can also use the autocorrect feature as a good shortcut for symbols. See "AUTOCORRECT – SYMBOLS". I have a few more useful ones under this function. (Didn't want to use CTRL plus a letter, because I'm running out of easy-to-remember letters.)

Shortcut Key Forgotten

If you forget what you previously ordered as a shortcut key for a particular symbol, click Insert > click Symbol dropdown arrow > click More Symbols > click on that symbol > Shortcut Key box at lower left, and then it tells you what the shortcut key is, in the "Current keys" box at middle left.

SHUT DOWN – See "START" > "Shut Down Options" and "COMPUTER ON / OFF – SIMPLIFY"

SIDE BY SIDE – DOCUMENTS OR WINDOWS – See "VIEW DOCUMENTS SIDE BY SIDE"

SIDEBAR – See "GADGETS"

SIDEWAYS PAPER ORIENTATION – See "LANDSCAPE ORIENTATION"

SIZE – TEXT – Home tab at top > Font box > click the dropdown arrow in the box next to the font type at upper left of the box > click on the size number you want. That will make the text from that point on, entered in that selected size. Text sizes are typically in the 9-point to 12-point range. *Newsweek* is in 9 or 10-point size, I think. Most of this manual is in 11-point size, though reduced to 90%.

If you block a section of text and then select a size, it will put that blocked text into that size. If you put your cursor into a random text and continue typing from there, it will continue in the same size.

Besides selecting a size from the box at top, you can also increase or decrease a size by pressing CTRL+ a bracket key (either the] key to increase size by one point at a time, or the [key to decrease it one point at a time). Note that if you have different sizes in your text, using this one-point-at-a-time increase/decrease function, will increase/decrease sizes yet keep the differences. In other words, if you have a mixture of 9-point and 10-point text, and increase it one point, you'll now have 10-point and 11-point text. Very useful feature if you want to retain different sizes throughout a document.

Wherever you put your cursor in your text, that small font-size box up there will show what your font size is at that point. Scroll your cursor down thru your text of different sizes and you'll see how it changes.

If you block a text section, that box shows what size you have. If that blocked section includes different sizes, then that box shows no number.

Half-sizes

You can do half sizes, but instead of selecting a point-size number at top, you need to type it in – click on the number in that small size box, delete it, then type in your desired number (like 9.5 or 10.5), then press Enter. Cannot do less than half-sizes, like 8.3, for example. If you have a mixture of sizes including half-sizes, the increase/decrease-by-one-point (CTRL+bracket key) function works nicely. Your 9's become 10, your 9.5s become 10.5.

SLEEP MODE – This is a state you can put the computer in so that it is not completely off but only in "Sleep" mode. You can wake it up very quickly to work on tasks, instead of having to wait for the computer to power up.

You can order up Sleep (or Hibernation) as a one-time deal: Start > Shut-off arrow > Sleep or Hibernation. To have Sleep as your default setting when pressing the power button or closing the lid, see "COMPUTER ON / OFF – SIMPLIFY"

SLOW COMPUTER – If you are doing too many things at once – like running a virus sweep, and making a movie with Windows Movie Maker, etc., all at the same time – it DOES slow down the computer.

Also, after a few years, I believe, the computer tends to pick up stuff that slows it down. Your computer is like a closet – the more cluttered it is, the longer it takes to find things.

They do sell commercial programs that claim to clean up your computer to speed it up. Don't know how well they work. I'm wary. Many companies try to scare you into buying stuff you don't really need. Myself, my computer is speedy enough. Rule of thumb: if it's not broken, don't try to fix it. If it ever slows down too much, I plan to bring it to Best Buy, Geek department; they'll be able to do a clean-up for me, or give me the best advice. Staples also provides clean-ups, for about $10.

There are a few things you can do to speed it up a bit:

– Start > right-click Computer > Properties > Advance System Settings, in left pane > in Performance area, click "Adjust for Best Performance" [i.e. speed] > wait. Now things should move a bit faster, though graphics are lower quality.

I tried this, but then the text on my screen was no longer crisp and clear, so I went back to the same window, and clicked instead "Let Windows Choose What's Best for My Computer."

– You could move large files (especially audio and video) to an external computer. See "EXTERNAL HARD DRIVE". (When I had 50 GB free space left out of 160 GB on my old computer, the speed was fine.)

– You can do a defragging, which organizes file locations on the hard drive better – See "DEFRAGGING" (under "MAINTENANCE").

– You can set your graphics to be basic rather than fancy. Basic is fine; "Aero" and others are overkill, and may slow things down a bit. Right click blank part of desktop > Personalize > Window Color and Appearance > choose Windows Vista Basic > OK. (You may have to click "Open classic appearance properties for more color options" to get that window up.)

– Or, you could un-install Vista (or Windows 7) and re-install it; that tends to give things a fresh start. Just remember that you have to make a copy of everything on an external hard drive, and then re-install ALL your programs and files, after re-installing Vista.

If you're uneasy about doing this, as I would be, I think having Best Buy do it for you, is a good route. I talked to them recently and they do an Operating System installation for $160. And they have a one year service contract for $200 (including the installation) that covers all kinds of things. But, for now, my computer is fine.

I note that it's much better to visit Best Buy during the day on weekdays, rather than weekends; weekends are very busy.

See also – "VIRUS – PROTECTION"

Speed/Performance Index

You can explore this feature. Windows rates your computer's performance. While online, Start > Control Panel > System and Security > System > next to "Rating" (middle of page) is your computer's rating and "(Your) Windows Experience Index (needs to be refreshed)"; click that > "Refresh Now" > and it gives you your current rating. 1 is lousy; 7.9 is tops. Your overall rating is actually not an average but is the lowest of your rating categories.

I refreshed mine. Changed from 4.6 to 4.7. And the other categories stayed at 5.0, 5.9, 5.9, 6.8. My thought – as usual, much ado about nothing; if it ain't broke, don't bother trying to fix it.

SOFTWARE PROGRAMS – CDs – A software program usually comes on a CD disk, which you insert into your computer; it gives you instructions on how to install the program into your computer, and then the program is on your hard drive and you can use it.

Some software you can install only once; some a few times. Companies don't want people to lend their programs to all their friends to install for free.

Many old CD programs will not work for Vista. They were made for older OS's (operating systems), i.e., Windows 98, 2000, ME, XP. Some new programs come on a DVD disk instead of a CD, since they need more disk capacity. If you have an old computer without a DVD-playing bay, you're out of luck.

SOLID STATE COMPUTERS – Don't know much here, but I understand that they are much less susceptible to physical shock and damage than regular computers, since they have no moving parts. But, they usually have less capacity. You might look into them, if your laptop is often subject to bumps or drops. Check with Best Buy. Guy there showed me one.

SONY PRODUCTS – PHONE NUMBER – 1 877 865-7669

SORTING (ALPHABETIZING & NUMBERS) – See "ALPHABETIZING"

SORTING – FOLDERS OR DOCUMENTS – You can have your list of folders or documents sorted by different categories – by name (alphabetically), by date, by size, by type. You have to click Views tab [W7 – "Change your view" at right] dropdown arrow and "Details", to get those 4 categories up. (Then later, you can go back to your preference for how you want those icons to appear – I like "List".)

While in a folder window, click one of those 4 categories at top; that will sort documents or folders by that category. Click the same category again and it will put them in reverse order.

I like documents alphabetically ordered and folders listed before documents, which I think is the default setting anyway. Occasionally clicking Date is helpful, if I can't remember which document of several is the one I just worked on recently.

You can sort by more advanced categories. Click View at top between Edit and Tools, Sort By. Or, right-click on any empty spot in a folder and click on "Sort by" to open these same options. But I think going beyond those 4 basic categories, is overkill, unless you've got some special situation.

Filtering

Filtering is getting a list of documents or folders according a particular date or date limitation. While in a folder, put the cursor on a category at the top (Date modified, Type, etc.), a dropdown arrow now appears, click on it, make your selection. I don't find this function particularly useful at all. I suppose every once in a while you need to know what you worked on, on August 12, or "earlier this month," but not usually.

SOUND RECORDER ON COMPUTER – You can record audio sound directly into your computer, either from a device, or with a microphone, or even without a mic. See "MUSIC" > "3. Recording Directly into Computer"

SOUND VOLUME – COMPUTER – I usually adjust volume by pressing the + or – buttons on the computer, upper left, over the keyboard (on my Sony Vaio laptop). (The Mute button is just to the left of those.)

You can also adjust volume by pressing the Fn key at lower left and, at top, the F2 key for mute, F3 for decrease, F4 for increase. (I have to do it this way on my new computer, because it does not have separate buttons at top like my old Sony Vaio.)

You can also adjust volume by clicking on the speaker icon at the lower right of your taskbar; that brings up a vertical bar which you can raise or lower. Often, other programs (like my Studio one) have their own volume controls. So occasionally you'll lose your sound volume because one of these has been adjusted, automatically or by accident. Or you accidentally pressed a Mute button somewhere. Then you look everywhere for any volume controls, mess around for three hours, click something by accident, and it's fixed. It's just that simple!!

(Recently, my + and – volume buttons suddenly, after 4 years of working fine, stopped doing anything. I had to use the speaker icon. Three days later, the buttons suddenly worked again. Didn't do anything, as far as I know. Maybe when I did a re-start, that fixed it.)

Different Volumes for Different Programs

Overkill, for me. But to set different volumes: Start > Control Panel > Hardware and Sound > Sound.

SPACE (ON THE COMPUTER) – See "MAINTENANCE TASKS"

SPACE (IN A TEXT) – See "HARD SPACE"

SPACING BETWEEN LINES – See "LINE SPACING"

SPACING BETWEEN LETTERS – You can squeeze letters in, or expand them.

Block text > click Home tab at top > Font box > dropdown arrow at lower right > Character Spacing tab [W7 – "Advanced" tab] > dropdown arrow for Spacing > select Condensed or Expanded > OK. To the right of Spacing you can condense or expand letters more by choosing higher numbers; the default number is 1 point. But if you do go that route, I think it doesn't really look that good. In fact I'm not a big fan of this feature. I think fonts never really look right if they are condensed or expanded.

On the other hand, I recently tried selecting 90% next to the Scale option, and it looks pretty good.

Here's an example of text at 100%.
Here's an example of condensed text – naw.
Here's an example of expanded text – naw.
Here's an example of text scaled at 80% – naw.
Here's an example of text scaled at 90% – not bad... not bad.

In fact, this manual is typed in 11 point and 10 point font, reduced to 90%.

Microsoft automatically "kerns" letters (adjusts the amount of space between certain combinations of characters) above a certain size, so that letters look more evenly spaced.

SPAM – Very hard to avoid. Once you order something over the internet, or if you order something for free, your email address might become available to many marketers. You just have to check your spam emails quickly and delete them. (For me, clicking on the word "Empty", deletes them all at once.) See also "E-MAIL PROBLEMS" > "SPAM".

I recently took perverse pleasure in letting my spam folder build up to over 1,000 spams, and then deleted them all, without ever looking at them. I'm at the point of feeling that there is no point in even looking at them; so seldom is anything of significance in there. From this point on, I think I'll only check my spam folder if I'm expecting a particular email, but don't get it.

Scams

Learn to identify them! AR writes, how do you know a finance-related email asking for personal financial info, is real or fake? Answer – they are ALL fake! No real financial institution asks for your ID, password, account numbers, etc., unless you contacted them first!! Scammers try to dress themselves up as legit. If you have ANY suspicions, play it safe.

Interestingly, for me, a former teacher, I can spot them almost 100% of the time based SOLELY on grammar, spelling, and use of idiom. It's incredible how badly scammers do here. They repeat letters, capitalize when they shouldn't, leave extra spaces, etc., etc. Legit institutions ALWAYS have solid grammar, spelling, typing, and proper idiom.

I don't remember for sure, but when you first start with Internet Explorer, I think it offers you a "Phishing Filter." (Phishing means trying to find out info on you.) Have it on. AR says it's a "very non-obtrusive safety net." While on the internet, click Safety tab at right, SmartScreen filter, Turn On/Off SmartScreen Filter, OK.

SPEED – See "SLOW COMPUTER"

SPELLING – Windows automatically underlines in red any word that is misspelled (if it doesn't correct it automatically in the first place, which it does for many, many words). For such an underlined word, put the cursor on it, and right-click. It gives you a list of suggested corrections, and if you click on one, it puts that one into your text, replacing your misspelled one. Try it, for example, on the word "mispelled"; at the top it will show the correct spelling with two s's.

Right-click on the word, Add to Dictionary, to get a name or other word you know IS spelled correctly (like a foreign name) into the spelling dictionary; that's it, and thereafter it no longer gets underlined in red.

Checking a Finished Document

Instead of scrolling thru a document to check all the underlined-in-red words, you can also click the Review tab at top, Proofing box, Spelling & Grammar. That will show you your red-underlined words in a window at the right, and you can fix each one and move to the next. A little less eye strain this way.

(Sometimes when you click on Spelling & Grammar, it won't give you an option window; it just checks your spelling and that's all. Press F7 key at top; that usually gives you the option window. Or, keep fiddling around, switching documents, go to the bathroom and come back, and usually, suddenly, that window is back.)

See also "GRAMMAR".

Spelling in a Website Search, or E-Mail

In a website search, spelling does not have to be exact. Search engines will offer you corrections, suggestions, good guesses. But, for eMail addresses, you need to be exact in your spelling or else the eMail will NOT go through!

For spelling within one of your emails, I think some email providers have a spell check button at left; I looked everywhere, and I could not find one in my email setup. What I do, is write important letters in a regular word document (so it will redline errors), and then copy it to the email.

SPLIT SCREEN – See "VIEW DOCUMENTS SIDE BY SIDE"

SPORTS ALERT!! – If you've taped a big sports event and you plan to sit down and watch it later, be careful when you open up Yahoo (or whoever your server is) to check your email! The result may be already shown prominently on the opening page, ruining your watching pleasure!

SPORTS – YAHOO – There's great info here. Click on what you want. For example, for baseball, click on MLB, and then on yesterday's date at upper left, to get results, which they give in summary or detailed format (box scores), etc.

Also, I really like the Stats icon at top. It shows you the league leaders in order, all the way down. Click on a particular stat at top, like Steals, and it shows you, in order, the leaders all the way down. (It also shows all the stats for each player).

SPREAD-OUT WORD SPACING – See "JUSTIFYING TEXT"

SQUEEZING TEXT – See "SPACING BETWEEN LETTERS"

START ICON – The "Start" button is the Windows four-colored flag icon at farthest bottom left. This is a normal way to access your programs, (though not for me, because I prefer keeping shortcut icons of my most frequently used programs on my desktop, and accessing them from there). (Instead of clicking on that Start icon, you can also press the flag key at the lower left of your keyboard to open up the same Start options.)

When you click on Start, Windows shows you your list of programs, supposedly with your most frequently used programs at the top of the list (I say "supposedly" because I find no consistency here at all). If you click "All Programs," you can scroll down to see your entire list. Click on your choice to open it. (Note that there is an alphabetical list, followed down below by yet another alphabetical list of programs under folders as you scroll further down!)

On the right of the Start window, are major categories to click on and open. The one I use most frequently here is "Control Panel," to make adjustments to my computer settings for hardware, appearance, programs, internet, clock, etc. Besides "Control Panel," I rarely use any of the rest of the categories listed here, because they are redundant. I prefer getting to programs thru my desktop shortcut icons rather than the list here.

Start Search Box

The search box on the lower left is very useful for helping you find stuff. It's my go-to place for finding things. Best Buy Geek guy confirmed its value to me; he said he uses it "all the time." See "SEARCH BOX – 'START' ICON".

Shut Down Options

Besides just shutting down by clicking Shut Down, you have several options after clicking the arrow to the right of Shut Down: "Switch User" (if someone else wants to use the computer for a while, it keeps your programs open), "Log off" (Windows saves your work and your settings and returns to the Welcome screen), "Lock" (no one else can access your material), "Restart", and "Sleep".

Start Button Disappears

I never had this happen to me, but I read that if the Start button disappears, you can get it back by pressing the Esc and CTRL keys at the same time.

Deleting a Program from the Start List

The list of programs on the left are essentially shortcuts to the programs. If you want to delete one, right-click on it and click "Remove from this list." The program itself remains somewhere, should you want to access it later on. Type its name into the Start search box, and it should appear up at the top of the Start panel. (Or, type it in and press Enter key to bring the program up immediately.)

STATUS BAR – This is the narrow bar just above your taskbar at the bottom. At the left, it shows what page, out of how many, you are on, and the total number of words in your document. At the right, it shows you zoom level controls. If you right-click on the status bar, it brings up a "Customize Status Bar" window.

It's usually best to stick with the default setup here, but you can change stuff if you want. Like if you want to know, besides word number, what line number, or section number you're on.

STILL CAPTURE – See "DVD – STILL CAPTURE"

STRIKETHROUGH FONT – If you want to have a text "crossed out" with a single line through it, that feature is right up on the top in the Font box – the ~~abc~~ icon. (That icon shows a double line strikethrough, but it actually gives a ~~single line strikethrough~~.) For an actual ~~double line strikethrough~~, click the arrow at lower right of the Font box > Font tab > click Double Strikethrough > OK.

STOCK MARKET – ON DESKTOP – Click the gadgets icon (+ sign in oval icon at extreme upper right; or, click Start, type in "Gadgets"); right-click stock market icon, and click Add. It shows the current Dow Jones number ($INDU).

STOPPING A PRINT JOB – Most printers now have a button on the printer itself that stops a print job immediately. Mine has a "Cancel" option on the display screen of the printer. (My printer years ago did not have such a button and you'd have jump hoops in the computer to stop a print job.) See also "Cancelling a Print Job" under "PRINTING"

STUDIO – This is a movie-making program that you can buy. $100 or so. Takes a while to learn. Would not recommend it if you like to make only relatively simple family movies; use Windows Movie Maker instead. But if you are into making films, I think this program is the best out there. Can do all kinds of things. Pinnacle, now under a company called Avid, puts it out. I have their latest version – "Studio 14."

It can be supremely frustrating though. Two big concepts to know:

1) Make your movie in segments. The more complex your film is, the more things can go wrong. But if you take a 5-minute segment, and burn a video file of that segment to your computer hard drive, that sets it with all its effects (sound levels, slo-mo, music, transitions, etc., etc.) so that the program does not have to laboriously re-render those effects every time you work on it. Re-import that set segment into your movie line, as a set segment, and go on to your next segment. Otherwise, things get exponentially more complex, time-consuming, and subject to anomalies and glitches.

2) Don't re-name or move your clips from their original storage location. Otherwise, the program can't find them and they disappear from your movie line, and the hours of work you did are lost, unless you can find those clips and put them back where they were, with their exact original names.

For strictly audio editing using the Studio program, see "MUSIC / AUDIO TRANSFERS THRU A COMPUTER" > 6) STUDIO .

STYLES – These are standard styles of formatting text, under the Home tab and Styles box. You select one of the formatting styles (or block a text and then select a style) and it will put the text into that set format, with titles, line-spacing, etc. I never particularly liked these; never use them; like to do my own formatting.

SUDDEN UNWANTED FUNCTION – If you accidentally hit a key and it performs some function you do not want – and this happens quite often, because you hit the CTRL key and a letter, instead of the Shift key and letter – usually just CTRL+Z it back to what you had. Or x out the function window you accidently ordered.

SUBSCRIPT – Subscript is text that runs lower and smaller than normal text. Subscript is used, for example, for chemical formulas – $C_6H_{12}O_6$. To order subscript, click Home tab > Font box > click the subscript icon – x_2 – to get the next character in subscript size and position. Click that same icon again to return to regular text.

SUPERSCRIPT – Superscript is text that is smaller and slightly higher than your normal text. Exponents in math, or numbers indicating a footnote[13], are examples. Click on the Superscript icon to get the next letter or number in superscript. (Home tab > Font box > x^2) Click on that icon again to return to regular text.

Note that Windows automatically superscripts certain items, like 1st and 2nd.

SURGE PROTECTION – You definitely should have one of those power strip surge protectors. Was once told power surges are a common problem for messing up computers. But Geek gal told me what happens if there is a power surge, is that your power cord black box gets ruined as it protects the computer, rather than the computer itself getting ruined. Geek gal says it's designed to self-destruct, to protect the computer, if too much power is coming thru.

Try to avoid using the computer when there is a thunderstorm. (Or use it on battery power, unplugged.)

SYMBOLS / CHARACTERS – To insert a symbol or odd character, click Insert tab at top > Symbols box at far right > click the Symbols dropdown arrow > click More Symbols > Symbols tab > find and click on desired symbol, and that inserts it into your text at the point of your cursor.

Next to Font, you have Normal Text, where you can find most things, but you can find other odd stuff, like different kinds of arrows, at the end of that list, under Wingdings.

Hard-to-Find Ones

Symbols are often surprisingly hard to find; there are so many of them. Overkill, as usual. If you use certain ones frequently, it's a good idea to note somewhere where they are located (how many columns over, how many columns down) for future reference. The initial window that opens up when you click Symbols does list 20 of your most recently used choices, which you can click on without going thru a long search.

¢ is 6 down, 2 over.

ñ is 12 down, 1st column.

pi – Π – 23 rows down, 2nd last column. You could block it and change it to Times New Roman font, for a nicer-looking one – π .

SYMBOL SHORTCUT KEYS – See "SHORTCUTS – CUSTOM SHORTCUTS FOR SYMBOLS"

SYNC – Refers to transferring music to an external device, like an iPod or MP3 player. It means synchronizing, or matching, your music from your computer to the music on your external device.

SYSTEM RESTORE – See "RESTORE SETTINGS"

TABS – IN YOUR TEXT – When you press the Tab key at upper left of your keyboard, the text indents itself for that line. The default indent is .5 inch. Each time you press Tab, the line moves over another half-inch.

You can change the size of the tab: Home tab at top > Paragraph box, click drop-down arrow at lower right > click Tabs at lower left > click "Clear All" at lower right > enter desired tab distance under "Default Tab Stops" at upper right > OK. That's it; from that point on, all your tabs will be the size you ordered. (I like .2)

You can change all the tabs in a document at once, by blocking the whole document, click Clear All in the dialogue window, then select your new size, OK.

You can delete an individual tab just like you would delete a letter, with the Backspace or Delete keys.

You can also use your mouse to set tabs, or indents, by dragging a slider on the ruler at top. See "RULER AT TOP". I don't like this technique; very inexact.

Automatic Tab Indent for First Line of Paragraphs

I prefer doing tabs manually, but automatic tab indents can be quite convenient. When you press Enter to end a paragraph, a tab indent is automatically inserted for the first line of your new paragraph.

Took me a long time to figure out how to do this. I do not think you can do it thru the paragraph box (where you can set tabs and whole-paragraph indents, but not automatic first line tabs). Turns out you need to use the ruler at top:

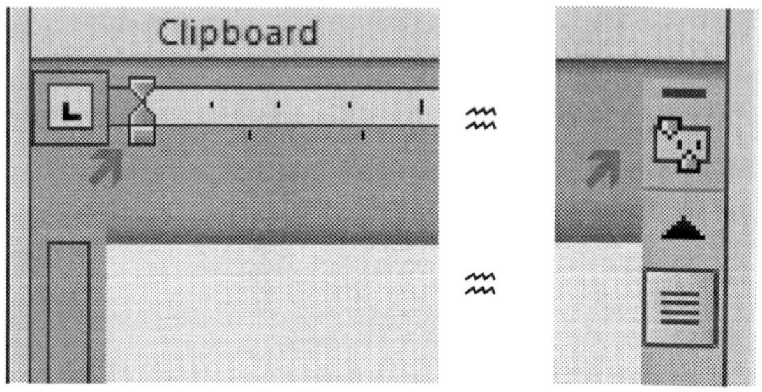

At upper right, click the small "View Ruler" icon just above your vertical scroll bar arrow, to show the ruler > at upper left, click on the top part of the slider (looks almost like an hourglass; shows "First Line Indent" if you hover the pointer on it) > drag that top part to your desired spot > that's it. Now the first line of each new paragraph will be indented the distance between the bottom slider and the top slider, without your having to press the Tab key.

The concept is this: That left slider has lower (Left Indent) and upper (First Line Indent) sections, sitting on top of each other, so that the left edge of your text and of the first line of a paragraph, are the same; if you drag the upper part over to the right, now the first line of each new paragraph will jump over to the right, automatically indented that distance, each time you press the Enter key for a new paragraph.

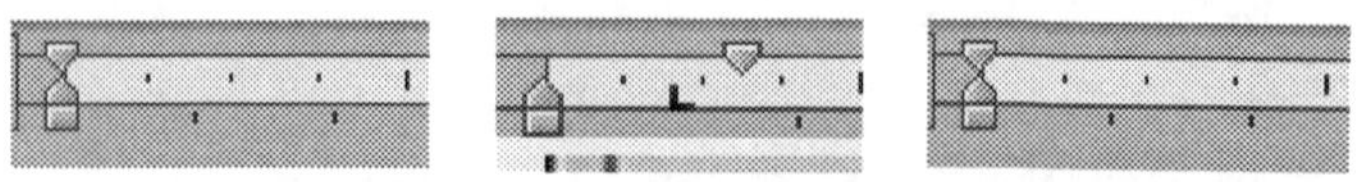

If you want to get rid of that automatic action, you must drag that top part back over on top of the lower part of the slider at the left, so that they again match exactly.

TAB KEY – TO MOVE TO NEXT INFORMATION FIELD – When you're filling out a form online – your name, address, whatever – pressing the tab key moves the cursor to the next category. Easier than using the touch pad or mouse.

Tab Key in a Table

If you are in a table, pressing the Tab key likewise, instead of indenting the line, moves your cursor to the next cell.

(At one point, when I was not in a table, every time I pressed the Tab key, it would move me down a paragraph, as though it were in a table. I remembered that I had originally moved that text from a table, so I figured that even though the table was no longer there, the text I had moved from the table came with an embedded invisible table. I started over, blocking each paragraph individually and moving it, and then it was OK. Tab key now produced an indent like it's supposed to. The key factor is that when you move text out of a table, you need to block only the text, not one space past it, or else the embedded table (invisible) will come with it.)

TABBED WEBSITE BROWSING – When browsing websites I've always use the big left and right arrow icons at the far upper left, to get back to a site; that is still my preference.

However, you can also navigate among websites by clicking on the folder tabs for sites that appear at the very top, going across... except that in order to get successive site tabs to go across, you have to first click, each time, the New Tab blank box just to the right of your latest tab (or, press Ctrl+T), then bring up a new site. Same for links you click on – click New Tab first and the site will appear in a new tab; whereas, if you don't click New Tab, the new site will simply replace your current tab... usually.

With those tabs going across, you can click on any one of them to get back to a particular site. (Or, click the "x" at the upper right of a tab, to close it.)

Tabbed browsing is ON as a default setting. If you want it off: Tools > Internet Options > General tab > Tabs > Settings > uncheck "Enable Tabbed Browsing" > OK > OK. Now, those site tabs no longer appear and you have to use the big left/right arrows to browse to sites you've visited. Note that you have to re-start the computer to have your new setting take effect.

(Even with your tabbed browsing off, you can still make use of your Favorites bar, the next toolbar down from the top. Those tabs stay there.)

With the tabbed browsing on, there are other options to check if you wish, under Tabs > Settings, but to me it's just typical Microsoft overkill, far more confusing than helpful.

TAB CHOICES AT TOP – See "TOOLBAR"

TABLES (GRIDS) – Using tables (grids) can be very useful for keeping information organized. For example:

Name	**Month**	**Income**	**Expenses**	**Notes**
Bill	Jan	$951	$125	Good month
Bob	Jan	$630	$112	Needs improvement
Bruce	Jan	$845	$119	Good
Bozo	Jan	$23	$2,457	Boss's son, humph

To insert a table into your text: With your cursor at the point you want the table inserted, click Insert tab at top > Table dropdown arrow > click Insert Table > pick the number of columns and rows you want, select Fixed width or Autofit > OK. I usually like Autofit; that way the cells expand as you type inside them.

It does take some practice to get familiar with how to make adjustments and get exactly what you want.

A	ab	abc	abcd	abcde	Cells expand automatically
					Pressed Enter here↓ to expand down.

Add or Delete Rows or Columns

While under the Insert tab, position the cursor somewhere within the current table and left-click; that automatically puts up at very top center the "Table Tools" tab, which consists of two tabs below it: Layout and Design. Click Layout tab > Rows & Columns box at left > click on Delete dropdown arrow > and make your selection, to delete rows or columns, or to add them to top, bottom, left, or right of your cursor.

You can also add rows by positioning the cursor at the end of a row and pressing the Enter key. Pressing tab key at the end of a row and holding it down, will add rows more quickly. Pressing the F4 repeat key at top will delete further rows or columns more quickly.

You can delete text using the Backspace or Delete keys, but to delete a whole table with its grid lines, you need to block it first, then press the Delete key. Note that whenever you delete a row, column, or table, you delete all the text inside also. Do a CTRL+Z if you delete something accidentally.

Adjustments

You can make various adjustments to your table. For example, to make a cell bigger, right click anywhere inside the table > Table Properties > Cell tab, up the number in the "Preferred width" box > OK.

Or, you can also make a cell bigger, horizontally, without text inside it, by pressing Shift, CTRL, and Space key all at once to enter "hard" spaces. You'll see the cell line move over just as though you were typing text in under Autofit. If you press the Enter key, then the cell will expand downwards.

To change the size of all the cells at once, either width or height, with cursor inside the table, under Layout tab, go to "Select" [W7 – "File"] dropdown arrow at upper left > Select – "Table" > make adjustment using the scroll arrows inside the Cell box; you can see the cells change size as you use the arrows. You can also type in an exact desired width and height, then press Enter key.

If you want to manually erase certain lines, making certain individual cells bigger than others, under Table Tools > Design tab > Eraser icon at right > you can drag the eraser down and literally erase lines by dragging the icon directly onto a line you want to erase and clicking, to eliminate them, one by one. Here, I knocked out three lines to make my top row cells bigger:

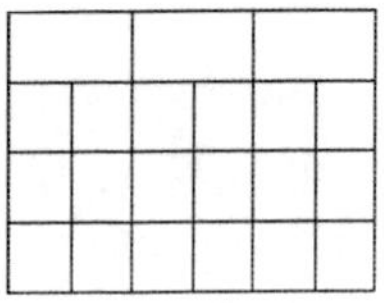

You can also shade cells or rows or columns. Or, under the Design tab, you can change the width or color of the lines.

Converting Text into a Table

You can put a table around existing text: Block your text first > Insert tab > Table > Convert Text to Table > pick number of columns > separate text at paragraphs > and it puts each paragraph of text into a separate cell. Takes some practice to get what you want. Don't know if it's worth the trouble, but if you have, for example, a list of animals, and you decide you want to get them in a grid, with each having its own cell into which you can type further info –

Dogs, Cats, Horses, Pigs, Wolves

Block that line, do the convert operation, picking AutoFit to contents, three columns, separate text at commas (in this case), and you automatically get:

Dogs	Cats	Horses
Pigs	Wolves	

Removing a Grid Already Around a Text

Block the table > Table Tools > Layout tab > Data box > Convert to text > Separate text at (pick the character you want to use; usually it's Tab) > OK. That removes the grid and leaves the text spaced as it was but without the grid lines.

Misc. Tips

Instead of moving your cursor slowly thru the text to get to the next cell, simply press Tab to move thru faster.

If you suddenly get a row that's bigger than others (happens sometimes, don't know why), then delete that row, and add a (proper-sized) row by simply going to end of the previous row and pressing Enter.

TABLE – CORRUPTED – Once in a while, after working on a table extensively, it will show "...cannot complete save due to a file transmission error." It might make a "rescue" document, which will show up under your "Documents" folder, but it may not have saved all you recently did.

At any rate, once this "corruption" occurs, the document from then on will, intermittently, do the same thing, and you have close the document without saving it. And open it up again and enter those changes again. Real pain. Sometimes it's easier to just redo the whole table from scratch. Once that "flaw" gets into your table, I think it's there for good.

What I do is this: When working on a big table, especially one where I've gotten this "file transmission error" message in the past, I save very frequently, so that if it refuses to save at one point, I can close the document and I'll have everything OK except for the last bit. Then I re-open it and redo that last bit. Most often, at that point, it does allow Saving; the "file transmission error" rarely shows up twice in a row.

Or, if I've entered new info, go to save it, and it refuses, I block the new material, CTRL+C it, close the document without saving, open it up again, and then paste in the new material. And then it allows me to save the document, with the new material. At least that way, usually, I don't have to re-type the new material.

TABLES – GRAPHS – You can make some nice-looking graphs – bar graphs, pie charts, etc. – by clicking Insert tab > Illustrations > Chart, choose a style, click OK, and it puts up a basic graph on the left and a data entry window on the right. For example, in the bar graph below you can enter new data for each colored bar and the bar will automatically move up or down to reflect your entry. Makes for a more professional presentation.

Now, it takes considerable practice to learn all the ins and outs of this feature. If you use graphs frequently, you may want to spend the time. Personally, as neat as they look, it's not worth it to me. I would spend hours learning it, for what? One chart per year?

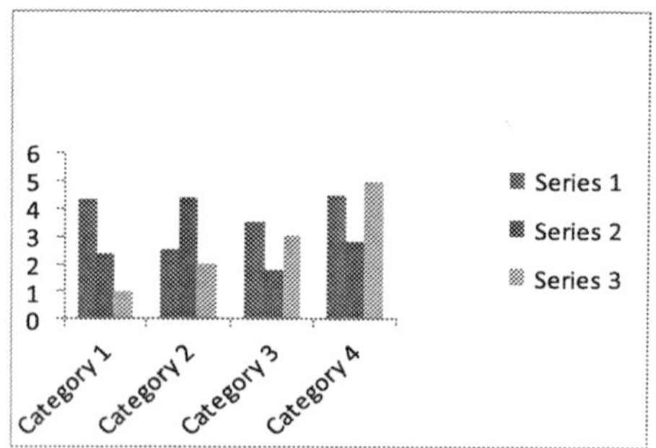

"Chart Area" Popup Icon

A small rectangular icon, saying "Chart Area", kept popping up all over my document. If you click on it, it disappears, but it still keeps popping up elsewhere later. Very annoying. After experimenting for a while, it seems that once you position your pointer any place inside a chart, that icon just keeps popping up everywhere, like it's saying ANYWHERE in your document is a "chart area," UNTIL you click in your text somewhere and start typing. Then it disappears, and stays gone until you put your pointer again into a chart... No, wait, it's still popping up every time I put the pointer on the scroll bar slider at the right!

Looked everywhere for a setting somewhere; no luck. Finally figured a way to get rid of it: Click inside the chart > press the Delete key at upper right, to temporarily delete it > move your pointer several paragraphs away from the chart > then CTRL+Z to get the chart back. Now you don't get the "Chart Area" icon when your pointer touches the scroll bar slider. And from that point on, you should avoid putting the pointer into the chart, or it will start all over again.

Typical Microsoft: Marvelous skill in creating an extremely complex program, but no concern for the cries of anguish from the consumer being terrorized by the "Chart Area" icon.

Update: Tried putting a section break before and after the chart. Nope, that didn't work either. I'm going ahead and cutting the chart, putting it into a separate document, then when my big document is all finished, I'll transfer it back into the big document.

TABLE OF CONTENTS – When typing a table of contents, numbers right-align at the end of the line better if you extend your periods from the word to the page number by alternating periods and spacebars, rather than just pressing on the period key.

Atoms..17
Atoms 17

Hah, NO! They lined up perfectly on screen, but printed out just as crooked. Tried all kinds of things. No luck.

Ho ho. Here's how to do it (I googled the problem and found an answer):

Home tab > Paragraph box > dropdown arrow > Tabs at lower left > set Tab Stop Position at the number of inches from the left margin you want the page number to land (for my table of contents for this manual, 2.4"; I also set my 3 columns .3" spacing apart) > set Default Tab Stops at 0 > set Alignment at "Right" > pick #2 leader > OK.

Now when you hit Tab, dots go instantly right across to the spot, and you just type in the number. If it's a single, double, or triple digit number, the dots adjust automatically, and you end up with the column of numbers perfectly aligned.

TASKBAR – This is the bar along the very bottom of screen. At far lower left, it has the Start button (colored Microsoft flag); in the middle, it shows programs, files, or websites you're currently working on; on the right, it has active program icons; and then on the far right, it has the time of the day.

Whenever you open up a program (Microsoft Word, Windows Media Player, a website... whatever), its icon automatically gets put onto the taskbar. Then, as you continue to work with other items, it puts each one's icon, in turn, onto the taskbar. Put your pointer on an item icon there on the taskbar and up pops up a thumbnail image, or the name, of that item. Click it, and it brings the program up onto the screen, replacing what is currently there. To delete an icon from the taskbar, right-click it, Close [W7 – Close Window].

So, basically, the taskbar shows items you're currently working on, so you can click on them and get them up on the screen quickly.

Over on the right also is an arrow pointing left [W7 – pointing up]; click on that and it reveals more programs that are normally hidden.

You can right-click on a taskbar blank spot, click Properties, and check or uncheck options. If you're happy with what you have, forget it, just leave it alone. [W7 – Has larger icons than Vista as the default size. I right-clicked the taskbar > Properties > Taskbar tab > Use small icons, to get the smaller ones I prefer.]

You can pin frequently-used programs onto the taskbar, so that they stay there, by simply dragging its desktop icon onto the taskbar. Now the shortcut icon is in both places, desktop and taskbar. To unpin it, right-click on the icon and click "Unpin this program from taskbar." I prefer to keep frequently-used programs up on my Desktop only.

Icons I never use sometimes appear on the taskbar also. I don't know why! Some of the icons seem to come and go on their own.

Tip – If you think you're going to work on a document or program again during the same work session, don't close it when you are temporarily done, but minimize it ("–" icon at upper right corner), so that that icon goes to your taskbar, and can click on it to bring it up again quickly to resume work on it. That, in fact, is the main purpose of the taskbar.

TASKBAR – HIDE – Right-click on taskbar at an empty spot > Properties > Auto-hide the taskbar > OK. Then it stays hidden. If you put your pointer on that area at the bottom, it will still pop up temporarily for you to use.

To get it back to stay: Right-click on the taskbar when it's popped up > Properties > uncheck Auto-hide the taskbar > OK.

Movie Control Icons

Note that the control icons (Play, Stop, etc.) that show at the bottom when you watch a movie, will disappear automatically once you take your pointer off them. And will reappear if you put your pointer into that bottom area.

TASKBAR – MOVE – If you prefer, you can position your taskbar at the side, or top, of your screen instead of at the bottom: Right-click an empty spot, uncheck "Lock the Taskbar," and then (from its middle) drag and drop it to the edge you want.

TASKS – See "MAINTENANCE TASKS"

TEMPLATES – You can find and use preset formats for letters, or business cards, or resumés: Microsoft Office Button at far upper left [W7 – File] > New > Installed Templates > select a preset format > then click "Create" > then fill in info. Some you can just go ahead and fill in (if it has a "Create" button there at lower right); others you have to download (if it has a "Download" button there instead of "Create.")

I don't like these at all. Overkill. More trouble to learn how to use them than to simply do it on your own. Sure, I'd like to see 2 or 3 sample templates for something, but when I see hundreds of choices, fuhgeddaboudit, leave me alone. But, I suppose if you need a professional-looking resumé, it might be worth the trouble.

TEXT – FONT SQUEEZING – See "SPACING BETWEEN LETTERS"

TEXT FORMATTING – REMOVING ALL – Say you've done a lot of formatting to your text, but you don't like it after all. You want to start over, but don't want to undo all that formatting piece by piece. You can remove all formatting, leaving only plain text, in one operation: Block the text > Home tab > Font box > click on the eraser icon at upper right > that's it.

Quite convenient. Not only removes bolding, italics, etc., but also color, shading, size changes.

THESAURUS – Right-click on the word, then click Synonyms; it lists a few synonyms. The website "Dictionary.com" is much better and more extensive.

TIME – SETTING – The time and date should automatically show correctly at the lower right of your screen. But, if it's not correct, you can adjust it:

Left-click the time at the bottom right of the taskbar > Change Date and Time Settings > Date and Time window shows > make your adjustments, including Time Zone if you need to, OK. (It also has here automatic adjusting for daylight savings time. That box is already checked as a default setting.)

TIPS – GENERAL CONCEPTS

Time Restraints

Whenever you're under a tight time restraint for a project, DO NOT attempt some unfamiliar operation or try experimenting as you work on that project. You're very likely to get stuck in things you cannot get out of easily, leading to disaster and missing your deadline. Exploring, in the long run, leads to knowledge, but in the short run, it leads to problems.

Undoing

Instead of deleting complex stuff you accidentally put in a text, or changed your mind about, use CTRL+Z to get rid of it. A bit easier, because it gets rid of bigger chunks of work at a time. You can CTRL+Z repeatedly to get back to something you had, even many dozens of changes ago. (And CTRL+Y if you went too far and want to undo that undo.)

Sudden Weird Stuff

If you're typing along and suddenly some function pops up, it's usually because you accidentally pressed CTRL and a letter rather than the intended Shift and the letter.

Help

You can click on the F1 key at top, for help in Windows when on the internet, and for help in Microsoft Word when in a document. Every so often these features are actually helpful. See "HELP" for more info on the efficacy of various "help" routes.

TITLES – FANCY – See "HEADINGS"

TITLE PAGES – They have some preset cover pages: Insert tab at top > Pages box > Cover Page dropdown arrow > select. It puts that cover page right into your document and you can enter your desired text into that cover page. They're professional-looking, but it depends on your taste if you like them. I generally don't.

TOOLBAR – Refers to a bar of icons to click, enabling you to perform various functions. There are all kinds of different toolbars. (Note that a toolbar at top when you are on the internet, is different than the one at top when you are working in MS Word on a document. See "The Internet Explorer Toolbars", just below.) But the main toolbar, the one usually referred to as the "toolbar," is the MS Word one at the top of your screen when you work on a document. It's a wide bar, heavily loaded with icons under each tab (Home, Insert, Page Layout, etc.) Often called the "Ribbon."

To minimize it (hiding all but the tab labels themselves), you double-click on the name of the active tab at top; click it again (single left-click), to get it back. [W7 – you can also click the caret arrow at upper right, right next to the question mark icon, to hide or show the full ribbon.] Myself, I like having the full mode ribbon up there all the time.

Customizing the Toolbar

You can add or hide specific items from this toolbar: Right-click anywhere on the current tab > Customize the toolbar > click the group (at right) you want to edit (for me it was the "Styles" group, never liked it) > click Remove, OK.

To get it back, you have to go thru the same procedure but click New Group and Add along the way, etc., etc. I couldn't do it and I refuse to spend more time trying to figure it out. You have so many choices, and you have to click things in the right order. One selection worked, but another did not, etc., etc.

Recommendation: As usual, it's absolute overkill. Don't fiddle with this unless you are really keen on customizing your toolbar. For me, it's fine as is, especially now that the one I never had any use for – the big "Styles" box in the Home tab – is removed. I mean, you could spend weeks customizing all the tabs and options to your preference.

The Internet Explorer Toolbars

If you right-click on an empty spot in any of the toolbars at top, you get the option to check or uncheck for showing or hiding these toolbars:

Very top: the ADDRESS bar – shows the back and forward navigation arrow at left, and the internet address and name of the current website.

Second from top: MENU bar – shows File, Edit, View, Favorites, Tools, Help tabs.

Third from top: FAVORITES Bar – shows your favorite websites (that you selected to put there) on the left, AND Command bar items (Page, Safety, Tools, etc.) on the right.

SAME third from top also: COMMAND bar – shows Page, Safety, Tools, etc. on the right. If you uncheck the Favorites toolbar, the Command bar items shift over to the left.

Positions and items of these toolbars may vary on other computers or setups, but that's how they are set up on my old computer (Vista) and my new computer (Windows 7).

The STATUS bar (just above taskbar at very bottom) showing pages and words at left and screen zoom percent at far right, only appears when you are in a Word document, not when you are on the internet.

Command Bar Disappeared

I was fiddling around with "Manage add-ons" (under "Tools") one day and added a Google toolbar. Next time I opened the internet, my Command bar was gone (Page, Safety, Tools, etc.). Tried to get it back by right-clicking the toolbar area, but did not get the usual options, just a couple of Google options. A day later I tried again and the desired options were back; I checked the unchecked Command bar choice and I got my Command bar back.

Finally figured out that I had clicked on a Google toolbar blank extension area, instead of an actual empty spot. When I clicked on an actual empty spot, I did get my normal options back. (Note that you can reach some of the Command bar options also under the Gear icon at far upper right.)

TOOLBAR vs STATUS BAR vs TASKBAR – By my understanding:

TOOLBAR usually refers to the wide bar of icons at the top which enable you to do all kinds of operations – the Home, Insert tabs, etc., and the Font, Paragraph boxes, etc. The toolbar is also called the "ribbon". I think of the "toolbar" as the bar of functions you can perform.

STATUS BAR is the narrow bar, second from the bottom just above your taskbar. This is the one that shows what page you're on at the left, and what zoom level you're in at the right. I think of "status bar" as the bar that shows where you are in a document.

TASKBAR refers to the narrow bar of labeled icons (documents, folders, programs) that get put along the very bottom of your screen after you minimize them or move to a different item. That's where they go, at the bottom, ready to be called up again if you want to continue with them. I think of "taskbar" as the bar of tasks you are currently working on.

- Toolbar, at top, is what you can do to your stuff
- Status bar, second from bottom, is where you are in your stuff
- Taskbar is the stuff you're working on.

TRACKING TEXT CHANGES – This feature, when on, enters any new text you type in a document in underlined red. Review tab at top > Tracking box > Track Changes dropdown arrow > Track Changes. To get rid of it, click it again. I never liked this feature, mainly because it used to be hard to get rid of. (I would accidentally order it by clicking on some odd icon at the bottom, and then I could never remember where to go to get rid of the red typing.)

I never use it, but it can be very useful for making corrections and notes on a document, so that one can distinguish the original text from corrections or commentary. Good for a professional editor, or maybe an English teacher.

See also "FONT – AUTOMATIC RED CORRECTIONS", especially for how to get rid of this setting!

TRANSFERRING INFO FROM OLD COMPUTER TO NEW COMPUTER – Transferring data (documents or picture or music files) may be easy enough – copy them onto a DVD, a flash drive, or an external hard drive, by dragging and dropping; then copy them to the new computer by dragging and dropping. See "BACKING UP YOUR MATERIAL" and "DRAGGING AND DROPPING".

However, PROGRAMS are a different story; you can't just drag and drop those over. You have to re-install them all in your new computer by using their CDs. There may be some software programs to make this process easier. Or, when buying your new computer at, say Best Buy or Staples, they can do it for you for a fee, or, sometimes, free as a promotion. See also "COMPUTER – SETTING UP A NEW COMPUTER".

TRANSLATION TO OTHER LANGUAGES – You can set your computer to enter text in languages other than English (Start > Control Panel > Clock, Language and Region > Region and Language > Change keyboards or other input methods > Formats tab > Format dropdown arrow, choose language, Apply and OK), but most computers do not have a language translation feature for full texts.

However, you can use the internet to translate text from one language to another. I found that most site offerings are too complex for my tastes, or cost money, or send you in circles, or do something other than what I want – which is simple translation of English sentences to another language and vice versa. I'm sure some of the $200 dollar software programs you can buy work pretty well, after you spend hours figuring them out.

I finally found what I want when I googled: "Google Translation Gadget". Just type in your sentences, and it translates it into any language of your choice in seconds. Then you can write to a foreign friend by blocking the translation you got and dropping it into your email.

This site has a limit of 300 words. If you want to translate more, use: translate.google.com. You simply choose the language from and the language to, and type in your text, then click a button. It does a fair basic job of translating, but idiom, expressions, choice of words, etc., often come out weird. For example, I was communicating with a woman in China for a bit, and to see how well it was translating, I blocked my result (in Chinese characters) and put it back in, to translate back to English. And it translated my sentence "What do people call you?" to "Who has done this to you?" Hah.

Sometimes you have to try to paste a text section more than one time to get it in. Keep trying; it should go. Also, it seems easier to block a text section by dragging the pointer from the end of the section to the beginning rather than from the beginning to the end.

Update – Actually the computer DOES have some translation capacity; it can translate individual words for you. Right-click the word > Translate > Translate, "Research" panel opens at right > pick language to and from, and it gives info on the word from a bilingual dictionary. On my computer I have only the default languages of English, French, and Spanish.

Alternate method: You can click Review tab > Proofing box [W7 – Language box] > Translation ScreenTip dropdown arrow [W7 – Mini Translator] > pick a language, and then when you hold the pointer over a word, it gives you the translation. [W7 – the info shows extremely light, until you slide the pointer up a line or two, then it turns into a small window with readable black text.]

I would say, if you use it a lot, keep that translating feature on (it toggles on and off each time you click it); otherwise, the right-clicking method is more convenient. Either method accesses the same information.

Update – Actually I notice both Vista and Windows 7 do have a full document translation feature, if you're on the internet: Right-click any random word in your document > Translate > "Translate the whole document" > click the green arrow > click Send > window (Microsoft-translator.com) pops up with the translation > CTRL+A and CTRL+V it where you want. Pretty neat! Translates very quickly. Works even if you have formatting or double columns in your source document. There might be a limit to the size; it wouldn't do a hundred pages for me, but it did do 42 pages. You can always do it in chunks.

TURNING ON COMPUTER – I think most computers have a simple On/Off button at upper right.

You should WAIT till it is fully booted up (desktop fully settled) before trying to open a document or go on the internet. Otherwise, it tends to get screwed up, or take significantly longer than usual, if you don't wait. See also "COMPUTER ON / OFF – SIMPLIFY"

TV – In the good old days, you could turn the TV on, pick a station, adjust the volume, and start watching. Today, there's no end to options, functions, setups, complexities. TV setups are beyond the scope of this manual. Just a few comments:

Setups

Setups vary. Myself, I have 4 machines: a TV, a DVR, a DVD player/recorder, and a DVD player-only. It gets extremely complex, but once you get used to it (your own particular setup), it becomes second nature to you, and you instinctively know which of a hundred buttons on different remotes you need to push to get what you want.

My basic wiring setup goes like this:

1. For normal live watching, or watching DVR-recorded material: Cable (coaxial) from wall to DVR. Cable (HDMI) from DVR to TV.

2. For recording material to disks, or watching disks: [I use blank DVD–RW disks, which replace the old VCR blank tapes that I used for years to record TV programs on.] Cable (coaxial) from DVR to DVD recorder (so I can record live or DVR-recorded material to a disk). Cable (a second HDMI) from DVD recorder to TV (so I can play a disk on the recorder and watch it on TV).

3. For making a copy of a disk: Wire (red, white, yellow) from DVD player to DVD recorder.

Note that the DVR essentially replaces one's old VCR and does everything much better; but, if you want to play <u>disks</u>, you need to add a DVD player to your setup; if you want to record DVR material to a disk, you need to add a DVD player/<u>recorder</u>; if you want to make a copy of a disk to another disk, you need both.

Big tip: Once you, or a Cable guy, have things set up, take a flash photo of how the wiring is set up in back, in case you get into a situation (like moving) where you have to set it up again. I found this very helpful.

<u>DVR – Digital Video Recorder</u>

DVR's are terrific. They allow timer recording and tremendous flexibility. Your cable company provides them. Mine, from Comcast, can record two programs at once. You can come home in the middle of a program and start at the beginning, etc., etc. It has a program guide. (I haven't seen a TV Guide <u>magazine</u> in years.)

The functions are relatively straightforward, though you do need to do some serious exploring to get familiar with them. Just recently realized the "Extended time" option for sporting events, in case they go long, is not limited to half an hour. You can up that time to as much as two hours.

What gets tricky is using the DVR remote functions <u>in conjunction</u> with your other machines; you have to press the right buttons in the right order, and get your sources and modes and whatnot correct.

Unlike most DVD players, the DVR (I assume others are like mine) <u>can</u> record hi-definition, which is just great, especially for sports and nature programs. (Note that most TV stations have both regular and hi-def versions. In my area, channel 4 is "4"; channel 4 hi-def is "804." Likewise there's "5" and "805", "33" and "833", etc.)

<u>"TV Ears"</u>

Those "TV Ears" they sell ($90, Radio Shack) are terrific. You can listen to TV at any volume and not bother anybody (as well as not be bothered yourself by external noise). Just handle them carefully; they're easy to drop or sit on accidentally; and the earbuds tend to fall off, if you don't push them down enough to settle into a solid position.

<u>TV RECORD DIRECTLY TO COMPUTER</u> – You can record TV signals directly to your computer. You need to buy a separate tuner device, to get the stations. (Pinnacle Pro TV Tuner Stick and Sling Box are two such tuners.) You detach your cable wire from your TV and attach it to the device instead, then plug the device into a USB port of your computer.

<u>ATI TV Wonder</u>

I had an old one called ATI TV Wonder, and it worked pretty well. Needed Geek guy to come over to set it up (could only get so far by myself and phone help). Once we got it installed, it puts a "Catalyst Media Center" icon onto the desktop.

<u>ATI TV Wonder</u>

<u>Record TV onto Computer</u>

1. Don't need internet, but do need coaxial cable from wall.
2. Attach tuner to TV cable wire from wall. Take the top cap off the tuner and attach it to the one foot connection wire, which goes into a USB port of the computer.

(One foot extension wire is partly for reach, but mainly to provide flexibility for wire; less likely to get damaged with movement).

3. Open "Catalyst Media Center" icon (the name of this program)
4. Click TV (wait)
5. Click Channel List (limited). Scroll (using arrow keys) to pick and click on station desired.

Can watch TV live that way.

Can maximize the picture by clicking on maximizing icon at upper right.

6. On lower left you have the controls (they come up when you put the cursor on that area).
7. Press red Record square to record what is currently on. (It pauses a few seconds, then comes up to record.)
8. Press black Stop square at lower left to stop recording.
9. To access it later on to watch it: Home (red house) > TV > Recorded TV > brings up thumbnails > click on what you want to watch.

(Can also burn to disk.)

10. Right-click thumbnail, to delete.

<u>Timer Record</u>

1. Open "Catalyst" icon > 2. TV at left > 3. Schedule > 4. New Schedule > 5. Pick station > 6. Set times > 7. Click "Apply." That sets it. > 8. Be sure to leave the computer on, the program open, and the tuner attached. > 9. To view the program → Catalyst icon > TV at left > Recorded TV > click on the clip > click Stop button at lower left when done.

<u>Notes</u>

1. You still need the tuner thing attached in order to pull up the program you recorded; you need it for <u>playback</u> also, not just for recording!

2. You can improve the picture a bit by: Settings > TV > Recording Settings > Recording Quality > Best (instead of Good or Better). Note that in Maine, for recording US Open tennis, it was mediocre. It would keep fading in and out every 2 seconds from good to splotchy. It was barely watchable.

3. I rarely use it. But, it's nice to keep the tuner in my laptop case, when I'm away from home and I suddenly come across something I really do want to record. (<u>Other</u> than tennis, which really requires a higher quality picture to enjoy.)

<u>Pinnacle PCTV HD Mini Stick</u>

I recently bought a newer one, a different model from Radio Shack – PCTV HD Mini Stick (Pinnacle TVCenter Pro), $50. Looks like a flash drive.

Online help: <u>support@pctvsystems.com. Phone help:</u> 1 631 434 3197 (M-F 9-6 EST)

After hours and hours of effort, 4 downloads, 6 phone calls... the device did not work for me. Apparently because it only works with unencrypted <u>"clear QAM"</u> signals, and my cable company signals are not that type.

Recommendation: If you buy such a tuner device, get Best Buy to install the program and get it to work, if it can work. (May have to pay for this.)

Radio Shack guy, since he himself has one that works, promised to get it going for me if I bought my laptop in. Well, he got it working... after three hours and 15 minutes of working on it!!

Can't tell you exactly what he did, something along the lines of doing a channel scan on Windows Media Center rather than on the PCTV program. (The scan itself took an hour.) And we finally got about 12 stations in, but they were stalling and breaking up – he thinks because inside the Mall reception is poor.

Told the guy about reviews on the net on this product, how some people were quite satisfied, other very dissatisfied. It was all over the place. I'm guessing different areas, different signals, different computer contexts, make a difference.

At any rate, it was gratifying and vindicating that he couldn't get it going in two minutes, but took over three hours to do so. Every so often I think to myself maybe I'm just not good with this kind of stuff, but I really don't think that's the case. I don't think it's me; it's the nature of the Beast – the computer world is very complex, and if you don't do the right steps, in the right order, with the right components, stuff doesn't work.

This guy was very knowledgeable. Went to school for computer stuff; designs websites also. And it took him over three hours to get it working.

So, I tried it at home.

First I had to figure out how to do a channel scan. You have to go to the initial Windows Media Center screen and scroll down to "Tasks," which is below what normally shows on the screen. Then click TV > TV Signal > Scan for more channels, Yes > Scan again → nothing > tried Set up TV signal, Yes, Next > put in zip code, Next > I agree, Next > shows "Downloading setup data" (for my region), wait 3 minutes > showed "Unable to detect" but the blue light on the tuner stick was not showing; re-attached it and tried again > showed "Examining TV signals" > no go again > backed up and selected "Manual" instead > showed TV signal providers in my area > picked Lawrence Comcast, OK... it started working! It scanned in 39 channels in about 35 minutes, and then downloaded a TV program guide. I clicked Next, then Finish.

Then went back to TV and clicked "Guide", clicked on desired channel, and, hooray, got a beautiful picture! It's finally working!

So I figure these are the keys: 1) I needed to use Windows Media Center, not the PCTV Center. 2) Had to scan in channels locally. 3) Had to scan in channels "manually."

The actual operation of the program, getting channels, watching, timer-recording, etc. is much more straightforward and you can figure it out on your own logically; everything is analogous to regular TV controls. If you put the pointer on the screen, it brings up the controls; take the pointer off the screen and it shows a nice, junk-free, full-screen picture. And, the picture quality is excellent!

In theory, you can also use an antenna they provide, instead of your cable wire.

Update: Tried the antenna outdoors in a different location. Well, it worked the same way as at the Mall – beautiful picture for a few seconds at a time, but then constant breaking up, stalling. I conclude the antenna route is worthless unless you happen to be in just the right location.

Bottom Line

I normally won't use it, since I prefer watching TV on a regular TV when at home. And if I want to watch something on my laptop, I'll do it the way I've been doing it for years – record it on a DVD–RW on my DVD recorder, and then play the disk in my laptop.

If I'm away from home, I can use the device, as long as I have access to a TV cable wire, as I normally would in a motel. Unscrew the cable wire from their TV, screw the wire into my device, attach the device to my laptop, set it to timer-record, go out for the day, then watch my material at night on my laptop.

I tried installing my old device onto my new computer (I still had the CD), but it wouldn't even install. A progress bar at one point just stayed stuck in one spot. Plus some spots to click did not even respond at all. Most likely the thing is out of date for my new computer, or is just not compatible in some way. At any rate, this old one works in my old computer; the new one works in my new computer. That's good enough for me; I've reached the point of diminishing returns. I'm done.

TWITTER – This is social networking website where you can send and read messages called tweets. Wikipedia: "Tweets are text-based posts of up to 140 characters displayed on the user's profile page."

I think of 1) email as messages you send to another person, 2) Facebook as messages you send to a group of approved friends, and 3) Twitter as messages you send to anyone who signs up to follow your tweets. And all of them can be powerful tools, or, colossal wastes of time.

UNDERLINE – CTRL+U, or, Home tab at top > Font box > **U** icon. To double underline, or to use another underline style, click the arrow at lower right of Font box, then chose options under Underline Style.

UNDO (CTRL+Z) – When you press CTRL+Z, it undoes the last thing you did to a text. In a Word document it erases the last word, or, group of words. (I couldn't establish just what amount of your latest text it erases each instance you press CTRL+Z; seems to vary. I found that if I do just straight typing and no part of that text gets any formatting by me (like underlining one word) or any automatic adjustment (like a misspelled word automatically corrected), then one CTRL+Z erases that whole chunk. But if a word got formatted, or automatically corrected, then the CTRL+Z only goes back to that word, and you have to press CTRL+Z again to undo the text previous to that word.)

CTRL+Z can also undo the last formatting you did. If you just did a CTRL+I to italicize a paragraph but then decide you prefer its original format, CTRL+Z will change that italicization back to what you had.

You can repeatedly press CTRL+Z to keep going back, dozens of times, thru previous Saves, in chronological order, all the way back to what you had when you opened the document. But once you close the document, then you can't use CTRL+Z to undo anything you did before closing the document.

One other big thing: If you do 5 CTRL+Z's, looking to find something, and then you change something at that spot, you can no longer do 5 CTRL+Y's to get back to where you were. In other words, you have now lost your latest 4 entries!! Once you make a change in that progression back, your progression forward is gone!

Therefore, if you use CTRL+Z to find something, once you've found the thing you want to change, don't change it, just note where it is, CTRL+Y yourself forward to your current spot, and THEN simply scroll back to the spot to make your change, instead of using

CTRL+Z to get back there.

"Redo" – Undoing an "Undo" (Restoring) – CTRL+Y

If you went back too far erasing things, to undo your undo, press CTRL+Y ("restore" or "redo"). CTRL+Y works like CTRL+Z except on the opposite direction, chronologically, restoring (instead of erasing) each chunk of text you did, in order.

Undoing a Document Name Change

If you change a Document name and then immediately do a CTRL+Z, it will put the previous name back. For most other operations CTRL+Z has no effect. Its main use is for undoing Word text, and it gets a lot of use.

UNINSTALL A SOFTWARE PROGRAM – Start > Control Panel > Programs > Uninstall a Program, wait till all programs show up, scroll down and click on the program (which puts a check next to it), "Uninstall" shows up at the top > click "Uninstall" > may need to click a couple more straightforward boxes, and, in some cases re-start your computer, but that's it. Blessedly simple, compared to installing.

UNSUBSCRIBE TO EMAIL NOTIFICATIONS – Almost every company you deal with on the internet, when you buy something or sign up for something, tries to sell you more stuff and services by emailing material to you in the future, since they now have your email address. Before you click on the final transaction button, check to see if they have a line to uncheck their offer to send you other offers, updates on products, etc. (By default it is checked.) Almost all companies have such a line. I always uncheck it; otherwise, my email box would constantly be clogged up with these annoying emails.

Also, if you do start getting such emails, most companies have a line to check at the bottom to unsubscribe to such offers and not receive them anymore.

Despite the tenor of their presentations, most sites and companies are not trying to be helpful and look out for your interests; they're trying to sell you more stuff.

UPLOAD vs DOWNLOAD – Uploading is sending material from your computer to a remote system; you're sending material out. Downloading is receiving material to your computer from a remote system; you're receiving material.

Downloading implies receiving and saving, whereas streaming means you're getting material to your computer, but you can't necessarily save it.

URGE – This is the Microsoft store for music. A competitor to iTunes. I don't use it. Pretty satisfied with iTunes. According to AR, URGE does not seem a good choice anyway. You pay a monthly fee, but then if you discontinue, you can no longer play those songs! I don't know if you can simply burn your songs to a disk, to save them permanently. I assume you can. That's what I do for my iTunes songs, to bypass the iTunes 7-plays limit.

URL – A URL (Uniform Resource Locator) is the exact address of a website on the internet. It includes the ending ".com" or .net, .gov. (government), or .edu (school), etc. The box for it is usually located at upper left. If you put a URL in and click the arrow just to the right of the box, that website should come up. (The "https://" prefix automatically gets put in when you put a URL in.) I tend to just use Google for finding sites, rather than the URL box, although the URL box is more accurate, assuming you put the right address in.

For example, if I google "Dictionary.com" it will show me a list of sites that most closely match; in this case, the Dictionary.com site is right at the top of the list, and then I click on it to open it. But, if I put in their exact URL address – http://dictionary.reference.com – into the URL address bar, their website will open up directly.

Pasting Addresses

Usually, for accuracy, it's good to copy (CTRL+C) an address and paste (CTRL+V) it into the box, rather than to type it in. For email, especially, you have to get the address exactly right or it doesn't send.

Website Address vs Email Address

When you have an @ symbol, that is an email address rather than a website address, though they both usually end in ".com."

USER ACCOUNT – Sometimes you want someone else to be able to use your computer on a regular basis, able to access their own material and folders, but not yours.

To add or subtract a User Account: Start > Control Panel > User Accounts and Family Security > User Accounts (click on green) > Manage another account > Guest > Create an account > type in the name, select Standard or Administrator, click "Create account". Click on the icon for that person to create a password for that person. Type in the password twice, Create password. Now, an icon for that person's account shows up at center of screen when you open up the computer, and they can put in their password to open up their account, their account only.

Note that a guest user account has its own desktop icons, as managed by that person, after the computer's "Preparing your desktop" sets up a few basic icons/programs.

To delete a user account, you have to restart the computer and open up your "owner" or "Administrator" account, and go thru the route described above, clicking on that user's icon, and then "Delete the account". I don't know if you can remove the Administrator account, but you can remove its password so that you, the owner, don't have to put in a password each time.

Typical situation: The parents of a family hold the "Administrator" account, the kids "Standard" accounts, and the babysitter a "Guest" account.

See also "PASSWORDS"

VERSIONS – WHICH WINDOWS VERSION YOU HAVE – Besides the different versions of the Windows operating systems ("XP", "Vista", "Windows 7"), each operating system has several "editions" ("Home Basic", "Home Premium", "Professional" etc.).

I had "Windows Vista Home Premium"; now I have "Windows 7 Home Premium." Built to fill most consumer's needs, these are the versions most people have.

To determine which version and edition you have, click Start > right-click Computer > Properties. It gives you the info at the top of the window. To get a nice listing and description of the various versions and editions, type "Windows versions" into the Wikipedia website search box.

<u>VIDEO</u> – See "DVD – MAKING A DVD FROM CAMCORDER VIDEO"

<u>VIDEO – DVD PLAYING</u> – You can choose which program opens your DVD (or CD) under Start > Control Panel > Hardware and Sound > Autoplay > "Choose what happens when you insert each type of media device, dropdown arrow, pick the one you want > Save.

I've been warming up to Window Media CENTER a bit. I like the full-screen picture, and I'm getting used to the controls. Of the various programs that play video (Windows Media Player, Windows Media Center, QuickTime Player, the Sony Vaio player, etc.) you can try them all out to see which one gives you the picture and controls you prefer. Right now, for me, I like my Sony Vaio player, which is a separate video-playing program that comes with Sony Vaio computers.

<u>VIDEO CLIPS FROM INTERNET</u> – When you visit a website, and they have a video clip to play, there's usually a Play icon (triangular arrow) right in the middle of the clip. Click on that to play it. Usually, at the lower right, there is also an icon (usually four outward-pointing arrows) to click, to bring the screen to full size.

Sometimes you can save a clip to your computer. (Right-click the clip > Save target as...; pick save location (usually Downloads folder) > Save.) Other times you cannot. You Tube clips, for example, you can't save.

AR – *"Some Websites only stream their video to your computer – you can't save the video to play later... After watching a streaming Web video, choose Save from Media Player's File menu. If that option is grayed out, the Website has forbidden you from saving the video."*

<u>VIDEO RECORDING WITH THE COMPUTER ITSELF</u> – My Sony Vaio computer, and I think most laptops, can act as a <u>camera</u> or as a <u>camcorder</u>. The lens is right at the center top of your computer lid.

Start > All Programs; might have to search your computer manual to find the actual name of the program; for me it's "ArcSoft WebCam Companion 3" > "WebCam Companion 3" > Capture > window comes up which, thankfully, is pretty straightforward (picture and video buttons are at bottom (may have to click a whitish arrow at middle left to get rid of panel and show video camera button at bottom); click them to take a picture or record video; click video button again to stop the recording) > puts an icon of the picture or clip at left (may have to click the whitish arrow again, now at left, to bring up the panel) > right-click on desired pic or clip > Find Target > check the icon and CTRL+X and CTRL+V it into your desired folder (Pictures, or Videos folder, normally).

I hardly ever use it; if you're going to use your laptop as a camera you'd have to carry it and then point it at your subject. But for in-house stuff, it's pretty neat. As you sit in front of the computer, you see yourself on screen looking back at yourself. It's an easy way to take picture of yourself.

As usual, you have to spend time with it, in order to get to know all the options here. But also as usual, the default settings for the casual user are fine.

<u>Skype</u>

The "Skype" feature is also launched from this program. Skype is like video telephone service over the internet; you can talk to friends and see them on your computer at the same time. Never tried it myself, since I have no friends. I'm kidding, I'm kidding. I think Skype must be a great program. Talking to, and seeing, loved ones on the other side of the planet. Pretty great. It's basically what you used to see in futuristic movies 20 years ago, now a reality.

<u>VIEW DOCUMENTS SIDE BY SIDE</u> – Right-click the taskbar at the bottom on an empty spot, click "Show windows side by side." That puts the two documents up, side by side, each with its own toolbar ribbon at top. Good for moving selected chunks of text over from an old document to a new one.

To get rid of the side-by-side setup, right-click the taskbar again and click "Undo Show side by side." Often you have to fiddle around with it for a while to get what you want, playing with the "Maximize"/ "Restore down" icon at upper right. And if you have more than two documents in the taskbar, often it does nothing.

I find a more stable method, is to do this, exactly: Open a document > minimize ("–" icon) it to the taskbar > open the second document (document, not folder) > with that second document on screen, click View tab > Window box > View Side by Side. That puts the two up side by side, every time, consistently. If you want to switch left/right sides, you can grab each document at the top part of it, and drag it to the other side. If you have more than two documents on your taskbar at the time, it brings up a dialogue box where you can select which one you want, to go with the one you currently have on your screen.

I like this View tab method much better. You turn it on and it works for that session; next time you use it, you click on it to use it again. Whereas the taskbar method retains – offscreen – its turned-on state for the next session, yet often doesn't work, until you fiddle with it for a while. I find the View method far less confusing.

Again, the <u>stupid</u> MS redundancy – you end up not knowing which operation overrides the other, which one is on, what order to do what, etc., etc. I'm not positive of the math here, but this overall point is valid: If you have one way to do one thing with five steps, you can mess up 25 different ways by doing one of the five steps out of order. But, when you have <u>two</u> ways <u>in play at the same time</u>, to do that five-step thing, you can mess up <u>125</u> different ways! **That's what Microsoft doesn't get. They think they are making things easier by providing different methods, when in fact they are making it harder!**

[W7 – The above commentary notwithstanding, hooray for Windows 7. They have a new, easy, consistent way to get two windows side-by-side: Drag one (by its top) deep into the right edge and the other deep into the left edge. Presto, each fills half the screen. And, this feature also works for <u>internet</u> windows! (You <u>do</u> need to have the two browser sessions open, not just two tabs open on the same browsing session.)]

<u>Internet Windows Side by Side</u>

I think the taskbar method is supposed to work for displaying <u>internet</u> pages side-by side as well, but it never does for me; it seems to start to work, but it never completes. Not a big deal for me, since I've never felt the need to compare internet pages; I use it only for Word documents.

However, you can always do it manually. Get one site up, drag it down a bit from the top bar so you can see the corner of the page, drag that corner in so that the page window gets small. Open your internet browser (Internet Explorer for me) again and do the same for the second site (you must open the second one separately, by clicking on the Internet Explorer browser a second time). Then position them side by side.

You can get more than two pages up with this method if you want. Then arrange them any way you want, manually.

Or, if you have Windows 7, use the method described above in the blue box, dragging a reduced window of each site deep into the left and right sides of the screen.

"VIEW" TAB – IN A DOCUMENT – When you are in a Word document, your basic toolbar at top includes, besides "Home", "Insert", etc., the tab labeled "View." It has options for how to make things appear on the screen.

I stick with default settings here and rarely use anything in this tab (except, lately, the "View Side by Side" option for two documents).

See also "ZOOM" for making text on screen appear bigger or smaller.

"VIEWS" BUTTON – IN A FOLDER – The dropdown arrow of the "Views" (plural) tab at the upper left [W7 – at upper right] of a folders window, gives you options for how you want your document list to appear – small icons, big icons, etc. I usually like "List" (the smallest) so that I can see all of them at once. If you click on the word "Views" itself, it cycles through all your options at each successive click.

See also "SORTING – FOLDERS, OR DOCUMENTS IN THOSE FOLDERS"

VIEW – INTERNET – To see an internet page at a different size, click the dropdown arrow beside the "100%" at the lower right, and make your choice.

VIRUS – A computer virus is a program that gets onto your computer and messes it up. They are designed by tech-savvy lowlifes, to get either money or information from you.

Normally you can't get one by just opening your email, or copying some website page. But you can get one by opening an attachment to an email (so never do that if you are not sure of the sender), or by downloading a malicious program (which they cleverly disguise as a legitimate one). See "VIRUS SAGA" below for a typical instance of a virus, as experienced by me.

AR: Viruses can also travel inside files, flash drives, add-ons, even screen savers.

Anti-Virus Programs

Usually when you buy a computer, you are also sold an anti-virus protection program (like Webroot or Norton) for about $40 per year. And you really do need one. The yearly subscription keeps defenses up-to-date. The newest viruses often cause the most damage.

Somehow, shortly after I bought my laptop in 2007, I found I had two virus protection programs on my computer – Trend Micro and Webroot ("Spysweeper"). The Geek guy where I bought it, said I needed both of them. BUT, every expert I've consulted since then says do NOT run two anti-virus programs simultaneously. They tend to interfere with each other, like two baseball players going for the same fly ball. So I uninstalled Trend Micro and went with Webroot.

Asked RS which is better, Trend, or Webroot. He said they're all just about the same.

Your computer needs to be turned on for anti-virus programs to work, or to be in "sleep" mode at least.

You can set how often it does a scan/sweep. Double-click on its icon to open windows with options. I picked daily for updates and monthly for a scan/sweep, at an off time (5AM) when I'm normally asleep, so it doesn't interfere with any work I may do on the computer. Though normally you can minimize that window, and you can continue working on something else at the same time, no problem.

You can order it to do a full scan immediately. My Webroot full scan would usually take about an hour and half. Then I would select "Quarantine" and it would get rid of any cookies or interfering junk.

I changed to Norton for my newest computer. With Norton, it seems things are even more automatic. I seldom check it. It will only bother you occasionally, like if it's been unable to get an update because you've not been connected to the internet recently, or if something came in and it can't identify it and needs to ask you permission to do something, like delete it, or whatever.

Also, I like how, whenever I open an attachment to an email, it specifically shows you at the bottom that it is running an anti-virus check on that attachment.

Suggestion: Buy a computer from a solid place like Best Buy, and then ask the salesperson if your virus protection is set, and at default settings, and then... don't touch a thing.

Windows Automatic Updates

Windows provides automatic updates (for its operating system), so that your computer will maintain good reliability, security, and compatibility, in the face of constantly new problems. These updates get installed in the background, and you don't have to do anything. I don't think your computer even needs to be on; it just needs to be online for these automatic uploads.

Just make sure that this updating feature is on: Start > Control Panel > Systems and Security > Windows Updates > "Change settings" at left > "Important updates" dropdown arrow > "Install updates automatically (recommended)" > OK.

See also "WINDOWS UPDATES"

6/09 – Problem – Keeps Saying One of My Protections Is Off

At one point I kept getting a message that one of my protections was off. Turns out there is a time delay, and it was not really off. The tech guy assured me that that message (from Windows Security Center, not Webroot!) just lags behind, before Webroot is fully turned on, and that the message will soon disappear on its own (as it did, every time, in a matter of seconds). Still, it's very annoying, having it appear consistently and pointlessly!

Using Windows "Help" icon, I typed in "Windows Security Center", and under the first entry, I went over to the left and clicked "Change the way security center alerts me." And clicked "Don't notify and don't display icon." That worked. Hooray.

[I couldn't find the above option the same way on my new computer (Windows 7). I think one has to go now to Start > Control Panel > Systems and Security > Action Center > "Change User Account Control Settings" on the left > select degree of notification > OK.]

MY VIRUS SAGA

Chapter 1 – The Gathering Storm

My disk bay started acting up. I brought my laptop to a small computer repair place with "Same Day" service. Left it there, came back in the evening. They replaced the bay with a new one that worked fine. $150 total. OK.

Chapter 2 – I Take the Bait

I had just seen an ad on TV about cleaning up one's computer to make it run better. Mine ran fine, but it is 4 years old. This shop offered a cleanup service for $75. Well, OK, I'll do it.

Chapter 3 – I Am Nailed to the Hull

Came back to pick it up. I was a bit peeved that they had replaced my Webroot anti-virus program with theirs, but the guy assured me theirs was the latest and much better. OK.

As soon as I got home and checked my email, I saw I had more spam now than usual, and different spam than usual. I was getting lots of stuff on cars now. Not happy about that, getting additional spam after my laptop was in their place for one day.

Less than a week later I got an alert notice of some sort for a virus. The alert window was titled "Windows Restore," so I assumed that that was my new anti-virus program. The shop had given me instruction sheets and the title of their program was "Microsoft Windows Essentials." So I figured that was their program, and I clicked the "Fix" button.

Big mistake.

I think that was the moment I let a virus in, clicking that "Fix" box. It went thru an impressive "fixing" process and then gave me these messages: "Failed to fix" and "Advanced module required to fix detected errors." $79. I tried the "Fix" button again, tried a few other things, but got additional messages: "Critical error. Damaged hard drive cluster detected. Private data is at risk," "Hard drive failure." "5 errors left. PC is in danger." "Hard drive failure. The system has detected a problem with one or more installed IDE/SATA hard disks."

I had no intention of buying additional software when the shop's program was supposed to be so good. And, because Webroot had always worked well for me, quarantining "cookies," etc., and I never had a serious problem. But, within minutes my computer was being wiped out. Not only was it totally frozen, my desktop icons were disappearing on their own, until only a few were left!

Brought it back to the shop. They looked at it and confirmed that I definitely had a virus. So they worked on it, and, despite being a "same day" service shop, kept it for four days, repeatedly putting me off, as I checked twice a day. They'd tell me they're working hard on it, but it's the worst virus they've seen in four years, etc., etc. Finally they told me they were not able to save the data; the best they could do is "restore/rebuild" the hard drive, so that I could use it. $150. OK, that's my only option.

Now, I had backed up all my data just before I brought it in for the first time, so I had all my important stuff saved. But now I would be losing an entire week's worth of work that I had done on one document! About 20 hours of work! Ugh.

The main guy there was very smart, and smooth, and obviously he knew more about computers than me. But, after another day of no progress, he said he really couldn't do anything more, and would not charge me. I asked if I could at least use the thing. He said yes, but he couldn't guarantee the virus was gone. So, basically... I'd have to buy a new computer.

Now, I don't know if these guys are scam artists or not. I thought it was very suspicious that, after being there for 4 years, they do not accept credit cards but only cash or check. I thought it was very suspicious that they denigrated Webroot, which has worked fine for me, and which Best Buy offers on a regular basis for new computers. And when I hear "the worst virus we've ever seen," I tend to think they say that to a lot of people, to cover up for their slow progress. But, other than the clean-up, they weren't angling to get more money out of me.

Yet, there was something not quite on the up-and-up with them, the way they kept putting me off, indicating they were working on it, it's just about ready... yet it wasn't. My best guess is that they were swamped with work, played it by the seat of their pants and kept coming up with excuses to put me off. But, they seemed competent and knowledgeable enough.

Chapter 4 – Disaster Options

What to do? Be stoic, and buy a new computer?

Not yet!

I immediately took the laptop, directly from their shop, to Best Buy. Best Buy was pretty sure they could fix it, and retrieve my data. OK, I said to myself, now we'll see who's right – Best Buy ("fixable") or the small shop ("unfixable").

Day and a half later, Best Buy had it all fixed, virus gone, data all retrieved (including my most recent 20 hours of work!), programs all retrieved.

Chapter 5 – Lessons Learned

Unless you have good specific reason to do otherwise, stick with the big, well-established places. Avoid the small shops. As I've said, I don't know for sure about this small shop, but the bottom line was that they weren't as competent as Best Buy. Not to mention that fact that it turns out "their" anti-virus program was simply the standard program that comes with Windows, with maybe one or two additions to it.

I hate to say it, but when you think about it, a computer repair shop is a thief's playground. First of all, it's like a car repair place – they can say all kinds of things need to be done for your car, and you can't refute them; you're pretty much at their mercy. And the other big thing is that a computer repair shop has your computer and all the information in it! Very likely personal info, financial info, etc.

So, bottom line, I say stick to the trusted big places. (Staples is the other big place that comes to mind, though I've not had any computer dealings with them.)

Best Buy has been a life-saver for me. Knowledgeable staff. And they usually speak in plain English. (Which is not to say the store doesn't have employees who are more attuned to yakking with co-workers than to being aware of customers who need help.)

Incidentally, I decided to buy a new computer anyway. And, even though I know it's a good rule of thumb to decline service plans for most items, for a computer I think it's a very good deal. Couple hundred bucks and you get all kinds of free repair, maintenance, and help from them. (Although, if you want unlimited help from them, or if you want them to come to your house in person, you'd have to pay per hour.)

My computer repair for the virus did not cost me anything extra, because their service plan includes up to 3 of your computers.

For really serious data retrieval, there's a place called "Excalibur" (1 800 466-0893), but that runs into really big bucks. I guessing it's for stuff like a flooded business with computers under water, or maybe a dropped computer, etc.

VISTA INCOMPATIBILITY – If you're trying to send material as an email attachment and the recipient can't open it, because it's the wrong file type, you can convert the file type to their type, in many cases. I had a situation where a company needed my attachment in "Word 97-2003" instead of Vista, and they told me how to convert it:

Open your file, click Office icon at uppermost left (colored icon) [W7 – "File" icon] > Save As > "Save as type" dropdown arrow > select the type you want to convert to > type in new document name > Save > then send THAT document as the attachment.

VOICE – COMPUTER NARRATOR READING STUFF ALOUD
See "NARRATOR – COMPUTER TALKS TO YOU"

VOICE RECOGNITION SOFTWARE – Such a program enables you to speak into the computer and have it type what you say onto the screen, instantly. "Dragon Naturally Speaking" (Nuance company) is the most popular one. Comes with a mic that you plug into the front of your computer, if I remember right.

Sounds like a fantastic program. But, I bought it years ago and there are serious limitations. It's neat seeing your words automatically appearing on the screen as you speak. But, it's not as accurate as one would wish; I found 10-20% of the text came out in Martian! Which means the time you spend correcting the text may well surpass the time it would have taken you to just type it out in the first place!

Now, you're supposed to fine-tune it. You can fix mistakes by speaking clearly the particular word or phrase, and matching it to the correct word or phrase, so that next time, being tuned in to your particular voice and pronunciation, it's supposed to enter them correctly from that point on. But, it's a lot of work to get to the point where it doesn't make too many errors. And, I found it just won't correct certain words or phrases. For example, no matter how often or carefully I pronounced it, it still would put in "Andy..." for the intended "And he..."

Like so many programs, I don't think it worth it for the casual user, but it may well be worth it for the heavy user – if you don't type well, if you have carpal tunnel syndrome, whatever.

VOICE RECORDERS – DIGITAL – See "1. Digital Voice Recorders" under "MUSIC".

VOICE RECORDING – See "MUSIC / AUDIO TRANSFERS THRU A COMPUTER" > "Recording Directly into Computer"

VOLUME OF SOUND – See "SOUND VOLUME – COMPUTER"

WALLPAPER – See "SCREEN – DESKTOP BACKGROUND"

WARNING WINDOW – Sometimes a warning/permission window titled "User Account Control" pops up. It says, "Do you want to allow the following program to make changes to this computer?" As a general rule of thumb, if it suddenly popped up out of nowhere, or you weren't trying to make any changes, click NO; it might be a virus. If you were trying to change something specific with your computer, click YES, so you can proceed with what you were trying to do.

You can change the level of security here by going to Start > Control Panel > System and Security > "Security Center" [W7 – "Action Center"] > Change User Account Control Settings > move the scroll bar up or down > OK. AR recommends leaving the level at the default setting. I do.

AR: Windows 7 doesn't have a virus checker, but it checks to see if you've installed one (Webroot, Norton, etc.), and notifies you if you haven't or if your subscription fee is not paid.

WEATHER – See "GADGETS"

WEBCAM – This is the computer's video and picture taking utility. Its lens is usually located at the top center. See "VIDEO RECORDING WITH THE COMPUTER ITSELF"

WEBSITE FOR YOURSELF – How to set up a website for yourself is beyond the scope of this manual. You can google "website building" or "Adobe Dreamweaver" (a web development site), for information on how to set up a basic website. You need a site name ("domain name") and a host server (a company that keeps it on the internet for you).

Setting up a site that sells products, is more involved. I would recommend getting an expert to help you. Last I checked, Best Buy does not offer website-building help. I was lucky that a friend of a friend was an expert; I paid him to help set up my site. Mine costs about $350 total per year to keep it up and running. I use a company called "1&1 Internet" and I've been pretty satisfied with them. (Keep in mind when choosing a host server, that internet reviews vary quite a bit; any big company will have at least some nasty reviews. You have to consider the majority of customer reviews, not the worst ones.)

Recurrent theme: If you're going to try some major operation – using an OCR program, using a speech-recognition program, setting up a website, etc. – dabbling usually doesn't pay off; only sticking with it does.

Websites for Dummies Book
I found the book way too detailed. Shows all kinds of details for how to design your website, rather than just how to set it up, to get it going.

WEBSITE – TABBED BROWSING – See "TABBED WEBSITE BROWSING"

WEBSITE – BROWSING HISTORY – See "BROWSING HISTORY – WEBSITES"

WEBSITE – SAVING A PAGE OR TEXT – You can make a copy of a website page by CTRL+A, CTRL+C, and then CTRL+V it into a Word document. Formatting (columns, spacing, etc.) tends to get changed, but the target copy usually will retain all the details, in some form.

I usually just want to copy a paragraph or portion of a page, so what I normally do is highlight (hold left of the touchpad down, drag right finger across the right of the touchpad), copy (CTRL+C), go to an empty Word document, and paste it in (CTRL+V).

Now, this type of highlighting, of a website page (as opposed to a document page or text, which is more straightforward) can be tricky. Parts of text or pictures, etc. sometimes do not get included, or too much gets included. Takes some practice to get better at it. And sometimes you just can't isolate the section you want, so you copy more than you want and then, once pasted in a regular word document, delete the sections you don't want.

See also "LINE-SPACING" > "Website Text"

You can usually copy just a picture alone, by highlighting it, CTRL+C, and then CTRL+V into a Word document.

Saving JUST Text Thru "Notepad" Program

In theory, there is another way to save website text without any pictures or text formatting: CTRL+A the page > CTRL+C > find "Notepad" Program (type it into the Start search box if you can't find it... it's actually under All Programs, "Accessories") > open it > CTRL+V into it. That puts just the plain text in. From there you can transfer it to a Word document.

I have to say though, it's pretty hinky; chunks get left out, both from what it drops into Notepad and what it transfers to regular Word. I'll stick with manually blocking chunks of text, then transferring to a Word document.

Saving an Audio or Video Clip

Sometimes a site has a "Download" button to click. Other times, you can right-click the file > Save Target As > send it to "Downloads" (select "Downloads" from the left panel if it's not already selected; or select "Music" or "Videos" if that's where you prefer to land it; the heading at top tells you what is currently selected) > Save. [W7 – downloading progress shows at bottom] You can play it immediately, by clicking Open on that progress bar once it's done downloading. Or, you can play it later, by double-clicking it under the target folder.

Warning: Be sure you have your anti-virus program on. Downloading material includes the possibility of downloading a virus.

Saving a Website

You can save a website, as a file, as an active website: Click Page tab (at upper right) > Save As > send it to where you want > Save. Then when you click on that file, it opens up as an active website. Basically it's like saving a shortcut. In fact, if you send it to your Desktop, that's exactly how it functions, like a Desktop shortcut. See also DESKTOP" > "Adding a WEBSITE Icon onto Desktop"

WELCOME SCREEN – [Also called "logon screen"] When you turn your computer on, the first thing that comes up is a greenish Welcome screen which has icons on it for each User Account. The user clicks on his or her account to open it up. For me, since I'm the only one using my computer, it has just 2 icons – "Administrator" (me, the owner), and "Guest".

Since I am the only user, I got rid of this screen by right-clicking desktop empty spot > Personalize > Screen Saver at lower right > unchecking "On resume display logon screen" > OK.

Getting Rid of Welcome Screen – Problem

I was fiddling with the Welcome screen options, just to get familiar with them, so I could see what other people who have more than one computer user go thru. I checked "On resume display logon screen" and set it at 1 minute. So next time I used my computer, every time I did not do anything for one minute, the screen went black for two seconds and then the green Welcome screen popped up. I just needed to click my account icon to resume work, but, OK, enough, now I know how it works, I want to get back to the way I had it.

I spent the next two hours trying to figure out how to do so. I went thru every option under Start > Control Panel > User Accounts, but could not find that window where I made that one-minute setting. The Windows "Help" icon was, as usual, worse than worthless. I checked the internet and read thru half a dozen complex procedures on how to do so, involving accessing the registry, typing in esoteric technical words, buying software to get rid of the Welcome screen, etc., etc. I knew it couldn't be that complex, because I had made that simple setting under a simple dialogue window. But I just couldn't find that window again!

Finally, I found it: Start > Control Panel > Appearance and Personalization > Personalization > Change screen saver. It was not under User Accounts, but under Appearance and Personalization! (Or, as noted above, right-click the desktop > Personalize > Screen Saver.) I had forgotten how I had reached that window originally.

WHITE INK – There is no white ink. When you order up white, it just means no ink, and assumes you are using white paper. Of course, that means you have to have some shading around letters to make them visible as "white" text... like this.

Tip: You can keep material secret by changing it to white so it's invisible. Then, to see it, Ctrl+A the document and order black font, to make it visible again.

WHITEOUT A WORD, OR AREA OF AN IMAGE – Insert > Illustrations > Shapes, pick a rectangle > right-click it > Format Auto Shape, to format it, making the black lines white, under "Line", "Color" > and then drag the white rectangle over the spot.

WIFI (WIRELESS FIDELITY) – Refers to connectivity between different wireless devices. For example, if you have a router and a computer with wireless capability, the router can send signals to the computer without being connected by a wire. iPhones and many modern handheld devices can receive signals wirelessly also, over the air. So you can get the internet as you walk around, as long as you're in an area that receives decent signals and you have a cell phone contract, to get those signals. I think that's how it works.

WIDOWS AND ORPHANS – These are single lines of text sitting by themselves, at the bottom or top of a page, separate from the rest of their paragraph. You can allow this, or prevent it – See "FORMATTING – EMPTY SPACE AT BOTTOM OF PAGES"

WIKIPEDIA – This is a website that serves as a giant encyclopedia, for virtually everything – academics, celebrities, products, etc., etc. The great thing about it, I find, is that for any subject it focuses on the basic info one normally is looking for, but, also gives references if you want more in-depth info. In the old days, I remember going to the library and plodding thru 20-page encyclopedia articles struggling to find some basic info. Wikipedia is very good at giving you, right up front, the basics, which is what the normal person normally wants!

It's quick, succinct, and people-oriented rather than technical. I love it. I use it constantly. (Is Glenn Ford still alive? What's the definition of "twitter"? How do you checkmate with only two bishops left?) In fact, I have a Wikipedia icon on my desktop, and I use it as often as I use Google. I used to use Google for a topic and frequently scroll down to Wikipedia on their list, but now I often find it easier now to go directly to Wikipedia thru its icon and its search box.

WINDOW – DRAGGING OR MOVING – Sometimes a small window sits in front of something you want to see. Usually you can put the pointer on the title bar at top and drag that window wherever you want, off to the side, whatever. With Vista I used to use this fairly frequently while doing a word search (CTRL+F); I'd drag the dialogue window over to the right so it wouldn't sit on top of text I was trying to read.

WINDOW SIZE – You can change a Word document window size, from small to full screen, by clicking the "Maximize" icon at upper right icon between the – and x icons. Then to get back to a small size, click the same icon, now labeled "Restore Down".

You can drag almost any window less than full screen size, to any size you want, by clicking on any of its corners and dragging it out or in. Or you can click on an edge and drag just that single edge out or in.

[W7 – You can also bring a window to full size by pressing the Windows Start key + up arrow. Or, drag a small window into the top edge of screen and it pops into full size.]

See also "SCREEN SIZE"

Opens Up in Wrong Size

If a window keeps opening up in a size you do not prefer, MANUALLY adjust it by dragging the corner or edge handles, and then close it. Theoretically, Windows remembers, and the next time you open it, it will be at the size you closed it in. (Have to do it manually; "Maximize" button at upper right will not set it.) I set my "My Documents" folder to a size just big enough to show all the items in it, but no bigger.

Update: Seems to work fine with folder windows, but with a document window, I keep getting mixed results – sometimes it works, other times not, other times it works partially.

I spent hours and hours researching and experimenting, with no final resolution, other than leaving window size alone if you get the size you want, and adjusting it when you don't.

Some Internet Comments on This Issue

"There sure does seem to be a lot of confusion. There are people out there that are still saying that there is a workaround for this but there isn't that I can see. This is one of the stupidest things I have found in Windows 7. How did this issue make it through beta testing?"

"I'll give you a straight answer. Are you ready? Answer: individual window size and position is not saved as it should be. Code error, no workaround."

And the thread of this forum here continued forever, with all kinds of solutions, and all kinds of responses that those solutions didn't work! I've resigned myself to just playing it by ear. If what I get is OK, fine; if not, I change it.

"WINDOWS" – Refers to Microsoft's operating system for computers; it controls the way your computer works. The term "windows" refers to the square or rectangular panels that appear on your screen containing the information of whatever item you opened up.

The Windows system has been around for 20 years. The most recent (2009) version that comes preinstalled on nearly every computer sold, is "Windows 7." I've read that the previous version – "Vista" – can be upgraded to Windows 7 relatively easily using the Windows 7 disk. (You don't have to erase all your material from your hard drive, as you do with "Windows XP," the version before Vista.)

Usually, even though an MS operating system comes preinstalled in your computer, you also get a disk in case you need to re-install it. Note that the XP version came on a CD disk, whereas Vista and Windows 7 come on a DVD disk.

"WINDOWS 7" – This is the most recent operating system put out by Microsoft, superseding Window Vista. As I understand it, reviews for Vista were generally negative, but for Windows 7, generally positive. I find Windows 7 has some improvements, but it's pretty much the same system and I don't find it that much better.

For specific comparisons, see "COMPUTER – GETTING A NEW COMPUTER" > "DIFFERENCES – VISTA AND WINDOWS 7"

WINDOWS – CASCADING – If you click open, say, four documents in a row, then right-click an empty spot on the taskbar, and select Cascade Windows, it puts all four up top on your screen, cascading one in front of the next, so you can read the top part of each one. Seems like pointless overkill to me. Who works with four documents at the same time? And, if you do, why not just keep them on the taskbar and call them up as you need them?

Note that when you have more than one window on screen at a time, with one covering part of another, if you click on any part of a window, that one jumps to the front.

WINDOWS DVD MAKER – A program for making a DVD from either downloaded video or camcorder-imported video. See "DVD – BURNING DOWNLOADS ONTO DVD" or "DVD–MAKING FROM CAMERA, OR CAMCORDER, VIDEO"

WINDOWS – "HELP AND SUPPORT" – ROTS! Enough said. Put a topic in the search box (Start, Help and Support), it gives you 30 topics only remotely related, if at all, to what you want. Consistently it does this! Once in a great while I'll find an answer there, but it's usually no help at all.

WINDOWS MEDIA *CENTER* – AR says Windows Media *Center* tends to duplicate Windows Media *Player's* functions. I believe most people don't use Windows Media Center regularly; I know I don't. Every time I try something there, I tend to get sent in circles and get nowhere. I think it's one of those typical computer programs where you can do all kinds of things... except get it working to begin with. You have to click all the right buttons, in the right order. And just recently I found out a key button called "Tasks" (for setting up things) is located off screen – you have to scroll down to see it. I never even knew it existed before! The scroll-down arrow doesn't appear unless you put your pointer into that area at lower left of screen under the listed options.

But, Windows Media Player is where you can access TV and record programs directly to your computer. See "TV RECORD DIRECTLY TO COMPUTER"

You can access Windows Media Center instructions, by pressing the F1 key while on the internet > type "Windows Media Center" into search box > click on Getting Started with Windows Media Center.

I believe Windows Media Center is also used to hook up TVs to the computer for video games thru Xbox. But, my interest in Xbox is even less than my knowledge of it. Seems like a huge waste of time to me, playing video games for hours. But then, I play computer chess for hours. Equally pointless, one could argue.

WINDOWS MEDIA *PLAYER* – Will play a DVD or CD that you insert into the disk bay. Will also play video or audio files that you have on your computer hard drive.

Playing DVD or CD DISKS

If WMP is your default player, just put a disk in and it should start playing. If it doesn't, double-click Windows Media Player icon on your desktop (or find the WMP program under Start, All Programs). That opens the WMP window. On the left should be something representing the disk, like "Unknown DVD (E)" or "Unknown Album (E)" (or, click the dropdown arrow under Now Playing, and then click "Unknown DVD (E)"). When you click on that, it puts what you have on the disk, into the panel at the right. Click on your desired choice, press Play button at bottom middle.

Or, after you insert the disk, double-click Computer, double-click Drive E (the disk bay), and it should open up WMP with clip icons/pictures to click, and a Play icon at bottom. If you want more detailed info for that DVD, right-click the clip picture > Show List, to see titles and chapters, to select something on that disk.

Full-Screen Size

Click the small slanted arrow at lower right to get a full-screen view. Or, right-click on the video as it's playing > Video > "Fit video to Player on resize". Or, hold down the ALT key and press Enter; again to get it back to smaller window size. Also, pressing the ESC key at upper left brings the view back down to smaller size.

Playing Video or Audio FILES

If you double-click on any video file in your computer (or audio file, other than iTunes songs), WMP starts to play it automatically (for me, anyway, since it is my default program to play such files). Note that you often have to wait a full 10 seconds before it starts. Just be patient here.

If it doesn't start playing automatically, you can open WMP first by double-clicking on it. That brings up the WMP window with your video library showing (or click "Video" at left to bring your video library up). Click on the clip of your choice, press Play button at bottom middle. Of course, Windows has a pile of their own arbitrary clips there; it's so annoying. I just go straight to my Videos folder and click on my desired clip there.

I've had WMP not open up for me once in a while. Rebooting the computer fixed that.

For CDs, if you have iTunes, the iTunes program may show up instead and start playing the CD.

Getting Rid of Control Bar

For all the video-playing programs (Sony Vaio player, QuickTime Player, Windows Media Center, Windows Media Player), to get rid of the control buttons bar along the screen bottom, just leave your pointer on the screen anywhere except at the top or bottom (I leave it at the right edge so that the pointer itself is out of the way), and the control bars disappear after a few seconds. If you move the pointer, the control bars get brought up again. If you store your pointer at either top or bottom, the control bars stay visible.

Actually for my Sony Vaio player, the above applies to Windows 7. I notice on my old computer (Vista), for my Sony Vaio player, I click on the screen to bring up the bar, and click again to hide it. Some variation of holding the pointer in particular areas and/or clicking should show, or hide, control bars for all these video-playing programs.

Also note that when playing website video clips, the first procedure described above usually applies – you move your pointer onto the video area, the control buttons appear; you take it off, the controls disappear.

Finding Video Files

Not sure, but I think if you use any of these programs and you browse for a clip to play, usually to "My Videos" folder, if the program does not show that clip in the folder, even though you know it's there, that means that particular program cannot play that particular type of video clip. I usually get around this by using one of the other programs instead.

Playing Audio FILES

Same deal as with a DVD, except click "Music" instead of "Videos" if WMP doesn't automatically play it.

WMP automatically puts any ripped music (music copied from a disk to your computer) into the WMP library and into your Music folder (under Owner [W7 – under File]).

Downloaded iTunes are handled separately, under the iTunes program instead of WMP. iTunes is a competing company to Windows! See elsewhere, under "MUSIC" section (a big section) for how to work with music on your computer.

When ripping songs, WMP compresses songs to 1/10 size, to keep things manageable. AR: *"Many people can't tell the difference between a CD and a song ripped at 128 Kbps (kilobits per second), so Media Player defaults to that standard."*

Portable music players, like iPods or MP2 players have their own software that you install to transfer music from your computer to the player. See "iPOD"

WINDOWS MEDIA PLAYER – SPYING ON YOU – I believe WM Player keeps track of every song, file, or movie you play (partly so that it can retrieve artist, song, etc. info to show on your playlists, I think). To adjust this:

In Windows Media Player, press ALT key to get menu up (if it doesn't come up, close WMP and try again; it usually works for me the second time) > Tools [W7 – "Organize"] > Options > Privacy tab, can leave the first five checked, but uncheck "Send unique Player ID to content provider" > OK. That, in theory, should prevent Microsoft from getting a lot of info on you.

Though I don't have much confidence they won't get info other ways even with this option unchecked.

WINDOWS MOVIE MAKER – It takes practice to produce anything complex in this program, but you can do a simple movie fairly quickly. Windows Movie Maker is set up very similarly to "Studio" (a movie-making program I bought). You import video clips to your computer; you open Windows Movie Maker and import the desired clips to the program; you drag the selected clips down from above into a movie line below. You split and trim and move them (by dragging) to your preferences. Add transitions (fades) between clips. Save and Publish, to a computer file, or to a DVD.

Note that when you edit the video clips that you've imported to your movie project, that does not affect your original clip; the original stays the same, in the folder where it is are stored.

[W7 – Windows 7 Movie Maker has reduced functionality compared to Vista Movie Maker.

There is no movie line below any more. Click on the center of the screen where it says so, to browse for and import material from your Videos, Pictures, and Music folders. Material gets put up on the right, in rows; that's the "movie line" now. Then, to add more material, you click at the top "Add Videos and Photos".

I couldn't find instructions anywhere. If you play with this program for a while, you'll see where and how you can do most of the same stuff as before, using the tabs at top, and the "Music tools" and "Video tools" tabs at very top.

I LIKED the movie line at bottom, with the sound volume bar ("waveform"). Now there's no more visual sound volume bar, which means audio editing is different, because you can't actually see the volume anymore. Damn them. Always messing up the customer with their "improvements"!

Once you get a video clip on, then you can add music by clicking Add Music at top > browse > Open. The Music-added sound bar (green) gets put on top of the video bar.

The added-music volume can be adjusted by clicking on the Music Tools tab at very top (which is there only once you've added music to your movie line), and then by clicking the volume icon at left. Likewise for the video clip's own volume under Video Tools tab.

The "Movie line" at right can be squeezed or expanded by the plus and minus icons at lower right. You click on either the video or audio clip to put the cursor there, and use the Edit tab at top to split, trim, delete, move, etc.

Don't see any Undo button, but you can do CTRL+Z to undo an action.

Click on File at upper left to save the project to a DVD or to the computer hard drive.

You can no longer produce an audio CD thru Windows 7 Windows Movie Maker the way you used to under Vista. As AR notes, Windows 7 version of Windows Movie Maker is a "stripped-down version" compared to the Vista one.

Importing Material

If you have videotape, you should get a DVD recorder that can transfer videotape material onto a DVD. Then you can make use of Windows Movie Maker, importing the DVD material, editing it, and making a movie. (Of course, the simplest editing technique here is to bypass the computer and just use the player, playing the videotape and recording on the blank DVD, those sections you want from the videotape.)

There are other ways to transfer videotape material to your computer besides copying the material to a DVD first, but I have no experience here. eHow website says you *"need a video capture card to translate the analog video into a digital format and copy it to your hard disk."* I suggest taking your laptop to Best Buy and asking them exactly what you need.

I think you can also use a camcorder (connected to your TV with the three colored wires) to send signals from your TV playing the videotape, to the camcorder, to the computer. Check eHow website. I know my old camcorder could record material from TV, and then I could import it to the computer thru the Movie Maker program. But, my new camcorder cannot record material from TV.

Copyrighted material (like a commercial DVD of a movie) usually will not work in Windows Movie Maker. But material recorded from regular TV broadcasts, usually works fine.

Multi-tasking

Don't do other stuff when the computer is importing video or "publishing" a movie; it needs all its power to process material smoothly. For a lot of other stuff, you can do more than one thing at a time (like running your virus program while surfing the internet, that's OK), but for video, it's best to run just that one operation at that time.

Editing Audio

You can use Windows Movie Maker (Vista version), quite nicely, to edit audio files. See "MUSIC / AUDIO TRANSFERS THRU A COMPUTER".

Finding a File

When using WMM (Windows Movie Maker) and browsing for files, sometimes as you look for a file to import, you can't find it. It may well be because it's only showing certain files in certain folders. Click the dropdown arrow at lower right and select "All Media." Then it should show all the files. But even then, sometimes you can't find it; you know it's there, but it doesn't show, because, I think WMM just doesn't work with particular kinds of files.

Warning

Once you start working on a WMM project, don't move your clips from where they are stored. If your source clip is not still stored in the same folder and under the same name, the project becomes null and void, with red "X's"! The program can't find your clips to use if you rename them, or move them. If you send the clip back to its original folder with its original name, assuming you can remember that info, then it will work again.

Once you get a project saved to the computer hard drive (not just the WMM program), then you're OK. Then you don't need to worry about the material as a "project" under Windows Movie Maker, since it is now a set video or audio file.

Windows Movie Maker vs Studio

– In WMM, the features are fairly basic. Studio can do a lot more. (If you're into making movies, WMM is a good introduction to Studio. The setup, and a lot of the basic operations, are similar.)

– In WMM, once a clip is trimmed, you can't expand it back; you need to delete it and drag down the whole source clip again and start over. In Studio, you can drag beginnings and ends of clips back and forth freely.

– In WMM, sound levels get imported and set at top volume, so you can only lower the sound, not raise it! Studio imports sound clips at ¾ level, so you can raise the volume also if you want to. A key thing for me.

– In WMM, if you drag a movie clip to the audio line, Windows Movie Maker will freeze on you, and then you have to close and open it again to continue (and get that movie clip out of the audio line). Studio, at least Studio version 14, allows you to drag a movie clip to the audio line and will play it automatically as an audio clip.

– In WMM, you can split a track and drag each segment apart, to get silent space between them. You can do likewise in Studio, BUT in WMM you can't drag a last track farther to the right; you have to take out a chunk from the middle, move it to the end, leaving some empty space in the middle to get some operating space, and THEN fiddle around with segments.

– In WMM, you can adjust volumes in individual clips without affecting the neighboring clips. In Studio, the volumes of adjoining clips automatically get gradated – a loud one following a soft one makes the soft one become louder at its end, and the loud one become softer at its beginning.

I don't like this feature, but can get around it in Studio by separating the clips by a little empty space, so that each clip does stay fully at its own volume.

– In WMM and Studio both, the trimming capabilities are excellent. You can be very precise in trimming tracks – just expand the movie line to maximum, listen to the track and read the sound level graphs inside the track, and split the track at the precise point you want (between consecutive words, if you want!).

– Note this additional big difference between WMM and Studio (I'm not positive about this, but I think it's so): In Studio, once you publish ("Make Movie") a movie, you've got that full movie in your "Projects" folder, as edited, and you can delete the original clips, BUT with WMM, if you delete those original clips, even after publishing your movie in the WMM program, your published movie can no longer access those clips and you get the dreaded red "X"s, indicating you don't have the clips anymore! Your published project is ruined!

Solution: Do not delete, or rename, or move any original clip or track, until you have ripped that project onto the computer as an audio or video file (or have a final disk in hand). THEN you can delete stuff if you want, since you now have a final, set, copy on your computer hard drive.

WINDOWS PHOTO GALLERY– A Windows program that stores your photos, and enables editing of your photos. Essentially, your photos are stored in your Pictures folder, but Windows Photo Gallery accesses and displays them. Note that deleting a photo in EITHER place, deletes the photo to the Recycle Bin. See "PHOTOS / PICTURES – BASIC OPERATIONS"

WINDOWS – RE-INSTALLING – Sometimes re-installing your whole Windows operating system (Windows XP, Vista, Windows 7, whichever one you have) is the only way to fix a frozen or acting-up computer. I have not done this. Presumably, it is relatively straightforward; you put the disk in and follow directions.

BUT! It wipes out all your data (and all your settings, etc.), and leaves your computer as though you just bought it. Hopefully you had your important material backed up on a flash drive or external hard drive. I would only do this as a last resort; I'd bring my computer to Best Buy first for advice.

WINDOWS – SECURITY CENTER – To get to a window showing which protections are on: Right-click Computer > Properties > Security Center at lower left. Or, easier: Start > Control Panel > "Security Center" [W7 – "Action Center".] I just leave things at default settings. I think my Norton Anti-Virus program takes care of problems anyway. (I've mentioned you shouldn't have TWO anti-virus programs on at the same time, but I think this Windows basic security program, which comes with the Windows operating system, is OK to have going at the same time.)

WINDOWS – SIDE BY SIDE – See "VIEW DOCUMENTS SIDE BY SIDE"

WINDOWS – UPDATES – Windows provides automatic updates ("patches"), on an ongoing basis, so that your computer will maintain good reliability, security, and compatibility, in the face of constantly new problems. These updates get installed in the background, and you don't have to do anything. However, your computer needs to be online, and either ON or in "Sleep" mode.

Make sure that this automatic updating feature is on; I'm pretty sure it's on as the default setting, but to check it: Start > Control Panel > Systems and Security > Windows Updates > "Change settings" at left > "Important updates" dropdown arrow > "Install updates automatically (recommended)" > (Daily, 3 AM) or your selection (just pick a time you normally don't use your computer, because it automatically shuts it down if it's on, which can be very annoying if you're in the middle of working on something) > OK.

Open Windows Update – Slightly Quicker Route

Right-click Computer > Properties > Windows Update at lower left > Check for updates at upper left.

Update Installing Problem

At one point I did have a problem with Windows automatic updating. When I checked my update history [Start > Control Panel > Systems and Security > Windows Updates > View update history (at left)], it showed many of them were not successful in being installed. I got in touch with MS help – mssupport.microsoft.com.

I went thru a long, major hassle, but finally got it fixed. The notes below are sketchy but they describe what I had to do. (I leave out all the things I did that didn't work!)

Updating still failing.

Had me try again under a Clean Boot. [Start, type in "msconfig" in Start search box, Enter (or double-click that program when it pops up above the search box), Services tab, Hide All Microsoft Services, Disable All, Startup tab, Disable All, OK, restart computer. Then Start, type in Windows Update, Enter, Change Settings, choose "Download updates but let me choose whether to install them", OK, Continue, Check for Updates. Then install these updates, but ONE BY ONE!]

That worked (!), but only if I did it one by one. And, one of them would not work, even after my trying the whole procedure again, etc., etc.

So, the end result was that I got 7 of 8 updates done successfully.

What a hassle! Hours of supreme frustration. And the above is the short version! But I kept at it. More phone calls. Upshot: They've had problems with that particular update. It's a glitch. Even though it shows as not installed successfully, it IS installed successfully.

I haven't had any problems here since that one major episode.

Windows Help

There is information under the Windows Update window ("FAQ") and the History window ("Trouble-shooting") that may be helpful, but I get a headache just reading it.

WINDOWS – VERSIONS – See "VERSIONS – WHICH WINDOWS VERSION YOU HAVE"

WINDOWS – XP – See Rathbone's *Dummies* book, for issues related to this older version of Windows. Also see "OLDER PROGRAMS – COMPATIBILITY MODE" for a feature on your current version that allows you to run a program on an older version of Windows.

WIRELESS HOME NETWORK – See "ROUTER"

WORD COUNT – On the bottom left of your status bar (the second bar from the bottom of your screen), it gives which page, out of how many, you are currently on, and, just to the right of that, how many total words you currently have in your document. Very useful when your teacher wants a 500-word essay for homework.

If you want a word count for just a section of text, block the section, and that same spot at the bottom automatically tells you how many words are in that section, out of the total. For example, if you block a paragraph of 53 words out of your total of 512 words in your document, it shows "53/512."

Word Count for Specific Words

To get a word count for a specific word, use the Replace function (CTRL+H, Replace tab) and type in the same word on both lines, click Replace All (in effect making no change) and it tells you how many replacements it made, which of course is the number of instances of that word.

Warning: Just to play it safe, do a CTRL+Z after that, to undo what you just did, so that you don't get that replaced word saved... because you may have typed it in wrong!!! And that may lead to a nightmare, especially if it's a long document, and you can't recall, or didn't notice what your mistake was at the time. Say you wanted to count the instances of the word "is" and you accidentally put in "it" as your replacement word, you may end up with a thousand errors, errors stuck in the middle of words, etc., etc.

So for specific word counts, especially for small words, undo that operation right after you do it!

[W7 – A specific word count is easier: Just do a CTRL+F, type in the word, and it tells you right there just below the box how many instances of that word are in your document.]

Be aware of spaces – if you want a count of the word "his", you'll get a more accurate count if you put a space before and after it in the search box. Otherwise, it will include all the instances of the word "this" also, because it has the same three letters.

WORDPAD – This is a word processing program. I think it's a stripped down version of Microsoft Word; the toolbars are similar. But I don't go near it. Why would anyone need it if they already have MS Word (which is standard)!? You can access it thru: Start > All Programs > Accessories > WordPad.

WORD SEARCH – See "FIND (WORD SEARCH)"

"X" ICON AT FAR UPPER RIGHT – Clicking the "x" closes the window that you are in. It doesn't delete that file; it closes it. Windows automatically reminds you to save your document if you did not do so already.

See also "IMAGES NOT SHOWING – SHOWS RED 'x' "

YOU TUBE – YouTube is a popular website where anyone can put up a video clip. It's free; no cost. To watch video clips on You Tube, just go to their website, put a topic into their search box, and click on a clip to watch it. Click the 4-arrow icon at lower right put the image up to full screen. (Of course YouTube video quality is generally not the best.)

To put up a clip yourself, you need to sign up for an account. I don't have much experience here, but here's what I did to get a clip up:

Signing Up

I forget exactly how I signed up. Get on their website (type in "You Tube", click on "You Tube – Broadcast Yourself" site), click "sign up" to sign up for an account, follow their instructions, and jot down your user name and password, for necessary future reference.

If you forget your user name or password, click on Forgot Username, Enter Email Address, enter the temporary code of 5 letters/numbers; then they immediately email it to you. Then, do the same with your password if you forgot that.

Uploading Your Clip

Once you get an account, go to the "You Tube – Broadcast Yourself" site, click "Sign in" at upper right, and put in your username and password to get into your account. [There's some current deal where You Tube is partnering up with Google and they make you link the two and/or pick a new password. Confusing. Says old password no longer will work; but, it did for me... Good luck.]

Your account name is at the upper right and you can click on it to show a drop-down menu, including "Account," which is where you can upload a video clip, or make any changes you need to make. It's very well organized. Can change the title of your clip here, delete, change description or keywords, etc.

To put clip on: Account > click "Upload" at upper right > Upload Video > browse for it (of course you have to have put the clip into your computer first), check it > click Open. It works just like uploading an attachment to an email. You browse, and then click "Open." Took about ten minutes for a 2 minute clip.

Choose medium quality if it's too big. My video clip was 900 MB, but under medium quality it went down to 13 MB and was fine quality-wise and sound-wise (music sounded OK). (Don't forget to click "Save Changes" once you've put in all your video information.)

My tennis clip wasn't up there right away, but after searching for it under my username – most people pick a name, I picked a random number (2994485) as my username – I found it. Now I have a tennis clip up there ("Trick Tennis Shots") along with my religion clip ("Confronting Believers").

Restrictions

Limits – Fifteen minutes, 2 GB. I think a 2 GB file would take hours to upload. But, I think YouTube itself automatically converts (compresses) the material, so that it can be both uploaded, and downloaded and watched, more quickly. ("Download" here to means to watch it, not to put it onto your computer's hard drive.)

They are quite liberal about what you can put up there. Just no obscenity. Short clips of commercial music seem to be no problem; only a full song is a problem.

Downloading Clips TO Your Computer

Normally, you cannot download and save You Tube clips, the way you can some video clips, on some websites. See "VIDEO CLIPS FROM INTERNET"

Misc.

– There are no categories; people just search by keywords, and that's how the machines "categorize" clips (by keywords); there's no actual people checking and placing clips into categories. So naming your clip is important; you want it under desired, relevant keywords.

–"Responses" are written comments. And it also has ratings. Can't do a rating on your own clip.

– Can check any clip you watch as a favorite and it bookmarks it for you, so you can see it again later from under your "Favorites" instead of having to search for it.

ZERO vs THE LETTER "O" – One of many computer nightmares – spending hours getting nowhere, because you mixed up the number 0 with the letter O when entering your product number, serial number, whatever. The difference is that the number is more egg-shaped or oblong (0), the letter is more round (O). Maybe associate the idea of "number of eggs" with egg-shaped, in order to remember this.

ZIP DISK – Like floppy disks, zip disks are now outdated. The zip disk worked just like a floppy disk – you could transfer material onto it – except it had a much higher storage capacity – 100 MB or 250 MB – compared to the floppy disk capacity of only 1.4 MB. And most computers did not have a zip drive bay, so you had to buy a separate machine, with software. I used to do my backup of material with zip disks. But, as I say, they are now outdated. Today, it's flash drives (1, 2, 4, 8 GB capacity) or external hard drives (hundreds of GB's capacity).

Roughly speaking, 1,000 KB (kilobytes) = 1 MB (megabyte), and 1,000 MB = 1 GB (gigabyte).

ZOOM – To increase or decrease the size of the text you're looking at, click the + or – buttons at the far lower right. Or, click View at top, choose Zoom, then choose the percent size you want.

Note that doing so does NOT change the size of the actual text as entered, only how big your view of the text appears on screen. If you print it out, it comes out in the size you typed it in.

If you keep getting, say a 20% version of the screen, you can change the default zoom setting of that document by going to View at the top > click Zoom > check 100% > Save/OK, and then it will open up next time at 100%. [This was critical for me on my website – one of my essays kept opening up at 30%, because the page size I left it at, before transferring to the website, was 30%.]

If a website has print that is too small for you, click Page at upper right > Zoom > select size. Or, at lower right bottom of taskbar, click the dropdown arrow by the 100% icon and make a selection. Of course, for a web page, if you pick more than 100%, the whole page will not fit on the screen; you'll have to drag the position bar (the bar between the right and left arrows) to the left or right to see the left- or right-most sides of the page.

****